Beautiful Bodies

Beautiful Bodies

Gender and Corporeal Aesthetics in the Past

Edited by
Uroš Matić

 OXBOW | books
Oxford & Philadelphia

Published in the United Kingdom in 2022 by
OXBOW BOOKS
The Old Music Hall, 106–108 Cowley Road, Oxford, OX4 1JE

and in the United States by
OXBOW BOOKS
1950 Lawrence Road, Havertown, PA 19083

Paperback Edition: ISBN 978-1-78925-771-7
Digital Edition: ISBN 978-1-78925-772-4

A CIP record for this book is available from the British Library

Library of Congress Control Number: 2021950228

Printed in the United Kingdom by Short Run Press

Typeset in India by Lapiz Digital Services, Chennai.

For a complete list of Oxbow titles, please contact:

UNITED KINGDOM
Oxbow Books
Telephone (01865) 241249
Email: oxbow@oxbowbooks.com
www.oxbowbooks.com

UNITED STATES OF AMERICA
Oxbow Books
Telephone (610) 853-9131, Fax (610) 853-9146
Email: queries@casemateacademic.com
www.casemateacademic.com/oxbow

Oxbow Books is part of the Casemate Group

Front cover: Princess Akhtar al-Dowleh among harem female personnel (Institut for Iranian Contemporary Historical Studies (IICHS))

For Jan
Beauty is in the eyes of the beholder

Contents

List of contributors

UROŠ MATIĆ is a research fellow of the Austrian Archaeological Institute (Cairo Branch), Austrian Academy of Sciences, Vienna, Austria. He received his PhD from the Institute for Egyptology and Coptic Studies of the University in Muenster (Germany) in 2017. Since 2012, he has been a team member of several archaeological missions in Egypt (Tell el-Dabᶜa, Aswan, and Kom Ombo). He was Co-Chair of Archaeology and Gender in Europe (AGE) community of the European Association of Archaeologists (EAA) from 2016 to 2019. His most recent publications in gender archaeology include *Archaeologies of Gender and Violence* (co-edited with Bo Jensen, 2017), *Violence and Gender in Ancient Egypt* (2021) and *Gender Stereotypes in Archaeology – A Short Reflection in Image and Text* (co-edited with Laura Coltofean-Arizancu, Bisserka Gaydarska, 2021).
uros.matic@oeaw.ac.at

HELGA VOGEL obtained a doctorate in Ancient Near Eastern Archaeology from Free University Berlin in 2008 with a study on the intersections between material culture, mortuary practices and the formation of early state structures in Mesopotamia. She has taught courses with a focus on gender studies and visual culture at the Institute of Near Eastern Archaeology at Free University Berlin from 2000 to 2014. Funded by the Fritz Thyssen Foundation, she recently conducted an analysis of finds and findings from the Riemchen Building at Uruk-Warka, an important archaeological site in southern Iraq.
vogelhva@zedat.fu-berlin.de

KIRA ZUMKLEY is a cultural heritage imaging specialist with a background in archaeology and Egyptology (BA and MA, University of Muenster, Germany). Working with museum collections and on excavation her research focuses on gaining a better understanding of historic material culture by deploying both traditional humanities research methods as well as advanced imaging techniques such as photogrammetry or multispectral imaging.
info@kirazumkley.com

FILIP FRANKOVIĆ obtained his PhD in 2021 at the Institute for Prehistory, Protohistory and Near Eastern Archaeology in Heidelberg. He was temporarily employed as a research associate at the Archaeological Museum in Zagreb, Croatia, from 2016 to 2017. Franković was a holder of the Gerda Henkel Foundation scholarship (2017–2019) and the scholarship of Faculty of Philosophy in Heidelberg (2020). In 2021 he was awarded a DAAD PRIME postdoctoral fellowship for his project *Power of Images and Images of Power: A Historical Examination of the Reflective and Creative Role of Iconography in the Formation of Late Bronze Age Aegean Elite Identities*, conducted at the Universities of Heidelberg and Vienna. Since 2017 Franković has been directing an excavation project focusing on the Middle and early Late Bronze Age in Eastern Croatia (Lovas Archaeological Project). His research interests include the Bronze Age of the Balkans, the Aegean and Anatolia, with the focus on burial practices, iconography and interregional interaction.
frankovic.uni@gmail.com

ISABELLE ALGRAIN holds a PhD in History, Arts and Archaeology from the Université libre de Bruxelles and a master's degree in gender studies. After a post-doctoral fellowship at the University of Oxford (2011–2012), she became research fellow from the F.R.S-FNRS at the Centre de Recherches en Archéologie et Patrimoine at the Université libre de Bruxelles (2012–2015) and is currently a research associate in this Centre. She is specialised in the morphological study of Greek pottery from the Archaic and Classical periods and is currently working on the publication of the pottery from the southern complex of the sanctuary of Apollo at Despotiko (Paros). Since her doctoral thesis,

she has also been working on the representations of women on Greek pottery and gender in Greek societies. Her book *L'alabastre attique. Origine, forme et usages* (2014) received in 2016 the Joseph Gantrelle Prize of the Royal Academy of Sciences, Letters and Fine Arts of Belgium.
isabelle.Algrain@ulb.be

VLADIMIR D. MIHAJLOVIĆ is an associate professor in archaeology and cultural heritage at the University of Novi Sad, Serbia. His research focuses on issues of social structure and identity in the Late Iron Age and Roman period of the Balkans, reception of the past, history of archaeology and theoretical archaeology. His most recent publications include co-edited volumes *Reflections of Roman Imperialisms* (2018) and *Pervading Empire: Relationality and Diversity in the Roman Provinces* (2020), as well as the monograph *The Scordisci between Ancient and Modern Interpretations. A Question of Identity in (Proto)History* (2019, in Serbian with an English summary).
v.mihajlovicc@ff.uns.ac.rs

BO JENSEN is an archaeologist (PhD) educated in Copenhagen and working on rescue excavations in the Danish commercial sector for a variety of employers. His research focuses on Viking Age Scandinavia, more precisely, on issue of symbolism, identity and meaning, and on how these phenomena interact with economy and the exercise of power. His publications include the monograph *Viking Age Amulets in Scandinavia and Western Europe* (2010) and *Archaeologies of Gender and Violence* (co-edited with Uroš Matić, 2017).
bojensen_dk@yahoo.dk

MARYAM DEZHAMKHOOY is a researcher at University of Heidelberg, Alexander von Humboldt Foundation alumna and a former assistant professor of archaeology at the University of Birjand, Iran. She is a historical archaeologist with a broad interest in theory. Dezhamkhooy is mainly interested in the study of violence and conflicts, colonialism, nationalism, gender and sexuality. Her most recent publication is *Homogenization, Gender and Everyday Life in Pre-Modern and Trans-modern Iran. An Archaeological Reading* (with Leila Papoli-Yazdi, 2021).
mdezhamkhooy@gmail.com

KATHARINA REBAY-SALISBURY is an archaeologist with a research focus on the European Bronze and Iron Ages. After completing her PhD in 2005, she was a post-doctoral researcher at the Universities of Cambridge and Leicester in the UK, where she participated in research programmes on the human body and networks. In 2015, she was awarded the ERC Starting Grant for her project *The Value of Mothers to Society: Responses to Motherhood and Child Rearing Practices in Prehistoric Europe*. In her current FWF-funded Project *Unlocking the Secrets of Cremated Human Remains* she investigates gendered mobility and temporality at Late Bronze Age cemeteries in Austria and contributes to improving the bio-archaeological investigation of cremated remains. She directs the research group Prehistoric Identities at the Austrian Archaeological Institute of the Academy of Sciences and teaches at the University of Vienna.
katharina.rebay-salisbury@oeaw.ac.at

Preface

Uroš Matić

During 2018–2019, the editor of this volume held a post-doc position (DAAD P.R.I.M.E) at the Institute for Egyptology and Coptic studies of the University in Muenster (Germany), with a guest research period of one year at former OREA-Institute for Oriental and European Archaeology of the Austrian Academy of Sciences (now Austrian Archaeological Institute). This post-doc project dealt with the use of cosmetic substances and utensils in Nubia during the New Kingdom (c. 1550–1070 BCE), when ancient Egyptian state established firm control of this region and its population. The editor of the volume explored how beauty ideals can form, change and transform in the context of cultural contact and which role beauty ideals play in the formation of identity. This is a long-term study whose publication is planned elsewhere.

Inspired by the richness of comparative anthropological and archaeological data, together with Sanja Vučetić, then a doctoral candidate at University College London (UCL), we organised a session titled "Beautiful bodies: Gender, bodily care and material culture in the past" at the Annual Meeting of the European Association of Archaeologists (EAA) in Maastricht, the Netherlands, 30th August–3rd September 2017. This was the official session of the Archaeology and Gender in Europe (AGE) community of the EAA. As all AGE sessions at the EAA this one too was well visited.

Being in contact with other authors who deal with this theme, one of the organisers and the editor of this volume, contacted relevant scholars and invited them to contribute. This is how this volume was formed. It combines papers presented at the session (2) with papers submitted after the session on the invitation of the editor (8).

Although archaeologists and ancient historians extensively dealt with gender, they dealt less with it in relation to beauty. The aim of the volume is to explore the role of material culture in the formation of corporeal aesthetics and beauty ideals in different past societies and thus to contribute to the cultural relativity of bodily aesthetics. The volume does not explore beauty for the sake of beauty, but extensively explores how it serves to form and keep gender norms in place.

The editor would like to express his gratitude to: AGE members, who have supported the project; reviewers, whose suggestions significantly improved the arguments of the papers; Andrea Sinclair for proofreading the English of the papers; and last but not the least Katharina Rebay-Salisbury for accepting to read all the papers and write the Afterword chapter for the volume.

Chapter 1

Beauty is in the eye of the beholder: an introduction to gender and corporeal aesthetics in the past

Uroš Matić

This book in context

Writing an introduction for an edited volume on gender and corporeal aesthetics in past societies is a daunting task. Even the task of summarising previous works in gender archaeology (*e.g.*, Back Danielsson and Thedéen 2012; Díaz-Andreu 2005; Gero and Conkey 1991; Gilchrist 1999; Hays-Gilpin and Whitley 1998; Matić and Jensen 2017; Sørensen 2000), aesthetics and archaeology (*e.g.*, Chi and Azara 2015; Gosden 2001), or body centred research in archaeology (*e.g.*, Borić and Robb 2008; Hamilakis, Pluciennik and Tarlow 2002; Matić 2019; Meskell and Joyce 2003; Montserrat 1998; Rautman 2000; Rebay-Salisbury, Sørensen and Hughes 2010; Robb and Harris 2013; Sofaer 2006) is a challenge, not to mention the exploration of their intersection.

The challenge is even greater if one bears in mind that other disciplines, such as history and art history, have extensively dealt with beauty ideals in the past (*e.g.*, Davis 2010; Eco 2004; Gherchanoc 2016; Hau 2003; Martin 2009), and that theories of aesthetics have a special place in philosophy (Adorno 1997). Anthropology, an all-encompassing discipline dealing with diversity of cultural expressions, also counts numerous studies on gender and beauty (*e.g.*, Boone 1986; van Damme 1996; Popenoe 2004). Therefore, readers familiar with this topic should not be surprised if some works, theories or authors are omitted here. The selection I have made here rather reflects both the themes in which I have a personal interest, and themes that are addressed by authors of this volume (Chapters 2–9). The chapters are arranged chronologically, but their themes are contextualised in the broader research landscape in this introduction and in the Afterword (Chapter 10). This introduction is certainly not exhaustive or representative of all three previously mentioned disciplines (archaeology, history/art history and anthropology). Instead it serves to situate the chapters of this volume within current debates and provide those less familiar with this topic with an overview that they can use for further research. As is usually the custom in introductions dealing with intersections of several phenomena, I will begin with a notion familiar to all of us and develop the discussion further.

One often hears the proverb "beauty is in the eye of the beholder". Nowadays this proverb is often evoked in order to relativise bodily aesthetics and elevate other values beyond corporeal beauty. The underlying message is: "I am beautiful no matter what they say. Words can't bring me down. I am beautiful in every single way" (Christina Aguilera "Beautiful", song from the album "Stripped" 2002). These strong words from the American pop singer come as an answer to our society's judgmental attitudes towards external appearance. Bodies are both perceived and evaluated, and they may respond to perception by enhancing or modifying how they are perceived (Bunn 2018, 11). Some artists write songs to counter this pressure of normative expectations and encourage body positivity among their fans, others succumb to this pressure and do everything they can to fit in. Therefore, the corporeal aspect is central to aesthetics (Irvin 2016a; Saltzberg and Chrisler 1995; Siebers 2000a). We judge ourselves, we judge others and others judge us, consciously or not (Gilman 1999, 3; Irvin 2016b, 1). Whether or not we follow the normative beauty ideals of our society or we choose not to do so, we are doing this with our bodies. We either fully succumb to specific diet regimes, do exercise, tan, wear make-up, shave, trim, depilate, etc. or we do only some of this, or all only to a certain extent, or we simply do not.

The escape from the pressure of beauty ideals is often sought in the notion of inner beauty, aesthetic of morality, the pureness of the soul (for a case where outer appearance reflects inner beauty, see Chapter 2, written by Helga Vogel). In modern western society this dichotomy is a consequence of the work of the usual suspects; the Cartesian mind-body split (Thomas 2004, 18) and the Judeo-Christian notion of the importance of the soul in contrast to the transiency of the body. This insistence on inner beauty is a consequence of the fact that corporeal aesthetics can be woven into other discourses, such as the one that is produced by western media and the advertising industry in which fit and thin bodies are presented as healthy, beautiful and sexually attractive, whereas unfit bodies as the opposite. As a consequence, lack of fitness is interpreted as the feature of an individual who is lazy, idle and unvirtuous (Eaton 2016; Forth 2013, 148–149; Pylypa 1998, 25). In our society bodies that are not fit and sporty are considered not to be productive. Therefore, one can say that in contemporary Western society ideas of beauty have become closely tied to economy (Bunn 2018, 14) which affects all genders. However, corpulent bodies, that would be considered unfit, lazy and unproductive by our society are desired bodies in other societies. Among the Azawagh Arabs, for example, obesity is a consequence of closedness, a social ideal coming from an economic system in which the active labour of men is invested in the passivity of the women (Popenoe 2004, 2; see also Chapter 9 of Maryam Dezhamkhooy for the attractiveness of overweight royal women of Qajar Iran). Therefore, if beauty ideals are tied to economy, and gender plays an important role in division of labour, then beauty ideals reflect gender systems.

The entanglement of beauty ideals and economy is clearly historically and culturally contingent. In his *The History of Beauty* (2004), Umberto Eco traced the preoccupation with beauty in Western culture from classical times to the present. He argued that sexual aesthetics is only one of the many notions of beauty, next to proportion, sacredness, impossibility, gracefulness and romance. Eco explored the complex relations between beauty and moral goodness, physical and spiritual, body and mind, etc. For example, male athletic bodies as materialised in ancient Greek sculpture and its Roman copies were not just aesthetically pleasing images, they represented the bodies of athletes who had achieved a desired state of balanced and harmonious soul resembling the one of gods. As pointed out by Heather Reid, aesthetic experience is not merely a matter of the senses, but is also related to a set of beliefs and attitudes, personal, cultural and historical (Reid 2012, 283). Erotic associations with these statues have either shaped entire art historical studies, such as those by Johann Joachim Winckelmann (1717–1768), or have been entirely converted into non-sensuous moral admiration, as in the aesthetics of Immanuel Kant (1724–1804; Davis 2010, 42; also see the discussion further below).

However, to claim that there was never an erotic gaze involved in viewing these statues neglects the abundance of sources indicating the contrary, but to state that this gaze was the same then as it is now is a serious misconception. An entire tradition of classicism and art history privileging ancient Greek statues and their Roman copies was built on the notion of white racial supremacy and progress, a concept alien to ancient Greeks, at least in its modern form. This tradition formed the base for racial anthropology and craniometry by placing the proportions of the bodies and faces of ancient statues, and not all ancient peoples, on an aesthetic and racial pedestal (Mitter 2017). It also shaped entire fashions in Europe of the late 18th century which were inspired by "classical ideals", but only as understood by European scholars of that time (Rauser 2020). In a similar vein, cults of health and beauty in Germany developed from the 1890s to 1930s, and were essential for the constitution of both the German nation and "Aryan race" (Hau 2003). Historically contingent and gendered ancient beauty ideals were understood by classicists and anthropologists as natural beauty. Yet this supposedly ahistorical natural beauty is historical at its core (Adorno 1997, 65).

However, by defining corporeal aesthetics based on ancient statues representing unreal men (idealised bodies cast in bronze or chiselled in stone), very real men, women and children of different backgrounds were excluded from the notion of the beautiful. Therefore, corporeal aesthetics is seldom not gendered. "Aesthetic standards thus serve a disciplinary function, maintaining oppressive norms of race, gender and sexuality" (Irvin 2016b, 1). Tobin Siebers claims that dramatic changes in corporeal aesthetics appear at the passages between antiquity, modernity and postmodernity (Siebers 2000b, 1). However, such a history of beauty, like the one of Eco (2004) does not consider pre-Greek and Roman corporeal aesthetics, neither does it consider non-European societies. Just like European history, European corporeal aesthetics has to be provincialised in a postcolonial manner (Chakrabarty 2000; also see Dezhamkhooy in Chapter 9 of this volume). Therefore, the questions in the background of this book are: is there one history of beauty or are there many histories of beauty? Is there a "herstory" of beauty? What is the relation of gender and corporeal aesthetics in different societies and how can this be explored archaeologically?

Beauty, gender and charisma of the higher classes

In his _Critique of Judgment_ (_Kritik der Urteilskraft_) from 1790, Immanuel Kant (2000) laid out one of the earliest theories of aesthetics. For an object to be beautiful the viewer must completely detach themselves from any practical considerations of the object (Sharman 1997, 180). A thing is beautiful because it cannot be reduced to practicality, but instead may be solely admired. However, as demonstrated by Pierre Bourdieu (1984) in his seminal work _Distinction_ from 1979, the idea of disinterested appreciation is neither universal nor is it even entirely western. Kant's model of aesthetics comes from the lifestyles of the elites accustomed to the luxury of the disposable, or from spare time and resources. The association of beauty with wealth and leisure is socially constructed by members of the upper classes (Saltzberg and Chrisler 1995, 311; Sharman 1997, 182), for whom the more expensive an object is, the more beautiful it is considered to be. Therefore, in modern capitalist society, beauty is a product of social competition (Gronow 1997, 34–39). The gender background of this distinction made by Bourdieu is demonstrated by Yan Yan's and Kim Bissel's study of the portrayal of female beauty in modern fashion magazines such as _Vogue, Elle, Glamour_ and _Cosmopolitan_ in 11 countries (USA, UK, Spain, Germany, France, Switzerland, Slovenia, China, Korea, Japan and South Africa) from 2007 to 2010. This study showed that more expensive magazines, such as _Vogue_ and _Elle_ try to define a high-fashion oriented beauty (of disinterested appreciation), whereas the more affordable _Cosmopolitan_ and _Glamour_ reinforce their role as proxy neighbours and friends by using smiling and laughing models wearing more accessible clothing (Yan and Bissell 2014, 208). This is in line with Bourdieu's postulate that the popular aesthetic of the working class is a negative opposite of Kantian aesthetic of "that which gratifies" (1984, 41). In the Kantian sense, the "practical" men and women of the lower classes cannot be considered as beautiful.

Since both Kant and Bourdieu wrote about European capitalist societies, Kant on 18th-century western Europe and Bourdieu on Paris of the 1970s, the question that naturally arises is: how valid are their class-based distinctions to other cultures? It is argued that beauty ideals are created and maintained by the society's elite (Saltzberg and Chrisler 1995, 311). However, the Kantian concept of disinterested appreciation is, according to Russel Sharman, not found in small-scale non-state societies outside the West. Within non-Western contexts, concepts of beauty rarely have to do with the disinterestedness of Kantian appreciation and instead relate directly to social and ritual practices (Sharman 1997, 180–181). All of the contributions in this book have dealt with state societies (Sumer, ancient Egypt, Aegean Bronze Age states, 5th-century BCE Athens, ancient Roman provinces, Viking Scandinavia and Qajar to Pahlavi Iran). All of these clearly demonstrate that beauty ideals and their gender backgrounds are in state societies constructed by the elites of a given culture. It is also noticeable that all of the contributions rely on past societies that were either literate and have left rich textual record as well as material culture, or have produced representations allowing for iconographic study. It is therefore a valid question how many of the topics covered by this volume can be explored in other past societies, namely those which have not produced texts or did not leave numerous representations for archaeologists to study (see the Afterword). Consequently, the question arises whether beauty as a social distinction is an invention of a class society? Equally, does beauty pre-date gender or are they mutually constituted? However, the answers to these questions were beyond the scope of this volume.

Beauty, gender and space

Care for the self or others with the aim to achieve certain corporeal aesthetic effects often takes place in spaces specially determined or chosen for such activities (*e.g.*, gyms, hair salons, barbershops). In the process of creating beauty, different genders can create gender-defined spaces which build and solidify gender distinctions (Cahill 2003, 61; Matić this volume). In our society these places function as self-surveying and self-disciplining spaces, because of the all-encompassing gaze of power of the bathroom scale, the mirror, television and gym monitors, magazines and posters (Pylypa 1998, 27).

Sometimes both men and women can go to the same place in which there is a further division of space. Yet, sometimes these beauty salons or barbershops are strictly gendered spaces. For example, until recently a barber shop "The Barbers" in hipster town quarter of Savamala in Belgrade (Serbia) even had a sign on the door forbidding women to enter (Fig. 1.1). This sign was taken seriously by the owner and employees of this barber shop. Women who casually

Fig. 1.1 A sign which until late spring 2021 stood on the door of "The Barbers" barbershop in hipster town quarter of Savamala in Belgrade (Serbia), forbidding women to go in (photo of the author)

walked in, not noticing the sign on the door, were kindly asked to leave the shop, which sometimes left either a bitter look or a smile on their faces.

The message behind this sign is clear, the barbershop is a man's world, space and time. Women can be only a distraction both for the employees and the customers. No one wants a wrong cut or a cut in the wrong place. This is also a heteronormative statement which assumes that women are distraction for all men, although the customers themselves may be of different ages and sexualities. At the same time such spaces can be queered. Such a homosocial environment with an emphasis on heterosexual manliness is a perfect place for men who are interested in men in a town in which homophobia is strong and gay bashing is frequent. One only needs to turn up at "The Barbers" and turn on one of the online dating apps to see who is around and differentiate between those who are straight and those who have a straight-look (compare with Han 2016 who discusses racial implications of contemporary gay beauty ideals). A virtual queer space thus becomes materialised. Furthermore, being part of this brotherhood of men comes with a high price, as the services in this barbershop cost double than in any regular barbershop in Belgrade.

Similarly, there are examples of barbershops in other times and places which demonstrate the gendering of space through beauty treatments. Thus, Mark Albert Johnston demonstrated how an early modern barbershop in London was not only a place where one could get various cosmetic services, but also place where a rising number of male Londoners with venereal diseases could get a variety of medical treatments performed by the barbers. Barbershops were places where time was passed and where masculinity could be both fashioned and undone (Johnston 2010, 115–117). These were evenly distributed in London, but some of them concentrated in areas notorious for prostitution and their barbers also conducted illicit and immoral activities from the point of view of early modern Londoners, *e.g.*, brothel keeping (Johnston 2010, 119–121). London barbershops were places where one could catch and remedy certain sexually transmitted diseases, but they were primarily gendered spaces and spaces that can gender. However, gendered spaces in which beauty treatments are done are not an early modern invention. The Roman *tonstrina* (barbershop) was also a space for men. Of course, some Roman barbers (singular *tonsor*) practiced their craft in the streets, even after the edict of Domitian (51–96 CE) forbidding the occupiers to work outside and rashly draw their razors in the middle of dense crowds (Holleran 2012, 126; Toner 2015, 93–95). Barbers also played an important role for men in creating their public image. First shaving (*deposition barbae*) was an important rite de passage and took place about the age of twenty or when *toga virilis* was assumed. A barbershop was also a place for Roman men to enhance their sexual identity and attractiveness (Toner 2015, 97–98).

As I demonstrate in my paper in this volume (Chapter 3), similarly in ancient Egypt for several millennia men used both public and private space for their beauty treatments, whereas women used private spaces for most of the beauty treatments in which their bodies could be more exposed. Due to the structural domination of men in ancient Egyptian society public space was by default dominated by men, whereas private space could be temporarily devoid of men. The reason women did not use public space for their beauty treatments is because these treatments involve direct intervention on the bodies and are therefore eroticised. They may attract the male gaze and trigger desire by their observers. Not all of these looks are welcomed, as social norms defined women as properties of their fathers before marriage and of their husbands in marriage. Therefore, gender-structured space and time during beauty treatments both reflected and solidified the patriarchal economy.

Beautiful bodies are also often found in spaces for various performances. For example, Rosemary A. Joyce (2000) argued that among the Maya, young male bodies were exposed to admiration of mature noble men in public performances. Another good example comes from ancient Greece where both men and women showed off their bodies in beauty contests and where the act of winning was associated with leadership (Hawley 2000; for beauty and leadership see especially the contribution of Helga Vogel, Chapter 2 in this volume). Although not dealt with by the contributors in this book, one should also consider the difference in time that genders may take for beautification. As an example, in our society jokes are made about how long women take to "get dressed", but these clumsy jokes are based on the fact that there is a gender imbalance in expected and normalised beautification practices (Saltzberg and Chrisler 1995, 309).

Beautification tools and gender

Grooming and cosmetics involve the manipulation of one's physical structure to make a desired impression upon others. These manipulations include, but are not conditioned by or limited to, bathing, anointing and colouring the skin; cutting, shaving, plucking, braiding, waving, and setting the hair; deodorising and scenting the body; colouring or marking the lips, hands, nails, eyes, face, or other exposed regions; cleansing, colouring and filing the teeth; moulding, restraining and concealing various parts of the body, and so on (Wax 1957, 588). The typical use of the word "cosmetics" itself implies a trivial adjustment to the surface that does not affect the underlying structure (Power 2010, 75). However, these practices directly affect the materiality of the body as the exploration of material qualities does not apply only to objects, but also to bodies (compare with Sofaer 2006). For example, in England and France of the 18th century whiteness, softness and smoothness of the skin were not less valued, because their contrast was rough, freckled, red and pimpled skin, often with disfiguring marks left by smallpox and other diseases (Palmer 2008, 204).

Nothing demonstrates the capacity of grooming tools, toiletry artefacts and cosmetics in achieving certain bodily forms better than the culture of drag. "You're born naked and the rest is drag", a quote by RuPaul, the most successful drag queen in modern show business, will come as familiar to those acquainted with gender and queer theory (Butler 1990; 1993). It is often said that drag produces an illusion.

However, the productions of illusion are not limited to drag, they are quintessential for all bodies and all genders. Furthermore, femininity and masculinity are not essential properties of male or female bodies. They are the acts of doing. Namely, human bodies have been nature-cultural since the Upper Palaeolithic. In 2008, electronics company Braun advertised a new electric razor by placing images of a chimpanzee, a baboon and a gorilla side by side with an image of a human male (Fig. 1.2). In each case the primate face is captioned as "8:00 am" and the human face with "8:05 am", and the text underneath reading: "Braun Series 1–Brings out the human in men" (Oikkonen 2013, 1). The message here is clear, we cannot be human without tools, even where grooming is concerned. Consequently, we cannot be men and women, not masculine or feminine, without shaping our bodies into expected norms.

What we do to our bodies and how we do this is more often than not, among other things, gender, age, class or occupation specific. For example, eye make-up was in classical Greece a common element in the adornment of prostitutes, so that the emphasis on the eyes was according to ancient Greek men only appropriate to a prostitute and other disreputable women, because of Greek connection of gaze and sexuality (Glazebrook 2009, 236; for the power of gaze and its class connotations beyond gender differences see the contribution of Bo Jensen, Chapter 8 in this volume). In his *Oikonomikos* Xenophon (*c.* 430–354 BCE) presents us with the gender issues of

Fig. 1.2 Braun electric razor advert (https://www.adsoftheworld.com/media/print/braun_evolution_3)

an ancient Greek household, in this requiring that women transform from idle, unproductive and deceptive to active, productive and trustworthy participants. Interestingly one signifier of this change is restraining from the use of make-up (Glazebrook 2009, 233–234; Hawley 2000, 50; Totelin 2017, 138). Therefore, not wearing make-up meant being bound to the *oikos* (the family, the family's property and the house).

Similar notions of make-up being aesthetically deceptive, repellent and indicative of sexual immorality are found in the attitudes of Roman men (Olson 2009, 293; Totelin 2017; on androcentrism of beauty ideals in ancient Rome see also Chapter 7 by Vladimir D. Mihajlović). Furthermore, in a literary context, the choice of the kind of beauty (decent vs. excessive) faced by Paris and Heracles is a choice between lifestyles (Hawley 2000, 52). However, as excellently demonstrated by Richard Hawley and Laurence Totelin, the whole question of the use of cosmetics for the ancient Greeks and Romans was related to gender norms. Men, just like women, used cosmetic products, but male authors of cosmetic texts target women and effeminate men as using cosmetic products not as a *kosmetikon*-form of medicine, but as *kommōtikon*-embellishment (Draycott 2019, 77; Totelin 2017). Again, too much make-up differentiates a dangerous woman or a prostitute from a trustworthy woman (Hawley 2000, 41). Similarly, in her study of women as works of art in 18th-century England, Caroline Palmer showed not only that applying make-up and painting shared the same substances and vocabulary, but also that culturally appropriate way of wearing make-up influenced aesthetic choices of painters in England and France. Political animosity influenced English ladies in distancing themselves from the French way of applying make-up. In England an excess red made one look like a prostitute, whereas in France the opposite was considered true. The striving towards more naturalised look of the face among the protestant English was contrasted to the so-called French face, that was even associated with popery and the worship of idols (Palmer 2008). Therefore, beauty goes well beyond surface aesthetics and reaches out to the level of politics (Tate 2007, 305).

Nothing demonstrates this better than racism. We have seen at the beginning of this introduction that European beauty ideals were based on the reception of classical Greek and Roman art and then entangled with racial anthropology (craniometry). Since at least 1619, African American women and their beauty have been juxtaposed against white beauty standards. Unlike white women, black women were considered by white people to be either asexual, out of control or oversexed, but never beautiful (Craig 2002, 24). During slavery, black women with lighter skin and wavy or straight hair tended to be household slaves and black women with darker skin, kinky hair and broader facial features tended to be field slaves (Patton 2006, 26). Among some black women light make-up, hair straightening, highlighting and certain clothes can be understood as transformation of "natural black beauty" into an unnatural state. The truth is however that both "black beauty" and "white beauty" are matters of doing (Tate 2007, 304–308). Beauty emerges in doing and being, and it is relational (Bunn

2018, 11). When black women competed in USA beauty pageants in the 1960s, they did not represent individuals like their white competitors, rather they represented their race (Craig 2002, 70). Equally, African-American women have answered to white beauty standards in different ways over the recent past. Enslaved women covered their hair with bandanas, whereas freed women straightened their hair. Proud black women in the 1960s and 1970s used unprocessed black hair as a political statement against Eurocentric beauty ideals, but black women in the 1990s again began straightening theirs and the hair of their daughters under the pressure of advertisements privileging white beauty ideals (Mayes 1997). In a manner of speaking, if there were no "white" women, there would be no "black" women, my point being not to deny physical features of different people, but to question the racial associations people make.

That not only beautified bodies are gendered, but even cosmetic products can be entangled with gender norms is nicely illustrated by the numerous gender divisions of cosmetic products in the contemporary cosmetic industry. For example, the cosmetic company *Rituals* bases its offer on an *orientalist's* (Said 1978) take on bodily care. Collections such as "Rituals of Sakkura, Dao, Buddha, Ayurveda, Hammam, Karma, Anahata", etc. provide their customers with the feel and smell of these substances and their "oriental philosophies". Apart from predominantly female collections, *Rituals* also offers its male customers a collection named "Ritual of Samurai" that is centred on male grooming practices, such as shaving, but also offers modern men a "Samurai scent" for their car. The message behind this collection is that grooming was part of Samurai identity, as these warriors did not go to battle without preparing their bodies in an appropriate manner. Therefore, wrinkle controlling creams coupled with car scents prepare the modern Samurais for their battles at work in a proper consumerist manner. Therefore, modern men can pamper themselves only as long this is covered in the veil of discipline and warrior masculinity. A similar notion was present in ancient Greece, where beauty contests (*kallisteion*) favoured bodily statue and strength in men as a sign of heroism and martial prowess, whereas a pleasant appearance was favoured only in women and boys (Hawley 2000, 39–50).

On the contrary, the collection "Ritual of Cleopatra" of the company *Rituals* quite expectedly concentrates on make-up products. The choice of Cleopatra VII Philopator (69 BCE–30 CE), last ruler of the Ptolemaic dynasty in Egypt, is of course not accidental. Already Galen (129–200/216 CE) and other ancient Greek medical authorities attributed Cleopatra to authoring a treatise called *Cosmetics,* and in the Latin medieval tradition Cleopatra became an authority of gynaecology. A book on aphrodisiacs by Cleopatra is mentioned by the Arabic author Qusta ibn Luqa (820–912 CE). These three different traditions (cosmetology, gynaecology and sexual advice) were closely related in the writings of male ancient Greek and Roman authors (Totelin 2017) and it is indeed not surprising that they were attributed to a foreign woman. The ancient orientalist association of Cleopatra to beauty and cosmetics lives on in modern popular culture and the cosmetic industry. In conclusion, whereas men are supposed to be well groomed warriors in contemporary culture, women are supposed to be well painted seductresses.

All of the above demonstrates the centrality of things and materials for achieving beauty ideals. Therefore, archaeology, a discipline of things, is best equipped to explore the gender aspects of beautification processes. One of the most referenced archaeological study of the use of toilet artefacts for achieving certain ideals of beauty is the one by Paul Treherne. He argued that toilet articles such as horn, bone and bronze combs, bronze tweezers, razors and mirrors, and possibly tattooing awls appear as a coherent horizon during the mid-2nd millennium BCE in central, southern, Nordic and north-western Europe. These toilet articles appear to be exclusively male funerary goods. This and the evidence of usage lead Treherne to conclude that grooming, shaving, combing and plucking hair, together with scarification and tattooing played a crucial role in maintaining masculine warrior beauty during the Middle to Late Bronze Age in Europe (Treherne 1995).

Already Roberta Gilchrist in her monograph *Gender and Archaeology: Contesting the Past* (1999, 66) has stressed some related problems. She rightfully asks how aging and coming of age, with all associated bodily changes, such as growth of hair in puberty or loss of hair in old age, would affect the beauty of the warrior and if these changes are associated with gender. Gilchrist also asked if these ideals are accessible solely to biological males or not? The paper by Treherne even stimulated the publication of the special reflection article in a *European Journal of Archaeology* issue entirely devoted to it (Frieman *et al.* 2017). In her reflective paper, Katharina Rebay-Salisbury asked if the European Bronze Age toilet objects could have been used in identity transformations from civilian to warrior and emphasised other elements of bodily beauty, such as well-trained and defined muscles as evidenced by Bronze and Iron Age body armour (Frieman *et al.* 2017, 42). Similarly, Christopher J. Knüsel asked whether individual cases represent true warriors or rather mimic men who actually never fought (Frieman *et al.* 2017, 55). The point being that looking like a warrior, does not make one a warrior, just as looking straight does not make one straight.

That beautification tools are indeed crucial for certain occupations is nicely demonstrated by Julia G. Costello in her study of the material culture of prostitution in 19th-century Los Angeles. There she showed that prostitute's dressers were filled with large quantities of beauty creams, medicine for venereal disease, conception preventatives and pain-numbing tinctures of opium and morphine (Costello 2000, 162) illustrating all the substances necessary for taking care of a female sex working body. Beautification procedures also demonstrate the entanglement of people and things. According to Alun Withey shaving was as important for the construction of polite masculinity in 18th-century Britain as was wearing steel watch chains, steel coat buttons, crests and seals. This was directly related to the appearance of sharper and more durable steel razors which made closer and more comfortable shaving possible (Withey 2013, 239). Other examples demonstrate normalisation of changes occurring through aesthetics procedures. Not only can objects like prostheses be appropriated to became part of one's body, making it able and normal (Jensen 2009), but body parts originally belonging to other bodies or made out of other materials can be appropriated by one's body. One only has to think of hair, fat and skin transplantation done both for medical and aesthetic reasons. Furthermore, nails made out of acrylic and wigs made out of animal hair, synthetic fibres and even human hair can be appropriated to the level that they can be experienced as one's own. As Alaska Thunderfuck, a celebrated drag queen and winner of *RuPaul's All Stars 2 Drag Race* show would stress: "This is my hair, I don't wear wigs". Paradoxically, bodies using cosmetics became more natural than those which did not. However, prosthetic body parts that make bodies beautiful and aesthetic surgery are not affordable to everyone, as in our society beauty does not come without high costs (Saltzberg and Chrisler 1995, 311). There are good indications that this was also the case in some past societies. For example, a full wig in ancient Rome was known as *capillamentum* or a *caliendrum* and it was more expensive than a hair piece known as *galerus* or a *galerum*. Full wigs were affordable only to wealthier men and women in ancient Rome (Draycott 2019, 74–75).

Beautification tools are not only used to achieve certain desired looks but can deliver messages that regulate behaviour (see also Chapter 3 in this volume). Using an example of a Roman mirror from Viminacium necropolis Pećine, Vladimir D. Mihajlović discusses the use of the mythological episode of Venus and Mars adultery for expressing a moral message possibly associated with the right of passage of the deceased with whom the mirror was found (Mihajlović 2011; see also Mihajlović, Chapter 7 in this volume). Thus, an object used in taking care of one's body is here *par excellence* an object used in taking care of the self (*sensu* Foucault 1988), however the self was framed at that time. Cosmetic utensils can also have a secondary agency regulating behaviours of different genders. However, one should also bear in mind that the association of cosmetics and medicaments in ancient Rome, where the term *medicamentum* covered both, is at the same time a challenge and a warning, since many toilet items, such as spatulas, probes and tweezers, are used for both purposes and by different genders (Allison 2015, 110; see also Chapter 7 by Vladimir D. Mihajlović). As in many patriarchal societies what differentiates gender in the use of cosmetic practices is the extent to which one goes with the process.

On relativity of corporeal aesthetics

What is beautiful for one does not have to be beautiful for the other. Ideas of what is beautiful vary cross-culturally (Dezhamkhooy, Chapter 9 in this volume; Gronow 1997, 10; Saltzberg and Chrisler 1995, 306). For example, Germano Vera Cruz has dealt with ideals of facial beauty among students in Mozambique, Brazil and France and showed that the French preferred more slender and smoother facial features whereas the students from Mozambique and Brazil preferred a wider and textured facial configuration (Cruz 2014, 89). Another example is the preferred appearance of the genitals. According to representations of men starting from the Archaic period and according to the writings of Aristotle, a smaller penis was more valued than a larger one since the latter cools down the sperm due to its length (see Chapter 6 by Isabelle Algrain). The ideal prepuce in ancient Greece and Rome was longer with its distinctive taper because it covered the glans. It reflected a deeper ethos revolving around cultural identity (some non-Greeks practiced circumcision), also morality, propriety, virtue and health. It was an object of erotic gaze, so that it was often either deliberately or accidentally elongated using a *kynodesmē* ("dog leash"), a thin leather thong wound around the prepuce that pulled the penis upward and was tied in a bow around the waist (Hodges 2001). Another example is ancient Roman women who used wigs made of hair cut from Germanic captives. Some of the Germanic women had their hair shorn, which was a sign of an adulteress in their society, which begs the question, how was a wig made of shorn Germanic hair viewed when worn by a Roman woman (Draycott 2019, 85)?

Beauty ideals are also subject to change and are often reflected in the changes in gender system (Dezhamkhooy, Chapter 9 in this volume; Saltzberg and Chrisler 1995, 307). For example, female beauty adapted to different contrasting ideologies throughout Chinese history. Confucianism promoted the ideal of a woman as devoted to the household. In addition, she was supposed to look delicate and demure. Her skin was ideally fair and her feet were bound (Lotti 2018, 96). The custom of foot binding meant binding the feet of five-year-old girls, so that as they grew their toes became permanently twisted under the arches and would eventually shrink in size, but the big toe remained untouched (Saltzberg and Chrisler 1995, 307). However, Maoism intended to liberate women from the male-dominated system of private property and it put emphasis on the working class beyond gender. Group identity thus came in place of individual identity. Maoism rejected the Confucian ideals of frail feminine beauty. Male and female fashion was dominated by shapeless grey and blue working-class outfits which in comparison to the Confucian tradition defeminised women (Lotti 2018, 96). With the end of Maoism, a market economy became the dominant ideology and women experienced refeminisation. As a consequence, cosmetics, fashion and aesthetic surgery started to flourish.

However, the role of cultural encounters should also be considered. When the Chinese first saw Europeans, they did not consider them handsome, quite the opposite. However, when Europeans imposed their economic power over East Asia through colonisation their appearance slowly started to be considered beautiful. In the 1920s and 1930s western beauty practices, such as permed hair, high heels, make-up, tanned skin and western clothes became popular (Lotti 2018, 98–99). Nowadays in China, just as everywhere else in the "developed" world, the power to create social taste and dictate beauty standards is in the hands of celebrities using social media. A thin figure, fair skin, oval face with pointed chin and big eyes are considered to be ideal features. Aesthetic surgery (*e.g.*, double eyelid surgery) plays an important role for achieving them. Still, whereas Chinese women are able to exercise their femininity globally, this is not the case for Chinese and other East Asian and South-East Asian men who are more often than not feminised in western media or assigned the passive role in gay sexual intercourse (Han 2016). Clearly, even globalisation has different gender trajectories when beauty ideals and racial politics are concerned. In Chapter 9 Maryam Dezhamkhooy explores how beauty ideals changed in the process from Qajar to Pahlavi rule in Iran. With modernisation and westernisation in Iran during the Pahlavi dynasty, the government did not only introduce new styles in clothing and beauty treatments, it also introduced heteronormativity (see also Papoli-Yazdi and Dezhamkhooy 2021).

Just how conflicted archaeologists can be in interpreting bodily features in other cultures is nicely illustrated with one more example from ancient Egypt, that also demonstrates the importance of gender in archaeological interpretations. In her mortuary temple at Deir el-Bahari the female king Hatshepsut (*c.* 1479–1458 BCE) of the New Kingdom's 18th Dynasty depicted her expedition to the mysterious land of Punt from which Egyptians traditionally imported luxurious and exotic products such as incense and incense trees. In one of the scenes there is a depiction of the queen of the land of Punt and her daughter who would today by a majority of people probably be described as obese (Fig. 1.3). Egyptologists have interpreted this woman variously, namely as an ideal of beauty in her own country, or a caricature of a foreigner or even an ancient Egyptian observation of pathology (for overviews of interpretation, see Green 2001, 170). However, one should bear in mind that in this scene the king

Fig. 1.3 King and Queen of Punt, mortuary temple of Hatshepsut in Deir el-Bahari, relief block from Egyptian Museum in Cairo (photo, courtesy of Filip Taterka)

of Punt is not depicted as obese. If we are dealing with a high-class ideal of beauty in the land of Punt, then this ideal of beauty is relative, gendered and restricted to women (compare with Popenoe 2004). Therefore, the different scholarly interpretations of the queen of Punt and her daughter have clearly demonstrated that beauty is socially determined.

Beauty and gender trouble

Whether the beauty of one gender is judged by the same gender or by the other it is clear that gender plays a significant role in defining an appropriate bodily aesthetic. Very often we use the word beauty to refer to the female body, whereas the bodies of men are described as "handsome", derived from the word "hand" and referring to both action and appearance. Therefore, in our heteropatriarchy "Men are instrumental; women are ornamental" (Saltzberg and Chrisler 1995, 306). It is often argued that beauty practices act as means of social control of the female body in patriarchy (Edmonds 2008, 152). One example is provided by Sylvia Ardyn Boone's study of ideals of feminine beauty in Mende art from West Africa. Among the Mende people discussions about beauty only concern women, since men consume beauty, but are never a source of it (the similarity to ancient Greece is striking). Men are in competition for the most beautiful brides as having a beautiful wife was an indication of high status. However, Mende women are also part of this beauty economy, since Mende female leaders gain power through arranging marriages (Boone 1986, 82–102).

The desperate attempts of women in our society to meet the expectations of men where beauty ideals are concerned has led some feminist scholars such as Wandy Chapkis (1986) and Naomi Wolf (1990) to fiercely criticise practices, such as use of cosmetics and various forms of bodily modifications, including plastic surgery, in order to achieve such ideals (Davis 1991, 26–27: see also Saltzberg and Chrisler 1995, 313). Exposing the inherent symbolic violence of the gender background of such practices (compare with Matić and Jensen 2017) has been an increasingly important theme of feminist writings since the 1980s. However, although true, these practices are not restricted to female bodies. Rather, in order to preserve the heterosexual matrix, male bodies have to undergo such practices too. Thus, beauty industries have also affected the look of men. Erotic images of nude males are more and more prominent in popular culture. Furthermore, women and men have internalised societal norms of attractiveness and they also comply with them because they find them pleasurable or want to avoid the penalties of not meeting the norms (Irvin 2016b, 4).

This leads us to the notion of normative gender beauty. Like Judith Butler has argued, we act out the practices assigned to our sex at birth in order to conform to social expectations and by doing this we performatively strengthen the already existing gender norms, making them normal and natural (Butler 1990; 1993). Nonetheless, which performative practices are related to gender and beauty? For example, women crossing legs rather than sitting with their legs spread is considered to be appropriate and attractive, whereas, men not crossing legs or even spreading them unnecessarily wide is a proper expression of toxic masculinity. The use of cosmetic utensils and substances can be so routinised in our habitus, that we notice them only in cases of transgression. We are regularly reminded by our heteronormative society that certain looks we present or certain cosmetic practices we conduct do not fit our gender (*cf.* Butler 1990; 1993).

But equally, there is no beauty with ugliness, as the very concept of beauty relies on selection, distinction and production of otherness (Eco 2007). As Theodor Adorno wrote "beauty is not the platonically pure beginning but rather something that originated in the renunciation of what was once feared, which only as a result of this renunciation … becomes the ugly" (Adorno 1997, 47). Disgust plays an important role in demarcating and maintaining group boundaries (Eaton 2016, 43). People considered to be ugly in our society suffer from discrimination at school or at work (Saltzberg and Chrisler 1995, 312). However, discrimination on the basis of corporeal aesthetics was not unknown to past societies. For example, ancient Romans found overindulging in depilation, wearing too much perfume, curling one's hair or generally taking too much interest in one's look to be a mark of the effeminate. Therefore, in using cosmetic products, Roman men had to find a balance between effeminacy and untidy masculinity (Totelin 2017, 147–148; see also Chapter 7 of Vladimir D. Mihajlović). I have previously mentioned that the ideal prepuce for ancient Greeks and Romans was longer because it covered the penile glans and insured modesty. The adjective *psōlos* was used for men with an exposed glans and they were considered unsightly and indecent. Ancient Greeks represented old men, slaves, old satyrs and comics with large ungainly penises and exposed glans even without erection (Hodges 2001, 392–393). Therefore, as archaeologists we have to be bear in mind that the past was also inhabited with people who did not fit the normative beauty ideals of their gender.

This leads us to the question of disability. Nowadays, western beauty standards deny disabled bodies the notion of beauty. Disabled bodies are not considered to be physically attractive. They teach us that ablism can affect all, since western beauty standards also exclude people of colour and older generations (Ellington and Lim 2017). Furthermore, paradoxically, beautification practices aiming to normalise and enable certain ideal appearances can result in disabling. The side effects of beauty treatments can be severe, as many women have been poisoned by toxic chemicals in the cosmetics (*e.g.*, ceruse, arsenic, benzene and petroleum). Side effects from plastic surgery include haemorrhages, scars and nerve damage. Silicon implants trigger breast cancer, autoimmune disease and the formation of thick scar tissue. Dieting for the sake of losing weight produces a constant feeling of hunger leading to emotional changes. Long hair and dangling earrings often get caught in machinery or entangled in clothing leading to injury. High heels and tight skirts prevent women from running from potential danger (Saltzberg and Chrisler 1995, 308–309). Yet, many of these beautification practices are not considered unhealthy, whereas obesity is (Eaton 2016,

46). The side-effects of beautification were also known to past people, as for example Ovid (43 BCE–17/18 CE) devotes an entire poem to the hair loss of Corinna, a direct result of her following fashion and dying her hair (Draycott 2019, 73). Yet people then, just as people now, undertook various procedures to make themselves look beautiful.

Conclusion and outline of this book

When one mentions anthropology of beauty, or a cross-cultural study of beauty for that matter, it is silently assumed that the aim of such studies is to find an X which bizarrely finds Y attractive (Edmonds 2008, 151). This voyeuristic approach to beauty ideals of different cultures is inherently colonial and orientalist (Said 1978) because it operates within a predetermined notion of aesthetically appealing and revolting, and because it is privileging modern western beauty ideals. There is more to aesthetic than "historico-relativistic description of what beauty has signified in various societies and styles" (Adorno 1997, 51).

Beauty as a social construct can be complicated, it is eminently subjective, corporeal, gendered, racial, hierarchical and political, it can be performed in different ways, spaces and with different associated implements. Still, the contributors to this book tackle these problems in various ways. They come from different cultural backgrounds and archaeological disciplines. They are men and women, early careers researchers and senior scholars. Following this introduction, Chapter 2, written by Helga Vogel addresses the role of beauty and charisma in the context of leadership, focusing on Sumerian Queen Pû-abī. Drawing her theoretical inspiration from leadership studies, Vogel demonstrates how the beauty of Sumerian queens supported the claim to power of the Sumerian royal houses. Far from relying on disinterestedness of Kantian appreciation, beauty ideals in Sumer were directly related to gendered social roles and ritual practices (compare with Sharman 1997, 180–181). These were materialised in the outer appearance of Queen Pû-abī through the choice of radiating, gleaming and sparkling precious metals and semi-precious stones used to produce her attire. In my own Chapter 3, I am interested less in how beauty treatments are used to achieve certain gender specific ideals of beauty and more in how a gender system is organizing beauty treatments and the spaces in which they occur, and then how in turn beauty treatments performatively (*sensu* Butler 1993) reinforce this gender system. Using Old to New Kingdom Ancient Egypt as a case study, I demonstrate that whereas beauty treatments of men could be both public and private, beautification processes of women in most cases probably occurred in private all-female spaces, even if only temporarily. In Chapter 4, Kira Zumkley closely examines a curious ancient Egyptian tool to which numerous functions have been ascribed by previous scholars, but rarely based on a thorough investigation. Zumkley demonstrates how the tool might have been used by both men and women. In Chapter 5, Filip Franković attempts to grasp the general patterns in the change of beauty ideals in the Aegean during the Late Bronze Age. Children's hairstyles were closely related to their age categories, but not to their gender identities. When girls and women are concerned, this changed in LH IIIB2–LHIIIC when girls and women, and boys and men are differentiated in iconography only by size. Women always wore their hair long. During the LM IIIA, the hairstyles of male individuals seem to become shorter, except in the case of musicians, possibly indicating their feminization in iconography. In Chapter 6, Isabelle Algrain goes beyond the usual binary approach to the use of perfume vases in ancient Greece. Focusing predominantly on evidence from ancient Athens, she argues that the use of perfume was entangled with "politonormative" sexual relations. In Chapter 7, Vladimir D. Mihajlović investigates the burials with mirrors in the Roman province of Upper Moesia. Although used by both men and women in Roman culture, mirrors were usually associated with women in iconography and texts. However, in cemeteries of Upper Moesia mirrors were associated with the full material assemblage of feminine appearance only in a limited number of cases. Hence, they cannot be treated as an indisputable reification of the elite notion of female beauty in each particular case. It is therefore tricky to pinpoint mirrors (and other associated mediators of "female beauty") as absolutely gender-specific objects. The standard known from literary and visual representations was not strictly followed in burials of Upper Moesia, but rather adapted in a more relaxed manner, giving way to more haphazard gender activities and less fixed attachments to "normally" masculine or feminine items. This was increased by the immense local cultural varieties that, although operating within the global imperial structure, could distort the ruling customs (but stayed outside the thematic scope covered by elite writers). In Chapter 8, Bo Jensen examines beauty in Viking Scandinavia and argues that the primary concern was to achieve a flawless appearance. Looking differently was causing attention and trouble. Hair and beards were gendered, and although the artefacts of hair-care were not gender specific, toiletries were feminine and filed teeth masculine. In Chapter 9, Maryam Dezhamkhooy investigates transformations of beauty ideals in the late 19th- and early 20th-century Iran. She argues that economic circumstances enforced by imperial/colonial encroachments also reshaped notions of beauty. The Pahlavi government in the early 20th century dismantled plural understandings of gender and beauty. In Chapter 10, Katharina Rebay-Salisbury reflects on the volume from a point of view of prehistorian. Her concluding contribution balances the focus of the volume on societies which left rich textual and iconographic sources with a reflection on the most challenging societies to investigate gender in, those of prehistory. Rebay-Salisbury also tackles the challenge of balancing between evolutionary perspectives on beauty ideals and sexual attraction and socio-cultural constructions of beauty ideals in relation to gender.

The contributors to this volume avoid making judgements based on their own or their culture's or subculture's beauty ideals. Their aim, just as the aim of other scholars doing recent research on beauty, is not simply "to make pronouncements on what is beautiful" (Bunn 2018, 1). Instead, they explicate how various beauty ideals are both historically and culturally specific and how they were created, maintained and changed, for which purposes and in what relation to gender.

Acknowledgements

I would like to express my gratitude to the participants of the session "Beautiful bodies: Gender, bodily care and material culture in the past" organized as an AGE (Archaeology and Gender in Europe working community) at the Annual Meeting of the European Association of Archaeologists (EAA) in Maastricht, 30th August–3rd September 2017. The papers and discussion at this session inspired this volume and its introductory chapter. The work leading to this publication was supported by the German Academic Exchange Network (DAAD) with funds from the German Federal Ministry of Education and Research (BMBF) and the People Programme (Marie Curie Actions) of the European Union's Seventh Framework Programme (FP7/2007-2013) under REA grant agreement no. 605728 (P.R.I.M.E-Postdoctoral Researches International Mobility Experience). I would like to thank Angelika Lohwasser (University of Muenster, Germany) and Bettina Bader (Austrian Archaeological Institute, Vienna) for hosting my DAAD P.R.I.M.E project *Beautiful Kush: Cosmetic Substances and Utensils in Egyptian New Kingdom Nubia* (2018–2019).

Bibliography

Adorno, T. (1997) *Aesthetic Theory*. London and New York, Continuum.

Allison, P.M. (2015) Characterizing Roman artifacts to investigate gendered practices in contexts without sexed bodies. *American Journal of Archaeology* 119 (1), 103–123.

Back Danielsson, I-M. and Thedéen, S. (eds) (2012) *To Tender Gender: The Pasts and Futures of Gender Research in Archaeology*. Stockholm Studies in Archaeology 58. Stockholm, Department of Archaeology and Classical Studies, Stockholm University.

Boone, S.A. (1986) *Radiance from the Waters: Ideals of Feminine Beauty in Mende Art*. New Haven and London, Yale University Press.

Borić, D. and Robb, J. (eds) (2008) *Past Bodies. Body-Centred Research in Archaeology*. Oxford, Oxbow Books.

Bourdieu, P. (1984) *Distinction. A Social Critique of the Judgment of Taste*. Translated from French by R. Nice. Cambridge, Harvard University Press.

Bunn, S. (2018) Anthropology and beauty: introduction. In S. Bunn (ed.) *Anthropology and Beauty. From Aesthetics to Creativity*, 1–20. London and New York, Routledge.

Butler, J. (1990) *Gender Trouble: Feminism and the Subversion of Identity*. London and New York, Routledge.

Butler, J. (1993) *Bodies That Matter: On the Discursive Limits of "Sex"*. London and New York, Routledge.

Cahill, A.J. (2003) Feminist pleasure and feminine beautification *Hypatia* 18 (4), 42–64.

Chakrabarty, D. (2000) *Provincializing Europe. Postcolonial Thought and Historical Difference*. Princeton and Oxford, Princeton University Press.

Chapkis, W. (1986) *Beauty Secrets: Women and the Politics of Appearance*. Boston, MA, South End Press.

Chi, Yennifer Y. and Azara, Pedro (eds) (2015) *From Ancient to Modern: Archaeology and Aesthetics*. Princeton, Princeton University Press.

Costello, J.G. (2000) Red Light Voices: an archaeological drama of late nineteenth-century prostitution. In R.A. Schmidt and B.L. Voss (eds) *Archaeologies of Sexuality*, 160–175. London and New York, Routledge.

Craig, M.L. (2002) *Aint' I a Beauty Queen? Black Women, Beauty, and the Politics of Race*. Oxford, Oxford University Press.

Cruz, G.V. (2014) Cross-cultural study of facial beauty. *Journal of Psychology in Africa* 23 (1), 87–89.

van Damme, W. (1996) *Beauty in Context: Towards an Anthropological Approach to Aesthetics*. Leiden and New York, Brill.

Davis, K. (1991) Remaking the she-devil: a critical look at feminist approaches to beauty. *Hypatia* 6 (2), 21–43.

Davis, W. (2010) *Queer Beauty. Sexuality and Aesthetics from Winckelmann to Freud and Beyond*. New York, Columbia University Press.

Díaz-Andreu, M. (2005) Gender identity. In M. Díaz-Andreu, S. Lucy, S. Babić and D.N. Edwards (eds) *The Archaeology of Identity: Approaches to Gender, Age, Status, Ethnicity and Religion*, 13–42. London and New York, Routledge.

Draycott, J. (2019) Prosthetic hair in ancient Rome. In J. Draycott (ed.) *Prostheses in Antiquity*, 71–96. London and New York, Routledge.

Eaton, A. (2016) Taste in bodies and fat oppression In S. Irvin (ed) *Body Aesthetics*, 37–59. Oxford, Oxford University Press.

Eco, U. (2004) *History of Beauty*. New York, Rizzoli International.

Eco, U. (2007) *On Ugliness*. Translated from Italian by A. McEwen. London, Harvil Secker.

Edmonds, A. (2008) Beauty and health: anthropological perspectives. *Medische Antropologie* 20 (1), 151–162.

Ellington, T.N. and Lim, S.R. (2017) Rendered powerless: disability versus Westernized beauty standards. *QED: A Journal in GLBTQ Worldmaking* 4 (4), 170–176.

Forth, C.E. (2013) The qualities of fat: bodies, history, and materiality. *Journal of Material Culture* 18 (2), 135–154.

Foucault, M. (1988) Technologies of the self. In L.H. Martin, H. Gutman, and P.H. Hutton (eds) *Technologies of the Self. A Seminar with Michel Foucault*, 16–49. London, Tavistock Publications.

Frieman, C.J. (2017) Aging well: Treherne's 'warrior's beauty' two decades later. *European Journal of Archaeology* 20 (1), 36–73.

Gero, J.M. and Conkey, M.W. (eds) (1991) *Engendering Archaeology. Women and Prehistory*. Oxford, Blackwell.

Gherchanoc, F. (2016) *Concours de beauté et beautés du corps en Grèce ancienne. Discours et pratiques*. Bordeaux, Ausonius.

Gilchrist, R. (1999) *Gender Archaeology. Contesting the Past*. London and New York, Routledge.

Gilman, S.L. (1999) *The Body Beautiful. A Cultural History of Aesthetic Surgery*. Princeton, Princeton University Press.

Glazebrook, A. (2009) Cosmetics and Sôphrosunê: Ischomachos' wife in Xenophon's Oikonomikos. *The Classical World* 102 (3), 233–248.

Gosden, C. (2001) Making sense: archaeology and aesthetics. *World Archaeology* 33 (2), 163–167.

Green, L. (2001) Beauty. In D.B. Redford (ed.) *Oxford Encyclopedia of Ancient Egypt. Volume I*, 167–171. Oxford, Oxford University Press.

Gronow, J. (1997) *The Sociology of Taste*. London and New York, Routledge.

Han, C.W. (2016) From "little brown brothers" to "queer Asian wives": constructing the Asian male body. In S. Irvin (ed.) *Body Aesthetics*, 61–80. Oxford, Oxford University Press.

Hau, M. (2003) *The Cult of Health and Beauty in Germany: A Social History, 1890-1930*. Chicago, The University of Chicago Press.

Hamilakis, Y., Pluciennik, M. and Tarlow, S. (eds) (2002) *Thinking through the Body: Archaeologies of Corporeality*. New York, Kluwer Academic/Plenum Publishers.

Hawley, R. (2000) The dynamic of beauty in Classical Greece. In D. Montserrat (ed.) *Changing Bodies, Changing Meanings. Studies on the Human Body in Antiquity*, 36–54. London and New York, Routledge.

Hays-Gilpin, K. and Whitley, D.S. (eds) (1998) *Reader in Gender Archaeology*. London and New York, Routledge.

Hodges, F.M. (2001) The ideal prepuce in Ancient Greece and Rome: male genital aesthetics and their relation to "lipodermos", circumcision, foreskin restoration, and the "kynodesmē". *Bulletin of the History of Medicine* 75 (3), 375–405.

Holleran, C. (2012) *Shopping in Ancient Rome. The Retail Trade in the Late Republic and the Principate*. Oxford, Oxford University Press.

Jensen, B. (2009) Rude tools and material difference-Queer theory, ANT and materiality: an under-explored intersection? *Graduate Journal of Social Science* 6 (1), 42–71.

Johnston, M.A. (2010) "To what bawdy house doth your maister belong?": barbers, bawds, and vice in the Early Modern London barbershop. In A. Bailey and R. Hentschell (eds) *Masculinity and the Metropolis of Vice, 1550–1650*, 114–135. New York, Palgrave Macmillan.

Joyce, R.A. (2000) A Precolumbian gaze: male sexuality among the ancient Maya. In R.A. Schmidt and B.L. Voss (eds) *Archaeologies of Sexuality*, 263–283. London and New York, Routledge.

Irvin, S. (ed.) (2016a) *Body Aesthetics*. Oxford, Oxford University Press.

Irvin, S. (2016b) Introduction. Why body aesthetics? In S. Irvin (ed.) *Body Aesthetics*, 1–11. Oxford, Oxford University Press.

Kant, I. (2000) *Critique of the Power of Judgment*. Edited by P. Guyer. Translated by P. Guyer and E. Matthews. Cambridge, Cambridge University Press.

Lotti, V. (2018) The image of the beautiful woman: beauty ideals in modern urban China. *Asien* 147, 92–104.

Martin, M. (2009) *Selling Beauty – Cosmetics, Commerce, and French Society, 1750–1830*. Baltimore, The John Hopkins University Press.

Matić, U. (2019) *Body and Frames of War in New Kingdom Egypt. Violent Treatments of Enemies and Prisoners*. Philippika 134. Wiesbaden, Harrassowitz.

Matić, U. and Jensen, B. (eds) (2017) *Archaeologies of Gender and Violence*. Oxford, Oxbow Books.

Mayes, E.M. (1997) As soft as straight gets: African American women and mainstream beauty standards in haircare advertising. *Counterpoints* 54, 85–108.

Meskell, L.M. and Joyce, R.A. (2003) *Embodied Lives: Figuring Ancient Maya and Egyptian Experience*. London and New York, Routledge.

Mihajlović, V.D. (2011) Adultery in the mirror: Roman mirror from Viminacium, Myth, moral and rite(s) of passage. In K. Maricki-Gađanski (ed.) *Antika i suvremeni svet: religija i kultura*, 178–193. Beograd, Društvo za antičke studije Srbije i Institut za teološka istraživanja.

Mitter, P. (2017) Western theories of beauty and non-Western peoples. In K.M. Higgins, S. Maira and S. Sikka (eds) *Artistic Visions and the Promise of Beauty Cross-Cultural Perspectives*, 79–90. London and New York, Springer.

Montserrat, D. (ed.) (1998) *Changing Bodies, Changing Meanings. Studies on the Human Body in Antiquity*. London and New York, Routledge.

Oikkonen, V. (2013) *Gender, Sexuality and Reproduction in Evolutionary Narratives*. London and New York, Routledge.

Olson, K. (2009) Cosmetics in Roman antiquity: substance, remedy, poison. *The Classical World* 102 (3), 291–310.

Palmer, C. (2008) Brazen cheek: face-painters in late eighteenth-century England. *Oxford Art Journal* 31 (2), 197–213.

Papoli-Yazdi, L. and Dezhamkhooy, M. (2021) *Homogenization, Gender and Everyday Life in Pre- and Trans-modern Iran: An Archaeological Reading*. Münster, Waxmann.

Patton, T.O. (2006) Hey girl, am I more than my hair?: African American women and their struggles with beauty, body image, and hair. *The National Women's Studies Association Journal* 18 (2), 24–51.

Popenoe, R. (2004) *Feeding Desire: Fatness, Beauty, and Sexuality Among a Saharan People.* London and New York, Routledge.

Power, C. (2010) Cosmetics, identity and consciousness. *Journal of Consciousness Studies* 17 (7–8), 73–94.

Pylypa, J. (1998) Power and bodily practice: applying the work of Foucault to an anthropology of the body. *Arizona Anthropologist* 13, 21–36.

Rauser, A. (2020) *The Age of Undress: Art, Fashion, and the Classical Ideal in the 1790s.* New Haven and London, Yale University Press.

Rautman, A.E. (ed.) (2000) *Reading the Body: Representations and Remains in the Archaeological Record.* Philadelphia, University of Pennsylvania Press.

Rebay-Salisbury, K., Sørensen, M.L.S. and Hughes, J. (eds) (2010) *Body Parts and Bodies Whole. Changing Relations and Meanings.* Oxford, Oxbow Books.

Reid, H. (2012) Athletic beauty in classical Greece: a philosophical view. *Journal of the Philosophy of Sport* 39 (2), 281–297.

Robb, J. and Harris, O.J.T. (eds) (2013) *The Body in History. Europe from the Palaeolithic to the Future.* Cambridge, Cambridge University Press.

Said, E. (1978) *Orientalism.* New York, Pantheon Books.

Saltzberg, E.A. and Chrisler, J.C. (1995) Beauty is the beast: psychological effects of the pursuit of the perfect female body. In J. Freeman (ed.) *Women: A Feminist Perspective*, 306–315. Mountain View, CA, Mayfield.

Sharman, R. (1997) The anthropology of aesthetics: a cross-cultural approach. *Journal of the Anthropological Society of Oxford* 28 (2), 177–192.

Siebers, T. (ed.) (2000a) *The Body Aesthetic: From Fine Art to Body Modification.* Ann Arbor, The University of Michigan Press.

Siebers, T. (2000b). Introduction: defining the body aesthetic. In T. Siebers (ed.) *The Body Aesthetic: From Fine Art to Body Modification*, 1–13. Ann Arbor, The University of Michigan Press.

Sofaer, J. (2006) *The Body as Material Culture: A Theoretical Osteoarchaeology.* Cambridge, Cambridge University Press.

Sørensen, M.L.S. (2000) *Gender Archaeology.* Cambridge, Polity Press.

Tate, S. (2007) Black beauty: shade, hair and anti-racist aesthetics. *Ethnic and Racial Studies* 30 (2), 300–319.

Thomas, J. (2004) *Archaeology and Modernity.* London and New York, Routledge.

Toner, J. (2015) Barbers, barbershops and searching for Roman popular culture. *Papers of the British School at Rome* 83, 91–109.

Totelin, L. (2017) From technē to kakotechnia. Use and abuse of ancient cosmetic texts. In M. Formisano and P. Van Der Eijk (eds) *Knowledge, Text and Practice in Ancient Technical Writing*, 138–162. Cambridge, Cambridge University Press.

Treherne, P. (1995) The warrior's beauty: the masculine body and self-identity in Bronze Age-Europe. *Journal of European Archaeology* 3 (1), 105–144.

Wax, M. (1957) Themes in cosmetics and grooming. *American Journal of Sociology* 62 (6), 588–593.

Withey, A. (2013) Shaving and masculinity in eighteenth-century Britain. *Journal of Eighteenth-Century Studies* 36 (2), 225–243.

Wolf, N. (1990) *The Beauty Myth: How Images of Beauty Are Used Against Women.* London, Vintage.

Yan, Y. and Bissell, K. (2014) The globalization of beauty: how is ideal beauty influenced by globally published fashion and beauty magazines? *Journal of Intercultural Communication Research* 43 (3), 194–214.

Chapter 2

The queen's beauty: leadership as an aesthetic and embodied practice in ancient Mesopotamia

Helga Vogel

Abstract

Using Queen Pû-abī as an example, this contribution investigates the aesthetics of leadership in ancient southern Mesopotamia (modern South Iraq) around 2500 BCE. The study is guided by a theoretical framework that conceptualises leadership as an embodied, sensory and felt experience involving the active participation of the followers. I will demonstrate how the aesthetic leadership of Sumerian queens supported the claim to power of the Sumerian royal houses. The decisive factor being the close linking of religious, cultural and social ideas, as well as values and norms in the appearance of Sumerian queens. It is argued, that the resplendent inner and outer beauty of the Sumerian queens evoked strong positive feelings – like admiration, joy, hope and security – and substantiated the idealisation and sacredness of rulership.

Key words: *aesthetic leadership, Mesopotamian archaeology, gender studies, ancient Near Eastern art*

Introduction

When it comes to archaeological societies, and especially ancient Near Eastern societies, talking about power still means talking primarily about men and their achievements as rulers and warriors. This is even true for a period in the history of ancient Mesopotamia in which a substantial part of the written sources stems from the household of the queens of Lagaš, one of the city-states that governed today's southern Iraq in the middle of the 3rd millennium BCE. The important role of queens in the governance of the Sumerian city-states during the so called Early Dynastic Periods

(ED I–III) is further attested by their depictions on stelae, votive plaques and cylinder seals; their lavish funerals and richly equipped graves point in the same direction. Against this backdrop, I will examine in this paper how the appearance and the public behavior of Sumerian queens contributed to the consolidation and reproduction of existing social power structures and to their widespread social acknowledgment. There have been some studies on the political significance of the body of Mesopotamian rulers, mostly from an art-historical perspective (Suter 2010; 2012; Vogel 2013a; 2018). The social, political and symbolic-religious implications of the public appearance of Mesopotamian queens, on the other hand, have, to my knowledge, never been the subject of a detailed analysis (but see, for example, Suter 2016 and 2017 for a survey of images of queens and other women from 3rd-millennium BCE Mesopotamia, as well as Gansell 2014 for a study of images and conceptions of ideal feminine beauty in Neo-Assyrian royal contexts and especially Gansell 2018a for an interpretation of royal Neo-Assyrian dress elements in terms of identity and ideology; see also Gansell 2018b for a digital reconstruction of the appearance of Neo-Assyrian queens).

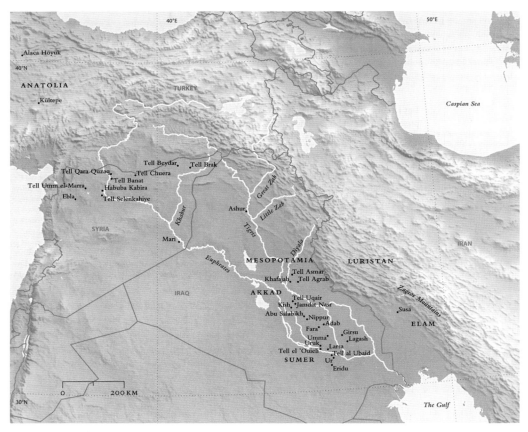

Fig. 2.1 *Map of the Near East during the Late Uruk and Early Dynastic periods. The city of Ur is located in the very south of Mesopotamia*

The study at hand focuses on the appearance of Queen Pû-abī of Ur at her funeral (for the location of Ur see Fig. 2.1). In the field of ancient Near Eastern studies until today, Pû-abī's spectacular burial (Figs 2.2 and 2.3), that was a world sensation at the time of its discovery in January 1928 (see Hafford and Zettler 2015), is only rivaled by the burials of Neo-Assyrian queens at Nimrud (see Damerji 1999; Hussein and Suleiman 2000).

In particular, Queen Pû-abī's very expensively worked golden headdress with beautiful details (Fig. 2.4) left most viewers with feelings of astonishment and great admiration, and this is still the case today. The same applies for her other jewelry, such as a cloak made of thousands of beads of semi-precious stones (Fig. 2.5) or her unique "diadem" (Fig. 2.6). The interment of Queen Pû-abī is therefore particularly suitable for a study on aesthetic leadership from an archaeological perspective.

The paper is organised as follows: within this framework the first section provides a brief overview of the historical and sociocultural context of Pû-abī's funeral. The

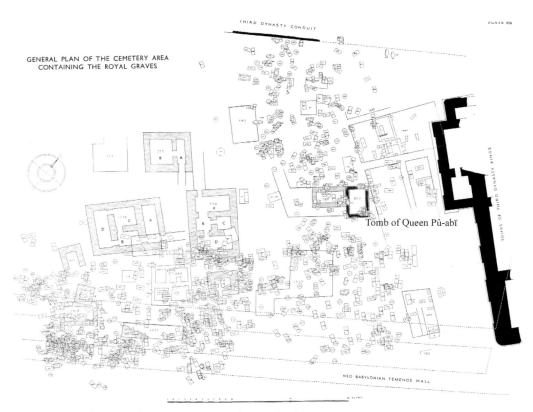

Fig. 2.2 Plan of the Royal Cemetery at Ur. The tomb of the queen Pû-abī (RT 800) is marked (after Woolley 1934, pl. 274)

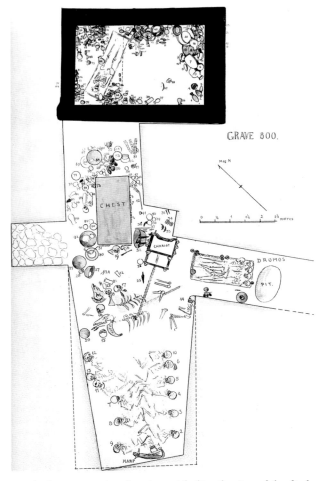

Fig. 2.3 Tomb of queen Pû-abī. Excavation drawing with distribution of the finds within the chamber (after Woolley 1934, pl. 36)

social status and the governmental activities of the Sumerian queens will be discussed at some length. Thereafter, I will summarise the archaeological remains of Pû-abī's burial in the Royal Cemetery of Ur. The analytical sections of the paper are based on a step-by-step analysis of the practices and procedures that were undertaken to create the queen's resplendent appearance. Based on these analyses I first discuss the reasons behind the beauty measures that were undertaken and second the emotional impact of the queen's beauty on a given audience and its political significance. The analytical part of the paper is conceptually anchored within the framework of current aesthetic leadership studies, the guiding principles of which are summarised below.

Fig. 2.4 Pû-abī's headdress (reconstructed by Katharine and Leonhard Woolley), side view. Top to bottom: (a) Gold comb with seven floral attachments. A lapis lazuli ball set in gold caps sits in the middle of each flower. L. 27.5 cm, W. 27 cm; 363.1 g. (U.10937) Benzel 2013, cat. no. 1. (b) Wreaths of 37 gold willow leaves with carnelian beads at tips and 13 gold flowers, strung with gold and lapis lazuli beads. The petals are inlaid with lapis lazuli and white paste. L. 66 cm, 255 g. (U.10936) Benzel 2013, cat. no. 4. (c) Wreath of 18 gold poplar leaves with carnelian beads at tips, strung with lapis lazuli and carnelian beads. L. 63 cm, 175.3 g. (U.10935bis) Benzel 2013, cat. no. 2. (d) Wreath of 20 gold rings, strung with lapis lazuli and carnelian beards. L. 36.5 cm, 277.6 g. (U10935) Benzel 2013, cat. no. 5. (e) Wreath of 20 gold poplar leaves, strung with lapis lazuli and carnelian beads. L. 70 cm, 216.3 g. (U.10935bis) Benzel 2013, cat. no. 3. (f) Gold hair ribbon (fragment). L. approx. 173 cm, W. 1.7 cm, 385.3 g. (U.10934) Benzel 2013, cat. no. 8. According to Woolley, the hair ribbon was 12 m long. (g) Pair of gold earrings, lunate-shaped. L. 10.5 cm, 84.7 g. (U.10933) Benzel 2013, cat. no. 8. (h) Two, three or four hair rings, gold round wire wrapped to form triple coils (U.10942) Benzel 2013, cat. no. 7 (Woolley 1934, pl. 127)

Conceptual framework

Traditionally, ancient Near Eastern studies have adopted the perspective of the ruling powers to describe social and political power structures in ancient Near Eastern societies. Against this backdrop, the premises and results of aesthetical leadership studies open up promising new research paths for the study of power phenomena in ancient Near Eastern societies in several ways.

First, the concrete practices of power making become the focus of scientific interest as aesthetic leadership studies focus on the investigation of micro practices in the

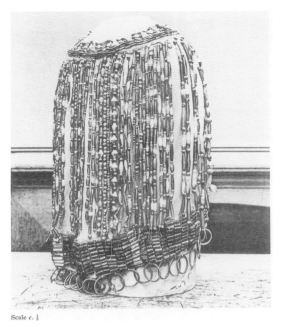

Scale *c.* ⅓

Fig. 2.5 The reconstruction of the bead cloak by L. Woolley (Woolley 1934, pl. 130)

context of specific leadership situations. This is entirely in line with Michel Foucault's (1995; 2001; 2002; 2005) and Pierre Bourdieu's (1984; 1998; 2005) ground-breaking research on the phenomenon of power. Aesthetic leadership studies assume that, as a matter of principle, leadership must be embodied. This includes the shaping of the surface and exterior of the leader's body according to social norms and values, control of the body's reactions, as well as the expectation that it performs certain actions and gestures, and a deliberate use of one's voice. The leader's body is seen as a carrier of emotion, desire, fantasies, bodily sensations and motivation (Pullen and Vachhani 2013, 315), causing powerful emotions and reactions in their

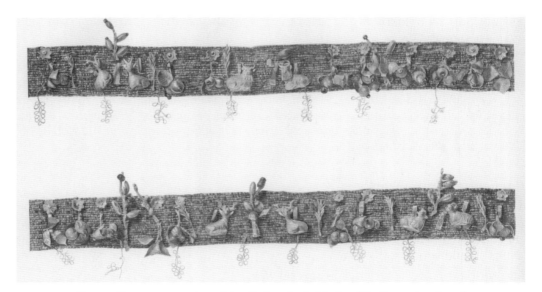

Fig. 2.6 The reconstruction of the diadem by L. Wooley (Woolley 1934, pl. 140)

followers. Ideally, the followers' experience will result in a deeply personal, emotional attachment and identification with a leader and his or her goals (Ford *et al.* 2017; Hansen, Ropo and Sauer 2007; Karlsson 2011; Ladkin 2008; Ladkin and Taylor 2010).

Second, as aesthetic leadership studies understand leadership as a relational and felt experience, research conducted in this field is often particularly interested in studying the complex relationships between followers and leaders (Hansen, Ropo and Sauer 2007). As opposed to leader-centric studies, here a leader is not understood to be a genuine leader, but to be a person to whom his or her followers ascribe specific leadership skills and by doing so make him or her "their leader" in the first place. Consequently, followers are not described as underlings who naturally need to be guided, but as persons who draw their own conclusions from perceived leadership phenomena by analysing the complex interplay between their bodily experiences, sensual observations, emotions, expectations and thoughts (Parry and Kempster 2014). In aesthetic leadership studies, the follower is thus one who actively contributes to the success or failure of a given leadership situation. However, for this to happen a leader and his or her followers must share the same (or very similar) social norms and values, traditions, images, narratives, mythologies, ideas, expectations and so on (*e.g.*, Zhang *et al.* 2011).

Third, if leadership is understood as an aesthetic experience, then it is to be expected that the environment, the design and atmosphere of a building or room, as well as physical objects, will have an impact on the perception and assessment of a given leadership situation. A growing body of literature has thus examined the interconnections between space, artifacts and individuals, addressing their feelings, perceptions, thoughts and interactions (Carroll and Smolović Jones 2018; Hawkins 2015; Ropo and Salovaara 2018; Zhang and Spicer 2014). It is argued, that space as well as material objects "play an active role in generating, transmitting, legitimizing and undoing meanings associated with leadership" (Hawkins 2015, 952). For example, the hierarchy of a company will typically take form and become visible as well as tangible in a sensual way through a rank-specific use of space and physical objects. However, only if those involved have the same knowledge about the meaning of objects and space, the "non-human agents" will positively contribute to the desired leadership effects.

Discussion

Applying the principles of aesthetic leadership studies to an archaeological case study may result in a research design as already outlined above. The first question that arises should concern which elements of the practice of aesthetic leadership can be determined in a particular case. As leadership is understood in aesthetic leadership studies as an embodied experience, one would probably start with analysing the appearance of a ruler or a queen, considering pictorial representations, written descriptions – if there are any – as well as archaeological remains of the beautification of the ruler's or the queen's body, such as cosmetics, fabric remnants, jewelry, or scent bottles and the like. With regard to the political significance of the ruler's or the queen's appearance, we can take a cue from Foucault's work and ask, why that way and why not in some other way? This question aims at the common socio-cultural background in a given archaeological society which provided the coordinates not only for the crafting, but also for the perception, and interpretation of the ruler's or the queen's appearance.

The conception of leadership as a multifaceted and mutual relationship between a leader and his or her followers may be of particular interest for studies of power phenomena in archaeological societies as it alters the meaning that is typically ascribed to common people in this kind of research. Put simply, according to the premises of aesthetic leadership studies, common people in preliminary states should be seen as persons with agency who actively contributed to the success or failure of leadership and not as mere objects suffering acts of domination. Yet, a structural characteristic of any hierarchical organisation/society is unequal access to material, social, cultural and economical resources. The subjective experience of aesthetic leadership and the objective reality of power structures are thus inevitably closely intertwined. The fact that perception and interpretation patterns are "power-based/shaped" is rarely addressed in aesthetic leadership studies (see Collinson 2014). However, this aspect should not be overlooked in archaeological case studies.

One other point is that aesthetic leadership studies may enhance our understanding of archaeological objects that are used in the processes of creating and maintaining power. With the exception of insignia, such objects have so far been addressed primarily as luxury goods or prestige objects that reflect the social status of the persons to whom they once belonged. One conclusion to be drawn from the results of the relevant research in the field of aesthetic leadership studies is that artifacts only gain importance as carriers of meaning, *e.g.*, of prestige, power, gender and so on, and that they do so only in certain settings and in regard to specific social groups. Thus, "being a prestige object" is solely the result of social conventions and convictions, past and present, and by no means an intrinsic feature of certain things. Otherwise put, the category "prestige object" is a social, not a material fact. Regarding the even more nebulous category "luxury good", Joanne Pillsbury (2017, 6) recently stated in the context of her research on such items from Mesoamerican ancient cultures:

> The concept of luxury varies over time and place, however, with the most common contemporary understanding identifying it with superfluous things. … But this simple distinction obscures the importance of cultural beliefs, where certain things, while not considered essential for practical purposes, according to our own beliefs, were nonetheless social necessities in particular times and places.

Thus, before categorising archaeological artifacts such as Queen Pû-abī's jewelry as prestige objects or luxury items, it needs to be demonstrated that they only served the purpose of an empty display of splendor and had no deeper meaning.

Historical context

At the time of Queen Pû-abī's funeral, today's southern Iraq was divided between powerful families who ruled over larger towns and their hinterlands. Despite the archaeological and written evidence of rivalries and military conflicts between the ruling families, southern Mesopotamia at that time constituted a cultural area with a unique writing system (cuneiform), a common system of calculation and measurement, a shared imagery, as well as common paradigms, narratives, beliefs, norms, traditions and customs (Bauer 1998; Nissen 2012, 62–74; see also the contributions in Crawford 2013 and Dittmann and Selz 2015). Each city-state was nominally ruled by a city-god or a city-goddess whose representative was the king (Selz 1998; 2005a, 49–55; Steible 2001). Still, power was not concentrated in the temples of the gods and goddesses, but in the palaces, which controlled weapons, key resources (*e.g.*, metals), long distance-trade and other aspects of economic life (Schrakamp 2013). In stelae and inscriptions, the rulers emphasised their divinely sanctioned power. At the same time, considerable efforts were made to establish close bonds between the ruling houses and their functionaries, as well as their families, and to unite the population under the leadership of the ruling families. In these efforts, the queens played an important role.

The queens' status and their governmental activities

We are particularly well informed about the governmental activities of the last three queens of the city-state Lagaš – Dimtur, Baranamtara and Šaša – as about 1,700 administrative tablets from the archive of the queens' household are at our disposal (Beld 2002; Mayerová 2015; Prentice 2010, 2–5; Sallaberger 2013, 225–227; Schrakamp 2013, 447–452; Selz 1995, 1–15). In Lagaš, the household of the queen, the so-called É-MÍ, literal "house [of[the woman [of the ruler]", was an institution with about 1,200 male and female employees of all ages who worked in agriculture, in fruit and vegetable growing, in timber and reed industries, in fishing and cattle breeding, as well as in processing and utilities units, in workshops and in other areas (Schrakamp 2013, 447). As far as may be gathered from the aforementioned administrative tablets – especially informative are offering-lists, ration lists and disbursement notes – the governmental activities of the queens were primarily aimed at enhancing and securing the power of the ruling house through peaceful means. We know, for example, that extra rations were given out to certain household members in the context of various religious festivals. On other occasions, rations of expensive wool or special foods were distributed to key staff members and their wives (Prentice 2010, 176–181). Particularly instructive is an annual ceremony at which certain individuals representing the queen's household ritually distributed "pure milk and malt" to the wives of men of the upper social stratum of the city-state, as well as to a few others (Prentice 2010, 181–185; Selz 1995, 73–78). These events, which took place regularly, formed a strong bond between the ruling house, its officials and functionaries, and influential families; the shared experience may also have created a common sense of identity among the participants that was oriented towards the ruling house.

At the level of the city-state and its hinterland the queens' regular journeys to important temples and their visits to the "drinking places of the dead" fulfilled the same functions. Sacrifices were offered to the gods and goddesses (*e.g.*, grain, beer, dates, cucumber, oil, wine, fish, sheep) and the dead were ritually provided with liquids and food, as was the custom (Bauer 1998, 506–507; Prentice 2010, 173–176; Vogel 2013b, 429–431; see also Selz 2005b; 2006). The care for the gods and goddesses was of utmost importance, as the gods were believed to determine the fate of men and thus also the fate of the city-state. The fulfillment of their cultic duties – which also included the donation of valuable votive offerings, temple equipment and additional sacrifices to the temples (Prentice 2010, 175–176) – offered queens therefore the opportunity to prove their reliability, uprightness, honesty and trustworthiness and thereby increase their reputation and, by extension, the reputation of the ruling house. In a more mundane sense, the cycles of ever recurring cultic events tied the local political, administrative and religious elites (and their followers) again and again to the ruling dynasty while at the same time reminding them of their obligations to the ruling house. Unfortunately, we do not know what a Sumerian queen looked like while performing cultic and religious duties. Yet, we can assume with some certainty that her "inner beauty", that is her impeccable morality and ethics, which enabled queens to establish their auspicious relationship with the gods and goddesses in the first place, became apparent not only in her activities, but also in her outer appearance.

According to our sources, a Sumerian queen's political agency was not limited to the ceremonial and ritual sphere. There is written evidence that the queens of Lagaš established diplomatic relationships with the queens of other city-states; on one occasion, donkeys, wooden objects, an ivory carved relief, copper and bronze were exchanged as diplomatic gifts (RTC 19: Prentice 2010, 162–163; see also Prentice 2010, 164–165, 172). Visual representations of two high-ranking women sitting opposite each other with drinking utensils and surrounded by female cupbearers, female musicians and female attendants could depict meetings between two queens or the reception of high-ranking women by the queen (Fig. 2.7).

The fact that the meetings of two Sumerian queens or the reception of high ranking women by the queen were considered just as worthy of artistic representation as the reception of male officials by the king or the royal couple may serve as further evidence for the significance of the Sumerian queens' governmental activities, as well as their high social status. In this respect, it should be noted that stelae, votive plaques and seal décors prove that the queen and the ruler met as equals at that time, at least on those occasions represented. An example is provided by the votive plaque below

Fig. 2.7 One of Pû-abī's three cylinder seals, showing a double-register banquet scene with only female participants and female staff (among others musicians, cupbearers, waitresses). The sitting female figure in the upper register, left, probably depicts the queen. Lapis lazuli. H. 4 cm, D. 2 cm (U.10872) (http://www.ur-online.org/subject/10782/)

(Fig. 2.8) which depicts a typical banqueting scene with the queen and the king occupying the same space, performing the same postures, gestures and attitudes, carrying the same type of insignia, and being attended in the same manner, but typically either by women (queen) or by men (king) (see also Asher-Greve 2013, 363–368; Crawford 2014, 13–18; Otto 2016, 114–121 and for the queens' administrative activities in the palace that resembled the activities of the rulers, Schrakamp 2013, 449–450).

We have further evidence of the high social status and the religious-political importance of Sumerian queens which needs to be mentioned here, as the preserved information will directly influence our discussion of Queen Pû-abī's appearance at her funeral. We know that at least two queens of Lagaš bore religious-ceremonial titles. Queen Baranamtara was addressed as PAP.PAP, that means roughly "the one who causes growth/cultivates sb./sth" ("die wachsen lässt/grosszieht"; see Selz 1998, 272). Baranamtara was also named the "mother of the city" or, in personal names, the "eternal mother" (see Selz 1998, 272–273). The latter is also true for Queen Dimtur, whose religious title Ni-a-a – the meaning is still unknown – was found, for example, in a personal name that reads "Ni-a-a (is) the eternal mother" (see Selz

Fig. 2.8 Votive plaque. Limestone. H. 20 cm. Mesopotamia, Khafajah, Sin temple. ED IIIA, c. 2500–2400 BCE. The Oriental Institute of the University of Chicago A 12417. Courtesy of the Wikimedia user Osama Shukir Muhammed Amin FRCP (Glasg) (https://upload.wikimedia.org/wikipedia/commons/7/77/ Sumerian_votive_wall_plaque_with_3_registers%2C_from_Khafajah%2C_Iraq%2C_c._2600-2370_BCE._ Iraq_Museum.jpg)

1998, 212). It is noteworthy that personal names which address PAP.PAP, on the one hand emphasise the close relationship between Queen Baranamtara and some of the most important goddesses of the city-state and her high reputation among the gods, see for example "PAP.PAP [is] really appreciated by [the goddess] Inanna", and on the other hand even ascribe a divine status to the queen as in the name "PAP.PAP [is] my personal goddess" (see Selz 1998, 273 nos. 13 and .14). It is therefore to be expected, that a Sumerian queen's official appearance conveyed at least to a certain extent not only her high social status, but also the distinctive features of Sumerian queenhood broadly outlined above.

The burial of Queen Pû-abī

The archaeological remains and the written records from the middle of the third millennium BCE indicate that the care for the dead was of utmost importance for the people living in todays southern Iraq at that time (see for example Vogel 2013b with references). The death of Queen Baranamtara was a public event involving a large mourning community who performed the necessary rites over two days (Prentice 2010, 185). Baranamtara was probably buried on the third day after her death, but we currently have no information about her funeral. Therefore it is the finds and findings of the Royal Cemetery of Ur that provide insight into the actual interment of a Sumerian queen.

The Royal Cemetery of Ur, which is located at the south-eastern slope of the later religious and political central area of the city, was continuously used for at least 500 years; and more than 2000 burials were excavated (see Fig. 2.2; Zettler and Hafford 2014–2016, 369, tab. 1, 375–379 with references to the dating of the graves). The excavator, Sir Leonard Woolley, designated 16 burials as the tombs of the ruling house of Ur during the Early Dynastic III based on their extraordinary wealth, their monumental construction (shaft graves with burial chambers) and the presence of mostly female co-interments (Woolley 1934, 33–37; see also Vogel 2014, abb. 6; the interpretation of the co-interments is controversial, Vogel 2014, 179–184; Zettler and Hafford 2014–2016, 377–378). The remains of Queen Pû-abī were found in a vaulted tomb on a bier (Woolley 1934, 83–91). She lay on her back, with her legs stretched out straight; this position had probably been preferred to the usual lateral position, due to her headdress and body ornaments. A large silver lamp was placed on her body, and a golden bowl and silver drinking tube were deposited next to her head. The bowl and the drinking tube enabled the deceased queen to ritually consume libations and foods with which the dead were regularly supplied, as already mentioned. Not counting the items that were part of the queen's jewelry or lay on her bier or belonged to the co-interments, at least 96 other objects had been placed in the burial chamber, made of gold (5), silver (51+), copper (37+) and clay (3). These were mostly vessels of various kinds, drinking tubes, sieves and ladles, that is, utensils necessary for banqueting. The burial equipment also included, among other objects, four ostrich eggs, parts of the decoration of a harp, another instrument (sistrum?) and containers for the storage of cosmetic pigments. To the left of the bier, a large quantity of minute pearls of lapis lazuli and figuratively designed pendants of gold, as well as lapis lazuli and carnelian "fruits" were discovered which Woolley (1934, 89) assembled into the queen's "diadem"(see Fig. 2.6, and for a different reconstruction Pittman and Miller 2015; Pittman 1998, 92–94).

Creating the radiant appearance of Queen Pû-abī

Applying the principles of aesthetic leadership studies to our specific case study, the first question to be asked is what measures were undertaken to create the resplendent beauty of Queen Pû-abī at her funeral. Three essential aspects will be thematised: body care and beauty treatments, the queen's dress and her jewelry.

Body care, make-up and hairdo

Archaeological evidence is only available for the make-up and hairdo of the queen. However, literary sources indicate that personal hygiene was of great importance in Mesopotamia (see Sallaberger 2011). Thus it can safely be assumed that the body of the queen was carefully nurtured both in life and in death. That might have included a bath in fresh warm scented water, the cleaning of her body and hair with soap-like substances, the removing of body hair with depilatory pastes, and the use of oil to care for the skin. It should be noted that only the ruling houses, the elite and perhaps to some extent middle-class families had access to the expensive utensils needed for the mentioned hygiene routines; this also applies for body care products, such as metal or obsidian mirrors, pedicure and manicure instruments, tweezers, razors, fragrances, or cosmetic pigments, and perhaps also sponges and combs (see Vogel 2016, 250–257). As already mentioned, the queen's grave equipment included an assortment of cosmetic containers, mostly cockleshells, but also imitations of cockleshells in gold and silver, as well as an unique silver cosmetic box with carved lid of lapis lazuli and shell (see Hansen 1998, 66, fig. 12). The cosmetics were based on expensive imported ores and minerals, which were powdered and processed with fats and other substances. Pigments in green and a delicate blue were probably used as eye make-up, black and brown pigments as eyeliner, the yellow pigments could have been used also as eye shadow or, together with brown pigments, as contouring powder (see Hauptman *et al.* 2016). The accentuation of the eyes with eye shadow, eyeliner and dark bushy eyebrows was without any doubt one of the most important features of female beauty at the time, whereas there is, to my knowledge, no evidence of the use of any kind of lipsticks or lip gloss, neither in archeological nor in written sources. It is noteworthy, that Woolley (1934, 245) assumed that cockleshells with cosmetic pigments were originally deposited in every woman's grave, an assumption that is not confirmed by the published material. Instead, cosmetics were also found in the graves of men (buried with weapons), not only in the Royal Cemetery of Ur, but also elsewhere (Danti and Zettler 1998, 144; Vogel 2015b, 52–53 with n. 66). It seems that in Mesopotamia back then, both men and women of a certain social strata could use cosmetic pigments, but they certainly did so to a varying extent and in different ways. The hairdo of Queen Pû-abī was primarily reconstructed by Woolley's wife, Katherine (Woolley 1934, 85–86; see Hafford and Zettler 2015, 96–101 for alternative suggestions). It refers to the hairstyles of more or less privileged women, who are known from stone statuettes dedicated to gods and goddesses during the Early Dynastic periods and later (Braun-Holzinger 1977; 1991). The represented group of women wore very elaborate hairstyles and also hair-accessories like headbands and ribbons. Thus, the voluminous hairdo of Queen Pû-abī – the diameter of her coiffure was deduced from the location of her 12 m long golden hair ribbon – referenced a broader socio-cultural pattern, according to which the artfully crafted hairstyles of women had a special, albeit unknown, significance.

Dress

Unfortunately, nothing of Queen Pû-abī's garment has survived. However, it is certain that she wore the usual women's attire, but surely made of a special fabric (for elaborately processed garments and wool fabrics dyed in certain colors which were reserved for the ruling houses see Sallaberger 2009; Waetzoldt 1984, 20, 26–27; 2010; Wright 2013, 400–402). This can be deduced from the findspot of three golden pins, three lapis lazuli cylinder seals and four small animal figures made of gold and lapis lazuli which were found against the right upper arm of the queen (Woolley 1934, 88). The previously mentioned votive statuettes, which are our best source for the female dress code of the time, prove that the usual calf-length wraparound garment was fastened on the right shoulder with a pin to which a seal could be attached; the left shoulder remained uncovered. Gold pins, especially with a pinhead made of lapis lazuli capped with gold caps, as is the case with Pû-abī's pins (see Benzel 2013, 217 cat. nos. 22–24), and personal pieces of jewelry such as the above mentioned animal figures, which Woolley (1934, 88) interpreted as amulets, are extremely rare finds, even in the context of the Royal Cemetery (see Vogel 2015b, 51 n. 58). Typically, silver pins and much more often copper pins, with and without lapis lazuli pinheads which may or may not be set in gold, were used to fasten the garment.

Based on the archaeological evidence, the queen's attire was completed by two extraordinary items, a cloak embroidered with beads and a belt. Woolley reconstructed the cloak from a large quantity of gold, silver, lapis lazuli, carnelian and agate beads that covered the upper body of the dead queen. The version of the cloak (Fig. 2.5) currently exhibited at the University of Pennsylvania Museum of Archaeology and Anthropology (USA) consists of 3,569 beads which together weigh 2,276.9 g (see Benzel 2013, 212 cat. no. 11). A second cluster of beads – tubes of gold, carnelian and lapis lazuli – and large golden rings were unearthed at waist level. As these beads ran across the body, Woolley (1934, 87) interpreted them as a belt. Golden rings were undoubtedly extremely valuable, as they are very rarely listed in the grave catalogue of the cemetery (see Vogel 2015b, 53 n. 67). Recently there have been doubts about Woolley's interpretation, since the golden rings have no loops for attachment (see Hafford and Zettler 2015, 95). According to Kim Benzel (2013, 213 cat. no. 13), "the so-called belt might have been the lower border of the cloak". This assumption is also supported by the fact, that, as far as I know, no depiction of a woman with a girdled gown is known from that time. It should only be noted here, that representations of women who wear a shoulder cloth are known so far only from northern Mesopotamia (see Aruz 2013, fig. 104a).

Jewelry

At her funeral, the queen's hair, ears, neck and hands were adorned with jewelry made of gold, lapis lazuli and carnelian. These were the most valuable materials available at that time, not only in economic terms, but above all in spiritual-religious-symbolic terms, as their processing in the manufacture of statues of gods and goddesses or in the jewelry of the gods indicates. Most of the queen's jewelry was individually made. However, hair ribbons, hair rings, lunate-shaped gold earrings and wreaths of gold poplar leaves were also found with co-interments and rarely in the graves of richly equipped female burials (see Gansell 2007, 31–34, 37; Vogel 2014, 177–179; 2015a, tab. 6). Yet, in such cases the number and/or the dimensions of the ribbons, earrings and wreaths and/or the processed raw materials differ from the pieces of jewelry worn by the queen (*e.g.*, Pû-abī's earrings have a diameter of 11 cm, whereas the earrings of the co-interments have usually a diameter of 7.5 cm approximately; see Pittman 1998, 90, 99, 107). The arrangement of the queen's headdress should obviously emphasise her face. This is reflected, for example, in the fact that the seven flower-bearing stems of her large gold comb were slightly bent forward and that her particularly valuable wreath with golden rings, which highlighted Pû-abī's forehead and eyes, did not reach the back of the head. The large lunate-shaped earrings accentuated her cheeks, her mouth and her neck and at the same time drew attention to her necklace made of three strings of gold and lapis lazuli beads and a gold rosette in the middle, the petals and center of which were inlaid with lapis lazuli. According to Woolley Pû-abī's hair band had been wrapped around her head seven times. Together with the wreaths it created a radiant, sparkling aureole around the queen's head that could probably be seen even from a distance. Worn during lifetime, the aural features of her jewelry – the sound produced by the oscillating flowers of her comb, the leaves of her wreath, the golden ring pendants and the beads, which collided with each other with every movement – certainly added to the dazzling effect of Pû-abī's appearance (see Pillsbury 2017, 7 in another context).

According to Kim Benzel (see the data to Fig. 2.4), Pû-abī's headdress weighed approximately 1,368 g, including the earrings, but without the weight of the hair ribbon. If her golden hair ribbon was originally 2 cm wide and 12 m long, as stated by Woolley, it would have weighed roughly 2,670 g, following again the measurements provided by Benzel (2015, 210–211 cat. no. 6). In this case the queen would have worn approximately 4,000 g of jewelry on her head. In order to wear her jewelry gracefully, Pû-abī had to adjust her posture as if wearing a crown. That is, as Melanie Holcomb (2019, 25) notes, the "spine must [be] elongate. The ears need to align with the shoulders. The eyes should look ahead, and the chin must be tucked in. Such are the small mechanical adjustments necessary to accommodate its [the crown's] weight, maintain its balance, and inhabit the royal role it implies". It is therefore likely that Pû-abī's jewelry not only played a major role in shaping the public perception of the queen, but it may also have had a significant impact on Pû-abī's physical embodiment of her queenhood and thus on her self-perception as a queen.

The reasons behind the beauty practices undertaken

Having provided an idea of the appearance of Queen Pû-abī at her funeral in the previous section we will now discuss the rationale behind opting for the beauty practices described above instead of others.

It has already become apparent that the queen's appearance was determined by two closely intertwined principles. On the one hand, her appearance was shaped by social values and standards, which she ideally fulfilled due to her exceptional status. On the other hand, her appearance communicated that she indeed was the queen. The point of intersection is the relationship of the then living people to their gods and goddesses and thus the influence attributed to the deities on the fate of the individual and society. A decisive factor here is that, according to the prevalent perception of the world at the time, the individual was surrounded by protective spirits and deities and was further corporeally connected with his or her personal god/goddess (or family god/goddess) and other gods and goddesses (see Selz 2004a and, for a general overview of the Mesopotamian concept of the person, Steinert 2012, ch. 2; 2017). It was assumed that the health, attractiveness, vitality and beauty of a person, all of which contributed significantly to the social recognition of an individual, depended on the presence of the gods and goddesses surrounding and directly associated with the person (Steinert 2017, 41–42; Vogel 2016, 242–243 with references). The unalterable requirement for the presence of the gods and goddesses and their favorable support was that an individual behaved in a manner consistent with society's expectations and values, as already noticed in the context of our discussion of the governmental activities of Sumerian queens. Misconduct and poor attitudes resulted in the gods and goddesses distancing themselves from one person, a situation that could lead to a faded, unattractive appearance, illness, unhappiness or impoverishment, thus leading to a temporary or permanent socially marginalised status (see Steinert 2012, ch. 13; 2017, 72–73; Vogel 2016, 244). The appearance of the individual in Mesopotamia was thus the manifestation of an indissoluble entanglement between the social conformity of a person, their moral state and ethical conduct, their proximity to or distance from the deities, and their social position. It follows that Pû-abī's magnificent appearance at her funeral provided both the visible and sensual evidence of her extraordinary closeness to the deities and her social conformity, integrity and decency.

While detailing the steps taken to create the radiant appearance of Queen Pû-abī at her funeral, we have already learned that in her day clothing and make-up choices depended on access to certain materials, fabrics and utensils. As was mentioned before, metals and semi-precious stones were among the goods that had to be imported into Mesopotamia and accumulated in the palaces. For all we know, these materials were used almost exclusively for the needs of the palaces and for the furnishing of the temples. The sole power of access to precious metals and semi-precious stones enabled the members of the ruling houses, of course, first and foremost the ruler and the queen, to adapt their appearance to the appearance of the (cult statues of the) gods and goddesses dwelling in the temples, thereby demonstrating their ideal relationship with the deities, on which, it was assumed, general prosperity depended. Evidence for this can be deduced from various texts from the middle of the 3rd millennium BCE. For example, King Urukagina of Lagaš, the husband of the above mentioned Queen Šaša, reports that the plundering enemy tore down gold and lapis lazuli from a large number of cult statues (see Steible 1982, 334–336, Urukagina Text 16). On the other hand it is also known that Šaša dedicated a statue depicting herself to the temple of the goddess Baba (see Selz 1992); this (composite-)statue was made mostly of purified silver and probably semi-precious stones and might therefore have looked very similar to the cult statue of the goddess. It should be noted, that the visual identity or similarity between the appearance of the ruler respectively the queen and the deities was not a superficial, but an intrinsic and substantial feature of their legitimate rule since it was believed that the aesthetic qualities of precious metals and semi-precious stones, especially lapis lazuli, actually manifested the presence of the deities (see Winter 1994; 1999). The key here is that anything that radiated, gleamed, sparkled and shone brightly or created an association to the abode of the gods, the sky, was thought to be evocative of divine powers, an idea that can be traced back to the 4th millennium BCE; in the earliest written records the name of a god or a goddess is determined by an additional character representing a radiating star, the sign AN (see Selz 2008, 18–19). Against this backdrop, we can safely assume that the resplendent appearance of Queen Pû-abī not only proved her exceptional intimacy with the deities, as stated above, but rather manifested her actual participation in the divine, thus bestowing divine powers upon the queen. We should recall here the personal names discussed previously, which name PAP.PAP, that was borne by Queen Baranamtara embodying a specific religious-ceremonial role, as the personal goddess of the respective name bearer.

Drawing on these findings, we may consider now some aspects of the iconography of Queen Pû-abī's jewelry. The aforementioned religious-ceremonial title of Queen Baranamtara, PAP.PAP, "the one who causes growth/cultivates sb./sth", will serve as a guideline. What immediately comes to mind in this context is the interpretation of blooming flowers, which decorate metal vessels from the Royal Cemetery of Ur, as "primal flowers", symbolising primordial vital energy/ life force (see Selz 2004b, 201). My assumption is that the blooming flowers in Queen Pû-abī's jewelry might have had a similar significance. Here, it might be informative to concern ourselves with the meaning of gardens in Mesopotamian literary texts. Considering the hot dry desert climate in southern Iraq, it is hardly surprising that lush and flowering orchards with shady trees are described in literary texts as places of great beauty, pleasure, joy, seduction and abundance (see Leick 1994, 73–75; Winter 2002, 14–15). The people of that time felt that flowering gardens and similar places emitted a particular energy, designated with the word HI.LI in Sumerian or with the word *kuzbu* in Akkadian texts. It is said that the sensory perception and aesthetic sensitivity of HI.LI energy aroused admiration and joy, bliss, passion and enthusiasm in people, which contributed to an increase in their love of life and filled them with renewed hope (see Leick 1994, 74; Steinert 2012, 408). The most important factor, however, for our discussion is that not only gardens but also magnificent examples of architecture, hence temples and palaces, as well as artifacts of superb quality, beautiful people and, of course, first and foremost the (cult statues of the) deities radiated HI.LI energy to a varying degree.

Against this backdrop, it could be argued that Pû-abī's jewelry conveyed in a unique way the interplay of divine and natural creative forces as well as human creativity, resulting in overwhelming beauty that appealed to all senses and beamed with HI.LI energy. The design of the queen's "diadem" fits perfectly with our line of argumentation. This exceptional artifact manifested HI.LI energy in every respect: precious materials that evoked divine powers, excellent craftsmanship, and on the iconographical level, the representation of a fertile "paradise garden" with flowering and fruit bearing trees, as well as the wild and tame animals which live in peaceful coexistence (see Selz 2010a for animal enclosures in the 3rd millennium BCE and for the symbolic meaning of some of the aforementioned animals). From there are only some steps to the declaration and experience of rulership as a divine mercy which gives life and salvation to the subjects. It is in this respect interesting to note again the religious-ceremonial titles of the queens of Lagaš, PAP.PAP, "the one who causes growth/cultivates sb./sth.", and "[the queen] is the eternal mother".

Conclusion: the public perception of the Queen

As we have seen in the previous section Queen Pû-abī's resplendent appearance displayed fundamental conceptions about social conformity, the affection of the deities for the queen and the nature of Sumerian queenhood. Her jewelry as well as her whole appearance was thus far from an empty display of splendor. To conclude, we will discuss some situational factors that might have influenced the public perception of the queen's appearance.

According to the results of aesthetic leadership studies, the social environment and the atmosphere of a building or a room will have a massive impact on the assessment of any given leadership performance. It is obvious that we have little knowledge about many details that might have influenced the perception of Sumerian queens while performing their official and cultic duties. Nevertheless, one might assume that the presence of the queen at cultic events which took place regularly during an annual cycle was a major influence on public awareness and understanding of Sumerian queenhood, and in a wider sense, the legitimacy of the dynasty's claim to power. The above mentioned visual identity or similarity between the official appearance of Sumerian queens and the appearance of (the cult statues of) the goddesses in the temples might have resulted in the transfer of habitual patterns of perception of the divine to the perception of the queen. The spectrum of emotions that the queen's sight might have provoked could thus have ranged from tremendous joy and collective bliss to amazement, gratitude, awe and reverence (Selz 2018, 362–265; Winter 2000; 2002, 12–14). The queen's radiating HI.LI energy might have increased the perception of positive feelings, stimulating vibrant excitement and enthusiasm as well as erotic tension, hope and peace of mind. Another key to the success of the negotiations of power in the setting of traditional Sumerian communities was undoubtedly the queen's respect for society's expectations and community norms, displayed in certain features of her make-up and hairdo, in her dress and also to some degree in her jewelry, as discussed in detail above. One may speculate that at certain cultic events the women present were adorned with chains and wreaths of flowers, resembling the queen's magnificent jewelry made of gold and semi-precious stones; the shared experience of such a joyous event might have strengthened the spirit of belonging and the (imaginary) togetherness of the local women and the queen. Yet, the vertical hierarchisation of Sumerian societies should not be overlooked; the economic and social marginalisation of certain population groups was certainly reflected in their spatial position on the fringes of cultic or public events.

Taking into consideration the then existing societal power structures and their material basis as well as the ideological superstructure, it is apparent that, on the one hand, the actual economic dependence of the larger population from the palace and, on the other hand, the dependence of the city state's total population from the auspicious relationship of the royal couple with the deities will also have had a great influence on the perception and appreciation of the queen's appearance. It has already been mentioned that it was the prerogative and the duty of the rulers of that time to build temples for the gods and goddesses and furnish them as magnificently as possible. It was believed that the more splendid and lustrous a temple and its interior, the more the temple reflected the radiant power and beauty of the divine, causing a god or a goddess to dwell happily in his or her temple and provide favorable support to the royal couple and their followers. In this respect, the magnificent appearance of Queen Pû-abī or any other Sumerian queen demonstrated that the ruling house had access to enormous resources which it could and would also use to maintain a fortunate and prosperous relationship with the deities. By circular reasoning, the wealth of the ruling family was proof of their close relationship with the deities, thus substantiating their claim to power and the legitimacy of their rule, as discussed above. Undoubtedly, we are dealing here with a monolithic ideological system in which social expectations, ideological convictions and religious beliefs, claims to power, and aesthetic sensibilities formed one inseparable entity, the objective basis of which, however, was the extensive control of imported resources and the economy by the ruling houses. This clearly shows, as Pierre Bourdieu (2005, 10) emphasised in another context, that the material world and the spiritual world are not alternatives and therefore cannot be analysed independently in a useful way.

Finally, I would like to discuss another thought. It has already been mentioned that the economic conditions at that time and the unequal access to resources led to a situation in which large parts of the population, the workers and their families, as well as other groups of the population of a city-state lived in social insecurity and, to a differing degree, in poverty. These individuals owned only basic equipment whose main characteristic was its functionality. One can argue that this group of people was existentially dependent on the proper operation of the economic system and thus on the maintenance of the existing power structures in society. Consequently, these people, who, from an objective point of view, had "nothing to lose but their chains", might have developed a particular receptivity for the radiating beauty of the Sumerian queens and its promises of happiness, abundance, peace and prosperity. Furthermore, strong group pressure ensured that autonomous actions and independent thinking were judged extremely critically (see Steinert 2017, 66–71), which, however, affected all population groups.

Nevertheless, there is evidence that the aesthetic leadership of Sumerian queens (and kings) were not at all appreciated by certain people, despite all the efforts made. For example, one Sumerian proverb states "There are countless fools in the palace" (see Selz 2010b, 11; SP 9 A 9). Another proverb addresses especially the personality of Sumerian queens; and reads: "The cities Idibi is their name. Their kings: Didibi is their name. Their queens 'No Good At All' is their name" (see Selz 2010b, 9; SP 1.75). Hard to believe that Queen Pû-abī, whose resplendent appearance still enchants and mesmerises us today, has ever been seen so negatively.

Acknowledgements

I would like to thank Uroš Matić for the invitation to contribute to this interesting topic. I would also like to thank Maresi Starzmann for correcting my original paper. Special thanks go to the two anonymous reviewers for their informed and fair comments. Sincere thanks also to Andrea Sinclair for her close review of the final manuscript.

Bibliography

Aruz, J. (2013) (ed.) *Art of the First Cities. The Third Millennium B.C. from the Mediterranean to the Indus.* New York/New Haven and London, The Metropolitan Museum of Art/Yale University Press.

Asher-Greve, J. (2013) Women and agency: a survey from Late Uruk to the end of Ur III. In H. Crawford (ed.) *The Sumerian World*, 359–376. London and New York, Routledge.

Bauer, J. (1998) Der vorsargonische Abschnitt der mesopotamischen Geschichte. In P. Attinger and M. Wäfler (eds) *Mesopotamien. Späturuk-Zeit und Frühdynastische Zeit*, 431–585. Freiburg, Switzerland and Göttingen, Universitätsverlag/Vandenhoeck Ruprecht.

Beld, S.G. (2002) *The Queens of Lagash: Ritual Economy in a Sumerian State.* Unpublished PhD thesis, The University of Michigan.

Benzel, K. (2013) *Pu-abi's Adornment for the Afterlife. Materials and Technologies of Jewelry at Ur in Mesopotamia.* Unpublished PhD thesis, Columbia University.

Benzel, K. (2105) What does Puabi want (today)? The status of Puabi as image. In J.Y. Chi and P. Azara (eds) *From Ancient to Modern. Archaeology and Aesthetics*, 132–160. New York and Princeton, Princeton University Press.

Bourdieu, P. (1984) *Die feinen Unterschiede.* Frankfurt/M., Surkamp.

Bourdieu, P. (1998) *Praktische Vernunft. Zur Theorie des Handelns.* Frankfurt/M., Surkamp.

Bourdieu, P. (2005) *Die männliche Herrschaft.* Frankfurt/M., Surkamp.

Braun-Holzinger, E. (1977) *Frühdynastische Beterstatuetten.* Berlin, Gebrüder Mann Verlag.

Braun-Holzinger, E. (1991) *Mesopotamische Weihgaben der frühdynastischen bis altbabylonischen Zeit.* Heidelberg, Heidelberger Orientverlag.

Carroll, B. and Smolović Jones, O. (2018) Mapping the aesthetics of leadership development through participant perspectives. *Management Learning* 49 (2), 187–203.

Collinson, D. (2014) Dichotomies, dialectics and dilemmas: New directions for critical leadership studies? *Leadership* 10 (1), 36–55.

Crawford, H. (ed.) (2013) *The Sumerian World*. London and New York, Routledge.

Crawford, H. (2014) An exploration of the world of women in third-millennium Mesopotamia. In M.W. Chavalas (ed.) *Women in the Ancient Near East*, 10–27. London and New York, Routledge.

Damerji, M.S.B. (1999) *Gräber assyrischer Königinnen*; mit einem Beitrag von Ahmed Kamil. Mainz, Verlag des Römisch-Germanischen Zentralmuseums Mainz.

Danti, K. and Zettler, R.L. (1998) Shell vessels and containers. In R.L. Zettler and L. Horne (eds) *Treasures from the Royal Tombs of Ur*, 143–146. Philadelphia, University of Pennsylvania Museum.

Dittmann R. and Selz, G.J. (eds) (2015) *It's a Long Way to a Historiography of the Early Dynastic Period(s)*. Münster, Ugarit-Verlag.

Foucault, M. (1976) *Überwachen und Strafen. Die Geburt des Gefängnisses*. Frankfurt/M., Surkamp.

Foucault, M. (2001) *In Verteidigung der Gesellschaft*. Frankfurt/M., Surkamp.

Foucault, M. (2002) *Sexualität und Wahrheit Bd.1. Der Wille zum Wissen*. Frankfurt/M., Surkamp.

Foucault, M. (2005) *Analytik der Macht*. Frankfurt/M., Surkamp.

Ford, J., Harding, N.H., Gilmore, S. and Richardson, S. (2017) Becoming the leader: leadership as material presence. *Organization Studies* 38 (11), 1553–1571.

Gansell, A.R. (2007) Identity and adornment in the third-millennium BC Mesopotamian 'Royal Cemetery' at Ur. *Cambridge Archaeological Journal* 17 (1), 29–46.

Gansell, A.R. (2014) Images and conceptions of ideal feminine beauty in Neo-Assyrian royal contexts *c*. 883–627 BCE. In B.A. Brown and M.H. Feldman (eds) *Critical Approaches to Ancient Near Eastern Art*, 391–420. Boston and Berlin, De Gruyter.

Gansell, A.R. (2018a) Dressing the Neo-Assyrian queens in identity and ideology: elements and ensembles from the Royal Tombs at Nimrud. *American Journal of Archaeology* 122, 65–100.

Gansell, A.R. (2018b) In pursuit of Neo-Assyrian queens: an interdisciplinary methodology for researching ancient women and engendering ancient history. In S. Svärd and A. Garcia-Ventura (eds) *Studying Gender in the Ancient Near East*, 157–181. University Park, The Pennsylvania State University, Eisenbrauns.

Hafford, W.B. and Zettler, R.L. (2015) Magnificent with jewels: Puabi, Queen of Ur. In J.Y. Chi and P. Azara (eds) *From Ancient to Modern. Archaeology and Aesthetics*, 86–105. New York and Princeton, Princeton University Press.

Hansen, D. (1998) Art of the Royal Tombs of Ur: a brief interpretation. In R.L. Zettler and L. Horne (eds) *Treasures from the Royal Tombs of Ur*, 43-72. Philadelphia: University of Pennsylvania Museum.

Hansen, H., Ropo, A. and Sauer, E. (2007) Aesthetic leadership. *The Leadership Quarterly* 18, 544–560.

Hauptmann, A., Klein, S., Zettler, R., Baumer, U. and Dietemann, P. (2016) On the making and provenancing of pigments from the Early Dynastic Royal Tombs of Ur, Mesopotamia. *Metalla* 22 (1), 41–74.

Hawkins, B. (2015) Ship-shape: materializing leadership in the British Royal Navy. *Human Relations* 68 (6), 951–971.

Holcomb, M. (2019) Head and hair. In M. Holcomb (ed.), *Jewelry. The Body Transformed*, 24–29. New Haven and London, The Metropolitan Museum of Art, New York.

Hussein, N.M. and Suleiman, A. (2000) *Nimrud. A City of Golden Treasures*. Bagdad, Al-Huriyah Printing House

Karlsson, J.C. (2011) Looking good and sounding right: aesthetic labour. *Economic and Industrial Democracy* 33 (1), 51–64.

Ladkin, D. (2008) Leading beautifully: how mastery, congruence and purpose create the aesthetic of embodied leadership practice. *The Leadership Quarterly* 19 (1), 31–41.

Ladkin, D. and Taylor, St.S. (2010) Enacting the 'true self': towards a theory of embodied authentic leadership. *The Leadership Quarterly* 21 (1), 64–74.

Leick, G. (1994) *Sex and Eroticism in Mesopotamian Literature.* London and New York, Routledge.

Mayerová, H. (2015) The Queens of Lagash in the Early Dynastic period. Especially the last three royal couples. In R. Dittmann and G.J. Selz (eds) *It's a Long Way to a Historiography of the Early Dynastic Period(s)*, 259–265. Münster, Ugarit-Verlag.

Nissen, H.J. (2012) *Geschichte Alt-Vorderasiens.* München, Oldenbourg-Verlag.

Otto, A. (2016) Professional women and women at work in Mesopotamia and Syria (3rd and early 2nd millennia BC): the (rare) information from visual images. In B. Lion and C. Michel (eds) *The Role of Women in Work and Society in the Ancient Near East*, 112–148. Boston and Berlin, De Gruyter.

Parry, K. and Kempster, S. (2014) Love and leadership: constructing follower narrative identities of charismatic leadership. *Management Learning* 45 (1), 21–38.

Pillsbury, J. (2017) Luminous power: luxury arts in the ancient Americas. In J. Pillsbury, T. Potts and K.N. Richter (eds) *Golden Kingdoms: Luxury Arts in the Ancient Americas*, 1–13. Los Angeles, Getty Publications.

Pittman, H. (1998) Jewelry. In R.L. Zettler and L. Horne (eds) *Treasures from the Royal Tombs of Ur*, 87–122. Philadelphia, University of Pennsylvania Museum.

Pittman, H. and Miller, N.F. (2015) Puabi's diadem(s): the deconstruction of a Mesopotamian icon. In J.Y. Chi and P. Azara (eds) *From Ancient to Modern. Archaeology and Aesthetics*, 106–130. New York and Princeton, Princeton University Press.

Prentice, R. (2010) *The Exchange of Goods and Services in Pre-Sargonic Lagash.* Münster, Ugarit-Verlag.

Pullen, A. and Vachhani, S. (2013) The materiality of leadership. *Leadership* 9 (3), 315–31.

Ropo, A. and Salovaara, P. (2018) Spacing leadership as an embodied and performative process. *Leadership* 15 (4), 461–479.

Sallaberger, W. (2009) Von der Wollration zum Ehrenkleid. Textilien als Prestigegüter am Hof von Ebla. In B. Hildebrand and C. Veit (eds) *Der Wert der Dinge. Güter im Prestigediskurs*, 241–278. München, Herbert Utz Verlag.

Sallaberger, W. (2011) Körperliche Reinheit und soziale Grenzen in Mesopotamien. In P. Burschel and C. Marx (eds) *Reinheit*, 17–45. Wien, Köln and Weimar, Böhlau Verlag.

Sallaberger, W. (2013) The management of royal treasure. Palace archives and palatial economy in the ancient Near East. In J.A. Hill, P. Jones And A.J. Morales (eds) *Experiencing Power, Generating Authority. Cosmos, Politics, and the Ideology of Kingship in Ancient Egypt and Mesopotamia*, 219–255. Philadelphia, University of Pennsylvania Press.

Schrakamp, I. (2013) Die "Sumerische Tempelstadt" heute. Die sozioökonomische Rolle des Tempels in frühdynastischer Zeit. In K. Kaniuth, A. Löhnert, J.L. Miller, A. Otto, M. Roaf, M. and W. Sallaberger (eds), *Tempel im Alten Orient*, 445–465. Wiesbaden, Harrassowitz-Verlag.

Selz, G.J. (1992) Eine Kultstatuette der Herrschergemahlin Šaša: Ein Beitrag zum Problem der Vergöttlichung. *Acta Sumerologica* 14, 245–268.

Selz, G.J. (1995) *Untersuchungen zur Götterwelt des altsumerischen Stadtstaates von Lagaš.* Occasional Publications of the Samuel Noah Kramer Fund 13. Philadelphia, The University of Pennsylvania Museum.

Selz, G.J. (1998) Über mesopotamische Herrschaftskonzepte. Zu den Ursprüngen mesopotamischer Herrscherideologie im 3. Jahrtausend. In M. Dietrich and O. Loretz (eds) *Dubsar anta-men. Studien zur Altorientalistik*, 281–344. Münster, Ugarit-Verlag.

Selz, G.J. (2004a) Composite beings: of individualization and objectification in third millennium Mesopotamia. *Archiv Orientální* 72, 33–53.

Selz, G.J. (2004b) Early Dynastic vessels in 'ritual' contexts. *Wiener Zeitschrift für die Kunde des Morgenlandes* 94, 185–223.

Selz, G.J. (2005) *Sumerer und Akkader. Geschichte, Gesellschaft, Kultur.* München, Beck Verlag.

Selz, G.J. (2008) The Divine Prototypes. In N. Brisch (ed.) *Religion and Power. Divine Kingship in the Ancient World and Beyond*, 13–31. Oriental Institute Seminars 4. Chicago, The Oriental Institute in Chicago.

Selz, G.J. (2010a) Das Paradies der Mütter. Materialien zum Ursprung der "Paradiesvorstellungen". *Wiener Zeitschrift für die Kunde des Morgenlandes* 100, 177–217.

Selz, G.J. (2010b) "The poor are the silent ones in the country". On the loss of legitimacy; challenging power in early Mesopotamia. In P. Charvát and P.M. Vlčková (eds) *Who Was King? Who Was Not King? The Rulers and the Ruled in the Ancient Near East*, 1–15. Prague, Institute of Archaeology of the Academy of Sciences of the Czech Republic.

Selz, G.J. (2018) Aesthetics. In A.C. Gunter (ed.) *A Companion to Ancient Near Eastern Art*, 359–376. Hoboken, John Wiley & Sons, Inc.

Steible, H. (1982) *Die Altsumerischen Bau- und Weihinschriften. Teil I.* Wiesbaden, Franz Steiner Verlag.

Steible, H. (2001) Legitimation von Herrschaft in Mesopotamien des 3. Jahrtausends v. Chr. In G. Dux (ed.) *Moral und Recht im Diskurs der Moderne. Zur Legitimation gesellschaftlicher Ordnung*, 67–91. Opladen, Leske und Budrich.

Steinert, U. (2012) *Aspekte des Menschseins im Alten Mesopotamien. Eine Studie zu Person und Identität im 2. und 1. Jt. v. Chr.* Leiden and Boston, Brill.

Steinert, U. (2017) Person, Identität und Individualität im antiken Mesopotamien. In E. Bons and K. Finsterbusch (eds) *Konstruktionen individueller und kollektiver Identität (II): Alter Orient, hellenistisches Judentum, römische Antike, Alte Kirche*, 39–100. Göttingen, Vandenhoeck & Ruprecht.

Suter, C. (2010) Ur III kings in images: a reappraisal. In H.D. Baker, E. Robson and G. Zólyomi (eds) *Your Praise is Sweet. A Memorial Volume for Jeremy Black from Students, Colleagues and Friends*, 319–349. London, British Institute for the Study of Iraq.

Suter, C. (2012) The royal body and masculinity in early Mesopotamia. In A. Berlejung, J. Dietrich and J.F. Quack (eds) *Menschenbilder und Körperkonzepte im Alten Israel, in Ägypten und im Alten Orient*, 433–458. Tübingen, Mohr Siebeck.

Suter, C. (2016) Images of queens, high priestesses, and other elite women in third-millennium mesopotamia. In S.L. Budin and J.M. Turfa (eds) *Women in Antiquity: Real Women Across the Ancient World*, 35–47. Abingdon, Routledge.

Suter, C. (2017) On images, visibility, and agency of early Mesopotamian royal women. In L. Feliu, F. Karahashi and G. Rubio (eds) *The First Ninety Years: A Sumerian Celebration in Honor of Miguel Civil*, 337–362. Boston and Berlin, de Gruyter.

Vogel, H. (2013a) Der 'Große Mann von Uruk' – Das Bild der Herrschaft im späten 4. und frühen 3. vorchristlichen Jahrtausend. In N. Crüsemann, M. van Ess, M. Hilgert and B. Salje (eds) *Uruk, 5000 Jahre Megacity*, 139–145. Berlin and Mannheim, Michael Imhof Verlag.

Vogel, H. (2013b) Death and burial. In H. Crawford (ed.) *The Sumerian World*, 419–434. London and New York, Routledge.

Vogel, H. (2014) Der Königsfriedhof von Ur und das Problem der so genannten Gefolgschaftsbestattungen. In T. Link and H. Peter-Röcher (eds) *Gewalt und Gesellschaft. Dimensionen der Gewalt in ur- und frühgeschichtlicher Zeit*, 169–185. Bonn, Verlag Dr. Rudolf Habelt.

Vogel, H. (2015a) *Brim-Stirnketten-Träger*, Musikerinnen und *Dog-Collar*-Trägerinnen als Bestattungen und Mitbestattungen im *Royal Cemetery* in Ur. In R. Dittmann and G.J. Selz (eds) *It's a Long Way to a Historiography of the Early Dynastic Period(s)*, 461–507. Münster, Ugarit-Verlag.

Vogel, H. (2015b) Wer wurde in der Grabkammer der Royal Tomb 1054 im Royal Cemetery in Ur bestattet? *Zeitschrift für Orient-Archäologie* 8, 38–60.

Vogel, H. (2016) Doing Beauty. Schönheit als gesellschaftliche Praxis in Mesopotamien. *Studia Mesopotamica* 3, 237–267.

Vogel, H. (2018) 'Gewaltszenen' in der urukzeitlichen Glyptik. Möglichkeiten und Grenzen ihrer Interpretation. In K. Kaniuth, D. Lau and D. Wicke (eds) *Übergangszeiten. Altorientalische Studien für Reinhard Dittmann anlässlich seines 65. Geburtstages*, 85–107. Marru 1. Münster, Zaphon.

Waetzoldt, H. (1984) Kleidung. A. Philologisch. In E. Dietz Otto, E. Ebeling and E.F. Weidner (eds) *Reallexikon der Assyriologie und Vorderasiatischen Archäologie 6*, 18–31. Berlin, de Gruyter.

Waetzoldt, H. (2010) The colours and variety of fabrics from Mesopotamia during the Ur III Period (20150 BC). In C. Michel and M.-L. Nosch (eds) *Textile Terminologies in the Ancient Near East and Mediterranean from the Third to the First Millennia BC*, 201–209. Oxford, Oxbow Books.

Winter, I. (1994) Radiance as an aesthetic value in the art of Mesopotamia (with some Indian parallels). In B.N. Saraswati (ed.) *Art, the Integral Vision: A Volume of Essay in Felicitation of Kapila Vatsyayan*, 123–132. New Dehli, D.K. Print World Ltd.

Winter, I. (1999) The aesthetic value of lapis lazuli in Mesopotamia. In A. Caubet (ed.) *Cornaline et pierres précieuses. La Méditerranée, de l'Antiquité à l'Islam*, 43–58. Paris, Musée du Louvre.

Winter, I. (2000) The eyes have it. Votive statuary, Gilgamesh's axe, and cathected viewing in the ancient Near East. In R. Nelson (ed.) *Visuality Before and Beyond the Renaissance*, 22–44. Cambridge, University Press.

Winter, I. (2002) Defining "aesthetics" for non-Western studies: the case of ancient Mesopotamia. In M.A. Holly and K. Moxey (eds) *Art History, Aesthetics, Visual Studies*, 3–28. Williamstown, MA, Sterling and Francine Clark Art Institute.

Woolley, C.L. (1934) *The Royal Cemetery. Ur Excavations. Vol. 2*. London, Trustees of the British Museum and of the Museum of the University of Pennsylvania.

Wright, R. (2013) Sumerian and Akkadian industries. Crafting textiles. In H. Crawford (ed.) *The Sumerian World*, 395–418. London and New York, Routledge.

Zettler, R.L. and Hafford, W.B. (2014–2016) Ur. B. Archäologisch. In E. Dietz Otto, E. Ebeling and E.F. Weidner (eds) *Reallexikon der Assyriologie und Vorderasiatischen Archäologie 14 (5./6. Lieferung)*, 367–385. Berlin, de Gruyter

Zhang, H., Cone, M.H., Everett, A.M. and Elkin, G. (2011) Aesthetic leadership in Chinese business: a philosophical perspective. *Journal of Business Ethics* 101, 475–491.

Zhang, Z. and Spicer, A. (2014) "Leader, you first": the everyday production of hierarchical space in a Chinese bureaucracy. *Human relations* 67 (6), 739–762.

Chapter 3

Beauty treatments and gender in Pharaonic Egypt: masculinities and femininities in public and private spaces

Uroš Matić

Abstract

This paper examines beauty treatments, such as shaving, grooming and hairdressing, in ancient Egypt by focusing on the spaces in which they took place according to visual and written sources. While both the visual and the written sources clearly indicate that most men shaved in public spaces, such as markets and streets, and only upper-class men enjoyed beauty treatments in privacy, shaving and other beauty treatments for women took place in private spaces. Where men received beauty treatments from other men, depictions of beauty treatments of noble women show female servants attending them privately. It is argued here that beauty treatments were structured according to gender as a regulatory norm which dictated conduct, intimacy and access, all in the service of the patriarchal economy.

Key words: *beauty treatments, gender performativity, engendered space, ancient Egypt*

Introduction

Visiting a hipster barbershop "The Barbers" in a popular urban neighborhood of Belgrade (Serbia) called Savamala, made me think about hair cutting, trimming, shaving and grooming, not only as gendered practices, but also as practices which "engender" space and time. In this paper I use the verb "to engender" in a very specific way, namely as a process in which people, animals, objects, spaces, practices and times acquire gender specific connotations (for such use of the verb in archaeology see *e.g.*, Conkey and Spector 1984; Díaz-Andreu 2005; Gero and Conkey 1991; Gilchrist 1999; Jensen and Matić 2017; Sørensen 2000).

As discussed in the introductory chapter of this volume, a peculiar sign at the front door of the barbershop "The Barbers" is the one with a crossed out figure of a woman with the specific intention of forbidding women from entering. In fact, as I visited this barbershop several times as a customer myself, I experienced the reactions of employees when a woman or a girl would accidentally walk in, or follow a man into the barbershop without seeing the sign. The owners or the employees would then kindly ask her to leave and would show her the sign on the door. The message was clear, "this is a man's world".

Of course, as discussed in the introduction to this volume, there might be numerous reasons for this choice by the owners of the barbershop. It could just be "one more of those hipster things", a creation of difference for the sake of the creation of a community among members. One can also say that the sign is in fact just stressing what is actually obvious if one walks by or goes in, namely that this is a barbershop and not a hair salon for women. There are other icons one uses to signify a barbershop, such as a razor or a bearded face, and all of these are indeed present. But although women understand that they will not be served there, the question presents itself, why are they not allowed to be in this space?

The answer to this question is based on the fact that this being a barbershop, and therefore attracting and serving male clients, the majority of people inside are men. Hair cutting, trimming, grooming and shaving are practices which take time. Those who come usually have to wait some time to be served, as this particular barbershop does not do appointments. Such an arrangement of work is intentional, as the owners want to revive the "old school" barbershop and its experience. This means that some men would wait while others are served. They will, together with the employees, share time and space. In order for their time to pass men talk to each other and these topics in turn are highly gendered. Among these are the sports typically associated with men in our society, such as football or basketball, although no one denies that women can play and do play both, but this is not the point I want to make. Men in this barbershop share their views of the recent games, goals, scores and performances of different athletes. They argue, quarrel, use bad language and exchange opinions loudly.

Of course, they also comment on politics. They discuss music and music artists. The choice of music that can be heard inside is eclectic, from hip hop to reggae, from house to techno, from rock to metal. Although, I have never heard pop music inside, I also rarely heard female vocals. Among topics discussed are also ways to maintain a certain hair or beard style after receiving a cut in the barbershop. The owners and employees advise their customers on how to wash and handle both hair and facial hair. Customers are encouraged to try certain products. Some of these are already present in the barbershop. The barbers invite the customers to smell them. The beard waxes smell like cognac and Cuban cigars, like oriental spices or like mint and chocolate. The visit to this barber is a sensory experience through and through. The barbers and the customers also discuss women. Either the ones they are dating or those they would like to date, short term or long term. Some of these discussions sometimes get very descriptive, focusing on attractive female bodies and very specific beauty ideals. Yet, some of the customers are younger or adolescent boys, others are mature men.

There are also those who occasionally look at their phones, turning online dating apps on and off. Some of these dating apps are for men only. If the sound function is turned on, a peculiar sound for a notification of a just received message can be heard. Carefully, screens are turned down so that no one sees. Heads turn, faces meet, gaze is exchanged. The message is clear, this is a space for men, but not all of these men are the same. Some have interest in women, others have interest only in video games, and some are interested both in women and men, or solely in men. Yet, the dominant idea of masculinity is established through the most common topics, such as sports, politics and women, or a specific gendered bad language, and of course through receiving treatment towards a certain masculine look.

All of this behaviour falls into the category of performative practices of gender as they were defined by Judith Butler. Practices, such as body language, dressing, grooming and modes of speech, reiterate norms of gender, and in this way, they also produce and strengthen these norms (Butler 1993; Perry and Joyce 2001). As embodied beings, humans are also always gendered beings living in a reality formed by social norms (Zaharijević 2020, 33). The more we act like "men" or "women" according to society's norms, the more others have to do so too. In 2021, the Law on Gender Equality was voted through in Serbian parliament and the owners of the "The Barbers" were impelled to remove the sign forbidding women to enter their barbershop. They were afraid of accusations of male chauvinism.

Taking from Belgrade this idea that beauty treatments can be part of a complex network of practices which establish masculinity, and masculine time and space, and taking from *Bodies that Matter* by Butler (1993) the idea that these practices are performative, in the rest of the paper I will explore whether beauty treatments in ancient Egypt also took part in the formation of gendered bodies, time and space, and how these might be similar or different to the gendered times and spaces of beauty treatments I am (we are) familiar with. I will argue that beauty treatments were entangled with norms which regulated sexuality in the service of patriarchal economy.

Where did men shave, groom and cut their hair in Ancient Egypt?

The first evidence which I will discuss in this paper comes from the tomb of two men who were among other things the overseers of the manicurists of the palace (*m-r jr ʿn.t pr ʿ3*), Niankhkhnum and Khnumhotep, from Saqqara (Mousa and Altenmüller 1977). The tomb which contained the double burial of these two men is dated to the late 5th Dynasty (*c.* 2435--2306 BCE) of the Old Kingdom. This tomb is well known to archaeologists studying gender and sexuality due to frequent interpretations of its owners as a same-sex couple (Dowson 2008; Reeder 2000; 2008), for which several authors have argued and several against (Büma and Fitzenreiter 2015; Evans and Woods 2016; Vasiljević 2008; for the most recent overview with further references, see Matić 2018). Other scenes from this tomb are of equal interest for gender archaeologists and can perhaps even tell us more about gender in ancient Egypt than the depictions of the owners that have in the past stimulated this discussion (*e.g.,* them holding hands or embracing each other).

In the first of four registers depicting an ancient Egyptian market of the time, there is a scene of several men receiving beauty treatments (Fig. 3.1). Starting from left to right, they receive the shaving of their legs, face and genital area (Arafa 2010, 184). In continuation some receive a manicure and pedicure. The inclusion of these depictions is certainly also related to the occupations of the tomb owners, namely they were manicurists of the palace. It has also been suggested that allusions to their profession are also made using an unparalleled motif of double black kites (*Milvus migrans*) attacking each other with their claws (ˁn.t is the words used both nails and claws in ancient Egyptian) in one scene from this tomb, as a visual cue to the occupation of the deceased men in their title *jrj ˁn.wt* "manicurists" (Evans and Woods 2016, 61–62). The second, third and fourth registers depict the buying and selling of different goods at the market and they will not be described in detail here. What has attracted the attention of many scholars until now is the presence of a woman depicted on the right end of the third register and a woman in the fourth and lowest register of the scene on the left. The one in the third register seems to be a customer, whereas the one in the fourth register seems to be selling her goods.

However, although women are depicted in this scene, which indicates that women, just as men, could be seen at a market in Old Kingdom (*c.* 2543–2120 BCE) Egypt, but also later on, as clear from later New Kingdom (*c.* 1539–1077 BCE) depictions of market scenes (Eyre 1998; van de Beek 2016; Stefanović 1999; 2001), women are not shown receiving beauty treatments in the market scene from the tomb of Niankhkhnum and Khnumhotep. A scene with manicure, pedicure and shaving (genital area and the head) is also known from the tomb of Ptahshepses in Saqqara dated to the reign of Unas (*c.* 2321–2306 BCE) of the 5th Dynasty. Here also, like in the tomb of Niankhkhnum and Khnumhotep, the beauty treatments are conducted by men on men. Unlike in other Old Kingdom tombs in which scenes with beauty treatments are depicted, in the tomb of Ptahshepses the customers are identified by accompanying inscriptions.

Fig. 3.1 First register from above of a market scene from the tomb of Niankhkhnum and Khnumhotep, Saqqara, 5th Dynasty (after Mousa and Altenmüller 1977, Abb. 10)

They are the tomb owner Ptahshepses and his two sons (Soleiman 2014, 31–38). In fact, manicure, pedicure and shaving occupies its own register in a scene in which the dominant figure is the seated tomb owner on the left. To his right are registers depicting boats, and below him and these registers with boats is the register with cosmetic treatments (Soleiman 2014, 33, fig. 2). It is hard to interpret the registers with boats based only on the photo, as the entire tomb has not been published yet. In analogy with other similar scenes, we could cautiously conclude that in the tomb of Ptahshepses the beauty treatments occur outdoors, perhaps in a market, or mooring place, or a harbour. Men of the upper classes could have also received beauty treatments in private. For example, Ptahhotep, overseer of the pyramid town of Djedkare Isesi (*c.* 2365–2322 BCE) of the 5th Dynasty and overseer of the two treasuries is depicted in his tomb with three male servants engaged in his manicure, pedicure and hair/wig arrangement (Davies 1900, 9, pl. XXXb)

Only men receive shaving of different body parts, manicure and pedicure in these Old Kingdom scenes and the ones who offer these services are also men. How can this be interpreted? Traditional Egyptologists would probably look for the answers in decorum, and argue that for whatever reason beauty treatments of women were not depicted because they did not fit the context of the scene or because for whatever reason depicting nude women was not appropriate. This argument does not take into account that female nudity is depicted in other scenes and of course always in very specific contexts (Asher-Greve and Sweeney 2006; Goelet 1993; Serova 2018). Therefore, we are safe to say that ancient Egyptian women, just like men, did not normally run around naked or with intimate body parts exposed or alluded to through transparent clothing. There are also varying reasons for someone to be nude in different contexts and to be represented nude in different contexts. Workmen are sometimes depicted nude indicating their lower status (Asher-Greve and Sweeney 2006, 120). Children are as rule depicted nude which is an indication of their age (Feucht 1995; Janssen and Janssen 2007, 23). Male enemies and prisoners of war are depicted either nude or with exposed genitalia, an indication of their defeat and vulnerability (Asher-Greve and Sweeney 2006; Matić 2021, 94–122). Common to all of these is still the idea of exposure, vulnerability, subjugation and weakness vis-à-vis the observer or a different referent. Yet, the first register from the market scene from the tomb of Niankhkhnum and Khnumhotep depicts a mundane scene, and as much as the men are depicted here nude and receiving shaving treatment, the context does not permit us to read in other associations, without strong arguments to back this up.

In conclusion, in the Old Kingdom, most men received beauty treatments in a market or a street, but certainly in a public space in ancient Egypt, a place in which both men and women could find themselves. We do not know where Old Kingdom markets were located, but we know that they were crowded and lively, with merchants, people haggling, guardsmen with baboons on a leash, and men, women and children of different ages and backgrounds. Some of these selling and buying beer (van de

Beek 2016, 31–32). Whether or not there was a special secluded space at the market where men would go to receive beauty treatments, including shaving, is something we cannot say with certainty. However, it is evident that in the tombs of upper-class men beauty treatments occupy a separate register which depicts only this activity and that no women are depicted there. Therefore, the assumption of a secluded space within the market space cannot be excluded.

Of course, noble men could have received beauty treatments in the privacy of their homes or the royal palace, if they were the closest servants of the king, and the kings themselves will have received cosmetic treatments in the seclusion of the palace, whereby we must also differentiate between royal and palace hairdressers. This is indicated by the titles of numerous individuals who were in charge of a king's beauty treatments, such as manicure, pedicure, shaving and hair cutting. The beauty treatments of the king also had ritualistic overtones, at least during the late Old Kingdom, and were related to the cult of the Sun god Ra. The titles and professions of hairdressers could be passed from father to son, and men could progress in their careers from working as palace hairdressers to working as royal hairdressers and overseers of hairdressers (Tassie 2017, 260–263). Most of these men also carry other titles which indicate their close proximity to the king, as proximity to the king elevated the status of these men. Being in charge of beauty treatments of the king was an important duty, since the pharaoh was living God on Earth (Riefstahl 1952, 12).

On the other hand, there are reputedly not many women carrying similar job titles during the Old Kingdom (Arafa 2010, 177; Tassie 2017, 256), one exception being a lady called Meretites, overseer of the house of hairdressing (*imy-r3 is-šn pr*) from the reign of Neferirkare (*c.* 2415–2405 BCE) of the 5th Dynasty whose statue is kept in the Rijksmuseum van Oudheden in Leiden (Riefstahl 1952, 14; Tassie 2017, 259, fig. 2). According to Geoffrey J. Tassie, the fact that she also carried titles such as royal ornament, royal relative and mistress of ceremonies indicates that she was in charge of hairdressing for women in the court of the king (Tassie 2017, 259).

Fig. 3.2 Shaving scene, tomb of Khety from Beni Hasan (tomb 17) Senwosret I, c. 1920-1875 BCE (after Newberry 1893, pl. XIII)

From the Middle Kingdom (*c.* 1980–1760 BCE) there are two tombs of importance for this discussion. In both the tomb of Baket III from Beni Hasan (tomb 15) from the reign of Amenemhat I (*c.* 1939–1910 BCE; Fig. 3.2) and the tomb of Khety from Beni Hasan (tomb 17) from the reign of Senwosret I (*c.* 1920–1875 BCE), we find more or less the same scene (Newberry 1893, pls IV and XIII). Two pairs of men are depicted in the middle of a beauty treatment. The barbers are sitting on

Fig. 3.3 Recruits scene, tomb of Userhat (TT 56), royal scribe of Amenhotep II, c. 1425–1400 BCE (https://www.wikiart.org/en/ancient-egyptian-painting/barbering-tomb-of-userhat--1400)

chairs and their customers are sitting on the floor so that their heads are lower and easier for the barbers to work on. However, we are unable to clearly see the tools that the barbers use. But conveniently, the accompanying text identifies the procedure as shaving. The determinative (hieroglyphic sign with no sound value indicating meaning of a word) in the shape of a razor in the word ḫꜥḳ "to shave" does resemble the tools used by the barbers in these representations. Nothing indicates that this is occurring in a closed space, rather, on the contrary, it is to be assumed that the act of shaving is happening outdoors.

The next scene I would like to discuss is the one from the tomb of Userhat (TT 56), royal scribe of Amenhotep II (c. 1425–1400 BCE) of the New Kingdom's 18th Dynasty (Fig. 3.3). The scene has three registers. The largest register is the one on the top of the scene depicting an officer addressing recruits next to a tree, indicating that this is happening outside. The middle register has recruits biding their time sitting around trees. The third register depicts two men taking care of the hair of two seated men (Arafa 2010, 184). Other men in this register are also seated next to a tree, again indicating that this is happening outside. However, it is not entirely clear what kind of treatment these men are receiving. Clearly it is something to do with the head and hair, but the tools in the hands of the barbers are hard to recognise and identify. The one on the left in the register has a tool that does not resemble the razors of the time (Fig. 3.4). It also does not resemble the enigmatic Egyptian cosmetic tool that is

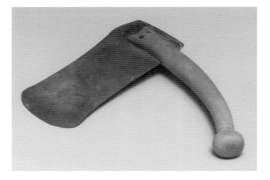

Fig. 3.4a mḫꜥk.t razor of Hatnefer, Tomb of Hatnefer and Ramose (below TT 71), Sheikh Abd el-Qurna, Upper Egypt, early 18th Dynasty MMA 36.3.69 (https://images.metmuseum.org/ CRDImages/eg/original/DP116027.jpg)

Fig. 3.4b dg3 razor of Baki, Tomb of Neferkhawet (MMA 729), east chamber, Burial of Baki (III), Asasif, Upper Egypt, reign of Thutmose I-Thutmose III (https://images.metmuseum.org/CRDImages/ eg/original/LC-35_3_65_EGDP026070.jpg)

Fig. 3.5 Scene in which workmen are depicted building a catafalque, tomb of Ipuy (TT 217), Deir el-Medinah, Ramesses II (c. 1279–1213 BCE), detail https://www.metmuseum.org/ art/collection/search/548572

discussed by Kira Zumkley in this volume (Chapter 4). It could be a comb.

Although unrelated to shaving, one more scene should be mentioned in connection to the cosmetic treatments conducted by men on men. In the tomb of Ipuy (TT 217) in Deir el-Medinah from the reign of Ramesses II (c. 1279–1213 BCE) of the New Kingdom's 19th Dynasty, there is a scene in which workmen are depicted building a catafalque. Although part of the scene is considerably damaged, among these workmen one can still recognise the figure of a seated man holding a long stick-like object towards the eye of another figure (Fig. 3.5). Above their heads is a depiction of an object that resembles a double kohl tube, with a kohl stick attached to it. Kohl was a galena-based (PbS) black eye make-up used in ancient Egypt by both men and women. Next to the object, on the right, is a box with a bag inside. Some authors have interpreted this scene as evidence for an eye cataract operation (Ascaso, Lizana and Cristóbal 2009), an interpretation which can be refuted bearing in mind the context and the details of the scene. Others have interpreted this as an application of make-up in order to prevent dust coming into the eye (Booth 2018, 33).

Where the barber occupation during the New Kingdom is concerned, one text is particularly informative. The Teaching of Kheti, or Satire on Trades, is a text entirely preserved on Papyrus Sallier II, partially on Papyrus Anastasi VII, both written in the 19th Dynasty, and in small portions on an 18th Dynasty writing board in the Louvre, Papyrus Amherst, Papyrus Chester Beatty XIX, ostracon British Museum EA 41650+47896 (paleographically dated to the 18th Dynasty), and numerous Ramesside ostraca. This text describes the hard work of a barber who shaves until evening and goes from street to street in order to find those who want to be shaved (Arafa 2010, 185; Hoch 1991/1992, 90–91; Lichtheim 1973, 184–186). Whether the barber is roaming through the streets looking for customers who would invite him to their homes to receive shaving or the shaving occurred on the streets is not explicitly stated. However, bearing in mind that the act of shaving requires light, and that the text states that barbers worked late until the evening, we can assume that they probably worked outside. If they worked in the homes of their customers, they would need the artificial light of lamps, which were of course also used in ancient Egypt. If the text informs us that barbers rather worked outside, then we should bear in mind that streets just like markets were public spaces with a lot of traffic. In fact, working in a public space would be a good commercial for the barber to attract more customers and could potentially form a cluster of waiting customers who could have, just as the customers in modern barbershops that I described in the introduction of this paper, shared stories about their lives, work, neighbours, wives, children or the women (perhaps even men) they find attractive.

If the barbers in the New Kingdom, like in the Old Kingdom, also worked in the markets, then we can add that New Kingdom markets were also located on the banks of the Nile, for example at Thebes, where even foreign trading ships could be docked (Wachsmann 1998, 42–43). Like in the Old Kingdom market scenes, in New Kingdom market scenes we also find women selling goods and men, women and children of different ages and backgrounds (van de Beek 2016, 34–36). In none of these New Kingdom scenes do we find men or women receiving cosmetic treatments, but the reasons for this could be various, for example the upper registers of the market scene from the tomb of Ipy (TT 217) are not preserved. A possible indication that men could have had haircuts or shavings in harbour areas or riverbanks is found on Ostracon Gardiner 197 from year 9 of Merenptah (1213–1203 BCE) of the 19th Dynasty. Here scribe Qenkirkhopshef is said to have returned from the riverbank. In the continuation it is said that the workman Rehotep shaved him. However, it remains unclear whether he received the treatment at the riverbank or after he had returned from the riverbank (Kitchen 2003, 119).

Fig. 3.6 Ostracon 32.1 from the Walters Art Museum in Baltimore, Maryland, USA (https://art.thewalters.org/detail/5104/ostracon-with-a-royal-head/)

Fig. 3.7 Ostracon Fitzwilliam Museum Cambridge EGA 4324-1943 (https://collection.beta.fitz.ms/id/image/media-24057)

Clearly, the well-groomed and shaved body of man was a masculine ideal of beauty advertised by the higher classes of society in ancient Egypt (Arafa 2010, 181; Volokhine 2019). Of course, not everyone was nicely groomed and clean shaved, at least not all of the time. Egyptian figured ostraca often depict a topsy-turvy world where not everything is shown according to social norms (Flores 2004), but much of which is a reflection of reality. These ostraca also depict men with beards in the form of stubble. Ostracon 32.1 from the Walters Art Museum in Baltimore, Maryland, USA (Fig. 3.6) depicts a 19th Dynasty king with what we would call a three-day beard (for other examples including those in other media than ostraca, see Czerkwiński 2014).

Ostracon Fitzwilliam Museum Cambridge EGA 4324-1943 (Brunner-Traut 1979, 40–41, pl. XII) depicts a bald man with large ears, three-day beard and muscular arms who is holding a chisel and mallet and working on a stone, which has led to his interpretation as a stonemason (Fig. 3.7). Such representations of unshaved men of lower classes are also found in other media. Another fragment of a wall painting depicting a carpenter at work from SPK/SMB Ägyptisches Museum und Papyrussammlung (inv.-no. ÄM 23731) also shows an unshaved man (Driaux 2020, 4, fig. 1).

These depictions remind us that for every shaved and well-groomed ancient Egyptian we have to imagine one who was not well-groomed and shaved. Egyptology tends to create an image of ancient Egypt populated by beautiful people according to both ancient and modern standards, often forgetting that there were also those who for various reasons did not comply to the norms, class being only one of those reasons.

Where did women shave and groom in ancient Egypt?

We have seen that most men shaved and groomed in public spaces, such as markets, streets or outdoors in general. Men of the higher classes and kings received beauty treatments in the privacy of their homes or the palace, because they had servants who regularly took care of them. Evidence for this practice spans from the Old Kingdom to the New Kingdom.

However, where cosmetic treatments for women are concerned, we have an entirely different picture. Noblewomen depicted receiving different beauty treatments (primarily hairdressing) are attended by female servants who mostly do not have specific cosmetic related-titles, like the male manicurists or barbers who treated men. The overall impression behind these representations of beauty treatments of women from the Old Kingdom to the New Kingdom is a more intimate atmosphere, in an unspecified space, but certainly a space and time shared by the mistress and mostly her female servants. Old Kingdom examples are interpreted as predecesorss of later First Intermediate and Middle Kingdom hairdressing scenes. On the false door of Senwehem from Giza and dated to the 6th Dynasty, the mother or wife of Senwehem called Nefer is represented standing with a small figure of a female servant behind her arranding her hair. Another example is the depiction of Inetites, wife of Ihy in the tomb of Ihy at el-Khokha from the end of 6th Dynasty. Inetites holds a mirror and behind her back is a female servant. Although not actually arrangeing the hair of her mistress, her presence indicates that beautification of women was a process done either by female family members or female servants (Hudáková 2019, 289). In one exceptional case, from the Saqqara tomb of princess Idut, daughter of Unas of the 5th Dynasty, the "hairdresser" is a man named Seshemnefer who was inspector of the physicians. He is depicted at a much smaller scale than the princess as he arranges the disc in her pigtail behind her (Macramallah 1935, pl. XVII). He is clearly not cutting her hair, nor is he providing her with a manicure or pedicure. It is also noticeable that he does not carry the title of barber or hairdresser. In a strict sense it therefore cannot be claimed that he actually provided beauty treatments to the princess.

First Intermediate Period examples of beauty treatments include a limestone slab from the Brooklyn Museum with the depiction of the female hairdresser (*jr.t šnj*-"maker of hair") Inenu (Riefstahl 1952, 7–8, fig. 1). Early Middle Kingdom examples include the sarcophagi of Kawit and Ashayet, priestesses of Hathor within funerary complex of Mentuhotep II at Deir el-Bahari (*c.* 2009–1959 BCE). Kawit is shown seated holding a mirror and drinking from a hemispherical cup as a servant girl adjusts her wig or hair (Riefstahl 1952, 9, fig. 2). Ashayet is depicted on the interior of her coffin in the company of her female servants. In one scene she is seated and beneath her stool is a small box, behind her a female servant with a kohl pot in one hand and a mirror in a leather bag in the other hand. In another scene on the interior of her coffin she is depicted seated on a stool under which a mirror is depicted above the small box. The female servant is depicted behind Ashayet holding a fan. In the same scene, other female servants bring her more mirrors (Liszka 2018). A fragment of a relief of Neferu, wife of Mentuhotep Nebhepetre II, originally from her rock-cut tomb at Deir el-Bahari depicts the hairdresser (*jr.t šnj*) Henut arranging the hair of Neferu (Stünkel 2015, 96). There are also Middle Kingdom examples in three-dimensional art in which women dress the hair of children or other women (Hudáková 2019, 220)

Therefore, the evidence from the First Intermediate Period and Middle Kingdom indicates that for women of higher classes at least, beauty treatments were the occupation of their servants who attended them in privacy. This continues into the later periods, although beauty treatment scenes, such as hairdressing, seem to disappear during the Second Intermediate Period (*c.* 1759–1539 BCE). In this context the hairdressers are private personnel and not high-ranking officials (Tassie 2017, 272). From the New Kingdom examples come from the 18th Dynasty tomb of Neferrenpet (TT 140) in which one woman tends the hair of another who is holding a mirror, and from Amarna tomb no. 5 of Ay (Fig. 3.8) in which a Syrian woman or girl tends the hair of another (Davies 1908, 20, pl. XXVIII; Gauthier-Laurent 1935, 682–683). It is important to stress here that the latter women shown tending their hair in the tomb of Ay from Amarna are depicted in a room of a house that is guarded by a man outside. Other women are also depicted in other rooms, but there are no men present.

This privacy in which women received their beauty treatments was the subject of literary fantasy during the New Kingdom, as indicated by the so called "love" poems. These also inform us on the ideal desirable female body from a very specifically male perspective. The protagonists of these poems can be described as unmarried adolescents (Sweeney 2002, 32). The first "love" poem of Papyrus Chester Beatty I

Fig. 3.8 Syrian woman or girl tends the hair of another girl, possibly also holding a mirror, Amarna tomb no. 5 of Ay, detail (after Davies 1908, 20, pl. XXVIII)

Group A (No. 31) from the 20th Dynasty (1190–1077 BCE) describes the female beloved as long of neck, luminous of chest, with hair of true lapis, arms of gold and fingers like lotuses (Darnell 2016, 28). A New Kingdom poem from Ostracon Cairo 25218 (8-14, A, 3) describes a woman while imagining she is bathing in front of her desired lover, she is wearing a dress of the finest royal linen, drenched with fragrant unguent (Landgráfová and Navrátilová 2009, 178). Stela Louvre C 100, an inscription in honour of princess Mutirdis, dating around 700 BCE, informs us that hair blacker than the black of night, teeth whiter than gypsum and flax fibres (?), and breast set firm on the chest were considered attractive in women (Quack 2016, 64–65). Therefore, we can indeed speak of the *longue durée* of an ideal female beauty, however, we should not forget that it is a product of the tastes of the literate Egyptian elite.

Interestingly, we are not similarly informed in texts about the desirable male body. In the *Tale of Two Brothers* (Papyrus D´Orbiney, British Museum EA 10183) a story which among other things thematises adultery and its social consequences, an older brother, Anubis, lives with his wife and his younger unmarried brother Bata. The wife of Anubis attempted to seduce Bata, who refused her advances, and in order not to be exposed as a seductress she falsely accuses Bata of trying to seduce her and of hurting her after she denied him. It is interesting in this case how the wife of Anubis expresses the way Bata supposedly approached her. He said to her: "Come, let's spend an hour lying together. You shall loosen your braids" (Lichtheim 1976, 205; Wente 2003, 83). Clearly, the desired female body as described in the "love" poems is a body encountered in the privacy of the home, within the constraints of marriage, or in secrecy as part of pre-marital or adulterous affairs. It is indeed no wonder that the male protagonists in the "love" poems express their wish to be the Nubian servant girls of the women they desire in order to be in their proximity. This is attested in song two of the Cairo love songs that is inscribed on a ceramic vessel and dating to 19th or 20th Dynasty. In it the boy speaks: "If only I were her Nubian maid, who attends upon her privately!" (Fox 1980, 103).

Cosmetic treatments and gendered space and time

Egyptological studies of gender usually focus on women and femininities (*e.g.*, Capel and Markoe 1996; Graves-Brown 2010; Robins 1993; Tyldesley 1995; Watterson 1991), and rarely on men and masculinities (Parkinson 1995; 2008; Matić 2021; Morris 2021). The focus on women and femininities was for a long-time endemic to gender archaeology, probably because of the general androcentrism in archaeology (Gilchrist 1999; Sørensen 2000). However, gender-informed studies of masculinities in the past have slowly appeared (*e.g.*, Alberti 2006; Knapp 1998a; 1998b; Treherne 1995), and they also have found their place in Egyptology. The danger behind this situation is that one is continuously focusing on women and the other on men, no matter how theoretically informed, rather than on gender which concerns both (Matić 2016; Meskell 1997). Only rarely are masculinities and femininities in ancient Egypt juxtaposed in order to better understand the gender systems and gender norms (Matić 2021; Meskell 1999).

Gender studies have a continuous focus on bodies and body related practices (Butler 1993; Meskell 2000; Meskell and Joyce 2003). Beauty treatments and ideals of beauty have been studied by numerous anthropologists, sociologists, historians and archaeologists (see Chapter 1 in this volume, but also other chapters). In this paper, I juxtaposed beauty treatments of men and women in ancient Egypt because I was interested less in how beauty treatments are used to achieve certain gender specific ideals of beauty (for this topic see other papers in this volume), but more in how a gender system is organising beauty treatments and the spaces in which they occur, and then how in turn beauty treatments performatively reinforce this gender system. My analysis for this purpose was based on iconographic and textual sources simply because most of the cosmetic utensils such as razors, tweezers, cosmetic knives, wig-tools, and cosmetic vessels for make-up, ointments and perfumes are found in tombs (Podvin 1997; Smith 1992, 207) and thus do not inform us on the spaces in which they were used in daily life and the people involved with both these tools and these spaces.

I propose a series of binary oppositions around the beauty treatments conducted upon men and women in ancient Egypt which are reconstructed using the limited number of sources we have, but which seem to indicate a continuous tradition, certainly a consequence of a long-term gender system (Table 3.1). Based on these sources we can argue that whereas men were shaved and groomed by other men who were barbers, manicurists/pedicurists and hairdressers by occupation, women were shaved and groomed by female servants who were mostly not professional barbers and manicurists/pedicurists. In fact, there is no woman attested with a title of a barber or manicurist, and only rarely do women carry the titles of hairdressers.

Finally, the most important question: why are we observing such a gendered structure of beauty treatments where the space used for them and those involved with them are concerned? In order to answer this question, we have to first understand that hair, the wigs worn by women and their skin were highly sexualised in ancient Egypt (Derchain 1975; Manniche 2003, 43; Matić, forthcoming). As I have mentioned previously, the so-called "love" poems of the New Kingdom inform us on the feminine beauty ideals which revolved around skin and hair. Therefore, being able to touch a woman's or a girl's hair or skin was the desire of men and boys, non-married in the "love" poems, and both married and unmarried in real life. Men and women desired

Table 3.1 A series of binary oppositions around the beauty treatments conducted upon men and women in ancient Egypt

Men	Women
Barber, manicurist, hairdresser (male)	Servant, hairdresser (female)
Group treatment	Individual treatment
Public, private	Private

other men and women outside of wedlock and there are numerous reports of adultery and rape (Matić 2021, 29–80). It was probably considered inappropriate for a male barber or manicurist/pedicurist to provide services to a female customer. A stranger, another man, touching the hair and skin of another man's wife, sister, mother or daughter, was most probably a taboo.

We know from Wisdom Texts such as the Maxims of Ptahhotep, a text which circulated at least since the Middle Kingdom, possibly even the Old Kingdom, that men were advised to beware of approaching the women in a house they enter if they want their friendship with the man of the house to endure. According to Maxim 18 where this warning is stated, women are also dangerous because one can fall into lust for them and death comes from knowing them (Matić 2021, 27–28). Adolescent girls, daughters transitioning from girlhood to womanhood, were probably particularly monitored by the family. This is also possibly indicated by the use of nude or semi-nude girls as a motif on cosmetic utensils, such as mirrors (Derriks 2001) and cosmetic spoons (Matić 2019; O'Connor 2020). They are often followed by marshland animals in these depictions. As demonstrated by Joachim Friedrich Quack, interpretations of these figures as representations of goddess Hathor are not well argued and iconographic parallels rather indicate that these are servant girls who were involved in the beauty treatments of their noblewomen (Quack 2003).

David O'Connor related the girls depicted on cosmetic objects to the world order, especially the continuous transformation of chaos into order and the image of the nude or semi-nude girl as part of the symbolic world (O'Connor 2020, 1107–1109). I agree with O'Connor that this imagery is related to the preservation of world order. However, I argued that the symbolic background of this imagery and the specific way of handling the objects ("to hold the nude girl in grip" *sensu* Quack 2003) come from the need to control "wild" adolescent sexuality threatening the patriarchal "world" order (Matić 2019). As I have mentioned, the sexual activity of the women of a household was monitored by men, which does not mean that some women, just as men, did not practice premarital sex or commit adultery, but this is exactly what men tried to control. We know from the New Kingdom love poems that sexual encounters of lovers frequently occurred in marsh-like settings (Darnell 2016; Landgráfová and Navrátilová 2009; Matić, forthcoming). Since married couples do not have to hide, clearly, we are dealing with sex out of wedlock, either because the involved were not married or because one or both committed adultery. This could also explain the motif of the swimming girl, fauna such as marsh birds (ducks and geese) and flora such as lotus and papyrus, that were frequently used in decoration of cosmetic objects with nude or semi-nude girls (O'Connor 2020, 1111).

Therefore, as indicated by Wisdom Texts, on the one hand men were advised not to get too close to women from other households if they wanted to stay on good terms with the man of that household, and on the other hand, as indicated by the "love" poems, unmarried men desired unmarried women and both men and women committed adultery. Beauty treatments are very much related to this, as these are practices that directly interfere with the body. They bring different bodies into close proximity to each other, with one being more exposed than the other. Maintaining boundaries in a situation where boundaries have to be crossed can be tricky. Ancient Egyptians clearly developed gender norms around beauty treatments, so that men were tended by men in public or private, and women were tended by women, mostly in private. This was done in order to mitigate the potential breaking of other already established norms, such as respecting the honour of other men and the institution of marriage and the right for father to give his daughter to another man. Therefore, we can recognise here an example of gender as a regulatory practice using the terminology of Butler (2004, 41) who rethought it based on the previous work of Michel Foucault (1990). Such practices produce the bodies they govern. Regulatory norms exercised through beauty treatments not only materialised ideal beautiful bodies (see other chapters in this volume), but also regulated the access to these bodies for different genders in the process of beautification. Ultimately, this is related to gender power relations and control of sexuality. No one is simply beautiful, but more beautiful for someone than for others. This simple fact can empower both the desiring and the desired subject, but it can also make them potentially vulnerable.

Conclusion

Unlike modern barbershops for men which create masculine spaces and times by excluding women from them, by prohibiting them entrance or simply creating an atmosphere in which women would not feel comfortable staying, ancient Egyptian men enjoyed services provided by barbers, manicurists/pedicurists and hairdressers both in private spaces, such as households and public spaces, such as streets. Public spaces were not strictly spaces for men, as women used them too, but we should not forget that as much as being different than our modern patriarchal societies in many aspects (Folbre 2020), ancient Egyptian society was patriarchal too (Matić 2021, 138). Therefore, although women were part of public spaces, these spaces were dominated by men, just like the private spaces, such as households in which the dominant figure was the oldest man, husband and father. This does not mean that at certain times distinct private household spaces could not become spaces of women, most certainly they could and they did.

However, as I have argued, this was done exactly in order to regulate access to women and their bodies, and this is why I argue that women were shaved and groomed by other women in all women's private spaces, as opposed to men who could be shaved and groomed in both private and public spaces. Spaces in which women receive beauty treatments which require greater exposure of their bodies, *e.g.*, body hair removal through various cosmetic practices, such as depilation, but also massage, are present in our societies and are also spaces to which men usually do not have access, unless they are tolerated by women, because *e.g.*, they show no sexual interest in them. These spaces are either temporary arranged women's spaces in individual households, like in ancient Egypt, or are created as permanent women's spaces in which women work as cosmeticians. The latter was not known in ancient Egypt.

Acknowledgements

The work leading to this publication was supported by the German Academic Exchange Service (DAAD) with funds from the German Federal Ministry of Education and Research (BMBF) and the People Programme (Marie Curie Actions) of the European Union's Seventh Framework Programme (FP7/2007–2013) under REA grant agreement n° 605728 (P.R.I.M.E.–Postdoctoral Researchers International Mobility Experience). I would like to thank Angelika Lohwasser, Bettina Bader, Christian Knoblauch and Barbara Horejs for our discussions on the topic of cosmetic utensils in ancient Egypt and Nubia, and for useful suggestions during my work on New Kingdom Egyptian cosmetic utensils in Nubia, conducted from 2018–2019 at the OREA-Institute for Oriental and European Archaeology of the Austrian Academy of Sciences (now Austrian Archaeological Institute) and the Institute for Egyptology and Coptic Studies of the University of Muenster, Germany.

Bibliography

Alberti, B. (2006) Archaeology, men, and masculinities. In S.M. Nelson (ed.) *Handbook of Gender in Archaeology*, 401–434. Lanham, AltaMira Press.

Arafa, N. (2010) Le Barbier en Egypte Ancienne. *Cahiers Caribéens d'Égyptologie* 13–14, 175–198.

Ascaso, F.J., Lizana, J. and Cristóbal, J.A. (2009) Cataract surgery in ancient Egypt. *Journal of Cataract and Refractive Surgery* 35 (3), 607–608.

Asher-Greve, J. and Sweeney, D. (2006) On nakedness, nudity, and gender in Egyptian and Mesopotamian Art. In S. Schroer (ed.) *Images of Gender: Contributions to the Hermeneutics of Reading Ancient Art*, 111–162. Orbis Biblicus et Orientalis 220. Fribourg and Göttingen, University Press and Vandenhoeck & Ruprecht.

van de Beek, N. (2016) Saqqara scenes: women in the marketplace. *Saqqara Newsletter* 14, 31–38.

Booth, C. (2018) *In Bed with the Ancient Egyptians*. Gloucestershire, Amberley Publishing.

Brunner-Traut, E. (1979) *Egyptian Artist's Sketches. Figured Ostraca from the Gayer-Anderson Collection in the Fitzwilliam Museum, Cambridge*. Istanbul, Nederlands Historisch/Archaeologisch Institut.

Butler, J. (1993) *Bodies that Matter: On the Discursive Limits of "sex"*. New York and London, Routledge.

Butler, J. (2004) *Undoing Gender*. London and New York, Routledge.

Büma, B. and Fitzenreiter, M. (2015) „Spielt das Lied der beiden göttlichen Brüder": Erotische Ambiguität und „große Nähe" zwischen Männern im Alten Reich. *Studien zur Altägyptischen Kultur* 44, 19–42.

Capel, A.K. and Markoe, G.E. (eds) (1996) *Mistress of the House, Mistress of Heaven: Women in Ancient Egypt*. New York, Hudson Hills Press.

Conkey, M.W. and Spector, J.D. (1984) Archaeology and the study of gender. *Advances in Archaeological Method and Theory* 7, 1–38.

Czerkwiński, P. (2014) The beard of Rameses VI. *Studies in Ancient Art and Civilization* 18, 195–203.

Darnell, J.C. (2016) The rituals of love in ancient Egypt: festival songs of the Eighteenth Dynasty and the Ramesside love poetry. *Die Welt des Orients* 46, 22–61.

Davies, N. de G. (1900) *The Mastaba of Ptahhetep and Akhethetep at Saqqareh. Part I. The Chapel of Ptahhetep and the Hieroglyphs*. London, The Egypt Exploration Fund.

Davies, N. de G. (1908) *The Rock Tombs of El Amarna. Part VI. Tombs of Parennefer, Tutu and Ay*. London, The Egypt Exploration Fund.

Derchain, P. (1975) La Perruque et le cristal. *Studien zur Altägyptischen Kultur* 2, 55–74.

Derriks, C. (2001) *Les miroirs cariatides egyptiens en bronze. Typologie, chronologie et symbolique*. Münchner Ägyptologische Studien 51. Mainz, Verlag Philipp von Zabern.

Díaz-Andreu, M. (2005) Gender identity. In M. Díaz-Andreu, S. Lucy, S. Babić and D.N. Edwards (eds) *The Archaeology of Identity: Approaches to Gender, Age, Status, Ethnicity and Religion*, 13–42. London, Routledge.

Dowson, T. (2008) Queering sex and gender in ancient Egypt. In C. Graves-Brown (ed.) *Sex and Gender in Ancient Egypt: "Don't Your Wig for a Joyful Hour"*, 27–46. Swansea, The Classical Press of Wales.

Driaux, D. (2020) Toward a study of the poot and poverty in ancient Egypt: preliminary thoughts. *Cambridge Archaeological Journal* 30 (1), 1–19.

Eyre, C. (1998) The market women of Pharaonic Egypt. In N. Grimal and B. Menu (eds) *Le commerce en Égypte ancienne*, 173–191. Bibliothèque d'étude 121. Cairo, Institut français d'archéologie orientale.

Evans, L. and Woods, A. (2016) Further evidence that Niankhkhnum and Khnumhotep were twins. *The Journal of Egyptian Archaeology* 102, 55–72.

Feucht, E. (1995) *Das Kind im Alten Ägypten. Die Stellung des Kindes in Familie und Gesellschaft nach altägyptischen Texten und Darstellungen*. Frankfurt and New York, Campus Verlag.

Flores, D. (2004) The topsy-turvy world. In G.N. Knoppers and A. Hirsch (eds) *Egypt, Israel, and the Ancient Mediterranean World. Studies in Honor of Donald B. Redford*, 233–255. Probleme der Ägyptologie 20. Leiden and Boston, Brill.

Folbre, N. (2020) *The Rise and Decline of Patriarchal Systems*. London and New York, Verso.

Foucault, M. (1990) [1978] *The History of Sexuality Volume I: An Introduction*. Translated from the French by Robert Hurley. New York, Vintage Books.

Fox, M.V. (1980) The Cairo love songs. *Journal of the American Oriental Society* 100 (2), 101–109.

Gauthier-Laurent, M. (1935) Les Scénes de Coiffure Féminine dans l'Ancienne Égypte. In G.C.C. Maspero (ed.) Mélanges *Maspero* I. Mémoires, 673–696. Institut Francais d'Archéologie Orientale du Caire 66. Le Caire, Institut Francais d'Archéologie Orientale du Caire.

Gero, J.M. and Conkey, M.W. (eds) (1991) *Engendering Archaeology. Women and Prehistory*. Oxford, Blackwell.

Graves-Brown, C. (2010) *Dancing for Hathor. Women in Ancient Egypt*. London, Continuum.

Gilchrist, R. (1999) *Gender and Archaeology: Contesting the Past*. London and New York, Routledge.

Goelet, O. (1993) Nudity in ancient Egypt. *Source: Notes in the History of Art* 12 (2), 20–31.

Hoch, J. (1991/1992) The teaching of Dua-Kheti. a new look at the Satire of the Trades. *The Journal of the Society for the Study of Egyptian Antiquities* 21/22, 88–100.

Hudáková, L. (2019) *The Representations of Women in the Middle Kingdom Tombs of Officials*. Harvard Egyptological Studies 6. Leiden and Boston, Brill.

Janssen, R.M. and Janssen, J.J. (2007) *Growing up and Getting Old in Ancient Egypt*. London, Golden House Publications.

Jensen, B. and Matić, U. (2017) Introduction. In U. Matić and B. Jensen (eds) *Archaeologies of Gender and Violence*, 1–23. Oxford, Oxbow Books.

Kitchen, K.A. (2003) *Ramesside Inscriptions. Translated and Annotated. Translations. Volume IV. Merenptah and the Late Nineteenth Dynasty*. Oxford, Blackwell.

Knapp, A.B. (1998a) Masculinist archaeology? *Archaeological Dialogues* 5 (2), 115–125.

Knapp, A.B. (1998b) Boys will be boys: masculinist approaches to a gendered archaeology. In K. Hays-Gilpin and D.S. Whitley (eds) *Reader in Gender Archaeology*, 365–373. London, Routledge.

Landgráfová, R. and Navrátilová, H. (2009) *Sex and the Golden Goddess I: Ancient Egyptian Love Songs in Context*. Prague, Agama.

Lichtheim, M. (1973) *Ancient Egyptian Literature I: The Old and Middle Kingdom.* Berkeley and Los Angeles, University of California Press.

Lichtheim, M. (1976) *Ancient Egyptian Literature II: New Kingdom.* Berkeley and Los Angeles, University of California Press.

Liszka, K. (2018) Discerning ancient identity: the case of Aashyet's sarcophagus (JE 47267). *Journal of Egyptian History* 11, 185–207.

Macramallah, R. (1935) *Fouilles à Saqqara, Le maṣṭaba d'Idout.* Le Caire, l'Institut français d'archéologie orientale.

Manniche, L. (2003) The so-called scenes of daily life in the private tombs of the Eighteenth Dynasty: an overview. In N. Strudwick and J.H. Taylor (eds) *Theban Necropolis. Past, Present and Future,* 42–46. London, British Museum Press.

Matić, U. (2016) Gender in ancient Egypt: norms, ambiguities, and sensualities. *Near Eastern Archaeology* 79 (3), 174–183.

Matić, U. (2018) Out of touch: Egyptology and queer theory (or what this encounter should not be). In A.-S.Naujoks and J. Stelling (eds) *Von der Quelle zur Theorie. Von Verhältnis zwischen Objektivität und Subjektivität in den historischen Wissenschaften,* 183–197. Leiden, Mentis.

Matić, U. (2019) Docile maids in the marshes: New Kingdom Egyptian cosmetic spoons in the form of swimming girls. Unpublished paper presented in the session "Getting into Shape: Reconsidering the Relationships between Perception, Skill, Cognition, and Materials in the Design of Ancient Figurines" organised by Celine Murphy and Alexander Aston at the Annual Meeting of the European Association of Archaeologists, Bern, Switzerland, 4–7 September 2019.

Matić, U. (2021) *Violence and Gender in Ancient Egypt.* London and New York, Routledge.

Matić, U. forthcoming. Sexuality in ancient Egypt: pleasures, desires, norms and representations. In M. Kuefler and M. Wiesner-Hanks (eds) *Cambridge History of Sexuality.* Cambridge, Cambridge University Press.

Meskell, L.M. (1997) Engendering Egypt. *Gender and History* 9 (3), 597–602.

Meskell, L.M. (1999) *Archaeologies of Social Life: Age, Sex, Class et cetera in Ancient Egypt.* Oxford, Wiley.

Meskell, L.M. (2000) Writing the body in archaeology. In A.E. Rautman (ed.) *Reading the Body: Representations and Remains in the Archaeological Record,* 13–24. Philadelphia, University of Pennsylvania Press.

Meskell, L.M. and Joyce, R. (2003) *Embodied Lives: Figuring Ancient Maya and Egyptian Experience.* London and New York, Routledge.

Morris, E. (2021) Machiavellian masculinities: historicizing and contextualizing the "civilizing process" in ancient Egypt. *Journal of Egyptian History* 13 (1–2), 127–168.

Mousa, A.M. and Altenmüller, H. (1977) *Das Grab des Nianchchnum and Chnumhotep.* Archäologische Veröffentlichungen 21. Kairo, Deutsches Archäologisches Institut, Abteilung Kairo.

Newberry, P.E. (1893) *Beni Hasan Part II.* London, The Egypt Exploration Fund.

O'Connor, D. (2020) "Objets de toilette" and the Egyptian world order. In J. Kamrin, M. Barta, S. Ikram, M. Lehner and M. Megahed (eds) *Guardian of Ancient Egypt. Studies in Honor of Zahi Hawass. Volume II.* 1105-1132. Prague, Charles University, Faculty of Arts.

Parkinson, R. (1995) 'Homosexual' desire and Middle Kingdom literature. *The Journal of Egyptian Archaeology* 81, 57–76.

Parkinson, R. (2008) Boasting about hardness: constructions of Middle Kingdom Masculinity In C. Graves-Brown (ed.) *Sex and Gender in Ancient Egypt: 'Don Your Wig for a Joyful Hour',* 115–142. Swansea, The Classical Press of Wales.

Perry, E.M. and Joyce, R.A. (2001) Interdisciplinary applications: providing a past for "bodies that matter": Judith Butler's impact on the archaeology of gender. *International Journal of Sexuality and Gender Studies* 6, 63–76.

Podvin, J.-L. (1997) *Composition, position et orientation du mobilier funéraire dans les tombes égyptiennes privées du moyen empire à la basse époque.* Unpublished PhD thesis, University of Lille.

Quack, J.F. (2003) Das nackte Mädchen im Griff halten. Zur Deutung der ägyptischen Karyatidenspiegel. *Die Welt des Orients* 33, 44–64.

Quack, J.F. (2016) Where once was love, love is no more? What happens to expressions of love in Late Period Egypt? *Die Welt des Orients* 46, 62–89.

Reeder, G. (2000) Same-sex desire, conjugal constructs, and the Tomb of Niankhkhnum and Khnumhotep. *World Archaeology* 32.2. Queer Archaeologies, 193–208.

Reeder, G. (2008) Queer Egyptologies of Niankhkhnum and Khnumhotep. In C. Graves-Brown (ed.) *Sex and Gender in Ancient Egypt: 'Don Your Wig for a Joyful Hour'*, 143–156. Swansea, The Classical Press of Wales.

Riefstahl, E. (1952) An ancient Egyptian hairdresser. *Brooklyn Museum Bulletin* 14 (3), 7–16.

Robins, G. (1993) *Women in Ancient Egypt*. Cambridge, Harvard University Press.

Serova, D. (2018) Entblößte Gestalten: Multifunktionale Nacktheit in Privatgräbern des Alten Reiches. In J. Aschmoneit, B. Backes and A. Verbovsek (eds) *Funktion/en: Materielle Kultur-Sprache-Religion. Beiträge des siebten Berliner Arbeitsjreises Junge Ägyptologie (BAJA 7), 2.12-4.12.2016*, 241–260. Göttinger Orientforschungen IV. Reihe Ägypten 64. Wiesbaden, Harrassowitz Verlag.

Smith, S.T. (1992) Intact Theban tombs and the New Kingdom burial assemblage. *Mitteilungen des Deutschen Archäologischen Instituts Kairo* 48, 193–231.

Soleiman, S. (2014) The hair-shaving and nail-cutting scenes in Ptahshepses' Tomb at Saqqara. *Journal of the American Research Center in Egypt* 50, 31–40.

Sørensen, M.L.S. (2000) *Gender Archaeology*. Cambridge, Polity Press.

Stefanović, D. (1991) Market-women and market-place in Pharaonic Egypt: according to Hdt, II, 35, Egyptian written sources and iconography. *Glasnik srpskog arheološkog društva/Journal of the Serbian Archaeological Society* 15–16, 145–151

Stefanović, D. (2001) Once more about MRYT and "market-place". *Glasnik srpskog arheološkog društva/Journal of the Serbian Archaeological Society* 17, 231–234.

Stünkel, I. (2015) Royal women: ladies of the two lands. In A. Oppenheim, D. Arnold, D. Arnold and K. Yamamoto (eds) *Ancient Egypt Transformed. The Middle Kingdom*, 92–119. New York, The Metropolitan Museum of Art.

Sweeney, D. (2002) Gender and language in the Ramesside love songs. *Bulletin of the Egyptological Seminar* 16, 27–50.

Tassie, G. (2017) The ancient Egyptian hairdresser in the Old Kingdom. *Mitteilungen des Deutschen Archäologischen Instituts Kairo* 73, 255–275.

Treherne, P. (1995) The warrior´s beauty: the masculine body and self-identity in Bronze-Age Europe. *Journal of European Archaeology* 3.1, 105–144.

Tyldesley, J.A. (1995) *Daughters of Isis: Women of Ancient Egypt*. London, Penguin Books.

Vasiljević, V. (2008) Embracing his double: Niankhkhnum and Khnumhotep. *Studien zur Altägyptischen Kultur* 37, 363–372.

Volokhine, Y. (2019) Barbe et barbus en Egypte ancienne. In Y. Volokhine (ed.) *Barbe et barbus: Symboliques, rites et pratiques du port de la barbe dans le Proche-Orient ancien et modern*, 59–87. Etudes genevoises sur l'Antiquité 5. Bern, Peter Lang.

Wachsmann, S. (1995) *Seagoing Ships and Seamanship in the Bronze Age Levant*. College Station, Texas A & M University Press.

Watterson, B. (1991) *Women in Ancient Egypt*. New York, St. Martin's Press.

Wente, E.F. (2003) The Tale of the Two Brothers. In W.K. Simpson (ed.) *The Literature of Ancient Egypt. An Anthology of Stories, Instructions, Stelae, Autobiographies, and Poetry*, 80–90. Third Edition. New Haven and London, Yale University Press.

Zaharijević, A. (2020) *Život tela. Politička filozofija Džudit Batler*. Novi Sad, Akademska knjiga.

Chapter 4

An unknown ancient Egyptian tool (for wig maintenance?)

Kira Zumkley

Abstract

This article focuses on a group of metal objects commonly known in Egyptological jargon as "hair-curlers". Found in ancient Egypt and Sudan and dating from the Middle Kingdom (c. 2100–1700 BCE) to the New Kingdom (c. 1500–1000 BCE), these objects were deposited with the deceased along with other funerary equipment. No thorough analysis of these has so far taken place, therefore the primary aim of this article is to investigate whether they are indeed hair-curlers or if they were used in a different context. Appearance, handling, material, archaeological context and chronology are discussed to narrow down possible usage scenarios. In a second step, usage scenarios are evaluated taking into account both of the above, as well as known ancient Egyptian corporal aesthetics and bodily care. Results indicate a strong likelihood of these objects being used as tools to make and maintain wigs. A catalogue of the specimen studied for this research can be found at the end of this article.

Key words: *Egypt, hair curler, toilet article, wig*

Introduction

Every now and then one can come across an ancient Egyptian object group that has yet to be analysed. Such was the case with a group of implements that can be found in most major ancient Egyptian museum collections. These delicate tools consist of two metal components attached together by a hinge. Their most characteristic attribute is a trough/pin feature at one end and a blade of various shapes and sizes or a figurative embellishment at the other (Fig. 4.1).

Fig. 4.1 Specimen 15 currently held in the Ashmolean Museum collection, Oxford (Ashmolean Museum, University of Oxford | Kira Zumkley)

The largest corpus of these is kept at the Petrie Museum in London where several are currently on display with labels identifying them as "hair curler". Although their trough/pin feature does resemble the curling section of modern hair curlers, their small size, as well as their being made of heat-conductive material without insulating handles suggests otherwise. Looking at the few comments published on these implements it becomes clear that their usage is far from ascertained. First labelled as hair curlers at the dawn of the 20th century, this assumption has since often been repeated without further inquiry. In the few cases where the specimens' usage was questioned (Kozloff 1992, 429), no in-depth analysis followed, leaving the question unanswered until today. Indeed, very little is known about this group of implements and there is great potential of gaining new and exciting insights into ancient Egyptian life by conducting a comprehensive analysis.

Research history

The implements discussed in this article have been known to Egyptologists for over a century. However, their unusual appearance puzzled excavators, and for a number of years they were described as strange "knives" (Petrie 1890, 34) or simply put in the category of "miscellaneous objects" (Petrie 1891, 19). It was in 1901 that the hitherto unidentified devices were labelled as objects "possibly for the toilet, as combined hair-curlers and trimmers" (Garstang 1901, 12). Although John Garstang seems to be in favour of his theory he also mentions other interpretations such as the implements being models of obstetric instruments (Garstang 1901, 12). However, he does not mention his source for this statement. After intensive but unsuccessful search in publications pre-dating 1901, one can assume that he must have heard this theory in a personal communication rather than having read it in a published script.

The idea of usage as hair-curlers was further supported by William Matthew Flinders Petrie (1917, 48) who states that "the two hinging points were for winding little curls of the wig". In 1911, fellow archaeologist David Randall-MacIver (1911, 144) came up with a new idea and published this in his work on Buhen, a Middle Kingdom military fort in Lower Nubia. Here he refers to specimens 18 and 56 as "surgical instruments" and in one case adds a question mark. The next scholar to offer a view on the objects is George A. Reisner who mentions them in his publication on Kerma, where he found three specimens and lists them in a chapter titled "scissor-shaped implements" (Reisner 1923b, 184). Neither mentioning Petrie's, Garstang's or

Randall-MacIver's idea in his reports nor in his subsequent publication, Reisner seems to have been unaware of other theories. Petrie's older publications are quoted numerous times by Reisner whereas *Tools and Weapons* (Petrie 1917) goes unmentioned throughout his five volumes as does Garstang's work on Arabah (1901) and Randall-MacIver's work on Buhen (1911). His omission of the idea of the implements being used as hair curlers or surgical instruments could therefore be put down to ignorance rather than an objection to the theory. Instead, he points out that there is no evidence of a spring and that apart from the curved cutting blade, the only other useful appliance is the trough/pin feature which could either be used as tweezers, or as a utensil to pierce through fabric. The latter is dismissed almost immediately by Reisner (1923b, 185) who argues that:

> the smallness and lightness of the implement is against its use for leather or cloth, and the occurrence with razors and other toilet articles is practically conclusive proof that it also was intended for some toilet purpose. [This toilet purpose might have been] cutting and lancing boils and ... removing deep-lying splinters or thorns.

For several decades the thus far voiced theories are repeated whenever such a specimen is published ("hair curler", Hayes 1935, 28; "shears" or "knives", Peet 1923, 28–30; "scissors", Schiaparelli 2007, 76). Slight variations are proposed by William C. Hayes (1959, 21–189) who wants to see them as a multi-purpose tool combining the function of tweezers and razors, and by Rita Freed (1982, 193) who interprets the specimen as eyelash or beard curlers. In general, it seems as though around the later part of the 20th century it was accepted by most scholars that the implements were most likely used as some kind of toilet article. For example, as "scissors", "mummification device" or a tool of "unknown function" (Doyen 1997, 119), as "hair curler" or "coiffeur device" (Schoske 1990, 95–97), or as "hair curler" or "hair removal device" (Stead 1986, 51). The exception being Arielle Kozloff who wants to see them as a mummification device, but she does, however, point out the existing hair curler theory and the fact that the precise usage is yet to be determined (Kozloff 1992, 428). The most recent discussion can be found in John H. Taylor's and Daniel Antoine's publication from 2014 on life in ancient Egypt in which Taylor indicates that the function remains unknown, but the objects were most likely used as either a cosmetic device or a multi-purpose tool. Specimen 81, featured in the accompanying exhibition "Ancient Lives" at the British Museum in London, is labelled "tool for delicate cutting and shaving" by Taylor and his fellow curator Daniel Antoine.

Description and handling

The implements consist of two components (Fig. 4.2) with their main attribute being a trough/pin feature that can be opened and shut thanks to a hinge joining the two parts together. The trough component is characterised by a cross-section in the shape

Fig. 4.2 Close-up images of specimen 80 showing the trough, pin, hinge and pipe (Trustees of the British Museum | Kira Zumkley)

of a semicircle which remains open at one end and is closed to a hollow pipe, either ending in a stump or a sharp pointy tip, at the other end. The second component featuring the pin is attached with a hinge at the point of transition from trough to pipe such that the pin and the trough fit together. Most specimens show a high degree of sophisticated manufacturing and execution resulting in a tight fit of trough and pin. However, in some cases the trough and pin do not end at precisely the same point.

The trough component remains unornamented and plain without exception. The pin component, however, merges into a broader section which either features an elaborate figurative ornament or an undecorated blade which can differ in size and shape (for a selection of different types see Figure 4.5). While at first glance this often-embellished blade section is what characterises the implements, it appears to have been the less important part, as it is diminished in some and even entirely suppressed in others. For example, specimen 44 in this study does not feature a blade but does display the pin-trough feature. In contrast, the attribute that is invariably displayed by all specimens is the trough and pin. Thus, henceforth it will be referred to as the front end whenever such a distinction is necessary. The primary purpose of the front end seems to be the open and shut function which is triggered by moving the rear end accordingly. As the two parts are attached alongside one another and do not intersect as is the case with modern scissors, the movement is such that by pressing the rear end together the trough and pin open and by pulling the pipe and the blade components apart the front-end closes. This observation has prompted some Egyptologists to assume that it was used to pry things open rather than to catch something between trough and pin as others have suggested (Kozloff 1992, 428). Due to the construction of the two parts side by side rather than with an intersection, two things had to be considered when manufacturing the items in order for them to open and shut comfortably. Firstly, the closing of the trough to a pipe should not occur too close to the hinge as this prevents the implement from opening properly when the pipe is being pushed onto the back of the blade. Secondly, the further bent the pin is at the transition from pin to blade or figurative element, the wider the overall opening of trough and pin becomes (Fig. 4.3). A good example of this is specimen 45 which can be opened to 1.4 cm. Some specimens on the other hand only open as wide as 0.4 cm (Specimen 48) or even 0.2 cm (Specimen 38). This is mainly because either the blade section is not bent enough, as with specimen 38, or the rear end of the blade section is shaped like an umbel which gets in the way of the pipe and thus limits this from being pushed down further.

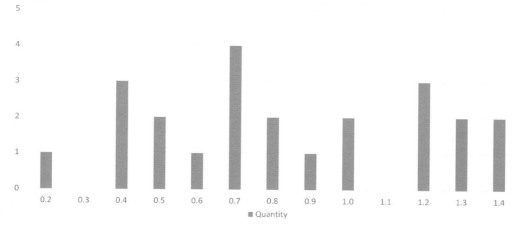

Fig. 4.3 Maximum opening of the trough/pin feature in centimetres. Only measurements of specimens from the British Museum, Ashmolean Museum, Fitzwilliam Museum and Petrie Museum are included in this figure as the author was not able to examine any of the other specimens listed in the catalogue herself. Furthermore, only specimens which are fully functional are included

The ancient Egyptians were clearly able to construct the implements in such a fashion that the trough and pin opens without restrictions. The fairly large number of specimens where this is not the case therefore begs the question whether a wide opening was necessary to fulfil the intended usage. Being able to open the front end more than a few millimetres is an advantage if not a prerequisite when an object is used to pry things open. Equally, a rather tight opening would prevent the specimens from being used to grasp anything thicker than the maximum aperture, which limits their usage considerably.

Another feature to consider is the actual shape of the implements' front end. If the specimens had been used to work with inflexible material, simple tongs or pincers would have sufficed to obtain the same result. Instead, a comparatively complicated tool was manufactured featuring a trough and pin. This has led to the idea that the front end was used to catch something flexible like hair, thread or cloth. This could then, if indeed needed, either be bent, wound around the pin or wound around both the pin and trough once they were shut. When viewing the implements in a photograph it is easy to misjudge their size and robustness and therefore their possible usage. Once examined in person, their thin blades, their intricately embellished rear ends, and the delicate hinge securing the two components offer a different picture. The average height of the specimens is around 2 cm as measured when the two movable parts are running parallel to each other. In addition, both are rarely thicker than 1 cm. In most cases, the thickest part is around the hinge pin except for figurative specimens such as specimen 46 or 66 where the embellished elements are thicker than the hinge. Specimen 55 is by far the thickest specimen, which could be because it might be a modern composite. The difference in the length of specimens is much more distinct as they can be as short as 5 cm or as long as 15 cm. The overall dimensions of the implements make them relatively difficult to handle, especially as most of these are equipped with a sharp blade. After examining them personally and with the understanding that the trough/pin section should be considered the front end, one can begin to develop ideas of how the devices could have been operated.

If taken into one hand like one would hold a pen, the open and shut function can be triggered by moving either the thumb back and forth over the hinge area, if the trough/blade component is at the bottom, or the index finger, if the specimen was flipped vertically so that the trough is on top. Thus, the device opens when moving the finger towards the rear end of the trough/blade component and closes by moving the finger towards the front. The idea of handling the implements in this way is further supported by many of them displaying a small bulge on the pin component directly behind the hinge section which helps to get a good grip and to prevent thumb or index finger slipping when opening and closing the device (for examples, see among others specimen 16, 75 or 81). A similar feature can be witnessed on specimens with a larger blade such as specimen 70 or 82 where the transition from pin to blade roughly follows a 45° angle thus allowing the thumb or index finger to be equally supported.

Held in the described way the rear end rests comfortably on the skin between thumb and index finger thus allowing a safe operation of the device without harming oneself. This is only the case, however, when the implement is of a certain length. Otherwise, the blade can slip and end up cutting the inner heel of the hand. When handling the specimens, I found that the minimum length that still felt comfortable was 7 cm. The author of this article is 1.74 m tall with a hand size of 17.5 cm. A survey of body size and physical constitution of ancient Egyptians has been performed by Masali (1972) and it shows a gracilised body build both in males and females and an average height of 1.66 m. Considering that most ancient Egyptians were smaller in build, it should be safe to assume that any implements shorter than 6 cm would have been rather difficult to handle. This assumption is supported by an analysis of the length of the implements which shows that most of them had a length between 7 and 10 cm with an average of 9.1 cm (Fig. 4.4). Specimen 39 has not been considered for this calculation as it is a special type of combination of a scraping razor and a trough/pin feature and therefore exceeds the normal length considerably.

Whereas the handling of the trough/pin feature is not obvious at first glance the interpretation of the use of the blade is much easier. One can simply grasp the blade section with the trough and pin either resting on the skin between thumb and index finger or under the heel of the hand as the tip of the trough and pin is too dull to do any harm. The blade can then be used in such a fashion that the sharp end is applied to whatever needs to be cut.

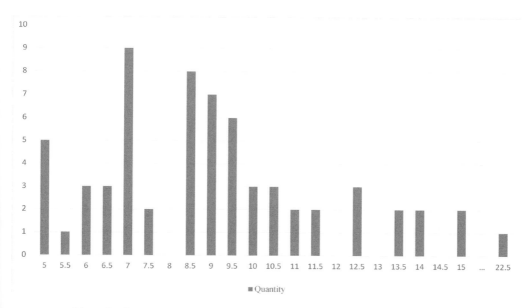

Fig. 4.4 Total length of specimens in centimetres. Only measurements of specimens from the British Museum, Ashmolean Museum, Fitzwilliam Museum and Petrie Museum are included in this figure as the author was not able to examine any of the other specimens listed in the catalogue herself

Identification of types

Having established the trough and pin feature as the singularity that distinguishes these specimens from other tools, it is necessary to look at discrepancies within the group itself. All exhibit the trough and pin in a similar style, so it is the rear section with its blade or figurative embellishment that allows for making further distinctions (Figs 4.5–4.7).

The first rear section and its blade that shall be discussed displays a large cut surface parallel to the trough/pipe. It features a curved arc in all cases and most of the specimens with such a blade show a straight spine. As this is the most common appearance amongst the devices with a total number of 13, the implements with such a feature will be henceforth referred to as Type A-I. Specimen 62 does have a slight dent in comparison to the other implements. Although not examined in person, from the available photograph that could be put down to traces of wear rather than an intentional feature. The object is therefore allocated to Type A-I. Very similar to this, and therefore designated Type A-II, are specimens with blades that have the same curved arc but in contrast to Type A-I these feature a slightly inward curved spine. Lastly a third subtype A-III can be identified which again features the same curved arc but with a spine transforming into an up-swept tip at the rear end.

Another group featuring blades with a cut surface parallel to the trough/pipe is assigned to Type B. The main characteristic of these is a small blade with horizontal

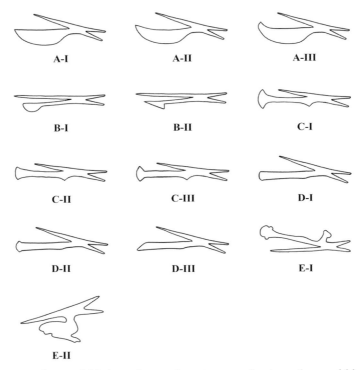

Fig. 4.5 A-I: *horizontal curved blade with straight spine.* A-II: *horizontal curved blade with inward curved spine.* A-III: *horizontal curved blade with upswept tip.* B-I: *semicircle blade.* B-II: *triangle blade.* C-I: *vertical umbel-shaped blade with distinct transition.* C-II: *vertical umbel-shaped blade with smooth transition.* C-III: *vertical-umbel shaped blade with angular transition.* D-I: *vertical blade, no distinct transition from bar to cut surface.* D-II: *vertical miniature umbel-shaped blade, no distinct transition from bar to cut surface.* D-III: *vertical rectangular blade, no distinct transition from bar to cut surface.* E-I: *figurative embellishment with vertical blade.* E-II: *figurative embellishment without blade*

cut surface either in the form of a semicircle (Type B-I) or a triangle (Type B-II) at the rear end of a thin flat bar.

In contrast to Type A and B all other specimens, except for the figurative implements without a blade, possess blades with a vertically oriented cut surface. The most common amongst the remaining unembellished specimens, and from now on referred to as Type C-I, is a blade with a cut surface in the shape of a semicircle with a very distinct and abrupt yet smooth transition into a thinner bar which then widens again on the side opposite the trough/pipe into the small bulge. Similar to this but without such a distinctive difference in width and with a much smoother transition from blade to bar are specimens allocated to Type C-II. In a final step specimen 53 must be considered as it fits neither Type C-I nor Type C-II since the transition from blade to bar is abrupt yet very angular in comparison to Type C-I.

Even though no other implement displays such a feature for future reference specimens exhibiting this attribute are categorised as Type C-III.

The last group of devices which does not belong to the figurative type is Type D. It features an elongated rectangular rear end that retains roughly the same width throughout and either shows no distinct transition from the bar to the cut surface (Type D-I) or exhibits a very small bulge at the end comparable to a miniature version of the umbel shaped blade of Type C-I (Type D-II). Just like with Type C, one specimen does not fit in either category and is thus ascribed to Type D-III. The object from Abydos features a long elongated rear end retaining the same width just as Type D-I and D-II but does display a small bulge and does not feature a vertical cut surface, but has a rectangular rear end cut at a 45° angle.

The last group that can be identified amongst the specimens are those with

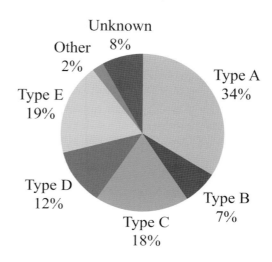

Fig. 4.6 Percentage of specimens per type

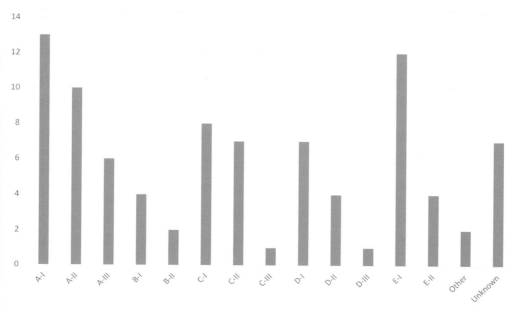

Fig. 4.7 Number of specimens within their allocated sub-types

figurative embellishments which henceforth will be referred to as Type E. Here again a further division is necessary into those with a blade (Type E-I) and those without a blade (Type E-II).

Material

Unfortunately, material analysis of the specimens was not possible and therefore the only available data is that which is provided by the museums, their online databases, publications and personal observation. The one exception being some specimens from the Ashmolean Museum in Oxford (Specimens 15, 20, 23, 25, 26 and 60) which according to their metadata sheet have been analysed by a museum conservator. An in-depth description of this analysis however is not available, and the only information given is that the former characterisation as "Copper Alloy" is crossed out in favour of a labelling as "Bronze". This does not come as a surprise, as bronze is by far the most frequently ascribed material within the group of specimens.

Forty-five of the 86 implements were made of bronze according to their museum catalogue entries which could, to a critical mind, be put down to the fact that most of them were dated to the New Kingdom during which bronze was the most commonly used material for tools, having largely superseded but not replaced copper (Auenmüller 2014, 33). As most of the specimen were given to the museums by private collectors, their date to the New Kingdom is not based on any scientific evidence. Therefore, being labelled as "Bronze" is equally questionable

The second most commonly assigned material in the group of implements is copper alloy or sometimes "copper alloy, bronze(?)" which can lead to confusion as technically bronze is a copper alloy. This can be put down to the fact that in old museum documents bronze and brass were at times used interchangeably and copper alloy, as the broad term for both, ensures that all objects made from bronze or brass can be found in the online database by searching for "copper alloy". It should therefore not be assumed that the term copper alloy automatically refers to bronze objects, as there were several copper alloys in use throughout ancient Egyptian times. It would be interesting to see the results of a material analysis of the specimens. If the results were positive for tin bronze rather than leaded bronze, it could narrow down their possible manufacturing date to any timeframe between the Middle Kingdom and the Late Period. Copper was the most commonly used main material for everyday objects – especially before the New Kingdom – with the earliest almost pure copper tools dating to the Badari Culture (4400–4000 BCE). Since copper is a rather soft substance with a hardness of 2.5 to 3 on the Mohs scale, it was desirable to mix it with other materials to improve its durability. Arsenic was the substance of choice which was smelted with copper to produce a copper arsenide with a hardness of 3 to 4 (Bladh 1990). The amount of available arsenic copper steadily decreased so that from the first half of the 3rd millennium onwards mixtures of copper with 5–10% tin – better known as tin bronze – came into use (Auenmüller 2014). Yet, copper tools remained widely used and it isn't until the 18th Dynasty that a substantial increase in tin bronze artefacts can be observed (Wilde 2003, 99). The new technology improved manufacturing processes and castability, but above all it became possible to produce a more durable material by increasing the allotment of tin (Fitzenreiter 2014, 24). From the middle of the 2nd millennium onwards artefacts of arsenic copper vanish completely, and tin bronze becomes the material of choice (Wilde 2003, 99). This changes again during the Late Period (*c.* 722–305 BCE) when leaded bronze was introduced with a mixture of 15–30% lead, only 5% tin and 65–80% copper resulting in improved plasticity (Auenmüller 2014, 33). Likewise, if the results were to show arsenical copper for those labelled as "Copper" or "Copper Alloy" it would suggest a strong possibility for an object having been produced before the New Kingdom. The latter supports Petrie's statement regarding specimens 1 and 2. Both are said to be made of copper (which should most likely be understood as arsenic copper or copper alloy) and are dated to the 12th Dynasty (Specimen 2) and the 6th–10th Dynasty (Specimen 1) by Petrie (1917, 49).

The third material used to manufacture these devices is gold. It is far less common than bronze and copper with only one specimen being made entirely of gold (Specimen 31) and another two having small inlays of said material (Specimen 55). Egypt was known for its vast abundance of gold, but this material mainly remained in the hands of royalty and the highest elites. The origin of specimen 31 is unknown, but it therefore most likely belonged to a high ranking official or a member of the royal family.

A thorough material analysis of all objects was not possible. The account given above should therefore be treated with caution as in almost all cases one has to assume that the information given in museum catalogues and publications is based on observation by eye and by drawing analogies in regard to their dating to the New Kingdom. In general, it can be summarised that the three main materials used when manufacturing these implements were (arsenical) copper, (tin) bronze and gold.

Provenance and archaeological context

Amongst the 86 specimens examined for this article 22 derive from a documented archaeological context. Specimen 5 from Mirgissa is not counted amongst these as its documentation is ambiguous. It is listed by B. Gratien and F. Le Saout (1994, 143) as having been found in Mirgissa, Cemetery MX, Tomb 83, but is not mentioned by J. Vercoutter (1975) along with the listed funerary equipment finds and it is therefore not possible to verify its precise archaeological context. However, Gratien's work is the more recent and is therefore more likely to be accurate. All other implements are unprovenanced, having been acquired by museums without any further information about the circumstances of their discovery.

Table 4.1 summarises information collated from various publications covering the specimens' archaeological context, associated finds that further help date the specimen and any other publication covering the excavation site or the life of the buried individual.

Kira Zumkley

Table 4.1 Overview of specimens with archaeological context

Cat. No.	Museum or Excavation No.	Type	Date	Provenance	Context	Gender of owner
3	MK38	B-I	Middle Kingdom	Kerma, Eastern Cemetery, Sector 24, Tomb 222 (Bonnet 2014)	In bag next to razor (Welsby and Anderson 2004, 86)	Unknown
4	MK660	Unknown	Middle Kingdom (Information provided by Charles Bonnet and Nora Ferrero)	Kerma, Sector 59, Secondary Settlement, EXVIII, salle de réunion (Bonnet and Valbelle 2014)	Foundation deposit	None
8	Unknown	B-I	Dynasty 12, post-Sesostris II (Dynasty 13 or 18) (Petrie 1898)	Rubbish heap, Kahun (Petrie 1898)	Rubbish heap	Unknown
9	SNM 31199	A-II	Early Second Intermediate Period 8 (Bonnet 2000)	Eastern Cemetery, Chapel C7, Kerma	Foundation deposit	Female (Bonnet 2000)
10	KXVI C:10	Unknown	Second Intermediate Period (Privati 1999, 49)	Tumulus XVI, Section C, Eastern Cemetery, Kerma (Reisner 1923a, 369)	With body H	Unknown
11	S111-6	AIII	Second Intermediate Period, Early Dynasty 18	Tomb S111, Cemetery S, Aniba (Onderka 2014, 87)	Unknown	Unknown
12	16.11.06.332	Unknown	Second Intermediate Period, Dynasty 18	Grave 198E, Esna	Unknown	Unknown
13	K440 viii	A-III	Late Second Intermediate Period, Early Dynasty 18 (Bonnet 2014a, 83 and Gratien 1978)	Tumulus KIV, Grave K440, Eastern Cemetery, Kerma (Reisner 1923a, 230)	Unknown	Unknown

Date

The dating of the specimens has thus far been obscure as there is little information on their archaeological context. Therefore, it seems that scholars often followed the dating given by early archaeologists such as Petrie and Garstang, with a preference for assigning the specimens to the 18th Dynasty or New Kingdom. This preference is most likely owed to the fact that most specimens with secured archaeological context date to the 18th Dynasty and it is the period most often referred to in essays and research papers. However, several specimens pre-date the New Kingdom, with three, possibly four of the analysed implements stemming from the Middle Kingdom (Specimen 3 and 4 and the unnumbered specimens from Kahun), and two from the Second Intermediate Period (Specimen 9 and 10). Another three come from contexts which either date to the Second Intermediate Period or the very early 18th Dynasty (Specimens 10, 11 and 12). It is thus clear that even though 16 out of the 22 specimens date to the 18th Dynasty, the invention of these implements goes back as far as the Middle Kingdom, if not earlier (Fig. 4.8).

An indication for an even earlier usage is given by Petrie in his publication on tools and weapons (Petrie 1917). It is here that he lists many specimens under the heading "Hair curler and razor", with one of these being dated to the 6th–10th Dynasty

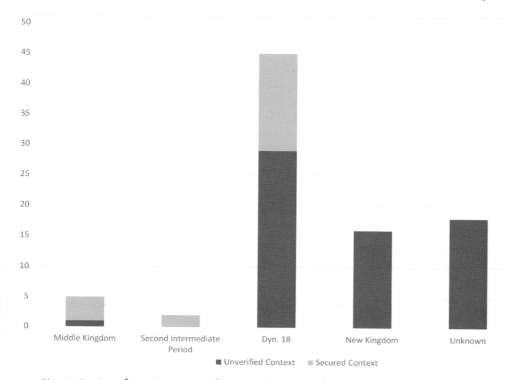

Fig. 4.8 Dating of specimens according to archaeological context and museum databases

(Petrie 1917, 49). According to Petrie, Specimen 1 was found in grave 395 in Mahasna, a site primarily known for its prehistoric settlement though its cemetery was in use until the 11th Dynasty (Beinlich 1980, 1164). Petrie never worked in Mahasna himself, but he was closely acquainted with Garstang who excavated the site from November 1900 onwards (Drower 1995, 261). Looking at Garstang's publication on Mahasna (Garstang 1903), Specimen 1 is neither mentioned in the text, nor is it pictured on any of the plates. Likewise, a grave with the number 395 does not appear anywhere. It is likely that Petrie acquired his information in an informal way from Garstang but seeing that there is no verifiable evidence for this specimen pre-dating the Middle Kingdom, it cannot be used to push back the implements' time of use any further.

Another specimen listed by Petrie in *Tools and Weapons* (1917) is Specimen 71, dated to the 22nd Dynasty and found in the Ramesseum. Petrie worked in this area during his campaign in 1895–1896 as did Quibell (Drower 1995, 218), but there is no mention of Specimen 71 anywhere within Quibell's publication and it is therefore not possible to verify the implements' time of use. The youngest precisely datable specimens thus remain the two objects from Amarna (Specimens 25 and 26) dating to either the reign of Akhenaten or Tutankhamun (late 18th Dynasty) and the oldest are Specimen 2 from Kahun (12th Dynasty) and Specimens 3 and 4 from Kerma (Middle Kingdom).

Usage scenarios

The archaeological context clearly shows that these implements were used as devices for bodily care. Therefore, Garstang's theory of them being models of obstetric instruments, Reisner's idea of them being used for cutting and sewing cloth and Kozloff's theory of the objects being used as mummification devices can be dismissed.

Further refinement of the specimens' potential usage could be made by looking at the gender of the associated burial. In five out of the seven cases where the gender is known, either due to an examination of the bones or inscriptions, the specimens have been found with male burials (Specimens 16, 17, 18, 22 and 24). Moreover, in the case of Kha and Amenemhet (Specimens 24 and 17) female relatives were buried in the same tomb but none of these were given their own implement with their personal funerary equipment. The two exceptions are Specimens 9 and 19. Specimen 9 however was not found amongst the personal items of the deceased female, but in the foundation deposit of the tumulus' chapel. Specimen 19 was found in the early 20th century when examination of bones and determination of gender was not as advanced. Nevertheless, the two specimens should not be ignored and five specimens out of 86 is a small subset. It is thus not feasible to only focus on usages associated with male hygiene habits and therefore the following three theories remain.

Firstly, the implements could have been used as knives, razors or trimmers with the front end mimicking the function of traditional tweezers. Secondly the implements could have been used as curling devices for either hair, eyelashes or beard hair. Lastly the idea of the specimens being used as scissors ought to be considered. In addition, after having studied the specimens found in the Petrie Museum, British Museum,

Ashmolean Museum and Fitzwilliam Museum myself, one more idea came to mind. Based on both modern and ancient Egyptian wig making techniques, the implements could have been used as a tool for making and maintaining wigs.

Tweezer-razor multi-purpose tool

The one feature easily identified and shared by most specimens is the blade. In the context of this being used to perform a daily hygiene act, it was most likely used for "delicate cutting and shaving" (Taylor and Antoine 2014, 131). Razors were used for the removal of facial, head and body hair throughout Egyptian history and the abundance of different knife types speaks volumes about the importance of this ritual and the utilisation of knives for shaving purposes can be traced back to the Old Kingdom (Odler 2016, 31–33).

However, as mentioned, not all specimens feature a blade whereas all have the trough/pin feature in common. A comparison with tweezers comes to mind. Ancient Egyptian tweezers were made of a long strip of metal which is bent in the middle to form an elongated U-shape. The two ends are usually flattened or bent to a 90° angle to get the best grip possible. Examples of Ancient Egyptian tweezers include 26.7.837c, Metropolitan Museum of Arts, New York; 07.447.1, Brooklyn Museum, New York; EA38151, British Museum, London. However, the trough/pin does not resemble any of the tweezer types currently known from ancient Egypt and while it can be used to pinch, the specimens' manufacturing method is often not precise enough to grip something that is only 1 or 2 mm long. This is due to the trough and pin not ending at precisely the same point in some specimens which would be necessary when attempting to grip something very short. Otherwise, the longer end, usually the trough, prohibits short splinters or hair from being grasped between trough and pin. Other than this restriction the tight fit of trough and pin allows the front end to pluck hair or splinters just as efficiently as tweezers do.

Hair curler

It was the specimens' physical appearance and their trough/pin feature which prompted the labelling of (scalp) hair curlers, as their close resemblance to modern hair curlers is undeniable. Petrie (1917, 49) argued that the implements' delicate nature reflects their usage for curling "the little curls of the wig". Looking at ancient Egyptian wigs, specifically wig EA2560 currently held at the British Museum and dating to the 18th Dynasty, one can identify small curls formed out of 18 cm of naturally curly human hair (Stevens Cox 1977, 67). This length corresponds with the average length of the front section of the implements which is 2.9 cm when shut (from front end to hinge). A test carried out by the author has shown that a strand of hair similar in thickness and length to the one used for EA2560 can just about be curled around the trough/pin of the specimens when shut. To set the curls, Petrie (1917, 49) suggested opening the trough/pin and stretching the hair, a movement which could explain their characteristic of opening when pressing the rear ends together. The resulting curls, however, would be uneven as the hair at the tip of the pin would be stretched much farther than the hair nearer to the hinge. This unevenness cannot be observed with the curls of EA2560.

In contrast, Kozloff (1992, 428) suggested that the curls were set by winding the hair around the pin and then pressing it into the trough much like one would do with modern hair curlers. However, there are two aspects which militate against this. Firstly, the average length of the pin when open from front end to intersection of trough and pin is only 1.9 cm, and secondly the trough/pin of the well-preserved specimens fit together snugly without allowing room for more than the thinnest strand of hair.

Lastly, one must consider that to curl hair with the specimens they would need to be heated (Durbin 1984, 29). Unlike the "29 ladles, of silver, handles of boxwood and ebony, with which one curls the hair" (Moran 1992, 31) mentioned in one of the Amarna Letters, all specimens lack handles and do not show any signs of handles being attached at any point in time. In addition, their delicate nature renders the idea of them being heated and then used to curl hair whilst having the rear end wrapped in protective fabric highly unlikely. The only other option available to the ancient Egyptians for setting curls without heat was curling the hair around a device whilst still wet and waiting for it to dry. For this they would have needed many round items, like burned clay bars or the shut trough/pin feature at the same time. This does not conform with the fact that only one specimen per burial was found.

Beard curler

Due to the specimens' intricate size, it has been suggested that they were used for curling beard hair rather than scalp hair. Most Egyptians shaved their head and body hair to discourage lice and other vermin (Fletcher 1994, 31). There is, however, evidence of beards being worn. For example, the statue of Rahotep dating to the Old Kingdom shows him sporting a neatly trimmed moustache and Middle Kingdom tomb imagery from the Qubbet el Hawa pictures the owner with a short chin beard (Edel 2008, 2058). The same can be said for depictions from the New Kingdom where short chin beards appear (Hoedel-Hoenes 2000, fig. 164).

Looking at the depictions of beards in ancient Egyptian art most of these appear to be either long and braided or very short. To make use of a beard curling device one would expect longer and/or fuller beards such as the ones known from ancient Near Eastern wall decorations. Furthermore, in the instance of Specimens 19 and 9 the device was not found with a male, but a female burial. Lastly, as with scalp hair the wet hair either would have needed to be curled around a round item and left to dry, or the device used to curl the hair would need to be heated to set the curls properly. It can therefore be concluded that the implements were not used to curl either scalp or beard hair.

Eyelash curler

Rita Freed (1982, 193) was the first to propose the idea that the specimens could have been used as eyelash curlers. This would indeed resolve two of the main objections voiced above. The first is the problem of the trough/pin fitting very snugly which prevents the feature from closing with a thicker strand of hair wound around it. Considering that eyelashes are very thin and seldom layered to any great extent, they certainly could fit between trough and pin when closed. The second problem is that of heat being needed to curl head or beard hair. Even though heat does help eyelashes to curl, it is not a prerequisite.

Further examination of the implements draws attention to another promising factor. As mentioned before, the average length of the pin when open is 1.9 cm which is not beneficial when trying to curl hair. However, looking at the size of a human eye and its eyelashes, this length is more reasonable and the orientation of the implements fits the eyelash theory equally well. The dimensions of the eye are reasonably constant, varying among individuals by only a millimetre or two; the vertical diameter is about 24 mm and is usually less than the transverse diameter (Encyclopaedia Britannica XXVII, 1997, 108). The specimens need to be held in such a way that the opening of the trough faces upwards, and the pin is pressed downwards. Only in this way is an upward curl of the eyelashes achieved. If the specimens were orientated the other way up, the eyelashes would be curled downwards. As mentioned, there is no restriction to the triggering of the trough/pin feature in either orientation. Yet, looking at the Type E specimens the figurative elements are fashioned in such a way that a usage with an upwards facing trough opening seems preferable (the only exception is specimen 44).

The physical character of the specimens therefore supports Freed's eyelash theory. However, looking at scenes of daily hygiene acts or the application of make-up, none feature a device such as the implements discussed in this article. In general, few depictions of facial treatments are known from ancient Egypt. If so, they show the application of make-up to the lips (Schoske 1990, fig. 21), the face (Schoske 1990, fig. 20) or the eye (Lembke and Schmitz 2006, fig. 39), with the latter depicting a black kohl make-up stick and not the implements. No figurative evidence of the specimens being used as eyelash curlers is known. A promising inscription can however be found on ostracon O. Wien Aeg. 1 which joins with O. IFAO 628 and dates to the 25th year of Ramesses III (Zonhoven 1979). The inscription gives an account of the remains of a ruined tomb amongst which several toilet articles are listed. One basket contains:

> One knife. One pin. One bowl. One libation vase. One razor case. One rotating razor. One scraping razor ... [and another basket contains] One alabaster k(3)b-vessel. One comb. One eye tweezer. One [alabaster] nmst-vessel. One h'r. Two pieces of scenting material (Zonhoven 1979, 91).

It is the word "eye tweezer" that immediately draws attention and needs to be examined further. Zonhoven (1979, 97) transliterates it as *T#y-/rt*, whereas Meeks (1982, 79.3455) suggests *T#jt-/rt* and Černy interprets the two reed leaves as a *tj*-pestle and transliterates it as *t#t/-/rt* (unpublished notebooks of Černy, courtesy of the Griffith Institute, Oxford).

The first element of the word strongly resembles that of the word *T#j* which is often followed by a tweezer determinative. One example can be found on the walls of the temple of Thutmose III in Abydos (Petrie 1903). The largely destroyed inscription lists offerings which include tweezers. The tweezer determinative – mimicking the form of the simple tweezers – identifies the word. The missing signs are assigned by looking at a very similar inscription from Kawa (Macadam 1949, pl.12). It can be found on a granite plate in the temple of Osiris which most likely list the temple's inventory. Here the duckling is followed by the eagle hieroglyph (G1), the t-bread (X1), and a tweezers determinative. In the case of O. Wien Aeg. 1 and O. IFAO 628 *T#j* is however not followed by this determinative. Instead, the hieroglyph N34, metal ingot, is used, which signals that the described object is made of bronze or copper alloy thus fitting perfectly with most of our specimens. Furthermore, the determinative is that of a knife or a blade and not tweezers which fits very well with the specimens' rear section. All of this combined presents compelling evidence of identifying the object mentioned on the ostracon as one of the specimens.

If the trough/pin feature was indeed used as an eyelash curling device, then the usage of the razor might have equally been restricted to the area around the eyes. One possibility could be that the blade was used to shave or trim eyebrows. "Baldness of the eyebrows" is described in an ancient Egyptian magic spell (Erman 1901, 20), however here it is not used in a context that would suggest that this state was worth achieving. Another reference to the treatment of eyebrows can be found in Herodotus' history (Book II, 66). Here he writes that "in whatever house a cat has died by a natural death, all those who dwell in this house shave their eyebrows". This again implies that ancient Egyptians did not shave their eyebrows and therefore, if the specimens were used as eyelash curlers, the blade was not used to shave eyebrows, but perhaps only to trim them.

Scissors

The idea of identifying the implements as scissors seems to provide a good solution for their ability to open and shut using the trough/pin feature. However, if examined more closely it becomes apparent that this is not the function performed by the implements. In order to cut fabric, papyri or thread normal scissors use two sharp blades which closely move past each other thus cutting whatever is caught between into two halves. If something were to be placed between the trough and pin and those were then subsequently shut, whatever was placed between would be pushed and bent into the trough by the pin without any cutting taking place due to the edges of the trough and the pin being blunt. Therefore, the only process applied is that of bending or possibly curling whatever is placed between the trough and pin.

Tool for making and maintaining wigs

The ancient Egyptian costume included elaborate wigs primarily worn by members of the royal household, as well as officials and members of the upper classes (Müller 2007, 1334). The oldest wigs are known from the Early Dynastic Period onwards and continued to be in use throughout pharaonic times (Müller 1982, 989). Research into wigs concentrates on their materials and whether they were made of human or animal hair or vegetable fibres. Most of the wigs were made of human hair and some were padded with vegetable fibre – such as date palm fibre (Lucas 1930, 190). According to Lucas, there is no evidence of horsehair or wool having been employed for this purpose (Lucas 1962, 30), whereas Müller states that some did contain animal hair (Müller 1982, 989). However, there have been two thorough analyses regarding their construction. The first one was conducted by James Stevens Cox in 1977 (Stevens Cox 1977). He was invited by the British Museum to examine EA2560, a wig dating to 1400 BCE and stemming from a tomb in Thebes. It features two main parts with the top one being formed of many curls of about 18 cm length and the lower consisting of plaited strands of 30 to 38 cm length. Stevens Cox also examined the substructure which consists of a fine net of human hair forming rhomboidal apertures. It is to this foundation that the strands of hair are attached to form the wig – a procedure for which one of the specimens could have been used in a similar fashion as modern wig beaders are used (https://www.youtube.com/watch?v=2MAe0gKrU5c&t=390s, accessed 27.09.2018; beader technique is shown from 6:50 mins to 8:10 mins). The construction of wigs out of a fine mesh as a basis to which either individual strands of hair are attached, or the hair is threaded on a cord which is then attached to the mesh is identical to that of modern wigs. The average thickness of human hair is 0.1 mm. Thus, a strand of 400 hairs has a diameter of about 2.3 mm. In a first step the strand of hair, usually containing about 400 individual hairs, is looped around the mesh of the substructure. This could be done by seizing the strand in between the trough and pin, thus holding them firmly in place. Then this strand is guided through one of the apertures and back. For this the front end of the specimens is much better suited than comparatively thick thumb and index fingers. As a next step the strand is pressed against the waxed hair stem which could be done by pressing them between the trough and pin (Fig. 4.9). To finish the attachment of the strand, a few hairs are separated, here either the front of the pin or the tip of the pipe could be used, and then wound tightly around the hair stem. When this is done, the hair is again pressed into the wax stem to seal it in place (Stevens Cox 1977, fig. 2). I was unable to examine EA2560 myself but during the examination of two detached

Fig. 4.9 Close-up of strand of hair from EA2560 and specimen 83 (Trustees of the British Museum | Kira Zumkley)

strands of hair from EA2560 a small dent could be observed in both cases of precisely the same size as the trough of the specimens (average width of trough opening is 0.18 cm).

In a final step any straying hairs are cut off, possibly with the blade section of the specimens, to achieve a clean look. Since the strands of hair are only attached by being sealed with a mixture of wax and resin, they easily could come loose through normal wearing of the wig. This would explain why the implements were needed on a regular basis as part of someone's toilet equipment.

The theory proposed above is based purely on the physical character of the implements. Looking at words like *bbwj.t* "wig" or *nbd.j* "wig maker", these do not feature a hieroglyph resembling our specimens, but rather feature either a strand of hair or a finger hieroglyph. The finger hieroglyph could undermine the theory of these implements being used as a tool for making and maintaining wigs as it corresponds perfectly with the few ancient Egyptian images showing hairdressers working on a wig. One of these is known from the tomb of Kawit, one of the wives of Nebhepetre Mentuhotep of the 11th Dynasty. The scene is found on her sarcophagus, Cairo JE 47397 (Lembke and Schmitz 2006, 91). Here the tomb owner is sitting on a chair whilst her hairdresser has secured some of the wig's locks in place with a bodkin and reworks the lock below with her fingers. A similar hairdressing scene is shown on wall fragments held by the Brooklyn Museum and the Metropolitan Museum of Arts and dating to the 11th Dynasty. This represents one hairdresser readying a separate strand of curled hair (Brooklyn 51.231) whilst another is reworking a curl (Brooklyn 54.49) on her mistress's wig (Riefstahl 1956, pl. X). Neither the first hairdresser, nor the second are pictured with a tool, but rather they work with their bare hands. The tomb of Nefermenu (TT 365), dated to the reign of Thutmose III, could yield figurative proof of the specimens being used as a wig tool. An inscription identifies Nefermenu as the "chief of the manufacturers of wigs of Amun in Karnak" (Kampp 1996, 591) and one could therefore hope that his grave might have been decorated with scenes of a wig workshop. However, the entrance to the tomb is currently blocked and the four existing images of the tomb's interior are currently unpublished (Porter and Moss 1960, 427).

Conclusion

The attribute that is unique to the specimens discussed in this paper is the trough/pin feature and its ability to grip and/or bend flexible material. Five specimens cited here derive from an undisturbed context giving great insight into their field of use, as without exception they were found together with other toilet articles, such as razors, tweezers and whetstones. On the other hand, restriction to users from only a certain kind of social status or gender cannot be made. The implements have been found in both female and male burials and in simpler burials, as well as elaborate ones.

It is now clear that these specimens were mainly used during the Middle and New Kingdom and that they were distributed throughout Nubia and Egypt. The items were either made of copper alloy, particularly bronze, or gold and were redesigned several times during their usage period, with some of the specimens showing a willingness to experiment with their physical nature.

The combination of a blade for either trimming or shaving and the front end of the specimens for pinching is best explained by these either being tools for making and maintaining wigs, by being eyelash curlers with trimmers or a multi-functional tool with pinching and trimming function. Contrary to this, the theory of the specimens being used as scissors can be ruled out as their physical nature does not allow for such a function. Likewise, the likelihood of them being used as either hair or beard curlers can be ruled out due to the lack of handles and the delicate size of the trough/pin feature. The multi-purpose character of the specimens would have been best utilised if they were used as devices for making and maintaining wigs. Here all necessary steps in the manufacturing process of wigs coincide with the different features: the trough/pin feature, as well as the blade would have been of equal importance during the work process and a quick switch from one function to the other would have ensured a fast workflow. Yet, whenever hairdressers are pictured, they work with their bare hands and not with one of our specimens. The combination of a multi-functional tweezers/razor tool would have allowed for shaving delicate areas of the body or face, and removal of any remaining hair instantly by plucking it without having to reach for another tool. However, as discussed, the plucking/pinching functionality is limited in some specimens due to their careless construction, and while specimens like Specimen 39 from the British Museum or Specimen 74 from the Hans Schwarzkopf collection show the ancient Egyptians' willingness to experiment with their tools, the question remains why ancient Egyptians would manufacture such a complicated device if they had traditional tweezers and razors readily at hand.

The inscription on ostracon O. Wien Aeg. 1 and O. IFAO 628 presents potential evidence for the idea of these implements being eyelash curlers. Particularly as it is the only written or depicted proof of a tool that comes close to the tools discussed in this article. On the other hand, the combination of eyelash curler and razor does not work as well as is the case with the two other theories. As a combination of tweezers and razor the two features work together to achieve the best possible result for one intended purpose. The same is true if the implements were used as a tool for making and maintaining wigs. A combination of eyelash curler and trimmer however would see the front end being used on the eyelashes, whereas the blade would not have been used on these, but probably on other facial hair.

Thus, the eyelash curler idea, while tempting, makes less sense due to the curling feature and the blade function not complementing each other as well. Likewise, since the Egyptians had perfectly functional tweezers and an abundance of different razor devices inventing yet another tool and placing it into graves in addition to other razors and tweezers seems excessive. A wig tool on the other hand would complement the typical toilet equipment well and since wigs were of great importance to the Egyptians, there was certainly a need to repair them whilst they were in use. Similarly, following the ancient Egyptians belief of life after death, a tool for making and maintaining wigs would have been a most welcome funerary addition.

Table 4.2 Catalogue of finds (Entries 1–25)

Cat. No.	Museum or Excavation No.	Museum	Date	Provenance	Dimensions	Material	Type	Publications
1	UC40535	London, UK, Petrie Museum	Unknown, Dynasty 6–10 (?)	Mahasna	Length trough: 6.7 cm Length: 7.0 cm Length blade (from hinge): 4.9 cm Height blade (vertical cut surface?): 1.0 cm Length pin (from hinge): 2.1 cm Length pin (when opened at maximum): 1.6 cm Maximum opening: 0.9 cm Average thickness pin: 0.08 cm Width trough opening: 0.2 cm Height: 1.2 cm Thickness: 0.6 cm	Copper	Unknown	Petrie 1917, 49, pl. LXI (no.1).
2	UC7249	London, UK, Petrie Museum	Dynasty 12	Kahun	Length: 10.8 cm Length blade: 7.1 cm Height blade: 3.2 cm Length pin (from hinge): 3.7 cm Average thickness pin: 0.1 cm Height: 1.2 cm Thickness: 0.3 cm	Copper	B-II	Petrie 1917, 49, pl. LXI (no.2).
3	MK38	Kerma Albeled, Sudan, Kerma Museum	Middle Kingdom	Kerma, Eastern Cemetery, Sector 24, Tomb 222	Unknown	Bronze	B-I	Bonnet 2014, 90.
4	MK660	Kerma Albeled, Sudan, Kerma Museum	Middle Kingdom	Kerma, Sector 59, Secondary Settlement, EXVIII, salle de réunion	Unknown	Unknown	Unknown	

(Continued)

Table 4.2 (Continued)

Cat. No.	Museum or Excavation No.	Museum	Date	Provenance	Dimensions	Material	Type	Publications
5	L.481	Lille, France, L'Institut de Papyrologie et d'Égyptologie de Lille	Middle Kingdom (?)	Mirgissa, Cemetery MX, Tomb 83	Length: 11.0 cm	Unknown	D-I	Gratien and Le Saout 1994, 143.
6	AF.531	Paris, France, Louvre	Dynasty 12 or 18	Unknown	Length: 8.9 cm	Bronze	C-I	Vandier d'Abbadie 1972, 160.
7	AF.6733	Paris, France, Louvre	Dynasty 12 or 18	Unknown	Length: 9.4 cm	Bronze	C-I	Vandier d'Abbadie 1972, 160.
8	Unknown	Unknown	Dynasty 12, post-Sesostris II (Dynasty 13 or 18)	Kahun, settlement, rubbish heap	Unknown	Copper	B-I	Petrie 1891, pl. VIII (no. 4).
9	SNM 31199	Khartoum, Sudan, National Museum of Sudan	Early Second Intermediate Period	Kerma, Eastern Cemetery, Chapel C7, Foundation deposit	Length: 9.1 cm	Bronze	A-II	Bonnet 2000, 39.
10	KXVI C:10	Unknown	Second Intermediate Period	Kerma, Eastern Cemetery, Tumuli XVI, Section C, with body H	Length: 6.2 cm	Bronze (?)	Unknown	Reisner 1923b, 185.

(Continued)

Table 4.2 Catalogue of finds (Entries 1–25) (Continued)

Cat. No.	Museum or Excavation No.	Museum	Date	Provenance	Dimensions	Material	Type	Publications
11	S111-6	Unknown	Second Intermediate Period, early Dynasty 18	Aniba, Cemetery S, Tomb S111	Length: 8.5 cm	Unknown	A-III	Steindorff 1937b, pl. 63.
12	16.11.06.332	Liverpool, UK, Liverpool Museum	Second Intermediate Period, Dynasty 18	Esna, Grave 198E	Unknown	Copper alloy, Bronze (?)	Unknown	Downes 1974, 102.
13	K440:viii	Unknown	Late Second Intermediate Period | Early New Kingdom	Kerma, Eastern Cemetery, Tumulus KIV, Grave K 440	Length: 8.6 cm	Bronze (?)	A-III	Reisner 1923b, 185, pl 49.
14	K317:8	Unknown	Early Dynasty 18, pre-Thutmose I	Kerma, Eastern Cemetery, Tumuli KIII, Grave K317	Length: 12.7 cm	Bronze (?)	A-II	Reisner 1923b, 185, pl 49.
15	1896–1908 E.2586	Oxford, UK, Ashmolean Museum	Early Dynasty 18	Abydos, Tomb E225	Length trough: 1,.9 cm Length: 12.3 cm Length blade (from hinge): 8.4 cm Height blade: 1.5 cm Length pin (from hinge): 3.9 cm Length pin (when opened at maximum): 2.9 cm Maximum opening: 0.8 cm Average thickness pin: 0.1 cm Width trough opening: 0.12 cm Height: 1.8 cm Thickness: 0.5 cm	Bronze	A-I	Garstang 1901, 12, 45 and pl. XVI.

(Continued)

Table 4.2 (Continued)

Cat. No.	Museum or Excavation No.	Museum	Date	Provenance	Dimensions	Material	Type	Publications
16	16.10/439	New York, USA, Metropolitan Museum of Arts	Thutmose I or II	Thebes, el-Asasif, Courtyard CC 41, Pit 3, Burial D 1, in bowl 16.10.439	Length: 9.0 cm	Copper alloy	D-II	Hayes 1959, 21, 64.
17	35.3.31	New York, USA, Metropolitan Museum of Arts	Thutmose II or III	Thebes, el-Asasif, Tomb of Neferkhawet (MMA 729),, east chamber, Burial of Amenemhat (V)	Length: 8.5 cm	Copper alloy, Bronze (?)	C-I	Hayes 1935.
18	185/260:1-3	Khartoum, Sudan, National Museum of Sudan | Uppsala, Sweden, Museum Gustavianum,	Dynasty 18, pre-Hatshepsut	Fadrus, Site 185	Length with lily ornament: 12.0 cm	Unknown	A-III	Säve-Söderbergh 1991b, 164.
19	E10303	Philadelphia, USA, Penn Museum	Dynasty 18, Hatshepsut to Thutmose III	Buhen, Cemetery H, Tomb 14	Length: 7.2 cm	Bronze	A-III	Randall-MacIver and Wolley 1911, pl. 64.

(Continued)

Table 4.2 Catalogue of finds (Entries 1–25) (Continued)

Cat. No.	Museum or Excavation No.	Museum	Date	Provenance	Dimensions	Material	Type	Publications
20	1896-1908 E.2602	Oxford, UK, Ashmolean Museum	Dynasty 18, Thutmose III (?)	Abydos, Tomb E268	Length trough: 9.5 cm Length: 9.8 cm Length blade (from hinge): 6.0 cm Height blade (vertical cut surface): 1.3 cm Length pin (from hinge): 3.8 cm Length pin (when opened at maximum): 2.5 cm Maximum opening: 0.7 cm Average thickness pin: 0.12 cm Width trough opening: 0.12 cm Height: 1.6 cm Thickness: 0.5 cm	Bronze	C-1	Garstang 1901, 12, 14, 45 and pl. XVI.
21	Unknown	Unknown	Dynasty 18, Post-Thutmose III	Abydos, North Cemetery, North of Mastaba 57, Pit grave D102	Unknown	Unknown	D-1	Randall-MacIver 1902, pl. XLVI.
22	Unknown	Unknown	Dynasty 18, Post-Thutmose III	Abydos, North Cemetery, North of Mastaba 57, Pit grave D113	Unknown	Unknown	D-III	Randall-MacIver 1902, pl. XLVII.

(Continued)

Table 4.2 (Continued)

Cat. No.	Museum or Excavation No.	Museum	Date	Provenance	Dimensions	Material	Type	Publications
23	1896-1908 E.2381	Oxford, UK, Ashmolean Museum	Dynasty 18 (Thutmose III to) Amenhotep II to III	Abydos, Tomb E143	Length trough: 10.3 cm Length: 11.3 cm Length blade (from hinge): 8,3 cm Height blade: 2.3 cm Length pin (from hinge): 3.0 cm Length pin (when opened at maximum): 2.4 cm Maximum opening: 1.2 cm Average thickness pin: 0.15 cm Width trough opening: 0.18 cm Height: 2.5 cm Thickness: 0.6 cm	Bronze	A-1	Garstang 1901, 12,13,14, pls XVI, XVIII.
24	S. 8376	Turin, Italy, Museum Egizio	Dynasty 18, Amenhotep II to III	Deir el-Medina, Tomb of Kha (TT8).	Height: 2.8 cm Length: 8.5 cm Width: 0.4 cm	Bronze	E-1	Schiaparelli 2007.
25	1921.1141	Oxford, UK, Ashmolean Museum	Dynasty 18, Akhenaten to Tutankhamun	Tell el-Amarna, Main City, South, House O 48.16	Length trough: 8.7 cm (heavily bend) Length: 8.7 cm (heavily bend) Length blade (from hinge): 4.9 cm Height blade: 1.1 cm Length pin (from hinge): 3.9 cm Average thickness pin: 0.15 cm Width trough opening: 0.18 cm Height: 2.5 cm Thickness: 0.5 cm	Bronze	Unknown	Peet and Woolley 1923, 28.

Table 4.3 Catalogue of finds (Entries 26–45)

Cat. No.	Museum or Excavation No.	Museum	Date	Provenance	Dimensions	Material	Type	Publications
26	1921.1143	Oxford, UK, Ashmolean Museum	Dynasty 18, Akhenaten to Tutankhamun	Tell el-Amarna, Main City, South, House O 49.24	Length: 6.3 cm Height blade (vertical cut surface): 1.2 cm Thickness: 0.2 cm	Bronze	C-I	Peet and Woolley 1923, 30 and pl. XIII.
27	UC40532	London, UK, Petrie Museum	Dynasty 18, Dynasty 12 (?)	Kahun (?)	Length trough: 6.0 cm Length: 4.6 cm Length blade (from hinge): 3.0 cm Height blade: 0.9 cm Length pin (from hinge): 1.6 cm Average thickness pin: 0.1 cm Width trough opening: 0.15 cm Height: 0.9 cm Thickness: 0.5 cm	Copper alloy	B-I	Petrie 1917, 49, pl. LXI (no.9). Petrie 1891, pl. VIII (no. 5) (?).
28	10.130.1308	New York, USA, Metropolitan Museum of Arts	Dynasty 18	Unknown	Unknown	Copper alloy, Bronze (?)	A-I	
29	12.182.7c	New York, USA, Metropolitan Museum of Arts	Dynasty 18	Thebes	Length: 13.3 cm	Copper alloy, Bronze (?)	D-I	

(Continued)

Table 4.3 (Continued)

Cat. No.	Museum or Excavation No.	Museum	Date	Provenance	Dimensions	Material	Type	Publications
30	1927.1295	Oxford, UK, Ashmolean Museum	Dynasty 18	Thebes	Length trough: 7.7 cm Length: 8.9 cm Length blade (from hinge): 5.7 cm Height blade: 1.4 cm Length pin (from hinge): 2.5 cm Average thickness pin: 0.1 cm Height: 2.2 cm Thickness: 0.4 cm	Copper alloy, Bronze (?)	A-II	
31	1977.169	New York, USA, Metropolitan Museum of Arts	Dynasty 18	Unknown	Length 8.6 cm	Gold	E-I	
32	37.654E	New York, USA, Brooklyn Museum	Dynasty 18	Unknown	Length: 5.9 cm Height: 2.2 cm	Bronze	E-I	
33	37.655E	New York, USA, Brooklyn Museum	Dynasty 18	Unknown	Length: 5.1 cm	Bronze	C-II	
34	5116	Hildesheim, Germany, Pelizaeus Museum	Dynasty 18	Unknown	Unknown	Bronze	E-I	
35	E.07348	Brussels, Belgium, Royal Museums of Art and History	Dynasty 18	Unknown	Length: 7.2 cm Height: 2.1 cm	Bronze	E-I	Doyen 1997.
36	E.07349	Brussels, Belgium, Royal Museums of Art and History	Dynasty 18	Unknown	Length: 7.1cm Height: 2.0 cm	Bronze	E-I	

(Continued)

Table 4.3 Catalogue of finds (Entries 26–45) (Continued)

Cat. No.	Museum or Excavation No.	Museum	Date	Provenance	Dimensions	Material	Type	Publications
37	E320	Unknown	Dynasty 18	Abydos, Tomb	Unknown	Bronze	E-I	Garstang 1901, pl. XVII.
38	EA17087	London, UK, British Museum	Dynasty 18	Unknown	Length trough: 9.3 cm Length: 11.7 cm Length blade (from hinge): 7.2 cm Height blade: 2.0 cm Length pin (from hinge): 4.5 cm Length pin (when opened at maximum): 1.7 cm Maximum opening: 0.2 cm Average thickness pin: 0.08 cm Width trough opening: 0.1 cm Height: 2.2 cm Thickness: 0.5 cm	Bronze	A-I	
39	EA67448	London, UK, British Museum	Dynasty 18	Unknown	Length trough: 13.7 cm Length: 22.4 cm Length blade (from hinge): 18.1 cm Height blade (vertical cut surface): 2.0 cm Length pin (from hinge): 4.3 cm Length pin (when opened at maximum): 2.9 cm Maximum opening: 0.7 cm Average thickness pin: 0.15 cm Width trough opening: 0.2 cm Height: 2.1 cm Thickness: 0.8 cm	Bronze	Other	

(Continued)

Table 4.3 (Continued)

Cat. No.	Museum or Excavation No.	Museum	Date	Provenance	Dimensions	Material	Type	Publications
40	O.C.2687	New York, USA, Metropolitan Museum of Arts	Dynasty 18	Unknown		Copper alloy, Bronze (?)	Unknown	
41	UC26935	London, UK, Petrie Museum	Dynasty 18	Unknown	Length trough: 1.1 cm Length: 5.4 cm Length rear part (from hinge): 3.7 cm Length pin (from hinge): 1.7 cm Average thickness pin: 0.2 cm Width trough opening: 0.25 cm Height: 3.0 cm Thickness: 0.4 cm	Unknown	E-II	Freed 1982, 194.
42	UC26936	London, UK, Petrie Museum	Dynasty 18	Unknown	Length: 5.9 cm Length rear part (from hinge): 4.3 cm Height blade (vertical cut surface): 1.0 cm Length pin (from hinge): 2.4 cm Average thickness pin: 0.15 cm Height: 2.3 cm Thickness: 0.5 cm	Unknown	E-I	Petrie 1917, 49, pl. LXI (no.16).

(Continued)

Table 4.3 Catalogue of finds (Entries 26–45) (Continued)

Cat. No.	Museum or Excavation No.	Museum	Date	Provenance	Dimensions	Material	Type	Publications
43	UC30134	London, UK, Petrie Museum	Dynasty 18	Unknown	Length trough: 8.6 cm Length: 9.6 cm Length rear part (from hinge): 7.0 cm Height blade: 1.3 cm Length pin (from hinge): 2.6 cm Length pin (when opened at maximum): 1.9 cm Maximum opening: 1.2 cm Average thickness pin: 0.25 cm Width trough opening: 0.2–0.3 cm Height: 2.3 cm Thickness: 0.4 cm	Unknown	E-I	Petrie 1917, 49, pl. LXI (no.15). Freed, 1982, 194.
44	UC36425	London, UK, Petrie Museum	Dynasty 18	Unknown	Length trough: 4.9 cm Length: 3.9 cm Length blade (from hinge): 1.9 cm Length pin (from hinge): 1.9 cm Length pin (when opened at maximum): 1.4 cm Maximum opening: 1.3 cm Average thickness pin: 0.1 cm Width trough opening: 0.1 cm–0.3cm Height: 2.0 cm Thickness: 0.4 cm	Copper alloy, Bronze (?)	E-II	Petrie 1917, 49, pl. LXI (no.17).

(Continued)

Table 4.3 (Continued)

Cat. No.	Museum or Excavation No.	Museum	Date	Provenance	Dimensions	Material	Type	Publications
45	UC40533	London, UK, Petrie Museum	Dynasty 18	Unknown	Length trough: 7.3 cm Length: 8.7 cm Length blade (from hinge): 5.0 cm Height blade (vertical cut surface): 0.9 cm Length pin (from hinge): 2.7 cm Length pin (when opened at maximum): 2.0 cm Maximum opening: 1.4 cm Average thickness pin: 0.1 cm Width trough opening: 0.2 cm Height: 1.0 cm Thickness: 0.6 cm	Bronze	D-I	Petrie 1917, 49, pl. LXI (no.12).

Table 4.4 Catalogue of finds (Entries 46–64)

Cat. No.	Museum or Excavation No.	Museum	Date	Provenance	Dimensions	Material	Type	Publications
46	UC40654	London, UK, Petrie Museum	Dynasty 18	Unknown	Length: 5,5 cm Length blade (from hinge): 1,7 cm Length pin (from hinge): 3,8 cm Average thickness pin: 0,1 cm Height: 2,2 cm Thickness: 0,9 cm	Bronze	E-II	Petrie 1917, 49, pl. LXI (no.20).

(Continued)

Table 4.4 Catalogue of finds (Entries 46–64) (Continued)

Cat. No.	Museum or Excavation No.	Museum	Date	Provenance	Dimensions	Material	Type	Publications
47	UC40658	London, UK, Petrie Museum	Dynasty 18	Unknown	Length trough: 7.0 cm Length: 7.1 cm Length blade (from hinge): 4.3 cm Height blade (vertical cut surface): 1.2 cm Length pin (from hinge): 2.8 cm Length pin (when opened at maximum): 2.2 cm Maximum opening: 1.3 cm Average thickness pin: 0.1 cm Width trough opening: 0.2 cm Height: 1.2 cm Thickness: 0.5 cm	Unknown	C-II	Petrie 1917, 49, pl. LXI (no.13).
48	UC40659	London, UK, Petrie Museum	Dynasty 18	Unknown	Length trough: 4.4 cm Length: 8.8 cm Length blade (from hinge): 6.4 cm Height blade (vertical cut surface): 1.3 cm Length pin (from hinge): 2.5 cm Length pin (when opened at maximum): 1.1 cm Maximum opening: 0.4 cm Average thickness pin: 0.18 cm Width trough opening: 0.3 cm Height: 3.3 cm Thickness: 0.7 cm	Bronze and copper	E-I	Petrie 1917, 49, pl. LXI (no.14).

(Continued)

Table 4.4 (Continued)

Cat. No.	Museum or Excavation No.	Museum	Date	Provenance	Dimensions	Material	Type	Publications
49	UC7784	London, UK, Petrie Museum	Dynasty 18	Gurob	Length: 9.7 cm	Bronze	A-II	Petrie 1917, 49, pl. LXI (no.6). Petrie 1890, pl. XVII (no.43).
50	UC7785	London, UK, Petrie Museum	Dynasty 18	Gurob	Length trough: 3.8 cm Length: 4.8 cm Length blade (from hinge): 3.2 cm Height blade: 0.9 cm Length pin (from hinge): 1.6 cm Average thickness pin: 0.1 cm Width trough opening: 0.2 cm Height: 1.1 cm Thickness: 0.7 cm	Bronze	A-I	Petrie 1917, 49, pl. LXI (no.7). Petrie 1891, pl. XIX.
51	UC7786	London, UK, Petrie Museum	Dynasty 18	Gurob	Length trough: 3.5 cm Length: 5.0 cm Length blade (from hinge): 3.4 cm Height blade: 0.9 cm Length pin (from hinge): 1.6 cm Average thickness pin: 0.08 cm Height: 0.9 cm Thickness: 0.5 cm	Bronze	B-I	Petrie 1917, 49, pl. LXI (no.8).

(Continued)

Table 4.4 Catalogue of finds (Entries 46–64) (Continued)

Cat. No.	Museum or Excavation No.	Museum	Date	Provenance	Dimensions	Material	Type	Publications
52	UC7787	London, UK, Petrie Museum	Dynasty 18	Gurob	Length trough: 7.5 cm Length: 4.3 cm Length blade (from hinge): 2.5 cm Height blade: 1.3 cm Length pin (from hinge): 2.1 cm Length pin (when opened at maximum): 1.6 cm Maximum opening: 1.2 cm Average thickness pin: 0.1 cm Width trough opening: 0.15 cm Height: 1.3 cm Thickness: 0.5 cm	Copper alloy, Bronze (?)	Unknown	
53	UC24338	London, UK, Petrie Museum	Late Dynasty 18	Amarna	Length trough: 6.1 cm Length: 6.8 cm Length blade (from hinge): 4.1 cm Height blade (vertical cut surface?): 0.9 cm Length pin (from hinge): 2.8 cm Length pin (when opened at maximum): 2.3 cm Maximum opening: 1.0 cm Average thickness pin: 0.1 cm Width trough opening: 0.2 cm Height: 1.3 cm Thickness: 0.5 cm	Copper	D-I	Petrie 1917, 49, pl. LXI (no.4).

(Continued)

Table 4.4 (Continued)

Cat. No.	Museum or Excavation No.	Museum	Date	Provenance	Dimensions	Material	Type	Publications
54	UC7783	London, UK, Petrie Museum	Late Dynasty 18	Gurob	Length trough: 5.9 cm Length: 7.0 cm Length blade (from hinge): 4.6 cm Height blade (vertical cut surface): 1.3 cm Length pin (from hinge): 2.5 cm Average thickness pin: 0.1 cm Width trough opening: 0.15 cm Height: 2.0 cm Thickness: 0.6 cm	Bronze	C-III	Petrie 1917, 49, pl. LXI (no.5).
55	UC8529	London, UK, Petrie Museum	Late Dynasty 18	Unknown	Length: 6.3 cm Length trough: 3.4 cm Width trough opening: 0.1–0.2 cm Maximum height: 1.3 cm Length dog with muzzle open: 4.6 cm Length god/gazelle: 3.7 cm Thickness: 1.8 cm	Copper Alloy, Gold	E-II	Petrie 1917, 49, pl. LXI (no.18).
56	E10308	Philadelphia, USA, Penn Museum	New Kingdom, Dynasty 18 (?)	Buhen, Cemetery H, Tomb 17	Length: 7.5 cm	Bronze	D-II	Randall-MacIver and Woolley 1911, pl. 64.
57	4713/23	Hildesheim, Germany, Pelizaeus Museum	Dynasty 18/19	Unknown	Unknown	Bronze	A-I	

(Continued)

Table 4.4 Catalogue of finds (Entries 46–64) (Continued)

Cat. No.	Museum or Excavation No.	Museum	Date	Provenance	Dimensions	Material	Type	Publications
58	909.80.517	Toronto, Canada, Royal Ontario Museum	Dynasty 18/19	Unknown	Length: 12.7 cm	Copper	A-II	Freed 1982, 194.
59	ÄS 2041	Munich, Germany, Staatliches Museum Ägyptischer Kunst	Dynasty 18/19	Unknown	Length: 14 cm	Bronze	A-I	Schoske 1990, no. 97.
60	1927.1296	Oxford, UK, Ashmolean Museum	New Kingdom	Unknown	Length trough: 11.1 cm; Length: 15.1 cm; Length blade (from hinge): 11.3 cm; Height blade (vertical cut surface): 1.8 cm; Length pin (from hinge): 3.8 cm; Length pin (when opened at maximum): 2.3 cm; Average thickness pin: 0.1 cm; Width trough opening: 0.12 cm; Height: 1.9 cm; Thickness: 0.4 cm	Bronze	C-II	
61	1933.1437	Oxford, UK, Ashmolean Museum	New Kingdom	Thebes	Length trough: 6.0 cm; Length: 6.3 cm; Length blade (from hinge): 3.9 cm; Height blade: 1.0 cm; Length pin (from hinge): 2.4 cm; Average thickness pin: 0.1 cm; Width trough opening: 0.12 cm; Height: 2.0 cm; Thickness: 0.4 cm	Copper alloy, Bronze (?)	A-II	

(Continued)

Table 4.4 (Continued)

Cat. No.	Museum or Excavation No.	Date	Museum	Provenance	Dimensions	Material	Type	Publications
62	22221	New Kingdom	Berlin, Germany, Ägyptisches Museum	Unknown	Length: 8.7 cm Height: 2.0 cm	Copper alloy, Bronze (?)	A-I	Schoske 1990, no. 95.
63	A634869	New Kingdom	London, UK, Science Museum	Unknown	Height: 2.5 cm Length: 14.0 cm	Bronze	A-II	
64	E.02258	New Kingdom	Brussels, Belgium, Royal Museums of Art and History	Unknown	Height: 2.9 cm Length: 9.1 cm	Bronze	E-I	

Table 4.5 Catalogue of finds (Entries 65-86)

Cat. No.	Museum or Excavation No.	Date	Museum	Provenance	Dimensions	Material	Type	Publications
65	EA26259	New Kingdom	London, UK, British Museum	Unknown	Length trough: 10.6 cm Length: 10.6 cm Length blade (from hinge): 7.3 cm Height blade (vertical cut surface): 1.5 cm Length pin (from hinge): 3.3 cm Length pin (when opened at maximum): 1.5 cm Maximum opening: 0.4 cm Average thickness pin: 0.15 cm Width trough opening: 0.2 cm Height: 1.5 cm Thickness: 0.4 cm	Bronze	C-II	

(Continued)

Table 4.5 Catalogue of finds (Entries 65–86) (Continued)

Cat. No.	Museum or Excavation No.	Date	Provenance	Museum	Dimensions	Material	Type	Publications
66	EA36314	New Kingdom	Unknown	London, UK, British Museum	Length trough: 2.2 cm Length: 10.5 cm Length blade (from hinge): 6.6 cm Height blade (vertical cut surface): 1.1 cm Length pin (from hinge): 3.9 cm Average thickness pin: 0.2 cm Height: 3.3 cm Thickness: 0.6 cm	Bronze	E-I	
67	Provv. 628 RCGE 46790	New Kingdom	Unknown	Turin, Italy, Museum Egizio	Length: 15 cm Height: 3 cm	Bronze	C-II	
68	UC40529	New Kingdom	Oxyrhynchus	London, UK, Petrie Museum	Length trough: 9.5 cm Length: 7.5 cm Length blade (from hinge): 5.0 cm Height blade: 1.4 cm Length pin (from hinge): 2.5 cm Length pin (when opened at maximum): 1.6 cm Maximum opening: 0.7 cm Average thickness pin: 0.1 cm Width trough opening: 0.2 cm Height: 1.1 cm Thickness: 0.5 cm	Copper	B-II	

(Continued)

Table 4.5 (Continued)

Cat. No.	Museum or Excavation No.	Museum	Date	Provenance	Dimensions	Material	Type	Publications
69	UC40530	London, UK, Petrie Museum	New Kingdom	Gurob (?)	Length trough: 6.3 cm Length: 6.8 cm Length blade (approx. as no hinge present): 4.5 cm Length pin (approx. as no hinge present): 2.1 cm Average thickness pin: 0.2 cm Height: 2.4 cm Thickness: 0.8 cm	Copper	A-I	
70	UC40664	London, UK, Petrie Museum	New Kingdom	Unknown	Length trough: 12.8 cm Length: 13.4 cm Length blade (from hinge): 9.3 cm Height blade: 2.1 cm Length pin (from hinge): 4.1 cm Length pin (when opened at maximum): 1.1 cm Maximum opening: 0.5 cm Average thickness pin: 0.1 cm Width trough opening: 0.15–0.3 cm Height: 2.5 cm Thickness: 0.6 cm	Unknown	A-II	Petrie 1917, 49, pl. LXI (no.10).

(Continued)

Table 4.5 Catalogue of finds (Entries 65–86) (Continued)

Cat. No.	Museum or Excavation No.	Museum	Date	Provenance	Dimensions	Material	Type	Publications
71	UC29811	London, UK, Petrie Museum	Dynasty 22	Ramesseum (?)	Length trough: 3.4 cm Length: 10.8 cm Length blade (from hinge): 8.5 cm Height blade (vertical cut surface): 1.5 cm Length pin (from hinge): 2.3 cm Average thickness pin: 0.12 cm Width trough opening: 0.25 cm Height: 1.7 cm Thickness: 0.7 cm	Bronze	C-II	Petrie 1917, 49, pl. LXI (no.11).
72	1950/56	Hannover, Germany, Kestner Museum	Unknown	Unknown	Length: 10.2 cm	Bronze	A-I	Hurschmann 1988, Tf. 4.
73	2769	Hamburg, Germany, Private Collection, Hans Schwarzkopf GmbH.	Unknown	Unknown	Unknown	Unknown	D-I	Hurschmann 1988, Tf. 4.
74	2770	Hamburg, Germany, Private Collection, Hans Schwarzkopf GmbH.	Unknown	Unknown	Length: 6.1 cm	Bronze	Other	Hurschmann 1988, Tf. 4.

(Continued)

Table 4.5 (Continued)

Cat. No.	Museum or Excavation No.	Provenance	Date	Museum	Dimensions	Material	Type	Publications
75	E.229.1954	Unknown	Unknown	Cambridge, UK, Fitzwilliam Museum	Length trough: 8.5 cm Length: 8.9 cm Length blade (from hinge): 5.4 cm Height blade (vertical cut surface): 1.5 cm Length pin (from hinge): 3.5 cm Length pin (when opened at maximum): 1.9 cm Maximum opening: 0.4 cm Average thickness pin: 0.1 cm Width trough opening: 0.12 cm Height: 1.6 cm Thickness: 0.4 cm	Bronze	C-I	
76	E.GA.3442.1943	Unknown	Unknown	Cambridge, UK, Fitzwilliam Museum	Length trough: 9.9 cm Length: 10.7 cm Length blade (from hinge): 6.5 cm Height blade: 1.3 cm Length pin (from hinge): 4.2 cm Length pin (when opened at maximum): 2.6 cm Maximum opening: 1.0 cm Average thickness pin: 0.12 cm Width trough opening: 0.18 cm Height: 1.7 cm Thickness: 0.5 cm	Bronze	A-III	

(Continued)

Table 4.5 Catalogue of finds (Entries 65–86) (Continued)

Cat. No.	Museum or Excavation No.	Museum	Date	Provenance	Dimensions	Material	Type	Publications
77	E.GA.3443.1943	Cambridge, UK, Fitzwilliam Museum	Unknown	Unknown	Length trough: 7.9 cm Length: 8.6 cm Length blade (from hinge): 5.4 cm Height blade: 1.5 cm Length pin (from hinge): 3.1 cm Length pin (when opened at maximum): 1.8 cm Maximum opening: 0.4 cm Average thickness pin: 0.18 cm Width trough opening: 02–0.4 cm Height: 1.9 cm Thickness: 0.6 cm	Bronze	A-1	
78	E.GA.3444.1943	Cambridge, UK, Fitzwilliam Museum	Unknown	Unknown	Length trough: 3.8 cm Length: 7.1 cm Length blade (from hinge): 5.1 cm Height blade: 1.4 cm Length pin (from hinge): 2.2 cm Length pin (when opened at maximum): 1.8 cm Maximum opening: 1.4 cm Average thickness pin: 0.18 cm Width trough opening: 0.2 cm Height: 2.4 cm Thickness: 0.6 cm	Copper alloy, Hinge made of gold	A-1	

(Continued)

Table 4.5 (Continued)

Cat. No.	Museum or Excavation No.	Museum	Date	Provenance	Dimensions	Material	Type	Publications
79	E.GA.4581.1943	Cambridge, UK, Fitzwilliam Museum	Unknown	Unknown	Length trough: 9.6 cm Length: 9.1 cm Length blade (from hinge): 5.1 cm Height blade: 1.5 cm Length pin (from hinge): 4.0 cm Length pin (when opened at maximum): 1.7 cm (does not open properly) Maximum opening: 0.5 cm (does not open properly) Average thickness pin: 0.11 cm Width trough opening: 0.15 cm Height: 2.1 cm Thickness: 0.5 cm	Bronze	A-II	
80	EA27730	London, UK, British Museum	Unknown	Unknown	Length trough: 9.0 cm Length: 9.6 cm Length blade (from hinge): 6.4 cm Height blade (vertical cut surface): 1.4 cm Length pin (from hinge): 3.2 cm Length pin (when opened at maximum): 2.2 cm Maximum opening: 0.8 cm Average thickness pin: 0.15 cm Width trough opening: 0.2 cm Height: 1.4 cm Thickness: 0.5 cm	Bronze	C-I	

(Continued)

Table 4.5 Catalogue of finds (Entries 65–86) (Continued)

Cat. No.	Museum or Excavation No.	Museum	Date	Provenance	Dimensions	Material	Type	Publications
81	EA37179	London, UK, British Museum	Unknown	Unknown	Length: 8.86 cm Height: 1.6 cm	Bronze	C-II	Taylor and Antoine 2014, 131.
82	EA67449	London, UK, British Museum	Unknown	Unknown	Length trough: 8.6 cm Length: 9.0 cm Length blade (from hinge): 6.9 cm Height blade (vertical cut surface): 1.3 cm Length pin (from hinge): 2.1 cm Length pin (when opened at maximum): 1.3 cm Maximum opening: 0.7 cm Average thickness pin: 0.1 cm Width trough opening: 0.2 cm Height: 1.8 cm Thickness: 0.5 cm	Bronze	D-I	

(Continued)

Table 4.5 (Continued)

Cat. No.	Museum or Excavation No.	Museum	Date	Provenance	Dimensions	Material	Type	Publications
83	EA67450	London, UK, British Museum	Unknown	Unknown	Length trough: 7.7 cm Length: 7.0 cm Length blade (from hinge): 4.0 cm Height blade (vertical cut surface): 1.3 cm Length pin (from hinge): 3.1 cm Length pin (when opened at maximum): 1.7 cm Maximum opening; 0.6 cm Average thickness pin: 0.1 cm Width trough opening; 0.15 cm Height: 1.1 cm Thickness: 0.5 cm	Bronze	C-I	
84	OIM E9912	Chicago, USA, Oriental Institute	Unknown	Unknown	Unknown	Unknown	A-III	
85	UC40531	London, UK, Petrie Museum	Unknown	Amarna (?)	Length trough part (large): 7.8 cm Length blade part: 6.9 cm Height blade part: 0.7 cm Thickness trough: 0.18 cm Average thickness pin: 0.2 cm Length trough part (small): 1.3 cm Length pin parts: 1.0 cm and 0.4 cm	Copper alloy	A-II	
86	Unknown	Paris, France, Louvre	Unknown	Unknown	Unknown	Unknown	A-I	

The different features and the physical nature of our specimens fit every step in the manufacturing process of wigs and the dent found in EA2560 provides compelling evidence. Even though there is no conclusive textual or figurative proof and only one strand of EA2560 could be examined, the results of the analysis above prompt me to favour the idea of the implements being used as tools for making and maintaining wigs, worn by both men and women in ancient Egypt.

Bibliography

Auenmüller, J. (2014) Metalle und ihre Verwendung im pharaonischen Ägypten. In M. Fitzenreiter, C.E. Loeben, D. Raue and U. Wallenstein (eds) *Gegossene Götter. Metallhandwerk und Massenproduktion im Alten Ägypten*, 31– 44. Rahden, Verlag Marie Leidorf.

Beinlich, H. (1980) Mahasna. In W. Helck (ed.) *Lexikon der Ägyptologie III*, 1164. Wiesbaden, Harrassowitz.

Bladh, K.W. (1990) *Handbook of Mineralogy I.* Tucson, Mineral Data Publishing.

Bonnet, C. (2000) *Edifices et rites funéraires à Kerma.* Paris, Errance.

Bonnet, C. (2014) Forty years research on Kerma cultures. *British Museum Publications on Egypt and Sudan 1*, 81–94.

Bonnet, C. and Valbelle, D. (2014) *La ville de Kerma. Une capitale nubienne au sud de l'Egypte.* Lausanne, Favre.

Brunton, G. and Engelbach, R. (1927) *Gurob.* British School of Archaeology in Egypt 41. London, British School of Archaeology in Egypt.

Downes, D. (1974) *The Excavations at Esna 1905-1906.* Warminster, Aris and Phillips Ltd.

Doyen, F. (1997) *Le Roman de la Momie. Les Amours d'une Princesse Égyptienne.* Brogne, Abbaye Saint-Gérard de Brogne.

Drower, M.S. (1995) *Flinders Petrie. A Life in Archaeology.* Madison, University of Wisconsin Press.

Dunham, D. (1967) *Second Cataracts Forts II. Uronarti, Shalfak, Mirgissa.* Boston, Museum of Fine Arts.

Durbin, G. (1984) *Wig, Hairdressing and Shaving Bygones.* Shire Album 117. Aylesbury, Shire.

Edel, E. (2008) *Die Felsgräbernekropole der Qubbet el Hawa bei Assuan.* Wiesbaden, Ferdinand Schöningh.

Erman, A. (1901) *Zaubersprüche für Mutter und Kind.* Berlin, Königliche Akademie der Wissenschaften.

Fitzenreiter, M. (2014) Metall und Kultur. Eine kurze Geschichte der "thermischen Revolution". In M. Fitzenreiter, C.E. Loeben, D. Raue and U. Wallenstein (eds), *Gegossene Götter. Metallhandwerk und Massenproduktion im Alten Ägypten*, 21 – 30. Rahden, Verlag Marie Leidorf.

Fletcher, J. (1994) A tale of hair, wigs and lice. *Egyptian Archaeology 5*, 31–33.

Freed, R.A. (1982) *Egypt's Golden Age. The Art of Living in the New Kingdom 1558-1085 B.C. Catalogue of the Exhibition.* Boston, Museum of Fine Arts.

Garstang, J. (1901) *El Arábah. A Cemetery of the Middle Kingdom. Survey of the Old Kingdom Temenos. Graffiti from the Temple of Sety.* London, Bernard Quaritch.

Garstang, J. (1903) *Mahâsna and Bêt Khallâf.* British School of Archaeology in Egypt 7. London, Bernard Quaritch.

Gratien, B (1978) Les cultures Kerma. Essai de classification, trente ans après. In V. Rondot (ed.) *La pioche et la plume. Autour du Soudan, du Liban et de la Jordanie. Hommages archéologiques à Patrice Lenoble*, 225–236. Paris, PU Paris-Sorbonne.

Gratien, B. and Le Saout, F. (1994) *Nubie. Les cultures antiques du Soudan.* Lille, Université Charles De Gaulle-Lille III.

Hayes, W.C. (1935) The tomb of Nefer-Khēwet and his family. *The Metropolitan Museum of Art Bulletin 30*, 17–36.

Hayes, W.C. (1959) *The Scepter of Egypt. A Background for the Study of the Egyptian Antiquities in the Metropolitan Museum of Art II. The Hyksos Period and the New Kingdom 1675-1080 BC.* Cambridge, Metropolitan Museum of Art.

Hoedel-Hoenes, S. (2000) *Life and Death in Ancient Egypt. Scenes from Private Tombs in New Kingdom Thebes.* London, Cornell University Press.

Holthoer, R. (1977) *New Kingdom Pharaonic Sites. The Finds and the Sites.* Scandinavian Joint Expedition to Sudanese Nubia Publications 5.1. Uppsala, The Scandinavian Joint Expedition to Sudanese Nubia.

Hurschmann, R. (1988) Zu Agyptischen Mehrzweckgeraten. *Studien zur Altagyptischen Kultur* 15, 165–169.

Kampp, F. (1996) *Die Thebanische Nekropole. Zum Wandel des Grabgedenkens von der XVIII. bis zur XX. Dynastie.* Mainz, Philipp von Zabern.

Kemp, B.J. (1978) The excavations at Esan 1905–1906. By Dorothy Downes. *Journal of Egyptian Archaeology*, 165–168.

Kozloff, A.P. (1992) *Egypt's Dazzling Sun Amenhotep III and His World.* Cleveland, Cleveland Museum of Art.

Lembke, K. and Schmitz, B. (2006) *Schönheit im Alten Ägypten. Sehnsucht nach Vollkommenheit.* Hildesheim, Theiss.

Lucas, A. (1930) Ancient Egyptian wigs. *Annales du Service des Antiquités de l'Égypte* 30, 190–196.

Lucas, A. (1962) *Ancient Egyptian Materials and Industries.* London, Edward Arnold.

Macadam, M.F.L. (1949) *The Temples of Kawa I. The Inscriptions.* London, Oxford University Press.

Masali, M. (1972) Body size and proportions as revealed by bone measurements and their meaning in environmental adaptation. *Journal of Human Revolution* 1, 187–197.

Meeks, D. (1982) *Annee lexicographique III.* Paris, Librairie Cybelle.

Moran, W.L. (1992) *The Amarna Letters.* London, Johns Hopkins University Press.

Müller, C. (1982) Perücke. In W. Helck (ed.) *Lexikon der Ägyptologie IV*, 988–989. Wiesbaden, Harrassowitz.

Müller, M. (2007) Braids for paradise from Dynastic Egypt to the Islamic Middle Ages. In J.-C. Goyon and C. Chardin (eds) *Proceedings of the Ninth International Congress of Egyptologists, Grenoble, 6–12 September 2004*, 1343–1350. Orientalia Lovaniensia Analecta 150.2. Leuven, Peeters.

Odler, M. (2016) *Old Kingdom Copper Tools and Model Tools.* Archaeopress Egyptology 14. Oxford, Archaeopress.

Onderka, P. (2014) Aniba. In P. Onderka and V. Vrtal (eds) *Nubia. A Land of the Crossroads of Cultures. Wad Ben Naga 2014*, 86–87. Prague, Národní museum.

Op de Beek, L. (2006) Shedding light on old excavations. Esna. *Chronique d'Égypte* 81, 94–115.

Peet, E.T. and Woolley, L.C. (1923) *The City of Akhenaten I. Excavations of 1921 and 1922 at el-'Amarneh.* Memoirs of the Egypt Exploration Society 38. London, Egypt Exploration Society.

Petrie, W.M.F. (1890) *Kahun, Gurob and Hawara.* London, K. Paul Trench Trübner.

Petrie, W.M.F. (1891) *Illahun, Kahun and Gurob.* London, D. Nutt.

Petrie, W.M.F. (1898) *Deshasheh.* Memoirs of the Egypt Exploration Society 15. London, Egypt Exploration Society.

Petrie, W.M.F. (1901) *Diospolis Parva. The Cemeteries of Abadiyeh and Hu 1898-9.* Memoirs of the Egypt Exploration Society 20. London, Egypt Exploration Society.

Petrie, W.M.F. (1903) *Abydos II.* Memoirs of the Egypt Exploration Society 24. London, Egypt Exploration Society.

Petrie, W.M.F. (1917) *Tools and Weapons Illustrated by the Egyptian Collection in University College, London.* London, British School of Archaeology in Egypt.

Porter, B. and Moss, R.L.B. (1960) *Topographical Bibliography of Ancient Egyptian Hieroglyphic Texts, Reliefs, and Paintings I. The Theban Necropolis 1.* Oxford, Griffith Institute.

Privati, B. (1999) La céramique de la nécropole orientale de Kerma. *Cahiers de recherches de l'Institut de Papyrologie et Égyptologie de Lille* 20, 41–69.

Randall-MacIver, D. and Mace, A.C. (1902) *El Amrah and Abydos.* Memoirs of the Egypt Exploration Society 23. London, Egypt Exploration Society.

Randall-MacIver, D. and Woolley, L.C. (1911) *Buhen.* Philadelphia, University Museum.

Reisner, G.A. (1923a) *Excavations at Kerma I-III.* Cambridge, Peabody Museum of Harvard University.

Reisner, G.A. (1923b) *Excavations at Kerma IV-V.* Cambridge, Peabody Museum of Harvard University.

Riefstahl, E. (1956) Two hairdressers of the eleventh dynasty. *Journal of Near Eastern Studies* 15, 10–17.

Säve-Söderbergh, T. (1991) *New Kingdom Pharaonic Sites. The Finds and the Sites.* Scandinavian Joint Expedition to Sudanese Nubia Publications 5.3. Uppsala, Läromedelsförlagen/Svenska Bokförlaget.

Schiaparelli, E. (2007) *The Intact Tomb of the Architect Kha in the Necropolis of Thebes.* Turin, AdArte.

Schoske, S. (1990) *Schönheit. Abglanz der Göttlichkeit. Kosmetik im alten Ägypten.* München, Lipp.

Stead, M. (1986) *Egyptian Life.* London, Harvard University Press.

Steindorff, G. (1937) *Aniba II.* Glücksstadt, J.J. Augustin.

Stevens Cox, J. (1977) The construction of an ancient Egyptian Wig (*c.* 1400 B.C.) in the British Museum. *Journal of Egyptian Archaeology* 63, 67–70.

Taylor, J.H. and Antoine, D. (2014) *Ancient Lives, New Discoveries. Eight Mummies, Eight Stories.* London, British Museum Press.

Vandier d'Abbadie, J. (1972) *Catalogue Des Objets De Toilette Egyptiens.* Paris, Éditions des musées nationaux.

Vercoutter, J. (1975) *Mirgissa II. Les nécropoles.* Paris, Presses Universitaires du Septentrion.

Welsby, D.A. and Anderson, J.A. (2004) *Sudan. Ancient Treasures.* London, British Museum Press.

Wilde, H. (2003) *Technologische Innovationen im zweiten Jahrtausend vor Christus. Zur Verwendung und Verbreitung neuer Werkstoffe im ostmediterranen Raum.* Göttinger Orientforschungen IV, Reihe Ägypten 44. Göttingen, Harrassowitz.

Zonhoven, L.M. (1979) The inspection of a tomb at Deir el-Medina (O.Wien Aeg.1). *Journal of Egyptian Archaeology* 65, 89–98.

Chapter 5

Fresco, fresco on the wall... changes in ideals of beauty in the Late Bronze Age Aegean

Filip Franković

Abstract

Iconographic representations on sealstones, frescoes and other media are some of the most recognisable features of the Late Bronze Age in the Aegean. Therefore, it is not surprising that Late Bronze Age Aegean iconography has often been considered to mirror reality. Since the beginnings of research in the area, costumes, hairstyles and the bodily features of human figures depicted on some of the objects (most commonly frescoes) have stimulated discussion about the beauty standards of the period. Unfortunately, previous research focused more on general trends on the basis of the entire Late Bronze Age Aegean or, at best, only differentiated between Minoan and Mycenaean spheres. It rarely focused on a more detailed examination of the material within chronologically and spatially smaller units. This chapter attempts to grasp the general patterns in the change of beauty ideals during the Late Bronze Age. It focuses mostly on hairstyles and beards (or the lack of them), but often addresses their relationships to costumes and bodies, as well as age and gender identities. As both hairstyles and beards are connected to hair manipulation, removal or grooming, it is argued that the changes to this aspect of the beauty ideal cannot be fully understood without the study of objects for personal care. Mirrors, razors and tweezers are studied separately and compared to the general conclusions arising from the study of the iconographic data.

Key words: *Late Bronze Age, Aegean, beauty, hairstyles, beard*

Introduction – an image in a mirror...

Despite its location on the edge of the eastern Mediterranean, where other large political powers, such as Egypt and the Hittites, dominated at the time, the area of the Aegean played an important role in the Late Bronze Age (LBA) from its beginnings between 1700 and 1600 BCE until the end of the palatial system around 1200 BCE. Since written sources are either limited to administrative economic texts (*e.g.*, in the case of Linear B) or still undeciphered (*e.g.*, in the case of Linear A and earlier scripts; see *e.g.* Davis 2014 for the context of some of the inscriptions), the rich iconographic sources have often been used to provide a more detailed insight into the social environment of the LBA Aegean. The iconographic sources from the LBA Aegean have often been understood as mirrors reflecting reality. Although one could argue that a certain degree of naturalism did exist (*e.g.*, Chapin 2007; 2009), it is clear that many of these representations are far from realistic (*e.g.*, Newman 2017, 217; Pini 1999; Weingarten 2005, 356). The same is the case with the representation of the body, which is consequently related to the perception of gender (*e.g.*, Alberti 1997; 2001; 2002; 2005; 2012; also Hitchcock 2000; 2009). Therefore, understanding LBA Aegean iconography as mirroring reality can easily cause misconceptions and oversimplified explanations of iconographic data, resulting in dubious and contradictory conclusions.

There are two characteristics of mirrors that are often neglected. First, when broken or missing a piece, mirrors distort the image of reality. Therefore, it should not be forgotten that many objects bearing iconographic representations have been recovered in a fragmented state. Second, even the reflection in the mirror is open to many interpretations and (re-)evaluations by the observer(s). When looking at their own image in the mirror, people often feel the need to alter their appearance so that the reflection appears more attractive. In other words, a mirror becomes an active factor in shaping one's appearance. The same characteristic is often neglected in LBA Aegean iconographic data. As a result, iconographic sources have often been interpreted as passive reflections of social relations rather than their active creators. Moreover, Aegean iconography is commonly seen as passive in discussions about beauty standards or representation of costumes, which often observe the context of the entire LBA (or, at best, the Minoan and Mycenaean sphere) and neglect subtler and chronologically more sensitive changes. Beauty standards and costumes were often treated as idealised, which in many cases has hindered serious discussion about their close relationship to various identities.

The creative power of iconographic depictions can be observed from two perspectives. First, the dubious character of some of the representations can affect archaeologists in their interpretation of data, thus creating new understandings of the past. Second, the same depiction might have been differently understood and evaluated by different consumers in the past, negotiating the old and creating new identities simultaneously. A signet ring from Grave 6 of the Isopata cemetery is one such example (CMS II 3, no. 56; Fig. 5.1).

The ring was found within the LM IIIA1 context, but can be stylistically dated to the LM I–LM II, which means that it was in use for a longer period of time and probably changed owners. The object represents two individuals in a pose similar to a handshake. The gesture in which two or more figures are joining hands is rarely depicted in Aegean art and can be linked to both male and female individuals. On the one hand, it can be compared to a scene representing two women joining their hands on a double axe (*e.g.*, CMS VI, no. 282; Fig. 5.2) or other objects (*e.g.*, CMS V Suppl. 1A, no. 178). On the other hand, it can be compared to a scene representing the leaders of two groups of warriors depicted on a recently discovered krater from Tiryns (Maran and Papadimitriou 2017, 40–41) or the two male figures represented on a sealstone discovered at Archontiki on Psara (Archontidu-Argyri 2006, 134). The possibility that the depiction on the Isopata signet ring represents a dancing scene should not be dismissed either.

A similar vagueness is visible in the depiction of their costumes. Both individuals are dressed in skirts, which are signified only by three horizontal lines at the bottom of the costume. The upper part of the body of both individuals seems to be undressed. Due to a high degree of schematisation, the costumes and bodies are open to different interpretations. The horizontal lines, probably representing layers of cloth, can be equally used to schematise flounced skirts that were worn exclusively by female individuals (*e.g.*, CMS I, nos. 17, 144, 145), as well as the kilts (*e.g.*, CMS II 6, no. 29; VI, no. 320; IX, no. 114) or long skirts (*e.g.*, CMS II 8, no. 237) worn by male individuals. It could be argued that flounced skirts

Fig. 5.1 Drawing of a signet ring (CMS II 3, no. 56) from Grave 6 of the Isopata cemetery representing two figures in a handshake gesture (after Platon and Pini 1984, 67. Image courtesy of the CMS Heidelberg)

Fig. 5.2 Drawing of a sealstone (CMS VI, no. 282) of unknown provenance representing two women joining their hands on a double axe (after Hughes-Brock and Boardman 2009, 461. Image courtesy of the CMS Heidelberg)

fall to the ankles (*e.g.*, CMS I, no. 159; II 3, nos. 16, 117) or cover the legs entirely (*e.g.*, CMS V Suppl. 1B, no. 114; V Suppl. 2, no. 106), while kilts end above the knee (*e.g.*, CMS II 6, no. 29; the Lion Hunt dagger). Therefore, this characteristic could be seen as a distinguishing factor. However, in certain representations of male individuals in kilts or skirts (*e.g.*, CMS II 8, no. 237; see also the representation of a kilt on a fresco from Ayia Irini in Abramowitz 1980, 58, 64, pl. 4, no. 62) and female individuals in flounced skirts (*e.g.*, CMS II 6, no. 24; X, no. 242; XI, no. 29), the costumes fall to the middle of the figures' calves. Consequently, their identification is in some cases far from certain. Moreover, breasts are the only clear marker of the female sex in Minoan art (see Alexandri 1994). Therefore, one could argue that the absence of breasts on the undressed upper part of the body might indicate that these are male individuals. However, breasts are sometimes excluded from the depictions of female individuals with an exposed upper torso (*e.g.*, CMS III, nos. 351, 352; V Suppl. 1A, no. 75; VI, no. 314).

The costumes, however, are never the only identity markers present. They are often combined into a homogenous unity with other identity markers, such as jewelry or hairstyles. If one of these markers were removed, the meaning of what is represented would therefore change. Unfortunately, the lack of details on the depicted scene does not allow for a sufficiently detailed comparison and the precise identification of its participants. In my opinion, it is more probable that the scene represented on the signet ring from the Isopata cemetery (CMS II 3, no. 56; Fig. 5.1) depicts two female individuals joining their hands on an object (as in CMS V Suppl. 1A, no. 178; VI, no. 282; Fig. 5.2), as these are the best contemporary parallels for such a gesture. The central object is probably missing from the signet ring from the Isopata cemetery (CMS II 3, no. 56; Fig. 5.1) due to the highly schematic nature of the depiction. However, the depiction is indisputably open to different interpretations. Moreover, it should be taken into account that scholarly research often assumed the bird's eye perspective on material culture, in this case the possible iconographic parallels. More precisely, it is quite probable that in many cases our knowledge about the possible origin of specific objects or iconographic parallels exceeds that of the LBA people. Although it could be argued that the aforementioned scene was comprehensible to the LBA people within their cultural context, it is equally possible that it was differently evaluated by different individuals in the past, much like it is today by different scholars. Therefore, I believe that the scene might have been variously interpreted and intentionally manipulated by different consumers during the LBA in order to match their own personal preferences and worldviews.

The recently discovered LH IIA "Griffin warrior" tomb from Pylos (Davis and Stocker 2016; Stocker and Davis 2017) is an interesting example for the discussion above. The individual was buried with multiple sealstones and signet rings depicting human figures. In three of these representations, the objects held by the individuals can be linked to the objects found within the tomb itself, suggesting that the deceased identified himself with the iconography placed next to him in the same context (Davis and Stocker 2016, 634, 650–652; Stocker and Davis 2017). The objects include a sword, a staff finial in the shape of a bull's head and a mirror. What is significant is the fact that the individuals holding the staff and the mirror on the representations can probably be identified as women (Davis and Stocker 2016, 643–646). Although primary sexual characteristics are not depicted, they can be identified as women when compared to other known iconographic sources. What is important to note, however, is the fact that in these two examples, the buried male individual is self-referenced through the representations of female individuals. It was shown earlier here that it is not always possible to precisely identify the costumes represented, which might have been the reason behind different understandings of the same depiction among their LBA consumers. However, in this case, other attributes of the figures could have been reinterpreted, as well. The pose and the long hair of the figures holding staffs can be linked to both male and female individuals in LBA Aegean art. Moreover, mirrors are connected to both male and female individuals in different LBA burial contexts in the Aegean. Therefore, it is not surprising that the gender of the depicted figures was mistaken, misunderstood or deliberately reinterpreted to better fit the needs of the final consumer. Such interpretation suggests that the character of certain bodily characteristics, beauty ideals or objects used for the interaction with the body can be understood as a more dynamic attribute, which can be easily manipulated and used for the creation of one's own identity, rather than as a predefined category.

As demonstrated above, iconography can sometimes mask or blur gender categories, allowing for multiple evaluations, both among present-day scholars and past societies. When it comes to the evaluation of gender in the LBA Aegean (*e.g.*, Alexandri 1994), it sometimes seems that gender was strictly based on a binary division (*e.g.*, Marinatos 1987; 2005), or that it was a completely fluid category (*e.g.*, Newman 2017; also Alberti 1997; 2001; 2002; 2005; 2012). However, neither of these two approaches successfully explains the inconsistencies within the iconographic data (see *e.g.*, Hitchcock 2000; also Hitchcock 1997). Although a more detailed study of the perception of gender in the LBA Aegean is beyond the scope of this paper, the study of the ideals of bodily beauty cannot be carried out successfully without looking at gender relations.

The beautiful heads – on the development of hairstyles in the Late Bronze Age Aegean

There are only a few beauty treatments which can be distinguished in LBA Aegean iconography, since large areas of the body are in many cases covered by costumes. Even when there is a glimpse of the body, it does not offer much information about possible beauty treatments. In opposition to the rest of the body, heads were depicted in multiple different ways to create beauty ideals closely related to gender, age and other identities. Consequently, different stylistic features of the head formed through different beauty treatments allow a more detailed analysis of the changes in beauty ideals between different age and gender groups. The following study should be taken as a general overview of the changes in beauty ideals, as it defines general patterns, rather than providing a detailed regional and chronological study.

Children's hairstyles

Hairstyles played an important role in the formation of identity in the LBA Aegean from the earliest childhood (for more on children in the LBA Aegean, see Rutter 2003). The most famous representations of young boys and girls (Fig. 5.3) are those on the frescoes found in the LM IA contexts on the island of Thera (*e.g.*, Chapin 2007; 2009; Davis 1986; Doumas 1986; 1987; 1992; Marinatos 1984, 35–37).

All boys (Yellow Ochre Boy, Boxing Boys (Fig. 5.3), Fisher Boys and Boys from Xeste 3) are represented in a similar way, with their varying sizes probably indicating age difference (Chapin 2007; 2009). They are represented naked, with their penises visible

in most of the cases. The boys' skin, except in the case of the Yellow Ochre Boy, is painted in red, which is typical for the representation of male individuals in Aegean frescoes. They also share the same hairstyle, a shaved scalp with locks of hair growing out of this (Fig. 5.3), similar to the contemporary Egyptian representations of boys. The number and length of locks vary between individuals. The shaved scalps are represented in blue, while the locks of hair (in most of the cases more than one) are usually represented in black. The Cretan examples of two LM I ivory figurines of naked boys with shaved scalps from Palaikastro and a bronze figurine of a baby from the Dictaean Cave dating to the MM IIIB–LM IB (Neopalatial) period (Rutter 2003, 37) are similar in representation to the boys from the Theran frescoes. To this group we should also add the famous Palaikastro Kouros (see MacGillivray, Sackett and Driessen 2000). Another individual with a shaved head is represented on a MM II–MM III sealing from Knossos (CMS II 8, no. 41), which might suggest that this

Fig. 5.3 Photo of the Boxing Boys fresco from House Beta at Akrotiri on Thera (https://upload.wikimedia.org/wikipedia/commons/8/84/The_Boxers_Fresco%2C_from_Akrotiri%2C_Thera_%28Santorini%29%2C_Minoan_Civilization%2C_16th_Century_BC%2C_National_Archaeological_Museum_of_Athens_%2814112030702%29.jpg. Image courtesy of the wikimedia user Butko)

tradition began already in the MBA. The ivory figure of a man carrying a calf from the Ayios Vasileios (Petrakos 2017, 20) is the latest of such examples. The figure was discovered in the LH IIIA2 context (Petrakos 2017, 20), but it cannot be excluded that it was produced earlier. He has a lock protruding from his head, which might suggest that the figure was a boy and not a man. More importantly, the boy might have been naked.

There is no iconographic evidence of the shaving practice itself. There have been attempts to identify the representation of boys with shaved scalps from Xeste 3 with the scene of the ritual shaving of the scalps (Doumas 1986; 1987; Karageorghis 1990). In these interpretations, the pottery vessels carried by some of the boys could be interpreted as ritual vessels used for washing the scalps after shaving. However, neither the process of shaving nor any tools used for cutting or shaving hair are represented, making this interpretation pure speculation without iconographic proof.

The same hairstyle is worn by young girls on LM IA frescoes from Thera (the Young Priestess fresco from the West House and young girls from Xeste 3). However, the girls are clothed in all of these representations, either in a version of a flounced skirt (Xeste 3 girls) or in a long garb covering the entire body (the Young Priestess). It is possible that the same hairstyle is depicted on female individuals in the MM IIIB–LM IA Sacred Grove fresco from the Palace of Knossos (*e.g.*, Immerwahr 1990, 173; Marinatos 1987, 2). The female individuals with this hairstyle in the fresco are again dressed in flounced skirts. Additional evidence of the same hairstyle comes from Mycenae in the Argolid and is represented by the 15th–14th-century BCE (LH II–LH IIIA phases) ivory group known as the Sacred Triad. The group represents two adult females and a little girl. The girl has a shaved scalp and is dressed in a skirt-like costume reaching the floor (Rehak 2007, 220–221; Rutter 2003, 39). In earlier research the child figure was interpreted as a boy (see discussion in Budin 2011, 284–287; Olsen 1998, 386–387), and thus the group has been explained as an early version of Demeter, Kore and Iacchos. However, an interesting comment was made by Stephanie Lynn Budin, who claims that the group might have been differently evaluated and interpreted within the context of consumption on the "Mycenaean" Greek Mainland and the context of production on "Minoan" Crete. As a result, the third figure might have been recognised as a girl on Crete and as a boy on the Mainland (Budin 2011, 287).

Several things can be concluded about the distinctions between representations of boys and girls. Boys are always represented naked, whereas girls never are. Furthermore, girls are always represented in costumes which are also worn by adult females. On the other hand, adult male individuals are never represented naked, except in the case of defeated warriors from the LM IA Naval Battle Scene fresco from Thera. However, this depiction probably has a different iconographic connotation, as, according to parallels in Egyptian iconography, flaccid penises on defeated enemies can be related to effemination in the iconography (Matić 2021). Gender distinction is also reflected in their skin colour, as male children are always represented in red, while female children are always represented in white, as are adults. The affiliation with a certain gender group was obviously clearly stated from earliest childhood and it is signified by skin colour in Aegean art. In representations of children, gender is also shown through the choice of costume (girls) or the absence of it (boys). The same hairstyles, however, are worn by both boys and girl, but are never worn by adults. In this respect, children's hairstyles are closely related to their age categories, but not to their gender identities.

Representations of children with clearly depicted hairstyles are rather rare in the later phases of the LBA (see Rehak 1997 for the change in the LBA Aegean art after the LM IB destruction on Crete). Consequently, it is difficult to make any comparison between earlier and later periods. However, certain representations might suggest that a change in the depiction of children took place. Some of the recently published LH IIIB2 fresco fragments from Tiryns represent at least one female figure carrying a smaller white figure (Fig. 5.4), possibly a girl (Maran, Paparimitriou and Thaler 2015, 109–111; Papadimitriou, Thaler and Maran 2015). In the publication the authors suggested that the carried white figure might equally be interpreted as a cult statue (Papadimitriou, Thaler and Maran 2015, 195–197, 202–206), which is an interpretation that this paper does not support. I believe that Papadimitriou, Thaler and Maran (2015, 203) are correct in attesting that the size of the figure and its depiction with dangling foot argue against its identification as a statue.

Fig. 5.4 Pomegranate Bearer fresco from Tiryns (after Papadimitriou, Thaler and Maran 2015, 176-177. Image courtesy of the authors)

The girl in the fresco (Fig. 5.4) is dressed in a flounced skirt and has long black hair. As shown by the Theran examples, flounced skirts are worn both by girls and adult women from the beginning of the LBA in the Aegean. However, the appearance of long hair on a little girl distances this representation from the earlier tradition. The girl's young age is no longer signified by the shaved scalp with locks. On the contrary, the hairstyle worn by the girl is obviously the same as on adult individuals on this and other contemporary depictions. In other words, hairstyle is no longer taken as an indicator of age on the representations of female individuals. Adult women differ from girls only in size. Although the same costumes appeared on both girls and adult women in the early phases of the LBA, the same hairstyles seem to be a feature of the later phases. This shows that female beauty ideals were no longer strictly related to age categories, as they had been in the earlier periods.

Representations of a child on each of the four gold foil sheets from the LH IIIC chamber tomb E at Kamini on Naxos (Zapheiropoulos 1966, 338, pl. 273b) might point to a similar development in the case of male children. All four sheets represent the same child, probably a boy. The child's sex might be indicated by an elongated triangle representing the penis. The boy is probably wearing a belt around his waist, as indicated by two parallel lines. It should be noted that the triangle could also represent the lower part of the boy's drawers, in which case it could be connected to the belt. The child has a full head of hair, although it is impossible to determine the exact hairstyle from the gold foil sheets. If the child is indeed naked, this would show a continuity in the depiction of male children as nude. However, similarly to representations of female children, the full head of hair distances the depiction from the earlier tradition, where a shaved scalp was the typical hairstyle for both male and female children.

Because of the scarcity of evidence, it is impossible to argue for the precise date for the change in children's hairstyle traditions. However, if the LH II–LH IIIA Sacred Triad ivory group from Mycenae and the boy from Ayios Vasileios still show earlier traits, while the LH IIIB2 fresco from Tiryns and LH IIIC gold foil sheet show clear distancing from the earlier tradition, the change must have taken place sometime late in the LH IIIA or early in the LH IIIB phase.

Adult hairstyles

Thanks to the large number of available depictions, the hairstyles of adults are a much broader topic. As a more detailed study of LBA Aegean hairstyles is out of the scope of this paper, this study will focus only on general changes. Adult women usually wear different variations of long hair (*e.g.*, Campstool fresco from Knossos), often decorated with several ribbons which can be used to shape hairstyles in different ways. However, it is impossible to generalise about female hairstyles for the entire duration of the LBA in the Aegean, as certain changes can be expected over time. Therefore, in order to fully understand the meaning behind the changes, a more detailed study is required. However, from a general observation of adult women's hairstyles it can be concluded that women always wear their hair long. Male hairstyles, however, show a different pattern.

There are several different types of male hairstyles appearing in the MM III–LM I period on Crete. The typical male figure of power and authority (Fig. 5.5) in this period was long-haired and dressed in a breechcloth (*e.g.*, Rehak 1995, 112–113; Matić and Franković 2017, 125). However, the male individuals dressed in other costumes, namely kilts, are represented with short hairstyles (Fig. 5.6). This shows a clear correlation

Fig. 5.5 Drawing of a sealing (CMS V Suppl. 1A, no. 142) from Chania representing a figure of power and authority (after Pini et al. 1992, 144. Image courtesy of the CMS Heidelberg)

between male hairstyles and costumes in the MM III–LM I. Furthermore, costumes and their corresponding hairstyles can be connected to certain activities in the iconographic sources. In this period, the combination of short hair and kilt can be connected to representations of warriors and lion hunters (Fig. 5.6; see also Franković and Matić 2020).

In the MH III–LH IIA on the Greek Mainland, which is parallel to the discussed period on Crete, the connection among costumes, beauty ideals and identities might have been more complex. Most of the iconographic examples found on the Mainland and dating to the early phases of the LBA are probably Cretan products. Consequently, these depictions might have been differently understood by Cretan and Mainland consumers. It is evident that the iconography of Cretan origin was abundantly used for the construction of identities on the Greek Mainland. However, possible multiple evaluations and consequently the significant regionality in the perception of these depictions should not be neglected. Again, the "Griffin Warrior" is relevant for the discussion.

Fig. 5.6 *Drawing of a sealstone (CMS I, no. 9) from Mycenae representing a lion hunter (after Sakellariou 1964, 20. Image courtesy of the CMS Heidelberg)*

As shown in the introduction, certain objects deposited in the grave were also depicted on some of the sealstones and signet rings accompanying the deceased. This type of self-referencing created a special connection between the deceased and the human figures using these objects in the representations. In two examples, self-referencing was clearly made in connection with a long-haired figure. The first example shows a female figure holding a staff (Davis and Stocker 2016, 643–645), while the second, known as the Pylos Combat Agate, shows a long-haired man dressed in a breechcloth and fighting other warriors with a sword (Stocker and Davis 2017). Although this is not a typical representation of an early LBA Aegean warrior and it can be historically evaluated in a different way (Franković and Matić 2020), it seems that in the context of the "Griffin Warrior" this depiction was taken as grounds for the creation of warrior identity. At the same time, this shows that the depicted scene was reinterpreted in the new context. In other words, although long hair was not one of the attributes of warrior identity on Crete, this example shows that through a reinterpretation of Cretan iconography, long hair could have been taken as a sign of warrior identity on the Greek Mainland in certain cases. Therefore, the analysis of the relationship between iconography and construction of identity in the early LBA Greek Mainland, in which bodily features played an important role, should focus more on specific case studies, rather than on generalised conclusions.

Although the LM II period on Crete brought about many changes, the long hairstyle was still used as the ideal of male beauty. This is visible on the depictions of male members of the elite on the Procession and Cup-bearer frescoes from the Palace of Knossos (Fig. 5.7; for the LM II date of the frescoes see Matić and Franković

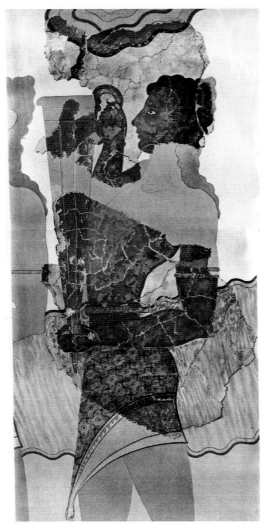

Fig. 5.7 Drawing of the Cup-bearer fresco from the Palace of Knossos representing an adult man in a procession (after Evans 1928, pl. XII)

2017, 113–115). However, we should be careful with the identification of long hair in the case of the Procession fresco from Knossos. The hairstyle of the Cup-bearer (Fig. 5.7) is the best-preserved hairstyle on the entire Procession fresco, but even in its case, the largest portion of the depiction is reconstructed. More importantly, the fresco is reconstructed in the lower part of the hairstyle, which would confirm its length. Nevertheless, according to the way the hair falls, which is paralleled in the contemporary Campstool fresco from Knossos, it seems more probable that the hair was long (see Koehl 1986, 103).

The same is suggested by the Egyptian 18th-Dynasty iconographic sources known from Theban tombs (TT), namely the tomb of Menkhepereseneb (TT 86) (Fig. 5.8) and the second phase of the tomb of Rekhmire (TT 100) in Thebes, which is dated to the LM II according to Aegean relative chronology. In these tombs, Aegean emissaries are represented in the same type of kilts as the figures from the Procession and Cup-bearer frescoes from Knossos (Matić and Franković 2017, 113). Long hairstyles are also worn by Aegean emissaries in earlier Theban tombs, those of Senenmut (TT 71), Useramun (TT 131) and Intef (TT 155), dating to the LM IB. This shows that the same hairstyle was used by the Cretan elite for their self-representation in the earlier LM IB and later LM II periods. This would not be problematic if there was not a clear change in the self-representation of Aegean emissaries in the transition between the LM IB and LM II (*e.g.*, Matić and Franković 2017). In earlier tombs (Senenmut, Useramun, Intef and the first phase of the Rekhmire), the Aegean emissaries are depicted wearing breechcloths, while they are wearing kilts in later tombs (Menkhepereseneb (TT 86) (Fig. 5.8) and the second phase of Rekhmire (TT 100)).

Fig. 5.8 Drawing of the representation of Aegean emissaries in the tomb of Menkheperreseneb (TT 86) at Thebes, Egypt (after Davies and Davies 1933, pl. V)

Although there is a clear change of costume, the issue of beauty ideals seems to be slightly more complicated. The figures wearing kilts in the MM III–LM IB always wear short hairstyles, which is not the case with the LM II, in which the figures dressed in kilts are represented with long hair.

Therefore, based on both Aegean and Egyptian iconographic sources, it can be concluded that the long hairstyle most probably continued to be used as the ideal of male beauty even after the transition from the MM III–LM I (Neopalatial) to the LM II (early Final Palatial) period. This continuation of beauty ideals is extremely important from the perspective of the noted change in the self-representation of elite members. Although antagonism between different groups existed in the iconography of the earlier period (Franković and Matić 2020, 365–367), it seems that with the beginning of the LM II, elite male iconography consists of a combination of old (*e.g.*, long hairstyles) and new (*e.g.*, the choice of kilt as the main costume) identity markers. Consequently, this new combination of markers resulted in the creation of a hybrid figure for the male elite member (Figs 5.7 and 5.8).

However, the new ideal of male beauty did not last for long in the Final Palatial period on Crete. It gradually moved towards a more pan-Aegean ideal, which dominated in the LM/LH IIIA–IIIB periods. During the LM IIIA, the hairstyles of male individuals seem to become shorter, as already noted on the so-called Captain of the Blacks fresco (Fig. 5.9), where male individuals dressed in kilts have short hair. The later example of the LH IIIA2 (*e.g.*, La Rosa 1999) painted sarcophagus from Ayia Triada depicts several male individuals dressed in different costumes. All except one have short hair. Importantly, the female individuals on the sarcophagus are wearing the same types of costumes as male individuals, but their hair is long. It seems that gender differentiation was made on the basis of hairstyle, while a certain costume might have been seen as appropriate for a certain activity and as such worn by both male and female individuals. The only male figure with long hair is the flute player. Nonetheless, the depiction of long hair on a musician might be significant, since the lyre player in the LH IIIB fresco from Pylos is also represented with long hair (Lang 1969, 79–80). There is another figure on the sarcophagus who is carrying a lyre and he is depicted

Filip Franković

Fig. 5.9 Drawing of the Captain of the Blacks fresco representing men dressed in kilts (after Evans 1928, pl. XIII)

with short hair. However, he is not playing the instrument, but only carrying it as part of the procession with gifts, unlike the long-haired musician. Therefore, it is possible that long hair was connected to the musical profession and it does not necessarily need to be understood as an indication of gender, although the possibility of effemination for a certain profession should not be dismissed. A similar interpretation of gender ambiguity can be found in Louise Hitchcock's (2000, 79–80) interpretation of the statue of the singer Ur-Nanshe found in the late 3rd-millenium BCE context at Mari on the Euphrates. In this case, gender ambiguity could have been culturally connected to specific segments of the religious sphere (Hitchcock 2000, 79–80). Similarly, the gender of the musicians in the LBA Aegean could have been created outside of the male-female division and could have had deeper cultural connotations. Despite the fact that it is possible to interpret the gender of the long-haired musician from the Ayia Triada sarcophagus in a context separate from the gendered depiction of hairstyles, it appears that the iconography shows a clear gender division between hairstyles from the LM IIIA1 on Crete, which did not exist in the earlier phases.

This claim can also be supported by the frescoes from the Greek Mainland, which confirm the gender division between male and female hairstyles. However, one should keep in mind that in many of the examples originating from the Mainland, the depictions of heads are not well preserved and do not provide complete information about hairstyle. In other cases, the hair is covered by warriors' helmets, which also makes the identification of hairstyle impossible. While some male hairstyles include longer locks of hair, they cannot be equated with the earlier long hairstyles known from the MM III–LM I and LM II in Crete. Rather, they represent a semi-long hairstyle which is clearly different from the elaborate hairstyles worn by female individuals, as well as the long-haired male individuals of the earlier periods. In the case of male individuals represented on the frescoes from the Mainland, the hair length never seems to go below the neckline. Possible exceptions from the LH/LM IIIA–IIIB are the already mentioned musicians, as well as bull-leapers, whose long hairstyles are inherited from earlier periods and are possibly related to this specific activity.

However, it is important to be aware that elite iconography was probably strongly influenced by trends. Therefore, the use of similar markers of identity by different elites in the Aegean might have created a common expression of bodily identity, in which the creative power of iconography played an important role.

Does a beard make a man?

The relationship of a beard to the male identity in the LBA Aegean has occasionally been mentioned by scholars, but not studied in detail. Marisa Ruiz-Gálvez and Eduardo Galán argue that beards are not worn by male figures in Aegean iconography before the LH IIIC, when the beard becomes a part of the warrior identity, as shown by the representations of warriors on the famous Warrior Vase from Mycenae (Ruiz-Gálvez and Galán 2013, 43, 46–47). However, there are several problems with such an interpretation.

In fact it is quite surprising that the beard has often been omitted from discussions about male identity in the Aegean, since one of the symbols of the Aegean LBA, the Mask of Agamemnon that was found within the LH I context of Grave Circle A at Mycenae, represents a bearded individual (for the discussion on the genuineness of the Mask of Agamemnon, see Dickinson 2005). While it is undoubtedly true that only a minority of the depictions show bearded men, as even the Mask of Agamemnon is the only bearded mask from Grave Circle A, there are still sufficient representations for an analysis. The earliest examples, dated between the MM/MH III and LM/LH I, are bearded heads represented on several sealstones found both on the Greek Mainland and Crete. These examples include sealstones from the Little Palace at Knossos (CMS II 3, no. 13), the Pediados region on Crete (CMS II 3, no. 196), Grave Gama of Grave Circle B at Mycenae (CMS I, no. 5) and a sealstone of unknown provenance (CMS VIII, no. 110). The last example mentioned has engravings on three sides. A bow and an arrow are depicted next to a head. The second depiction on the same sealstone represents an agrimi in the running pose, while the representation on the third side probably represents a bucranium. Three of these examples indicate a connection between bearded individuals and animal heads, which are represented either on the same or the opposite side of the sealstones. Ox heads are represented on the sealstone from the Little Palace at Knossos (CMS II 3, no. 13) and the sealstone of unknown provenance (CMS VIII, no. 110). Two deer heads and a boar head are represented on the sealstone from the Pediados region on Crete (CMS II 3, no. 196). A similar example of bearded male heads is found on a silver cup from Mycenae, which represents bearded male heads in profile facing left (Davis 1977, 297–300).

There are other examples of bearded individuals in clearly depicted scenes which allow for them to be contextualised. One such figure is represented on a signet ring (CMS I, no. 16) from Shaft grave IV of Grave Circle A at Mycenae. The decoration depicts a battle scene with four warriors, with the bearded individual sitting defeated on the floor. Another example is the bearded warrior fallen in battle, who is represented on the LH I Silver Battle Krater from Shaft grave IV of Grave Circle A at Mycenae (*e.g.*, Blakolmer 2007). Furthermore, there is a bearded archer on a fragment of a stone vase from Knossos (Evans 1930, 106, fig. 109; Fig. 5.10).

In addition, it is important to mention another possible representation. There is a possibility that the first figure dressed in a net-pattern coat leading the procession on the LM I Harvester vase from Ayia Triada might also be bearded. Unfortunately, this individual is carrying a staff which is blocking the view of his lower face. Another bearded individual is represented on a signet ring from the grave context at Mycenae (CMS I, no. 89), which is stylistically dated to the LH II. This representation depicts a bearded male figure in the Master of Animals pose, controlling two lions with the use of physical force.

Several things can be concluded on the basis of the analysis of the common features of bearded individuals. The beard itself does not cover the entire face, but rather grows only from the chin, while the moustache area on the upper lip seems to be shaved, which shows that this area of the face was carefully groomed. The only exception to this is the gold Mask of Agamemnon, which has a clearly defined moustache. In representations in which the hair is not covered by headgear (*e.g.*, CMS I, no. 16), bearded men share a common semi-short hairstyle (Fig. 5.10). This hairstyle is shorter than the long

Fig. 5.10 Drawing of a fragment of a stone vase from Knossos representing a bearded archer dressed in a kilt (after Evans 1930, 106, fig. 59)

hairstyles of contemporary elite members dressed in breechcloths (Fig. 5.5), but it is still longer than the short hair worn by non-bearded warriors dressed in kilts (Fig. 5.6; see above). A similar type of beard and hairstyle is worn by the bound prisoner from Keftiu (Crete), who is depicted in the Theban tomb of Kenamun (TT 93) in Egypt, which dates to the reign of Amenhotep II (Fig. 5.11). The connection of this particular hairstyle and the beard was noted already by Koehl (1986, 103), who links them to male individuals in later maturity.

Several different analyses of bearded figures in LBA Aegean iconography have been offered. Emily Vermeule (1983, 111–112) interpreted the beard as a sign of Mycenaean or Assyrian ethnicity, based on the bearded archer on the stone vase fragment from Knossos (Fig. 5.10). However, the beard cannot be interpreted as a marker of ethnic identity in this case. The figure is

Fig. 5.11 Photo of a detail from the tomb of Kenamun (TT 93) in Thebes, Egypt representing a bound prisoner from Keftiu (Crete) on the left (Davies 1930, pl. XI, A)

wearing a typical Aegean costume, which makes his identification as an Assyrian improbable (for more on the problem of identification of foreigners in Aegean art, see *e.g.*, Blakolmer 2002; 2012). Moreover, depictions of bearded individuals are found both on Crete and the Greek Mainland in the early stages of the LBA. Nanno Marinatos (1986, 43) proposed a different solution and argued that the bearded head combined with a bow and arrow on the sealstone of unknown provenance (CMS VIII, no. 110) represents a hunter. Marinatos argued that there is a close connection between hunting and sacrifice, and proposed that beardedness symbolises priests. While the three scenes depicted on this sealstone might be connected, there are several problems with Marinatos's conclusion. First, bearded individuals are often shown as bowmen on other depictions, which explains the depiction of the bow and arrow together with the head. Second, the costumes worn by bearded archers differ from those of individuals performing sacrifices, since archers usually wear early versions of kilts, while the individuals performing sacrifices wear long skirts and do not have beards (*e.g.*, CMS I, no. 80). More importantly, there are no representations of bearded individuals in the LBA Aegean iconographic sources which would connect them to the performance of any priestly activities.

Franković and Matić have suggested that the beards represented on male figures in battle scenes can be taken as indicators of their age (Franković and Matić 2020, 358; also Koehl 1986, 103). They conclude that bearded warriors are usually represented as archers when they are depicted with a weapon and they are never associated with any other kind of weapon. As such, bearded archers are placed at the bottom of the warrior hierarchy as expressed through the choice of weapon. Older warriors could have been removed from the physically more demanding center of the battle and used as archers (Franković and Matić 2020, 358). This considered, the bearded head represented with the bow and arrow can be understood as a bowman, rather than a priest, and can thus be connected to warrior iconography. A possible correlation of bowmen to hunting iconography also has to be mentioned. Two figures hunting a deer with bows from a chariot are represented on a signet ring (CMS I, no. 15) from Shaft grave IV of Grave Circle A at Mycenae. However, the deer hunters in this example do not have beards.

While Franković and Matic's conclusion (2020) is supported by the evidence of available battle representations, it is important to note that it cannot be applied to all representations of bearded individuals. Other representations of bearded men cannot be clearly related to the lowest rank of hierarchical relations, but rather seem to represent individuals closer to the top. For example, the Mask of Agamemnon can be related to the richest elite burials, while the representation of the Master of Animals on a signet ring (CMS I, no. 89) from Mycenae undoubtedly represents a figure of power and authority. Even the possible bearded individual from the Ayia Triada Harvester vase seems to be leading the group. Therefore, it may be concluded that bearded individuals can be equated with those individuals at the top of the hierarchy in certain cases, while in others they can be related to the bottom, depending on the context of the scene.

There are several different reasons why the beard could be understood as an attribute of age. First of all, age could have been seen as an advantage or a disadvantage in different contexts. At least in the iconographic context, older warriors might have been kept away from the main battle due to their inability to take part in the physically more demanding parts of the battle. On the other hand, older individuals might have been respected in terms of authority and leadership (*e.g.*, the Mask of Agamemnon; Harvester Vase; signet ring from Mycenae – CMS I, no. 89). Depending on the context of an activity, age might have had different connotations and was therefore differently represented in the iconography, although the meaning of a beard remained the same.

The second argument is that there are no unambiguous representations of elderly individuals in LBA Aegean iconography. Since there are representations of children from the LBA Aegean iconographic sources, representations of the elderly can also be expected. Except for the bearded men and possibly a few individuals with prominent abdomens (*e.g.*, the individual playing a systrum on the Harvester Vase from Ayia Triada or some of the bronze figurines from Crete; see Verlinden 1984, 78–79, pls 14–15, nos. 30–31), no other representations can be clearly identified as depictions of elderly individuals. Unfortunately, the available representations of individuals with prominent abdomens do not allow for a more detailed analysis. Nevertheless, obesity does not need to be connected with age and could have had various iconographic connotations. The beard and its correspondent hairstyle can be seen as the main markers of age of elderly individuals, similarly as hairstyles and sometimes the size of the body indicate age in representations of children. When observed in the context of all human figures represented in LBA Aegean iconography, there is a relatively small number of both children and elderly individuals. It can therefore be concluded that the general category of the adult probably represents the central beauty ideal, while children and elderly individuals appear only in specific contexts related to certain activities.

There are several problematic areas in the analysis of the representations of bearded individuals in the LH/LM IIIA–LH/LM IIIB. While beards do appear, they are mainly represented on the heads of figurines. Examples from this period include the head of a bearded male individual made of green schist, found in House A at Grotta on Naxos (Cosmopoulos 1998, 132) and heads of terracotta figurines with protruding bearded chins (French 1971, 148; Mayer 1892, 189–196; Mylonas 1937, 237). As there is no clear context for these examples, it is impossible to discuss the meaning of the beard in these periods. However, it is clear that representations of bearded individuals appear in a minority of the depictions and therefore cannot be interpreted as the beauty ideal of the time, which is further supported by the fact that there are no representations of bearded individuals from glyptic and frescoes.

Nevertheless, the later LH IIIC period shows a different pattern. Iconographic sources from the Aegean from the LH IIIC are scarce, with the exception of vase painting. This is quite problematic, since vase paintings show very few details. It can be argued that beards are represented on the warriors on the Warrior vase from Mycenae. This is quite important, as the back side of the same vessel represents bearded warriors wearing a spiky "hedgehog" helmet type. A recently discovered vase from Tiryns represents warriors wearing the same type of helmet (Maran and Papadimitriou 2017, 40–41), but they are not bearded. It can be observed that in the case of the Warrior vase from Mycenae, the beard comes straight from the helmets of the warriors. It therefore could be argued that the represented lines do not depict beards, but rather cheek-guards. However, it is not clear why cheek-guards would be depicted as a part of a certain type of helmet in some cases, while in others these would be left out, as is the case with the newly discovered vase from Tiryns (Maran and Papadimitriou 2017, 40–41). The reasons for the exclusion of cheek-guards could be various, such as the preferences of different artists or the more subtle and chronologically untraceable change to the helmet type. Nevertheless, while helmets are represented as black with white dots, the beards/cheek-guards are represented as completely black. If this feature represented a part of the helmet, it would probably have been represented in the same manner as the rest of the helmet. Even in this case, the representations of beards do not include a moustache, since these are limited to the chins and the lower jaws of the bearded individuals, which, as in earlier periods, indicates that facial hair was carefully groomed.

As both vases date to the same period, it is possible that after the fall of the palatial system different groups of warriors expressed their identities in a similar way, sometimes using the same attributes of the warrior identity. Considering this, the distinction between these groups is not based on specific identity attributes, but rather on their combination (Hitchcock and Maeir 2016). The beard might have been part of the expression of common identity in one warrior group, while it might have been neglected in another. In other words, while different warrior groups might have used the same military equipment and costumes, the beard might have been the distinguishing factor between them.

The connection between warrior identities and beauty treatments was observed by Paul Treherne (1995) and elaborated on in his influential article on "the warrior's beauty". However, the general theoretical framework introduced by Treherne (1995) is open to criticism (*e.g.*, Frieman *et al.* 2017) and his conclusions seem rather decontextualised. Nevertheless, Treherne (1995, 110–111, 114, 121, 123–127) correctly pointed out the importance of toilet articles in the formation of a warrior's identity through beauty rituals (during their life or even after their death). Moreover, Treherne's (1995, 125) conclusion that most of the representations from Bronze Age Europe depict men as either beardless or carefully groomed can well be applied to LBA Aegean iconography. Therefore, as recently shown on the example of the LH IIIC Crete (Tyree, Hitchcock and Barnett 2020), toilet articles used for shaving, tweezing and grooming must have played an important role in the formation of beauty standards and bodily identities in the LBA Aegean.

Objects for personal care in the Late Bronze Age Aegean

Objects for personal care have been found in different LBA contexts in the Aegean, although the majority of these come from funerary contexts. This broad category includes mirrors, razors, tweezers, combs, earpicks/earspoons and possibly even knives, often found as assemblages (for a general definition of objects for personal care in the LBA Aegean, see Papaefthymioy-Papanthimou 1979; also Dickinson 1977, 83–84; Hakulin 2013, 41, 46–47; Paschalidis 2012, 547; Salavoura 2012). Most of these objects can be used in hair treatment processes, such as cutting, grooming or shaving hair on different parts of the body. This paper presents separate case studies for mirrors, razors and tweezers, and considers the roles they might have played in the creation of different beauty ideals and gender identities.

Mirrors

In the LBA Aegean, mirrors are in most cases found in graves. However, even in funerary contexts, they do not appear everywhere with the same frequency. They appear mostly in graves around Chania and Knossos on Crete, in the Argolid and

Messenia on the Greek Mainland, and rarely in
other parts of Greece (Paschalidis 2012, 551–553).
Importantly, Cretan examples are usually found
in contexts dating to the LM II–LM IIIA, a time
often connected to the "Mycenaean" predominance
over the island (Hakulin 2013, 41–42; Paschalidis
2012, 551–553). LBA Aegean mirrors are usually
made of bronze (Fig. 5.12), often with the addition
of an ivory handle. However, there is also an
example of a crystal disc from the Temple
Repositories from the Palace of Knossos, that could
be interpreted as a mirror (Panagiotaki 1999,
124–125).

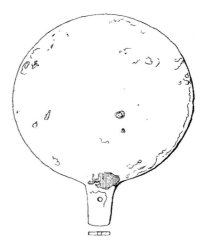

*Fig. 5.12 Drawing of the bronze mirror
discovered in Tomb 61 at Ialysos on
Rhodes (adjusted after Benzi 1992, pl.
180: g. Image courtesy of the author)*

Mirrors are also known from iconographic
sources. A representation of a woman sitting on a
throne and holding a mirror in her hand is
depicted on two signet rings. In both cases, there
is another female individual standing in front of
the enthroned woman. The first example is a
signet ring from the LH IIA tomb of the "Griffin
warrior" at Pylos (Davis and Stocker 2016, 645–
646). As argued earlier, the seated female figure
holding a mirror could have been used as a
representation of the buried male individual,
especially because the breasts are not depicted on
her exposed chest. The provenance of the second
signet ring (CMS XI, no. 30; Fig. 5.13) is not known,
but it can be stylistically dated to the LM/LH I–
LM/LH II. This signet ring depicts a slightly
different scene, as it seems that the enthroned
woman is handing the mirror over to the woman
standing in front of her, while the Pylos signet
ring represents the woman in front of the throne

*Fig. 5.13 Drawing of a signet ring
(CMS XI, no. 30) representing a seated
woman holding a mirror (after Pini et
al. 1988, 44–45. Image courtesy of the
CMS Heidelberg)*

holding a bull's horn (see Davis and Stocker 2016, 645) in her hands. Additional
depictions of women holding mirrors are found on both sides of an ivory handle
of a mirror found in a chamber tomb at Mycenae (*e.g.*, Paschalidis 2012, pl. CXLIa;
Vlassopoulou-Karydi 2000).

The available iconographic evidence always depicts the mirror in relationship
to female individuals, which might suggest that mirrors were gendered in
iconography. None of the depictions of women handling mirrors were discovered
on Crete, while both the signet ring from the tomb of the "Griffin warrior" (Davis
and Stocker 2016, 645–646) and the mirror with the depiction of two women

handling mirrors (*e.g.*, Paschalidis 2012, pl. CXLIa; Vlassopoulou-Karydi 2000) were found on the Greek Mainland. However, it is important to keep in mind that the two signet rings representing mirrors probably date to the LM I. They are probably Cretan products or at least represent Cretan topics. Therefore, it is possible that a certain association of females with mirrors in iconography existed both in their context of creation on Crete and on the Greek Mainland. As mirrors were not deposited in graves on Crete during this period, it is impossible to argue that they can be associated with a certain gender group. One could argue that on the signet ring CMS XI, no. 30 (Fig. 5.13), the mirror is being handed over by the enthroned female figure to the one standing in front of her. In that context, the mirror might have been understood as a symbol of status handed from one female individual to another. It could be speculated that such a practice is the reason why mirrors were not deposited in MM IIIB–LM IB funerary contexts on Crete. However, the scarce funerary data from this period does not allow further development of this argument. It seems that the deposition of mirrors in grave contexts on Crete from the LM II onwards occurs simultaneously with their disappearance from iconographic sources.

The deposition of mirrors in the graves on the Greek Mainland shows a completely different practice and possibly a different understanding of the object. As mirrors are present in both male and female graves in different phases of the LBA, they cannot be considered as objects gendered through burial practice. Kostas Paschalidis (2012, 555) notes that the mirrors in female burials outnumber those in male burials in the five to one ratio, with 71 reported examples in female and 15 in male burials. However, it is important to keep in mind that mirrors are often attributed to male or female individuals on the basis of other "typically" male or female finds found within the tombs (*e.g.*, Konstantinidi 2001, 247; Paschalidis 2012, 551), rather than on proper anthropological examination of skeletal remains. Even if the premise that certain assemblages point to certain gender groups in funerary contexts is true, it has been shown by Paul Rehak (1995, 102) that the "male iconography" connected to warrior ideology can be found in the burial contexts of female individuals. In addition, a possible reinterpretation of the female individual holding a mirror on the signet ring from the grave of the "Griffin Warrior" shows a different understanding of the status of mirrors in the iconography of the early stages of the LBA. As the woman holding the mirror was probably interpreted as a man in the context of the Greek Mainland, it can be argued that the iconography representing mirrors was not clearly gendered in this context.

Tweezers

Tweezers have been found both in female (*e.g.*, Paschalidis 2012, 547–548) and male LBA graves (*e.g.*, Paschalidis and McGeorge 2009, 92–93), often in combination with razors. Therefore, the claim of some authors (*e.g.*, Papadopoulos 1999, 269) that tweezers are associated with female and razors with male warrior burials cannot be sustained. Paschalidis and McGeorge offer an interesting viewpoint on the appearance of tweezers in male burials (2009, 93), interpreting them as tools for extracting arrowheads from wounded warriors, rather than as part of the bodily care equipment, as is usually suggested (*e.g.*, Cavanagh and Mee 1998, 52; Deger-Jalkotzy 2006, 152, 172–173; Eder and Jung 2005, 490). The use of tweezers as a medical instrument is supported by Paschalidis and McGeorge (2009, 93), due to the fact that tweezers have been found as a part of the assemblage of medical equipment in the LBA context (Protonotariou-Deilaki 1973, 92–93).

While the archaeological record cannot confirm this claim, it still provides an interesting perspective on the use of the object and its connection to gender categories. In other words, although the object itself might not have been gendered, its use might have had a gendered connotation. By being used in a certain context it would acquire its gendered meaning, which was later used in the construction of identity through burial practice. Finally, it is important to keep in mind that a single object might have been used for multiple purposes.

Razors

Razors, also most commonly found in burial contexts, have often been associated with the LBA warrior identity and male aesthetics (*e.g.*, Driessen and Macdonald 1984, 59; Papadopoulos 1999, 269–270; Ruiz-Gálvez and Galán 2013, 48; Treherne 1995), although they can be connected to female individuals as well (*e.g.*, Pachalidis 2012). The number of razors deposited in funerary contexts varies across different periods and regions. Only a minority of the Cretan examples found in funerary contexts date to the MM IIIB–LM IB, while most can be dated to later periods (Hakulin 2013, 64; also see Weber 1996). However, this is more indicative of the general trend for the deposition of bronze finds in the funerary context of LBA Crete (*e.g.*, Hakulin 2013, 90; Popham, Catling and Catling 1974, 252–257; Wilkie 1987, 131), than it has to do with bodily care. Some of the authors (Carter 1994, 136) have pointed out that the typological term razor expresses the modern understanding of this term, which has not been confirmed by the archaeological context. However, there are not many other classes of objects which can be associated with shaving and depilation procedures. In addition to knives (*e.g.*, Hakulin 2013, 64–65) and lithic artefacts (blades and flakes), bronze razors seem to have been the most probable tool for shaving.

LBA bronze razors can be divided into two main types, the leaf-shaped type (Fig. 5.14), and the single-edged type (Fig. 5.15) (for an overview of the examples from the Aegean see Weber 1996). These differ both typologically and chronologically, as the leaf-shaped type already appears in the Early Bronze Age (*e.g.*, Branigan 1970, 20, 71), while the development of the single-edged razor can probably be dated before the end of LM IIIA1, as shown by an example from the tomb at Sellopoulou (Popham, Catling and Catling 1974, 245; Wilkie 1987, 133). It seems that towards the end of LM IIIA the single-edged razor replaced the leaf-shaped one, which was used in the earlier phases of the LBA (Hood *et al.* 1958, 235; Weber 1996, 34–44).

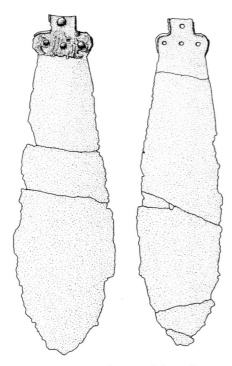

Fig. 5.14 Drawing of two leaf-shaped razors discovered in Pit 3 of the Nichoria tholos. Scale 1:2 (adjusted after Weber 1996, pl. 12, nos. 131–132. Image courtesy of the PBF series)

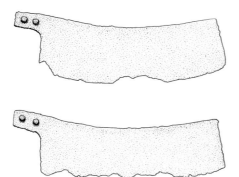

Fig. 5.15 Drawing of two single-edge razors discovered in Pit 3 of the Nichoria tholos. Scale 1:2 (adjusted after Weber 1996, pl. 34, nos. 295–296. Image courtesy of the PBF series)

Although these two types of razor rarely appear together in the same context (Hood *et al.* 1958, 235; Wilkie 1987, 133), it can be argued that the transition from the use of the earlier to the later type was a slow and gradual process. This is shown by their probable connection to the same individual in Tomb 4 of the Zapher Papoura cemetery at Knossos (Hood *et al.* 1958, 235) and their simultaneous appearance in the LH IIIA2 hoard of bronze artefacts from the MME tholos at Nichoria (Figs 5.14 and 5.15; see Wilkie 1987, 131–134). While it can be argued that the nature of the latter deposit does not allow any definite conclusions to be made about the simultaneous appearance of both razor types, since the objects in the hoard might have had different and complicated personal biographies, Wilkie (1987, 133) convincingly argued that there is no reason to believe that the single-edged razors were of later date than the rest of the hoard.

In addition, the change in the use of a certain type of object could have had other repercussions. The use of a razor is a bodily experience. The person using it can easily be injured/cut, therefore its proper use requires specific knowledge. Furthermore, the use of a razor changes/influences the perception of the body, as it is necessary to understand the interaction between the object and the body to avoid possible injuries. In other words, the razor becomes an active creator of someone's perception of their own body, rather than being a mere tool. As the use of leaf-shaped and single-edged razors require somewhat different skills, it is possible that the change of the razor type slightly changed the perception of its user's body. Consequently, the change in the razor type during the LH/LM IIIA might point to a gradual change in the perception of shaving and beauty procedures. A similar argument has recently been suggested for Italian-type razors appearing on Crete in the LM IIIC (see Kanta and Kontopodi 2011; Tyree, Hitchcock and Barnett 2020)

As razors in funerary contexts can be connected to both male and female individuals, it can be argued that the objects themselves were not gendered. However, the process of shaving can be considered gendered from two standpoints. First, as male and female individuals shave different parts of the body, either due to cultural conventions or biological differences, it can be argued that they also have a different perception of this process. Moreover, it is important to keep in mind that shaving can be performed on one's own body, sometimes with the help of a mirror, or by one person shaving another.

Second, the cultural preferences determining who is allowed to perform shaving can differ from one culture to another (also see Chapter 3 by Uroš Matić in this volume). An interesting ethnographic parallel was presented by Radcliffe-Brown in his overview of the hair-dressing tradition on the Great Andaman island (Radcliffe-Brown 1922, 483), where the same hairstyle, a shaved scalp with a skull-cap of hair left in place, is shared by male and female individuals, and both groups' heads are shaved by the same object. Therefore, it can be argued that neither the shaving objects nor the hairstyles are clearly gendered. The process of shaving, however, differs in this respect, as it is most often performed by female individuals, while male individuals perform it extremely rarely, which clearly makes it a gendered practice. Interestingly, it seems that on the Little Andaman island women and older men share the same hairstyle (Radcliffe-Brown 1922, 483), showing the correlation of an age group of one gender to another gender group, possibly effeminising older male individuals, at least through hairstyles.

In the context of the LBA Aegean it is hard to argue whether shaving practice was gendered, as no clear depictions of shaving are preserved. However, as shown by the iconographic sources in the MM IIIB–LM IB and the following LM II on Crete, the similar hairstyles of male and female individuals suggest that gender was not created through every aspect of bodily beauty, but rather through a combination of characteristics such as hairstyle, skin colour, costume, etc.

There is another group of objects that can be associated with the shaving procedure. Stone blades, mostly produced of obsidian, have often been found in Early Bronze Age funerary contexts in the Aegean and are usually interpreted as razors (*e.g.*, Bosanquet 1896, 54; Branigan 1970, 71; Carter 1994, 127–133, 136; 1998, 150, 174). The similarity of form between obsidian blades and bronze leaf-shaped razors cannot be denied, but interpreting them as analogous can be problematic (Carter 1994, 136). The use of obsidian blades as razors is also confirmed by ethnographic (Clark 1978; Gallagher 1977; Radcliffe-Brown 1922, 483) and historical data (Fletcher 1976; MacCurdy 1900, 421). One should not forget that even an ordinary flake can be successfully used as a shaving tool (see Radcliffe-Brown 1922, 483). While there are some problems in associating obsidian blades with razors (Carter 1994, 136–137), it is possible to determine whether a blade was used as a razor by using different methods, such as the analysis of the wear patterns (*e.g.*, Carter 1997) or the residues (of hair or blood) preserved on the edge (see *e.g.*, Loy 1983; 1985; Loy and Wood 1989).

Furthermore, in the Early Bronze Age, obsidian blades are sometimes found with other beauty utensils (Branigan 1970, 70–71; Carter 1994, 131), most commonly bronze tweezers (*e.g.*, Mylonas 1959, 78; Renfrew 1972, 531; Taylour 1972, 211). A burial from the cemetery at Ayios Stephanos might point to a continuation of this practice, or its recurrence in the transition between the Middle Bronze Age to the LBA (Taylour 1972, 218–219, 221), although it has been argued that such a depositional practice was abandoned in the Middle Bronze Age (Carter 1994, 133). Tristan Carter (1994, 137) argued that it would be hard to precisely say why the obsidian blades were placed with the deceased. However, their placement in relation to the body might be indicative. In some cases, the blades and flakes were placed close to the head (Taylour 1972, 211, 218–219), possibly symbolically showing a correlation to shaving or hair treatments.

Archaeological evidence also points to the importance of obsidian blades in the LBA, as for example the LM II–LM IIIA1 (Final Palatial) deposit of obsidian blades from the rooms to the north and west of the Throne Room in the Palace of Knossos (Carter 2004). Between 5–10% of the blades show traces of use related to linear cutting of soft or medium hard material, such as flesh, plant, textile or hair (Carter 2004, 274). Although the blades might have been used for cutting hair, the marks connected to linear cutting show that the blades were not used for shaving, as it would have shown a different motion pattern. The importance of obsidian blades in the Palace at Knossos, more precisely in its West Wing, is documented from the MM IB (Carter 2004, 278; Panagiotaki 1998, 178–80, pls 35–6; Panagiotaki 1999, 22–30). However, a larger portion of the material dates to the MM III - LM IA (Carter 2004, 278). Especially important is the Room of the Great Pithos, which was identified by Evans as "a barber's shop" (Carter 2004, 278; Evans 1935, 635, n. 2; Panagiotaki 1999, 30), due to the large quantity of obsidian blades found there. While this assemblage suggests that the production took place in the West Wing of the palace (Panagiotaki 1999, 30), Tristan Carter (2004, 280) rightfully pointed out that these deposits do not simply represent workshops, but rather specialised places where production was related to final consumption in activities such as shaving or cutting hair. This interpretation can be well related to the importance of hairstyles in the creation of elite identities in the MM III–LM I (Naopalatial) and LM II (early Final Palatial) periods, as argued earlier in the text on the basis of iconography.

Another interesting example was found at Praesos on Crete. Two obsidian blades were found in the Geometric tomb in association with toilet articles (Marshall and Bosanquet 1901, 251). The blades were probably originally produced in the earlier period, but were found and reinterpreted in the Geometric period (Carter 1994, 136). It seems that the association of obsidian blades with toilet articles continued in later periods as well.

Conclusion

While these are often neglected, the differences in the representation of human figures between different chronological phases of the LBA Aegean can be traced in the iconography. Consequently, the changes to the depictions of beauty ideals between different periods can also be traced. In the early stages of the LBA on Crete and the Cycladic Islands, more precisely, the LM IA–LM IB, beauty ideals do not seem to be highly gendered. Rather than showing a relationship to a certain gender group, hairstyles and beauty ideals in these periods tend to show the difference in age, as already suggested by Lee (2000, 118). However, this does not mean that the depictions of human figures were not gendered, but rather that gender identity was created through a specific combination of iconographic attributes, such as hairstyles, costumes or skin colour. Age groups seem to be more closed when it comes to hairstyles and beauty ideals, as some attributes seem to be age-specific. In other words, children belonging to both gender groups share a common hairstyle, which is never worn by adults. At the same time, both female and male adult individuals share the same hairstyles. Therefore, the difference in hairstyle between children and adults seems to be related more to their age identities than to their gender identities. A similar principle applies to older adults, as it seems probable that the beard and its corresponding hairstyle were used to indicate male individuals of an older age. In different iconographic contexts the beard, and consequently old age, could have acquired different connotations. While in the context of battle scenes old age might have been understood as a disadvantage, as shown by multiple examples (the Silver Battle Krater; a fragment of the stone vase from Knossos (Fig. 5.10); a signet ring from Mycenae – CMS I, no. 16), in other cases, such as the Mask of Agamemnon, the Harvester Vase from Ayia Triada or the signet ring from Mycenae (CMS I, no. 89), old age might have been taken as a sign of power and authority.

Such a view can be applied both to Crete and the Greek Mainland, as the objects with iconographic representations have been found on the Greek Mainland and the themes of these representations most probably originated from Crete. Therefore, it can be argued that Cretan ideals of beauty not only resembled those on the Greek Mainland, but also actively influenced the creation of identity of the new rising "Mycenaean" elite. As argued, the creation of identity on the Greek Mainland is sometimes carried out through self-referencing in burial contexts where iconographic representations on objects placed in graves usually represent other objects buried together with the deceased. It seems that the represented images have been reinterpreted as depictions of the deceased in some cases. This shows a close relationship between male and female beauty ideals, as self-referencing is sometimes carried out through the depiction of a person of the opposite gender.

In the LM IA–LM IB/LH I–LH IIA period the deposition of the utensils for bodily care in grave contexts differs on Crete and the Greek Mainland. Objects like mirrors, razors, tweezers or earpicks were abundantly deposited in graves on the Greek

Mainland, whereas this is not the case on Crete. Such a practice fits into the general trend of deposition of other metal finds, such as swords, in burial contexts. A similar deposition practice has been recently noted by Michael Galaty (2018) for Egyptian imports.

The later stages of the LBA show different patterns both in iconography and burial practices. First, the LM II period on Crete was a period of significant changes, probably caused by the change of the Knossos elite which took control over Crete. The new elite created a new and hybrid way of self-representation by using features connected to two different and parallel elite iconographies of the LM IA–LM IB (see Franković and Matić 2020, 366). The long hairstyle shared by men and women in the earlier period was used in combination with the kilt as a new way of representing male members of the elite, as shown both by Aegean and Egyptian iconographic sources. However, this seems to have been only a temporary change, as in the later LM IIIA phase significant distancing from the earlier tradition can be observed. The same applies to the LH IIIA on the Greek Mainland, which might again have been influenced by the iconography originating in Crete.

In the aforementioned LH IIIA period, male and female individuals no longer have the same hairstyles in iconography. At the same time, children and adults belonging to the same gender group begin to have the same hairstyle in representations. Such a change shows distancing from the older tradition and the creation of a new one, in which affiliation to a certain gender group in iconographic representations proves more important than affiliation to an age group, at least when it comes to beauty standards. Furthermore, representations of human figures with clear gender division in beauty ideals seem to move towards a more pan-Aegean tradition. A similar phenomenon can be traced in burial practices, where from the LM II onwards metal finds, especially beauty utensils, were deposited in funerary contexts. The fact that such a practice has often been interpreted as a sign of the "Mycenaean" predominance, which originated from the Greek Mainland, over the previously "Minoan" Crete points to the appearance of a vast number of similarities in the expression of identity. Therefore, it can be argued that the similar expressions of identity appear sometime in the LM II period on Crete and the LH IIB on the Greek Mainland, both in funerary and iconographic contexts, and reach their final form during the LH/LM IIIA in both regions. The creation of new and shared beauty ideals together with the development of a similar attitude towards burial practices suggest that there were similar perceptions of gender and age identities across the Aegean.

Acknowledgements

I am thankful to Ana Popović for revising the language of the paper. I am especially grateful to Gerda Henkel Foundation for financing my PhD studies at the University of Heidelberg.

Abbreviations

CMS I: Sakellariou, A. (ed.) (1964) *Die minoischen und mykenischen Siegel des Nationalmuseums in Athen.* CMS I. Berlin, Gebrüder Mann Verlag.

CMS II: Platon, N. and Pini, I. (eds) (1984) *Iraklion, Archäologisches Museum. Teil 3. Die Siegel der Neupalastzeit.* CMS II, 3. Berlin, Gebrüder Mann Verlag.

CMS V: Pini, I. (ed.) (1992) *Kleinere griechische Sammlungen. Ägina - Korinth.* CMS V, Suppl. 1A. Berlin, Gebrüder Mann Verlag.

CMS VI: Hughes-Brock, H. and Boardman, J. (eds) (2009) *Oxford. The Ashmolean Museum.* CMS VI. Mainz, Philipp von Zabern.

CMS XI: Pini, I., Betts, J.H., Gill, M.A.V., Sürenhagen, D. and Waetzold, H. (1988) *Kleinere europäische Sammlungen.* CMS XI. Berlin, Gebrüder Mann Verlag.

Bibliography

Abramowitz, K. (1980) Frescoes from Ayia Irini, Keos. Parts II–IV. *Hesperia* 49 (1), 57–85.

Alberti, B. (1997) *Archaeology and Masculinity in Late Bronze Age Knossos.* Unpublished PhD thesis, University of Southampton.

Alberti, B. (2001) Faience goddesses and ivory bull-leapers: the aesthetics of sexual difference at Late Bronze Age Knossos. *World Archaeology* 33 (2), 189–205.

Alberti, B. (2002) Gender and the figurative art of Late Bronze Age Knossos. In Y. Hamilakis (ed.) *Labyrinth Revisited: Rethinking 'Minoan' Archaeology,* 98–117. Oxford, Oxbow Books.

Alberti, B. (2005) Bodies in prehistory: beyond the sex/gender split. In P.P.A. Funari, A. Zarankin and E. Stovel (eds) *Global Archaeological Theory: Contextual Voices and Contemporary Thoughts,* 107–120. London and New York, Kluwer Academic and Plenum Publishers.

Alberti, B. (2012) Queer prehistory. Bodies, performativity, and matter. In D. Bolger (ed.) *A Companion to Gender in Prehistory,* 86–107. New Jersey, Wiley-Blackwell.

Alexandri, A. (1994) *Gender Symbolism in LBA Aegean Glyptic Art.* Unpublished PhD thesis, University of Cambridge.

Archontidu-Argyri, A. (ed.) (2006) Ψαρά. Ένας σταθμός στην Περιφέρεια του Μυκηναϊκού κόσμου. Psara, Hypurgeio Politismu kai Turismu, 20. Ephoreia Proïstorikon kai Klasikon Archaiotiton.

Benzi, M. (1992) *Rodi e la civiltà Micenea.* Incunabula Graeca 94. Roma, Gruppo Editoriale Internazionale.

Blakolmer, F. (2002) Afrikaner in der minoischen Ikonographie? Zum Fremdenbild in der bronzezeitlichen Ägäis. *Ägypten und Levante* 12, 71–94.

Blakolmer, F. (2007) The silver battle krater from Shaft Grave IV at Mycenae: evidence of fighting "heroes" on Minoan palace walls at Knossos? In S.P. Morris and R. Laffineur (eds) *Epos: Reconsidering Greek Epic and Aegean Bronze Age Archaeology,* 213–224. Aegaeum 28. Liège, Peeters Publishers.

Blakolmer, F. (2012) The missing "barbarians": some thoughts on ethnicity and identity in Aegean Bronze Age iconography. In A. Papadopoulos (ed.) *Recent Research and Perspectives on the Late Bronze Age Eastern Mediterranean,* 53–77. Talanta 44. Amsterdam, Dutch Archaeological and Historical Society.

Bosanquet, R.C. (1896) Notes from the Cyclades. *The Annual of the British School at Athens* 3 (1896/1897), 52–70.

Branigan, K. (1970) *The Tombs of Mesara. A Study of Funerary Architecture and Ritual in Southern Crete, 2800-1700 B.C.* London, Duckworth.

Budin, S.L. (2011) *Images of Woman and Child from the Bronze Age: Reconsidering Fertility, Maternity, and Gender in the Ancient World.* Cambridge, Cambridge University Press.

Carter, T. (1994) Southern Aegean fashion victims: an over looked aspect of Early Bronze Age burial practices. In N. Ashton and A. David (eds) *Stories in Stone*, 127–144. Lithic Studies Society Occasional Paper 4. London, Lithic Studies Society.

Carter, T. (1997) Blood and tears: a Cycladic case study in microwear analysis. The use of obsidian blades from graves as razors? In M.A. Bustillo and A. Ramos-Millan (eds) *Silicious Rocks and Culture*, 537–551. Monografica Arte y Aequeologia 42. Granada, Universidad de Granada.

Carter, T. (1998) *"Through a Glass Darkly": Obsidian and Society in the Southern Aegean Early Bronze Age.* Unpublished PhD thesis, University College London.

Carter, T. (2004) Transformative processes in liminal spaces: craft as ritual action in the Throne Room area. In G. Cadogan, E. Hatzaki and A. Vasilakis (eds) *Knossos: Palace, City, State*, 73–282. British School at Athens Studies 122. London, British School at Athens.

Cavanagh, W. and Mee, C. (1998) *A Private Place: Death in Prehistoric Greece.* Studies in Mediterranean Archaeology 125. Jonsered, Paul Åströms.

Chapin, A.P. (2007) Boys will be boys: youth and gender identity in the Theran frescoes. In J. Rutter and A. Cohen (eds) *Constructions of Childhood in Ancient Greece and Italy*, 229–255. Hesperia Supplement 41. Princeton, The American School of Classical Studies.

Chapin, A.P. (2009) Constructions of male youth and gender in Aegean art: the evidence from Late Bronze Age Crete and Thera. In K. Kopaka (ed.) *FYLO. Engendering Prehistoric Stratigraphies in the Aegean and the Mediterranean*, 175–181. Aegaeum 30. Liège, Université de Liège.

Clark, J.E. (1978) Contemporary obsidian use at Pachuca, Hidalgo, Mexico. *Lithic Technology* 7 (3), 44.

Cosmopoulos, M.B. (1998) Reconstructing Cycladic prehistory: Naxos in the Early and Middle Late Bronze Age. *Oxford Journal of Archaeology* 17 (2), 127–148.

Davies, N. de G. (1930) *The Tomb of Ken-Amūn at Thebes. Volume II.* New York, Metropolitan Museum of Art.

Davies, N.M. and Davies, N. de G. (1933) *The Tombs of Menkheperrasonb, Amenmosĕ and Another (Nos. 86, 112, 42, 226).* London, Egypt Exploration Society.

Davis, B. (2014) *Minoan Stone Vessels with Linear A Inscriptions.* Aegaeum 36. Leuven and Liège, Peeters Publishers.

Davis, E.N. (1977) *The Vapheio Cups and Aegean Gold and Silver Ware.* New York, Garland Publishing.

Davis, E.N. (1986) Youth and age in Thera frescoes. *American Journal of Archaeology* 90 (4), 399–406.

Davis, J.L. and Stocker, S.R. (2016) The lord of the gold rings: the Griffin Warrior of Pylos. *Hesperia* 85 (4), 627–655.

Deger-Jalkotzy, S. (2006) Late Mycenaean warrior tombs. In S. Deger-Jalkotzy and I.S. Lemos (eds) *Ancient Greece: From the Mycenaean Palaces to the Age of Homer*, 151–179. Edinburgh Leventis Studies 3. Edinburgh, Edinburgh University Press.

Dickinson, O.T.P.K. (1977) *The Origins of Mycenaean Civilization.* Göteborg, Paul Astroms.

Dickinson, O.T.P.K. (2005) The "Face of Agamemnon". *Hesperia* 74 (3), 299–308.

Doumas, C. (1986) Ανασκαφη Θηρασ (Ακρωτηριου). *Praktika tes en Athenais Archaiologikes Hetaireias* 141, 206–209.

Doumas, C. (1987) Η ξεστη 3 και οι κτανοκεφαλοι στην τεχνη τησ Θηρασ. In *ΕΙΛΑΠΙΝΗ - Τόμος Τιμητικος για τον Καθηγητη Νικολαο Πλατωνα*, 151–159. Herakleion: Βικελαία Δημοτική Βιβλιοθήκη.

Doumas, C. (1992) *The Wall-Paintings of Thera.* Athens, Thera Foundation and Petros M. Nomikos.

Driessen, J. and Macdonald, C. (1984) Some military aspects of the Aegean in the late fifteenth and early fourteenth centuries B.C. *The Annual of the British School at Athens* 79, 49–74.

Eder, B. and Jung, R. (2005) On the character of social relations between Greece and Italy in 12th/11th cent. BC. In R. Laffineur and E. Greco (eds) *Emporia. Aegeans in Central and Eastern Mediterranean*, 485–495. Aegaeum 25. Liège/Austin, Université de Liège/University of Texas at Austin.

Evans, A.J. (1928) *The Palace of Minos II, 2.* London, MacMillan and Co.

Evans, A.J. (1930) *The Palace of Minos III*. London, MacMillan and Co.

Evans, A.J. (1935) *The Palace of Minos IV, 2*. London, MacMillan and Co.

Fletcher, C.S. (1976) Torquemada's description of Aztec obsidian-working. In T.R. Hester (ed.) *Archaeological Studies of Mesoamerican Obsidian*, 25–27. Ballena Press Studies in Mesoamerican Archaeology and Ethnohistory 3. Socorro, Ballena Press.

Franković, F. and Matić, U. (2020) The lion, the weapon and the warlord: historical evaluation of the early Late Bronze Age Aegean iconography. *Ägypten und Levante* 30, 343–375.

French, E. (1971) The development of Mycenaean terracotta figurines. *The Annual of the British School at Athens* 66, 101–187.

Frieman, C.J., Brück, J., Rebay-Salisbury, K., Bergerbrant, S., Montón Subías, S., Sofaer, J., Knüsel, C.J., Vandkilde, H., Giles, M. and Treherne, P. (2017) Aging well: Treherne's "warrior's beauty" two decades later. *European Journal of Archaeology* 20 (1), 36–73.

Galaty, M.L. (2018) Prestige-goods economies: the prehistoric Aegean and modern northern highland Albania compared. In A.R. Knodell and T.P. Leppard (eds) *Regional Approaches to Society and Complexity*. Monographs in Mediterranean Archaeology 15. Sheffield and Bristol, Equinox Publishing Limited.

Gallagher, J.P. (1977) Contemporary tools in Ethiopia: implications for archaeology. *Journal of Field Archaeology* 4 (4), 407–414.

Hakulin, L. (2013) *Metals in LBA Minoan and Mycenaean Societies on Crete: a Quantitative Approach*. Unpublished PhD thesis, University of Helsinki.

Hitchcock, L.A. (1997) Engendering domination: a structural and contextual analysis of Minoan Neopalatial bronze figurines. In J. Moore and E. Scott (eds) *Invisible People and Processes. Writing Gender and Childhood into European Archaeology*, 113–130. London and New York, Leicester University Press.

Hitchcock, L.A. (2000) Engendering ambiguity in Minoan Crete: it's a drag to be a king. In M. Donald and L. Hurcombe (eds) *Representations of Gender from Prehistory to the Present*, 69–86. New York, St. Martin's Press.

Hitchcock, L.A. (2009) Knossos is burning: gender bending the Minoan genius. In K. Kopaka (ed.) *FYLO. Engendering Prehistoric Stratigraphies in the Aegean and the Mediterranean*, 97–102. Aegaeum 30. Liege, Université de Liège.

Hitchock, L.A. and Maeir, A. (2016) A pirate's life for me: the maritime culture of the sea peoples. *Palestine Exploration Quarterly* 148 (4), 245–264.

Hood, S., Huxley, G., Sandars, N. and Werner, A.E. (1958) A Minoan cemetery on Upper Gypsades (Knossos Survey 156). *The Annual of the British School at Athens* 53/54 (1958/1959), 194–262.

Immerwahr, S. (1990) *Aegean Paintings in the Bronze Age*. University Park, Pennsylvania State University Press.

Kanta, A. and Kontopodi, D.Z. (2011) Kastrokephala (Crete): strangers or locals in a fortified acropolis of the 12th century BC. In V. Karageorghis and O. Kouka (eds) *On Cooking Pots, Drinking Cups, Loomweights and Ethnicity in Bronze Age Cyprus and Neighbouring Regions*, 129-148. Nicosia, A.G. Leventis Foundation.

Karageorghis, V. (1990) Rites de passage at Thera: some Oriental comparanda. In D.A. Hardy, C.G. Doumas, J.A. Sakellarakis and P.M. Warren (eds) *Thera and the Aegean World III (1)*, 67–71. London, The Thera Foundation.

Koehl, R.B. (1986) The chieftain cup and a Minoan rite of passage. *Journal of Hellenic Studies* 106, 99–110.

Konstantinidi, E.M. (2001) *Jewellery Revealed in the Burial Contexts of the Greek Bronze Age*. BAR International Series 912. Oxford, Archaeopress.

Lang, M. (1969) *The Palace of Nestor at Pylos in Western Messenia 2. The Frescoes*. Princeton, Princeton University Press.

La Rosa, V. (1999) Nuovi dati sulla tomba del sarcofago dipinto di H. Triada. In V. La Rosa, D. Palermo and L. Vagnetti (eds) *Epípónton plazómenoi. Simposio italiano di studi egei dedicato a Luigi Bernabò Brea e Giovanni Pugliese Carratelli*, 177–188. Roma, Scuola Archeologica Italiana di Atene.

Lee, M.M. (2000) Deciphering gender in Minoan dress. In A.E. Rautman (ed.) *Reading the Body: Representations and Remains in the Archaeological Record*, 111–123. Philadelphia, University of Pennsylvania Press.

Loy, T.H. (1983) Prehistoric blood residues: detection on tool surfaces and identification of species of origin. *Science* 220, 1269–1271.

Loy, T.H. (1985) Preliminary residue analysis: AMNH Specimen 20.4/509. In D.H. Thomas (ed.) *The Archaeology of Hidden Cave*, 224–225. New York, Museum of Natural History Press.

Loy, T.H. and Wood, A.R. (1989) Blood residue analysis at Çayönü Tepesi, Turkey. *Journal of Field Archaeology* 16 (4), 451–460.

MacCurdy, G.G. (1900) The obsidian razor of the Aztecs. *American Anthropologist* 2 (3), 417–421.

MacGillivray, J.A., Sackett, L.H. and Driessen, J.M. (eds) (2000) *The Palaikastro Kouros: a Minoan Chryselephantine Statuette and its Aegean Bronze Age Context*. British School at Athens Studies 6. Athens, British School at Athens.

Maran, J., Papadimitriou, A. and Thaler, U. (2015) Palatial wall paintings from Tiryns. New finds and new perspectives. In A.-L. Schallin and I. Tournavitou (eds) *Mycenaeans Up to Date. The Archaeology of the North-Eastern Peloponnese – Current Concepts and New Directions*, 99–116. Skrifter utgivna av Svenska institutet i Athen. Series prima in 4°, 56. Stockholm, Svenska Institutet i Athen.

Maran, J. and Papadimitriou, A. (2017) Die aktuelle Unterstadt-Grabung und das Erbe palatialer Bauplanungen. In I. Marathaki, U. Schulz and U. Thaler (eds) *DAI ATHENEA*. Athens, Deutsches Archäologisches Institut.

Marinatos, N. (1984) *Art and Religion in Thera*. Athens, D. and I. Mathioulakis.

Marinatos, N. (1986) *Minoan Sacrificial Ritual. Cult Practice and Symbolism*. Acta Instituti Atheniensis Regni Sueciae 8, IX. Stockholm, Skrifter Utgivna av Svenska Institutet i Athen.

Marinatos, N. (1987) Role and sex division in ritual scenes of Aegean art. *Journal of Prehistoric Religion* 1, 23–34.

Marinatos, N. (2005) The ideals of manhood in Minoan Crete. In L. Morgan (ed.) *Aegean Wall Painting: a Tribute to Mark Cameron*, 149–158. British School at Athens Studies 13. Athens, The British School at Athens.

Marshall, J.H. and Bosanquet, R.C. (1901) Excavations at Praesos I. *Annual of the British School at Athens* 8, 231–270.

Matić, U. and Franković, F. (2017) Out of date, out of fashion – the changing of dress of Aegean figures in the Theban tombs of the Egyptian 18th Dynasty in the light of Aegean Bronze Age costume. *Studi Micenei ed Egeo-Anatolici*, Nuova Serie 3, 105–130.

Matić, U. (2021) *Violence and Gender in Ancient Egypt*. London/New York, Routledge.

Mayer, M. (1892) Mykenische Beiträge II. Zur Mykenischen Tracht und Cultur. *Jahrbuch des Kaiselich Deutschen Archäologischen Instituts* 7, 189–202.

Mylonas, G.E. (1937) A Mycenaean figurine at the University of Illinois. *American Journal of Archaeology* 41 (2), 237–247.

Mylonas, G.E. (1959) *Aghios Kosmas. An Early Bronze Age Settlement and Cemetery in Attica*. Princeton, Princeton University Press.

Newman, A.N. (2017) Queering the Minoans: gender performativity and the Aegean color convention in fresco painting at Knossos. *Journal of Mediterranean Archaeology* 30 (2), 213–236.

Olsen, B.A. (1998) Women, children and the family in the Late Aegean Bronze Age: differences in Minoan and Mycenaean constructions of gender. *World Archaeology* 29 (3), 380–392.

Panagiotaki, M. (1998) The Vat Room deposit at Knossos: the unpublished notes of Sir Arthur Evans. *Annual of the British School at Athens* 93, 167–184.

Panagiotaki, M. (1999) *The Central Palace Sanctuary at Knossos.* British School at Athens Supplementary Volume 31. London, British School at Athens.

Papadimitriou, A., Thaler, U. and Maran, J. (2015) Bearing the Pomegranate Bearer: a new wall-painting scene from Tiryns. In H. Brecoulaki, J.L. Davis and S.R. Stocker (eds) *Mycenaean Wall Painting in Context: New Discoveries, Old Finds Reconsidered,* 173–211. Meletemata 72. Athens, National Hellenic Research Foundation and Institute of Historical Research.

Papadopoulos, T.J. (1999) Warrior-graves in Achaean Mycenaean cemeteries. In R. Laffineur (ed.) *POLEMOS. Le contexte guerrier en Égée a l'Âge du Bronze.* Aegaeum 19, 267–273. Liège and Austin, Université de Liège and University of Texas at Austin.

Papaefthymioy-Papanthimou, A. (1979) *Σκεύη και Σύνεργα του Καλλωπισμού στον Κρητομυκηναϊκό Χώρο.* Unpublished PhD thesis, Aristoteleion Univesity in Thessaloniki.

Paschalidis, K. (2012) Reflections of eternal beauty. The unpublished context of a wealthy female burial from Koukaki, Athens and the occurrence of mirror in Mycenaean tombs. In M.-L. Nosch and R. Laffineur (eds) *Kosmos. Jewellery, Adornment and Textiles in the Aegean Bronze Age.* Aegaeum 33, 547–557. Leuven and Liège, Peeters Publishers.

Paschalidis, K. and McGeorge, P.J.P. (2009) Life and death in the periphery of the Mycenaean world at the end of the Late Bronze Age: the case of the Achaea Klauss Cemetery. In E. Borgna and P. Cassola-Guida (eds) *From the Aegean to the Adriatic: Social Organisations, Modes of Exchange and Interaction in Postpalatial Times (12th-11th B.C.),* 79–113. Roma, Quasar.

Petrakos, V. (2017) Άγιος Βασίλειος Λακωνίας. *Ergon* 63 (2016), 19–20.

Pini, I. (1999) Minoische "porträts"? In P.P. Betancourt, V. Karageorghis, R. Laffineur and W.-D. Neimeier (eds) *Meletemata, Studies in Aegean Archaeology Presented to Malcolm H. Wiener as he Enters his 65th Year,* 661–670. Aegaeum 20. Liège, Université de Liège.

Popham, M.R., Catling, E.A. and Catling, H.W. (1974) Sellopoulo Tombs 3 and 4, two Late Minoan graves near Knossos. *The Annual of the British School at Athens* 69, 195–257.

Protonotariou-Deilaki, E. (1973) Ανασκαφικαί έρευναι εις περιοχήν Ναυπλίας. *Archaiologikon deltion* 28 (B1), 90–93.

Radcliffe-Brown, A. (1922) *The Andaman Islanders.* London, Cambridge University Press.

Rehak, P. (1995) Enthroned figures in Aegean art and the function of the Mycenaean Megaron. In P. Rehak (ed.) *The Role of the Ruler in the Prehistoric Aegean,* 95–118. Aegaeum 11. Liège, University of Liège.

Rehak, P. (1997) Aegean art before and after the LM I B Cretan destructions. In R. Laffineur and P.P. Betancourt (eds) *TECHNE. Craftsmen, Craftswomen, and Craftmanship in the Aegean Bronze Age,* 51–66. Aegaeum 15. Liège and Austin, Université de Liège and University of Texas.

Rehak, P. (2007) Children's work: girls as acolytes in Aegean ritual and cult. In A. Cohen and J. Rutter (eds) *Construction of Childhood in Ancient Greece and Italy,* 205–225. Hesperia Supplement 41. Princeton, The American School of Classical Studies at Athens.

Renfrew, C. (1972) *The Emergence of Civilization.* London, Methuen.

Ruiz-Gálvez, M. and Galán, E. (2013) A meal fit for a hero. On the origins of roasted meat, spits and the male ideal. *Cuadernos de Arqueología Mediterránea* 21, 43–69.

Rutter, J. (2003) Children in Aegean prehistory. In J. Neils and J.H. Oakley (eds) *Coming of Age in Ancient Greece. Images of Childhood from the Classical Past,* 31–57. New Haven and London, Yale University Press.

Salavoura, E. (2012) Mycenaean "ear pick": a rare metal burial gift, toilette or medical implement? In M.-L. Nosch and R. Laffineur (eds) *Kosmos. Jewellery, Adornment and Textiles in the Aegean Bronze Age,* 345–351. Aegaeum 33. Leuven and Liege, Peeters Publishers.

Stocker, S.R. and Davis, J. (2017) The combat agate from the Grave of the Griffin Warrior at Pylos. *Hesperia* 86 (4), 583–605.

Taylour, W.D. (1972) Excavations at Ayios Stephanos. *The Annual of the British School at Athens* 67, 205–270.

Treherne, P. (1995) The warrior's beauty: the masculine body and self-identity in Bronze-Age Europe. *Journal of European Archaeology* 3(1), 105–144.

Tyree, L., Hitchcock, L.A., and Barnett, C. (2020) E-Qe-Ta: conceptions of warrior beauty and constructions of masculinity on postpalatial Crete. In B.E. Davis and R. Laffineur (eds) *NEWTOROS: Studies in Bronze Age Aegean Art and Archaeology in Honor of Professor John G. Younger on the Occasion of His Retirement*, 91–112. Aegaeum 44. Leuven, Peeters publishers.

Verlinden, C. (1984) *Les statuettes anthropomorphes crétoises en bronze et en plomb du III millénaire au VIIe siècle av. J.-C.* Publications d'histoire de l'art et d'archéologie de l'université catholique de Louvain 41. Archaeologia transatlantica 4. Providence, Brown University, Center for Old World Archeology and Art.

Vermeule, E. (1983) *Ελλάς, Εποχή του Χαλκού*. Athens, Εκδότης Καρδαμιτσα.

Vlassopoulou-Karydi, M. (2000) Ελεφάντινες Λαβές Κατόπτρων με Ανάγλυφες Γυναικείες Μορφές της Μυκηναϊκής Συλλογής. *το Μουσείον* 1, 39–50.

Weber, C. (1996) *Die Rasiermesser in Südosteuropa*. Prähistorische Bronzefunde VIII, Band 5. Stuttgart, F. Steiner.

Weingarten, J. (2005) Review of O. Krzyszkowska, Aegean Seals: An Introduction. *Studi Micenei ed Egeo-Anatolici* 47, 353–359.

Wilkie, N.C. (1987) Burial customs at Nichoria: the MME tholos. In R. Laffineur (ed.) *Thanatos: Les Coutumes Funeraires en Egee a l'Age du Bronze*, 127–136. Aegeum 1. Liège, Université de Liège.

Zapheiropoulos, N.S. (1966) Ανασκαφαι Ναξου. *Praktika tēs en Athēnais Archaiologikēs Hetaireias* 1960, 329–340.

Chapter 6

Gender, perfume and society in ancient Athens

Isabelle Algrain

Abstract

The use of perfume vases in ancient Athens is often presented in a binary way in research based on the iconography of Athenian vases. Images show us how perfume vases were used by both sexes to perform their gender, as part of their "identity". On the images, the aryballos is linked with the citizen-athlete, while the alabastron and the plemochoe appear mainly in scenes of bathing, dressing and adornment of women and brides. Yet, a close examination of images and archaeological contexts can help to nuance this interpretation and reveal a more subtle use of perfume vases and their content in Athenian society. This paper attempts to explain the social uses of perfumed oils and the norms associated with the bodies in ancient Athens. Particular attention will be paid to different aspects of Greek society from the construction of norms related to individuals, given that these norms are applied in the context of interpersonal relations (sexuality) to the study of their deployment at city level. Thus, I will draft an overview of Athens' social norms. Once this theoretical framework defining gendered social relationships in ancient Athens is laid, I will attempt to find out whether the uses of clay perfume vases can shed further light on these relationships in Archaic and Classical Athens.

Key words: *perfume, gender, Archaic and Classical Athens*

Introduction: defining gender in ancient Athens

Gender and heteronormativity are historically recent concepts. In the fields of classical history, art and archaeology, scholarly interest in these subjects developed in the course of the 1980s. At that time, the question of the place of women in ancient and modern societies was opening up to other fundamental aspects of social relationships, intimately interwoven with sex, such as socio-economic status, age, gender identity or "race" (Foxhall 2013, 4–14). Instead of simply "adding women and stirring" (Bunch 1987, 140) and thus writing a history of women superimposed on men's, the focus was a on analysing gender relationships – called "rapports sociaux de sexe" by French sociologists and feminists – in a detailed way, to understand how gender could shape relationships between women and men, at all levels of society, and among other things in artistic representations

Gender is, according to the historian Joan Scott's definition in her seminal article on gender as a useful category of historical analysis, "a constitutive element of social relationships based on perceived differences between the sexes, and gender is a primary way of signifying relationships of power" (Scott 1988, 1067). It is more than a social invariant: whatever the time or the society, the hierarchical relationship between men and women is always present. The only change is its modalities of expression. Heteronormativity is the belief that heterosexuality is the norm. These concepts help to explain gendered social relations, the hierarchy and relationships of domination of men over women, and the heterosexual norm which are an integral part of our societies. These are the tools the use of which is immediate and practical because they can be applied, unfiltered, to understand current social phenomena. But how about using these concepts to try to explain gendered social relations in past societies, namely in ancient Greece?

To take gender into account when studying ancient societies is a necessity. Indeed, applying modern conceptions related to the roles of men and women without thinking about notions of gender in ancient civilizations may lead to major interpretation problems. In the context of ancient Greek burials, the identification of the sex of the deceased was for a long time (and this is sometimes still the case) derived from the objects deposited in the tomb. Yet, objects do not have a gender and very few have proved to be discriminating: *e.g.*, mirrors and weapons are found in both women's and men's graves (Houby-Nielsen 1995). Osteological analyses were necessary to demonstrate this fact because the presence of weapons in tombs did not fit well with the vision of the "Greek" woman (an essentially Athenocentric vision), living secluded in the *gynaikeion*, the rooms of the Greek house devoted to women. In the same way, the interpretation of Greek vase-paintings, especially Athenian ones, has long been dependent on modern preconceptions projected on the life of ancient women. Thus, most women represented in everyday life scenes were interpreted for a long time as *hetairai* (courtesans) or *pornai* (low-life prostitutes/slaves) on the basis of criteria that are in fact non-discriminating (Algrain 2014, 153–215).

These frequent misinterpretations invite us to rethink the construction of both sexes and gendered social relationships in past societies. Can we apply some modern concepts from gender studies (including heteronormativity) to the study of ancient Greek societies to help us avoid these pitfalls? How were sex and gender relations constructed in Archaic and Classical Greek cities? Can one apply some of these concepts as is, or would one be risking misinterpreting the period-specific social relationships?

This paper attempts to answer some of these questions with the example of ancient Athens. Particular attention will be paid to different aspects of Greek society from the construction of norms related to individuals, given that these norms are applied in the context of interpersonal relations (sexuality) to the study of their deployment at city level. Thus, I will draft an overview of Athens' social norms. Once this theoretical framework defining gendered social relationships in ancient Athens is laid, I will attempt to find out whether the uses of clay perfume vases can shed further light on these relationships in Archaic and Classical Athens.

The normalised body

Biological differences between men and women were studied by many ancient philosophers and physicians. These two professions, difficult to distinguish in their analyses of the female and male bodies, approach the question of body functions in a similar way. Plutarch says that philosophy and medicine deal with the same domain (*De tuenda sanitate praecepta,* 122e). The binary vision of the world shared by Greek philosophers and physicians differentiates between male/female, right/left, clear/dark, good/bad, hot/cold, dry/wet, solid/porous, impermeable/permeable, etc. and these oppositions have different hierarchical values: positively connoted ideas are associated with men while those with negative connotations are associated with women (Parker 2012, 107–109). Biological differences between women and men are ranked hierarchically, a good example of the differential valence of the sexes was defined by French anthropologist Françoise Héritier:

> The differential valence of the sexes reflects the different place that is universally given to the two sexes on a table of values, and signs the dominance of the masculine principle over the feminine principle. The male/female relationship is built on the same model as the parent/child relationship, the elder/younger relationship, and more generally, the anterior/posterior relationship, anteriority meaning superiority (Héritier 1996, 127).

From Aristotle to Galen, many ancient authors sought to explain the differences between women and men and to naturalise the supposedly inferior status of women. For example, Aristotle says about reproduction:

> the contribution of the female to the generative product is not the same as that of the male, but the male contributes the principle of movement and the female the material. This is why the female does not produce offspring by herself, for she needs a principle, i.e., something to begin the movement in the embryo and to define the form it is to assume (Aristotle, *Generation of Animals,* 730b).

Aristotle repeatedly reaffirms the importance of man in reproduction, putting forward, for example, sexual relations between spouses as the trigger of childbirth.

The prevalence of this model should not come as a surprise with major myths like a version of the birth of Athena, tutelary goddess of her eponymous city, born motherless, armed and helmeted from the skull of Zeus. In Aeschylus' *Eumenides*, Apollo says:

> The mother of what is called her child is not the parent, but the nurse of the newly-sown embryo. The one who mounts is the parent, whereas she, as a stranger for a stranger, preserves the young plant, if the god does not harm it. And I will show you proof of what I say: a father might exist without a mother. A witness is here at hand, the child of Olympian Zeus, who was not nursed in the darkness of a womb, and she is such a child as no goddess could give birth to (Aeschylus, *Eumenides*, 657 sq.).

Plato is an exception because his texts do not differentiate between the biological status of women and men, nor between the virtues with which they were endowed (Smith 1983, 467–478). According to humourism and the theory of the four temperaments, the body was made of four different humours (blood, black bile, yellow bile, phlegm) whose proportions needed to be balanced and which had specific qualities (warm, cold, dry, moist). Hippocratic medicine considered that the male body was warm and dry and that the female body was cold and moist. A moisture imbalance (too much or too little) often causes a disease. The overabundance of warmth makes man a perfect being while the lack of heat prevents a woman's genitals from descending, condemning her to remain an imperfect being. Treatises on the diseases of women and girls describe the female body as a sick body, more easily subject to disturbances than the male body (Dorlin 2006, 20–21, 35–37). The detachment from the female subject or any type of medical examination is obvious in Aristotle's works, for whom women were inferior to men (Aristotle, *Parts of Animals*, 648a9–18), an assertion based for example on the fact that women were supposed to have fewer teeth than men (Aristotle, *History of Animals,* 501b19) or that a menstruating woman reddened the mirror into which she looked (Aristotle, *On Dreams*, 459b–60a). Diseases like gonorrhoea, defined as the involuntary excretion of sperm, were shameful because they threatened a man's manhood and made his body similar to that of a woman (Aretaeus, *On the Causes, Symptoms and Cure of Acute and Chronic Diseases*, II, 5). Different theories explained the bodily mechanisms occurring in reproduction, but it was the work of Galen that would have the greatest durability and would be in use until the 17th century. Galen explains the necessity to reproduce by a failure of the demiurgic work that aimed at immortality (Foucault 1984, 127–129). In line with the authors of medical and philosophical texts, he tended to consider that women and men were isomorphic, *i.e.*, in all points identical on an anatomical level, including their genitals. The latter were considered to be in an inverted position, outside men's bodies and inside women's bodies. Isomorphism was so prevalent that the vocabulary used to designate ovaries was the same as that used for the testes (Laqueur 1992, 31).

This ancient view of the (lack of) difference between the sexes is part of what the historian Thomas Laqueur has called, in his work on the evolution of our understanding of biological sex, "a one-sex model". Considering that an important conceptual shift took place in the 17th–18th centuries, he defines all conceptions before this period as models, according to which the assumed isomorphism of the male and female genitals implied that only one sex existed in the ancient common mindset. The evolution towards a modern and post-modern society would imply the passage from a conception of sex as a non-binary hierarchical continuum to a strict, irreducible and irreconcilable bicategorisation. For Laqueur, before the 17th–18th centuries, the difference between men and women was not ontological but anchored in gender and its social expression (Laqueur 1992, 36–37). Laqueur relies on medical texts, particularly those of Galen and his passage on the isomorphism of male and female organs. But as Elsa Dorlin and other scholars have already noted, Laqueur's explanatory model goes too far. While there is no doubt that the ancient conception of the difference of the sexes viewed the female body as an inverted version of the male body, it is impossible to consider that the difference between the sexes was purely social: ancient texts specify the biological differences, even if their explanations of these differences might seem fanciful today (Dorlin 2006, 20–23). The main distinction between ancient and modern texts written after the 17th century is that ancient authors set the anatomical difference between women and men only at the level of the gonads, whereas modern authors seek to differentiate them throughout the entire body. Aristotle (*Generation of Animals,* 716b; 724b–727b) thus relies on clear biological differences to explain differences in body mechanics: men produce sperm (because of their overabundance of heat that cooks food and transforms it into sperm), women have menstruation (being imperfect and cold, their lack of heat prevents them from cooking their sperm in the same way as men, which gives rise to menstruation). The woman is therefore not simply an inverted model of the masculine. It is an imperfect version of it and this view legitimises the hierarchical relationship established by men over women.

The biological difference between women and men, and the way in which this difference was constructed and essentialised in ancient discourses had important social impacts with regard to the differential valence of the sexes, the socialisation of women and men, and the way in which women and men performed their gender in society.

Performing gender

If masculinity, like femininity, has long been considered to be a social invariant, recent studies have shown that it is a phenomenon whose construction has varied over time. Among the social invariants, *i.e.,* universal categories at work in the construction of all societies, identified by Claude Lévi-Strauss and Françoise Héritier are the prohibition of incest, the sexual division of tasks, a recognised form of sexual union and the differential valence of the sexes (Héritier 1996, 27). At present, the definition of manhood is essentially based on sexuality, but other factors, such as honour, have prevailed in the past, showing that masculinity is a social construct (Duru-Bellat 2017, 113–114). Thus, the glorification of the idealised male body was clearly a part of male identity in ancient Greek societies. The body is shaped and "built" by exercises that took place at the gymnasium. The values associated with masculine beauty were not only physical and, in the many male beauty contests of the Classical period, manhood (*euandria*) and personability (*euaxia*) were exalted: masculine beauty was the reflection of military, political and civic values. These competitions allowed cities to assert their power and strength, through the victory of citizens with perfect physical and moral qualities (Gherchanoc 2016, 115–174).

In art, male beauty was represented through heroic nudity. From the figurative representations of the Late Bronze Age and the Geometric period, men were regularly represented naked in order to highlight physical qualities and beauty (Newman 2018). Standard elements begin to appear in the Archaic period, such as the small size of the male penis which was widely valued (Keuls 1985, 67–75). This convention could be explained by the idea, expressed by Aristotle, that men with large penises "are less fertile than when it is smaller because the semen, if cold, is not generative, and that which is carried too far is cooled" (Aristotle, *Generation of Animals*, 718b). Conversely, the representations of women show them dressed and, though naked women appear already on Greek pottery from the 6th century BCE, it is only with Praxiteles' Aphrodite of Cnidus in the 4th century BCE to see a female nude in sculpture. Women's beauty contests, less numerous than men's, focused not only on physical traits but also on behaviour and clothing. The goal of these contests was to introduce marriageable girls to the community who had the potential to safekeep the moral, political and religious order of the city or wives who already maintained this order. The beauty contests reserved for courtesans do not have a civic purpose but an erotic and sexual scope and focus on certain parts of the female body, especially the buttocks (Gherchanoc 2016, 77–114).

Although social class may have impacted their situation, young Athenian girls in citizen families had a strongly differentiated socialisation from that of boys and married around the age of 14 with men who were, on average, 30 years old. Gender domination was thus reinforced by age domination and the early entry of girls in married life ensured that their period of fertility was exploited to the full (Bozon 2013, 14–15). The patriarchal control exercised over young Athenian women was such that they could only leave paternal guardianship to pass under their husband's. In addition to ensuring the reproduction of the body of citizens, marriage symbolised the union of two families on a social and economic level (dowry), especially among the elite. The only aspiration of young girls (*parthenoi*) in wealthy families was marriage. Moreover, the term *gyne*, as in French femme, meant both "woman" as a female human being and "wife". In the *Oeconomicus* (6,17–10,9), Xenophon developed the idea that the husband educated his young wife to shape her into a good wife and housewife. Other authors also write on the transition from *parthenos* to *gyne* using terms relating to the wild and untamed nature of children, especially girls, who are not completely tamed until they are married (King 1993, 110–111).

In contrast to Athenian practices, Sparta seems to have been at the other end of the spectrum of gendered social relationships in ancient Greece. Although Spartan society was also patriarchal, women enjoyed greater freedom at all stages of their lives. Education was provided to both boys and girls, while the boys focused primarily on military skills. Girls also had access to arts and physical education and married later than other Greek women, on average at the age of 18. Spartan women could, with the consent of their husbands, have another partner it they thought they could produce better children for the city (Pomeroy 2002).

Norms and sexuality

The word "sexuality", just like the word "gender", is a modern invention that had no equivalent in antiquity. When ancient Greeks wrote about sexuality and certain practices, they distinguished between acts which conformed to the norm (*kata nomon*), that were contrary to the norm (*para nomon, e.g.,* incest) or contrary to nature (*para phusin, e.g.,* sex with animals, corpses or between women). These distinctions were not rigid and depended essentially on the person who performed the sexual acts and his/her social position (Foucault 1984, 30–50): the same practice could thus be *kata nomon* or *para nomon* depending on whether it was performed by a man, a woman, a slave, a prostitute, a younger or older person, a richer or poorer one:

> The ancient discourse on sexuality reveals an essential concern: that of knowing who does what, and how (who acts, who takes pleasure, who is submitted – the active-passive opposition is not in fact sufficient to account for the totality of oppositions and considerations linking such an act to a social interpretation). The idea of a sexual relationship where partners are equal, where a practice can be done by one or the other partner, does not exist (Boehringer 2010, 194).

Michel Foucault's analysis in *Le souci de soi* (*The Care of the Self*) confirms that inequality was compulsory in ancient sexual relations and that practices considered to be against the norm were those that implied a departure from this principle of inequality (Foucault 1984, 33). Practices contrary to the norm threatened the balance of the city, so, in the absence of any legal apparatus on sexuality, morality was in charge of regulating sexuality and public speeches on deviances to prove the immoral character of the accused (Lanni 2009, 706).

In Athens, the organisation of sexuality in the context of marriage was asymmetrical. In the case of men, Walter Scheidl uses the notion of "polygynous monogamy", which expresses the inequality of the relationship between husband and wife: male adultery is tolerated and men can maintain concubinage with *pallakes*, resort to *hetairai* or prostitutes, or to slaves of both sexes within the *oikos* (Scheidel 2011, 109–111). Monogamy could be flexible under exceptional circumstances since the Athenians were allowed to have legitimate children with a woman other than their own at the end of the 5th century due to significant male losses during the Peloponnesian War (Ogden 1996, 72–75). Female adultery was strongly condemned: in the context of the Athenian marriage compulsory monogamous heterosexuality was expected of married women. Marriage produced legitimate children (*gnêsioi*) – who would in turn be citizens in the case of male children – and their legitimacy could not be questioned at the risk of undermining the basic principles of citizenship. Marriage would become even more important to ensure the reproduction of the body of citizens from 451 BCE because it was that year that Perikles passed a law stating that the transmission of Athenian citizenship would have to be passed down by both parents, a citizen father (although previously the father could legitimise his children born out of wedlock (*nothoi*) and assure them citizenship), and a mother who had to be a citizen's daughter. Women were thus passive citizens, who did not enjoy citizens' rights but were able to pass them on.

It was therefore important for married women to remain chaste, which was difficult because women were considered insatiable and incapable, because of their lack of reason, of controlling their impulses and passions in the same way as men. This vision of women was abundantly used in the plays of the Old Comedy (King 1993, 110; Mitchell 2015; Topper 2012, 149–150). This notion of self-control was not limited to sexuality but was present in all aspects of Greek life. The Greek man was defined by his self-control; excess, immoderation and pride were the subject of much moral blame. *Hybris* attracted divine punishment, as shown by the myth of Pandora, fashioned by the gods to punish men and Prometheus. The myth is reported by Hesiod in the 8th century BCE: one of the oldest Greek texts preserved considers therefore woman to be "a plague to men", a punishment inflicted by the gods (Hesiod, *Works and Days,* 60-80). Seen as unreasonable beings, women have thus a limited role to play in the daily life of the city.

A gendered and socio-economic use of perfume vases

The Greek city was a social body, a collective institutional structure associated with a territory and defined as a group by participation in the defense of its territory and by common rites (such as processions, sacrifices, banquets, etc.). It is for this reason that one speaks not of the city of Athens but of the city of the Athenians because without its citizens, the city was nothing. Access to citizenship was in fact prohibited for women, minors and foreigners because they could not assume the dual identity of the citizen-soldier. Theoretically, citizenship allowed any citizen to participate in the political decisions of the city through its various civic bodies. Yet, only citizens who had a personal fortune or significant income could in fact participate in political life and contribute to the finances of the city.

Women were thus removed from the political life of the city, but they did participate in public life through religious rituals such as processions and funerals. Apart from these events and as stated by Thucydides (II, 45), women should not make themselves known: "To a woman not to show more weakness than is natural to her sex is a great glory, and not to be talked about for good or for evil among men". In ancient texts, the rejection of foreigners from the social and civic body was often reiterated by in the analogy between "foreigners" and "women", two categories of beings considered to be inferior. This system of thinking found an echo in the modern analogy between "sex" and "race" that was developed from the end of the 17th century, although the Greeks did not think about humanity in terms of races, but a Greek/non-Greek opposition. This opposition, however, fell within the Anglo-Saxon definition of race as a social construct on which discrimination is based. The work of the philosopher Elsa Dorlin on the history of racism shows "the assimilation of a population to the feminine temperament, to the 'nature' of women, in order to mark its difference and its inferiority" (Dorlin 2006, 223). Indigenous men were stripped of their manhood in stories of the 18th and 19th centuries because of their weak and unhealthy female temperament, their lack of body hair or the alleged insatiability of indigenous women that they could not satisfy.

In the same way, a very clear opposition emerged between Greeks and Barbarians. The barbarian was literally a man who did not speak Greek and uttered incomprehensible nonsense. This opposition was also expressed by comparing their bodies, clothing and the discourses attached to them (Gherchanoc 2008, 76–81). The otherness of the Barbarians was described by comparing them to women. See how Xenophon described the way Agesilaus of Sparta treated the troops of the Lydian satrap Tissaphernes towards 396–394 BCE:

> And again, believing that to feel contempt for one's enemies infuses a certain courage for the fight, Agesilaus gave orders to his heralds that the barbarians who were captured by the Greek raiding parties should be exposed for sale naked. Thus, the soldiers, seeing that these men were white-skinned because they never were without their clothing, and soft and unused to toil because they always rode in carriages, came to the conclusion that the war would be in no way different from having to fight with women (Xenophon, *Hellenica* III, 4, 19).

Here the text opposed the athletic ideal of the Greek citizen to eastern habits considered to be effeminate (not exposing oneself to the sun, not walking, not training). In artistic representations, nudity exalted the physical and warlike qualities of the hoplite while the garment of the Eastern warrior – where the only uncovered members were the face, hands and feet – hid his softness, overweight body, its whiteness and lack of training. The Greek heroic nudity only aimed to glorify its warriors since, in reality, they fought clothed. One example of this can be found on Fig. 6.1, where a Greek warrior fights against a fully clothed Persian soldier.

The Greek warrior on the reverse is naked in order to oppose heroic nudity to the fully clothed Persian hiding his body. To the Greek eye, the Persian warrior was a "figure de l'alterité", a symbol of otherness that included all those who were not citizens on Greek vases (Lissarrague 1990). If the whiteness of Oriental bodies is laughable to the Greeks, their contempt also extended to bodies that were too dark were also ridiculed, as reported by Frontinus about Gelo of Syracuse in 480 BCE:

Gelo, tyrant of Syracuse, having undertaken war against the Carthaginians, after taking many prisoners, stripped all the feeblest, especially from among the auxiliaries, who were very dark-skinned, and exhibited them nude before the eyes of his troops, in order to convince his men that their foes were contemptible (Frontinus, *Stratagems* I, XI, 18).

The social body was not only made of external oppositions but also internal ones. "Athletic nudity is an operator of distinction: of ethnicity, of gender and of age. ... it is an expression of the equality, at least theoretical, between citizens" (Gherchanoc 2008, 86) and this athletic nudity thus operated as a criterion of citizenship. Training in the gymnasium modelled the bodies of citizens towards an ideal that was inaccessible to others: in this context where nudity had its place, handsome, manly, muscular bodies were tanned by the exercises practiced in the open and covered with oil. This activity was the prerogative of citizens and free men since laws specifically prohibited slaves, as well as bastards, to practice naked and to anoint their bodies with oil at the palaestra, as stated by Aeschines:

"A slave," says the law, "shall not exercise or anoint himself in the wrestling-schools." It did not go on to add, "But the free man shall anoint himself and exercise;" for when, seeing the good that comes from gymnastics, the lawgivers forbade slaves to take part, they thought that in prohibiting them they were by the same words inviting the free (*Against Timarchus*, 138).

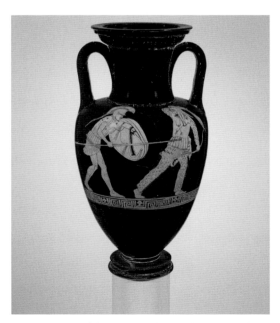

Fig. 6.1 Attic red-figured amphora. The Metropolitan Museum of Art, New York, inv. 06.1021.117. Rogers Fund, 1906. c. 480–470 BCE (www.metmuseum.org)

It was also the activity of a leisure elite, with time to spare for training (Filser 2017, 278 *sq.*). Archaic and Classical iconography depicting athletes with aryballoi, the container for oil associated with men, thus likely shows citizens – or at least free men – training, and the aryballos seems to be a marker of social and economic status. Attic clay aryballoi are particularly rare. We barely know 50 pieces from the Archaic and Classical periods (Algrain, Brisart and Jubier-Galinier 2008, 161). They were however manufactured over a long period of time, from the Geometric period until the 4th century BCE (Fig. 6.2).

This rarity is all the more surprising when one considers the numerous (over 800) representations of aryballoi on Attic vases (Fig. 6.3). It is therefore very likely that many Athenian aryballoi were made from precious and/ or perishable materials. We have many bronze aryballoi (Boix 2013, 54), but leather was probably also used to make small containers, sometimes with a mouth made of iron or bronze (Boix 2013, 55–60; Heinemann 2009, 164–165), as suggested by the discovery of a leather aryballos with a strigil in the tomb of a young man in Paestum (Carter 1998, 201). In addition, an Etruscan aryballos dating from the late 7th century BCE bears an engraved inscription that designated it as an *aska* containing oil (Maggiani 1972). This word, borrowed from the Greek *askos*, usually referred to a wineskin.

Fig. 6.2. Attic black-figured aryballos signed by Nearchos. The Metropolitan Museum of Art, New York, inv. 26.49. Purchase, The Cesnola Collection, by exchange, 1926. c. 570 BCE (www.metmuseum.org)

A vase associated with body care, the aryballos appears frequently in scenes where male or female characters are bathing. Its content was used to soften the skin and, in this context, it often appears in combination with the sponge and the strigil, two other objects frequently used when cleaning oneself or bathing. However, aryballoi were used in a context where the alabastron was rarely found because it was the athlete's vase. Men took the vase to the gymnasium, hung it in a corner of the palaestra and used it either before the exercise or after the bath. Oil was rubbed into the skin before training and the mixed oil, dirt and perspiration were scraped with the strigil before bathing (Fig. 6.4).

It was also sometimes applied after the bath to nourish the skin. The association of the aryballos with men is reinforced by the existence of a series of plastic oil vases in the form of male genitals (Algrain, Brisart and Jubier-

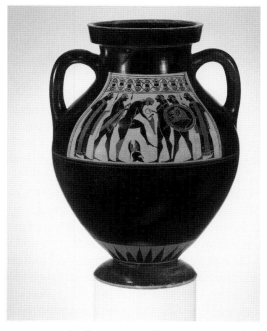

Fig. 6.3 Aryballoi are usually equipped with a leather strap to carry them to the palaestra and to attach them to the wall. Attic black-figured amphora attributed to the Amasis Painter. The Metropolitan Museum of Art, New York, inv. 06.1021.69. Rogers Fund, 1906. c. 550 BCE (www. metmuseum.org)

Fig. 6.4 Figures on the left and right are using a strigil to scrape dirt after training at the palaestra. On the wall, there are sandals on the left and an aryballos and a sponge on the right. Attic red-figured cup attributed to the Antiphon Painter. The Metropolitan Museum of Art, New York, inv. 96.18.67. Purchase by subscription, 1896. c. 500–475 BCE (www.metmuseum.org)

Galinier 2008, 158–159). More rarely, there are representations of aryballoi in funerary contexts, hanging on or around graves associated with an athlete. For example, on the *lekythoi* at the Agora Museum (inv. P10369; Beazley Archive Pottery Database, from now on abbreviated BA: 216342) and at Berkeley (Phoebe Apperson Hearst Museum of Anthropology, 8.37; BA: 216758).

The aryballos is one of the various vase shapes that contained scented or unscented oils in ancient Athens. Oils were used in a wide range of contexts, a bathing cosmetic by men and women or used by women to seduce men; a gift from men to women; an ointment for the ritual cleansing of corpses; an offering to the gods, sometimes used to anoint cult statues (D'Acunto 2012). The opposition between the use of oils by men and women is marked in imagery by a gendered use of vases. If the aryballos, which probably contained pure unscented oil (*elaion*), is usually associated with men, other vases such as the alabastron and the plemochoe are associated with women. The Attic alabastron is a perfume vase (for *muron*, scented oil) produced in Athens between the middle of the 6th and the beginning of the 4th centuries BCE (Fig. 6.5).

The contents of the Attic alabastron was relatively valuable. Indeed, in contrast to the aryballos, the contents of which was usually poured in the palm of the hand, the alabastron's content was extracted with a small stick that was then used to deposit the perfume on the skin, hair or clothing (Fig. 6.6). For example, a cup at London, British Museum, E 82 (BA: 217212). Odoriferous substances are also used to perfume clothes on a chous at New York, Metropolitan Museum of Art, 75.2.11 (BA: 220503). The use of substances to perfume clothing is also attested by textual sources, particularly in the Homeric epic (Shelmerdine 1995). Experiments have shown that the use of scented oil on linen garments makes them soft and shiny, and that they retain this appearance after being washed (Shelmerdine 1985, 129). Metal sticks for depositing perfume on the skin have been discovered (Hill 1965). The parsimony with which the contents were extracted from this vase suggests that it contained a valuable substance. Aryballoi are manipulated on several cups in Berlin (lost, F 2314; BA: 203450), Providence (Rhode Island School of Design, 25.076; BA: 200379), Ferrara (Palazzo Schifanoia, 269; BA: 200566), and on a crater (Berlin, Antikensammlung, F2180; BA: 200063).

As stated earlier, men using aryballoi in Attic iconography were probably citizens. The status of women using alabastra is, as we shall see, more problematic. The alabastron appears frequently in bathing scenes, as on Figure 6.6, and this use is also confirmed by ancient texts. In this context, women use the content of the alabastron to perfume both their body and hair. Bathing scenes involving alabastra are relatively few in Attic iconography and they appear mainly on red-figure vases from the 5th century BCE. These usually represent one or several naked women washing at a high basin (*louterion*). In some of these bathing scenes, women also use objects traditionally associated with men, such as strigils and aryballoi. Usually, the sponge is associated with the aryballos and, together with the strigil, they represent

Fig. 6.5. Attic alabastron. The Metropolitan Museum of Art, New York, inv. 06.1021.92. Rogers Fund, 1906. c. 510–500 BCE (www.metmuseum.org)

the traditional "athlete's package". However, it might be preferable to reinterpret this "athlete's package" as a simple package of toiletry items, because such representations are numerous. Indeed, at the end of the 6th century BCE, when the alabastron begins to be produced on a larger scale, washing scenes show aryballoi in the hands of men and women. From the 5th century BCE onwards, alabastra and aryballoi appear in bathing contexts, but only the aryballos remains associated with the world of the palaestra and the athlete's bath. It seems that these shapes become gendered during the late archaic period: the alabastron became associated with women, whilst the aryballos became associated with men, especially athletes.

According to Ulla Kreilinger (2007), bathing scenes with naked women were often related to marriage. In these scenes, women are shown naked, aside an obvious practical reason, to reveal their beauty, in the same way that athletic nudity revealed the beauty and physical qualities of

Fig. 6.6 Red-figured stamnos attributed to the Group of Polygnotos. München, Antikensammlung, 2411 (© Staatliche Antikensammlungen und Glyptothek München. Photo Renate Kühling)

young citizens. More generally, the alabastron is also present in images where women are getting dressed and taking care of their appearance: they do their hair, choose jewellery, look at their reflection in a mirror or use perfume vases. The alabastron in these scenes, like the mirror, can therefore be considered to be an attribute of femininity. The erotic dimension of the vase is particularly clear because of the recurring presence of one or several small Erotes. Such scenes of adornment or preparation are frequently associated with marriage ceremonies. From the second half of the 5th century until the end of the 4th century BCE, the number of representations related to marriage grows significantly. This increase may possibly be related to the law introduced by Pericles in 451 BCE, limiting access to citizenship only to male children whose father and mother were citizens (*i.e.*, whose mother was the daughter of a citizen). Marriage, which was already an important rite of transition for women, took on a considerable importance since it legitimised the union of two "citizen" parents and of course, their children. It was therefore natural that both vases and images associated with this important ceremony occupied a more prominent place in the typological and iconographic Athenian ceramic repertoire. In these scenes of women dressing, as in the more general preparation scenes, the bride is usually the central character of the composition, one to which all eyes turn to (Fig. 6.7).

She is most often in the company of many women, who help her prepare and bring her various objects, including alabastra, jewellery boxes, precious pieces of clothing, etc. Sometimes, the person who brings her the perfume vase is simply a small Eros, which reinforces even more the erotic symbolism associated with the perfume in the context of marriage. The alabastron and its contents are thus part of everyday life bathing activities as well as in the more ritualised bath of the bride. The scented oil in the vase becomes a weapon of seduction in the love arsenal of women and goddesses, an artifice whose effects are widely described in ancient literature. For example, in *The Bath of Pallas* (13–32), Callimachus opposes how Aphrodite and Athena use scented oils: Athena does not need a mirror or an alabastron filled with perfume. Pure olive oil suits her better. This simple observation highlights the fundamental differences between the two goddesses, a warrior without artifice and a seductress, using perfumes contained in alabastra as odoriferous love potions.

Several scenes include the alabastron in the context of seduction and the interpretation of

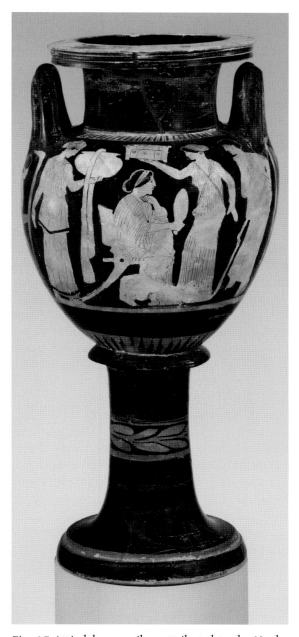

Fig. 6.7 Attic lebes gamikos attributed to the Naples Painter. Attendants of the bride bring different items, including an alabastron. The Metropolitan Museum of Art, New York, inv. 06.1021.298. Rogers Fund, 1906. c. 420 BCE (www.metmuseum.org)

these scenes is controversial. Many studies since the early 19th century present a negative and prudish image of women represented on Greek vases. When the context of the scene or the status of the characters are difficult to determine, women are often labelled as "courtesans" (*hetairai*) or "prostitutes" (*pornai*). As stated by Sian Lewis, this is particularly the case with scenes depicting naked women, but also women:

> who converse with men, women who receive any kind of gifts, woman who dance, play music, or drink, and those who engages in odd tasks such as spinning or textile work. In its most extreme form, this theory can label a woman who stands fully-clothed making a cushion, or who is alone in a room holding a mirror as a prostitute (Lewis 2006, 33).

The author also notes that some recent studies emphasise the erotic value of fully clothed, sometimes veiled, women. So, we can only wonder at the apparently considerable disproportion between the (huge) number of scenes showing prostitutes and the (very low) number of scenes showing "respectable" women. A good example of this type of interpretation is provided by an alabastron representing a woman holding a flower while another dances with rattles (Athens, National Museum, 1740, BA: 201531; Peschel 1987, 82). No other element, such as a piece of furniture, gives any reason to set the scene in a specific context. However, the young woman dancing with rattles is interpreted as a courtesan dancing during a banquet. Given the absence of any reference to the banquet in this scene, however, she could be dancing in a Dionysian context or at a religious event. Another good example of over-interpretation is a red-figure cup medallion with a woman holding an alabastron (Private collection, BA: 22047). There is a door behind her, one of her shoulders is naked and there is big vase at her feet. It has been said that the big vase was a krater related to a banquet happening behind the door and that, given the erotic value of the alabastron and its content, the woman is a prostitute about to engage in sexual intercourse with banqueters (Badinou 2003, 65). But she could simply be about to take a bath. Our goal here is not to deny the existence of representations of courtesans on Attic pottery. However, in some cases, the information provided by the image is too weak or ambiguous to allow us to identify with certainty the status of the represented figures.

The alabastron is closely associated with female body care, and its contents were used not only in daily baths, but also nuptial baths. In this last instance, the fragrance was used to increase women's beauty and sex-appeal, along with more traditional ornaments like jewellery and beautiful clothes. However, the alabastron is more than just a feminine vase: the alabastron and its fragrant contents belong to the set of objects that allow the *oikos* to show off its wealth, especially during wedding ceremonies, as noted by L. Bodiou and V. Mehl (2008, 169): "Luxurious fabrics, expensive perfumes, sumptuous gifts, plentiful food, numerous guests: during the wedding it is also the wealth of the family that is shown". The authors also point out that, in Aristophanes' *Ploutos*, poverty deplores the lack of perfume that could have been spread over the bride. So, it seems that the use of perfumes and of alabastra was sometimes linked to luxurious practices.

This seems to be the case with the plemochoe as well. The plemochoe is a vase with a wide opening, which has the particularity of having a curved inward lip, probably to avoid the spilling of its content. In archaeological literature, it is also called exaleiptron though this term is most often applied to the stemless Corinthian version (Rodríguez-Pérez 2016). This shape undergoes an evolution that will lead to a high-footed, lidded Attic specimen in the late 6th century BCE (Fig. 6.8). Its wide opening was probably not ideal for preserving precious perfumes. Although some authors have taken it for a lamp, it has often been considered to be a vase containing diluted perfume. It could also be a container for scented powders or make-up (Scheibler 1964).

Fig. 6.8 Attic black-glaze plemochoe. The Metropolitan Museum of Art, New York, inv. 07.286.46a, b. Rogers Fund, 1907. Late 6th century BCE (www.metmuseum.org)

There are numerous representations of plemochoai which helps us identify the contexts of use of this vase. Like the previous vases, the plemochoe was one of the objects that could be brought to the tomb as an offering during various rituals or be deposited on a funerary monument's steps. For example, on Basel, Antikenmuseum und Sammlung Ludwig, BS454 (BA: 389); Athens, Kerameikos (BA: 1358); Brussels, Musées Royaux d'Art et d'Histoire, R395 (BA: 4622); Gotha, Schlossmuseum, AHV71 (BA: 8001); Cambridge, Arthur M. Sackler Museum, 60.335 (BA: 209185); Taranto, Museo Archeologico Nazionale, 4567 (BA: 209199); Boston, Museum of Fine Arts, R449 (BA: 213982). It is often found in the *gynaikeion*, placed on the floor or on a shelf or in the hands of women that are bathing. Examples are Boston, Museum of Fine Arts, 00.340 (BA: 203180); Aberdeen, University, 706 (BA: 203181); Gela, Museo Archeologico, N110B (BA: 207910); Athens, Vlasto collection (BA: 208328); Compiègne, Musée Vivenel, 1090 (BA: 211213, plemochoe stored on a shelf). There are also examples in which the women are dressing, Gela, Museo Archeologico, N64 (BA: 207423); Munich, Antikensammlungen, J627 (BA: 210162). Like the alabastron, it also appears frequently in wedding scenes, which is not the case with the aryballos. For example, Berlin, Antikensammlung, 3373 (BA: 430); Copenhagen, National Museum, 479 (BA: 2093); Hanover, Kestner Museum, 1966.116 (BA: 8737); Athens, National Museum, A1877 (BA: 275718). It is especially used during the ritual bath of the bride or the future husband and during the preparation of the bride. For example, Hanover, Kestner Museum,

Fig. 6.9 Attic red-figured hydria attributed to the Washing Painter. The Metropolitan Museum of Art, New York, inv. 22.139.25. Rogers Fund, 1922. c. 430–420 BCE (www.metmuseum.org)

1966.116 (BA: 8737); Kiel, Antikensammlung, B270 (BA: 30046); Warsaw, National Museum, 142290 (BA: 206567); Athens, National Museum, 1681 (BA: 220566); Saint-Petersbourg, Hermitage Museum, ST1811 (BA: 220696). As stated before, perfume vases and containers, such as alabastra and plemochoai, are probably markers of economic status. The hydria attributed to the Washing Painter in Figure 6.9 is a good example of this.

As suggested by the flying Eros, the woman at the centre is a bride and she is surrounded by female attendants, one of them holding a fan. This accessory was introduced from the East during the 5th century and indicates just like the parasol (also imported from the East) the wealth of the main character on this image (Miller 1997, 198–206). It is worth noting that the daughters of metics, foreign residents in Athens, carried the parasols of the Athenian maidens at Panathenaea, a service called sciadephoria that marked them out as a class inferior in dignity to the citizens (Pollux, VII, 134). Thus, if perfume vases are obviously gendered in images, they are also clearly a sign of a higher socio-economic status, as some other objects. Alabastra and plemochoai are mainly represented in images related to body care and seduction, but other images show uses reinforcing this idea of a link with elite citizens. Men, like women, could be buyers of alabastra as shown by vases where scented oil is sold to athletes in the palaestra (Algrain 2014, 169–170). During the banquet as well, whether in Attica, Eastern Greece or Etruria, images often show the alabastron used by or for men and associated with "Eastern" practices: banqueting on beds, use of Eastern shapes of drinking vases like the phialai, and these practices can usually be associated with a wealthier part of the population. Another image of the uses of perfume vases emerges here, perhaps more related to an economic status than to a specific gender.

Archaeological contexts also show a more complex situation: perfume vases are found in graves of both sexes but it is difficult to determine whether they are associated with the dead or with the persons in charge of the cleansing of the body with scented oils, namely women in ancient Greece (Algrain, forthcoming). Women, already acquainted with the pollution (*miasma*) of birth, are, to the eyes of the Greeks, the most appropriate to deal with the pollution engendered by death. The preparation of the deceased's body before the funeral is part of their tasks (Parker 1983, 32–73). In graves, although the other vase shapes named above can also be part of funerary assemblages, the bulk of the offerings in the Archaic and Classical periods often consists of lekythoi. The lekythos is the Athenian oil vase *par excellence*, as evidenced by the particularly high number of these discovered in funerary, ritual or domestic contexts (Fig. 6.10).

The production of this shape and its variants dated from the beginning of the 6th to the 4th century BCE (Algrain, Brisart and Jubier-Galinier 2008, 148). In Classical Athens, the vase was not gendered when associated with the dead. In representations, the

Fig. 6.10 *White-ground lekythos attributed to the Bosanquet Painter. Lekythoi and other vases decorate the funerary monument; on the right, a mourner approach with an alabastron as an offering; on the left, a young man, probably the deceased, hold an aryballos. The Metropolitan Museum of Art, New York, inv. 23.160.38. Rogers Fund, 1923. c. 440–430 BCE (www.metmuseum.org)*

lekythos is brought by women who visit the graves of a family member. For examples see the lekythoi at Athens, National Museum, 1929 (BA: 209186, preparation of a visit to the tomb); Tampa, Museum of Art, 86.79 (BA: 209247) and the fragment of a hydria at Athens (National Museum, 17283; BA: 215027). It could also be placed on a funerary monument, functioning as a sign of previous visits and of the care taken in the maintenance of the tomb. For example, lekythoi at Athens (Vlasto Collection; BA: 212350 and National Museum, 2018; BA: 212364), New York (Metropolitan Museum of Art, 51.11.4; BA: 212352), Basel (Private collection; BA: 212392), Laon (Musée Archéologique Municipal, 37.955; BA: 215826) and New York (Metropolitan Museum of Art, 23.160.38; BA: 216333). During the second half of the 5th century BCE, it is often decorated with funerary scenes, mostly visits to the tomb (Schmidt 2005, 29–79).

Conclusion

The Athenian social body is built not only in opposition to foreign barbarians, but it also excludes some of the inhabitants of Attica. As shown by the example of slaves who cannot access the gymnasium, there is no homogeneous group of "Athenians" and a large social stratification defines the place and roles of each individual within the city. "Women" are not a more homogeneous group than "Athenians" because of the intersection of various social elements such as class, city of origin, ethnicity, age, etc. with gender, creating groups of women who experienced gender inequality differently (Brumfiel 2007, 2). Being a wealthy citizen's wife was a profoundly different experience from being a slave woman in an Athenian household. The low visibility and problems of identification of certain categories of women (for example poor women, slaves, non-Athenian women) in artistic and archaeological sources invites us to ask the question: are we really writing a history of Greek women or are we limited to write the history of only some Greek women?

A conceptual framework with a gender-sensitive analysis must therefore take into account the differences between old and modern norms, in order for us to not distort interpretations. Heteronormativity is more problematic because, although Greek society seems to be patriarchal in the same way as ours, the norms that regulate it in terms of body, sexuality and constitution of the social body do not only use the heterosexual couple as the basis of the society. Though it was one of the basic aspects of the social constitution of the city, the male citizen also constituted a strong norm. The perfect body is masculine, the most permissive sexuality is masculine as long as the man remains in a dominant position, the social body is constituted of men and rejects non-citizens. Marriage is the only heterosexual framework that is mandatory, but its ultimate goal is the reproduction of the body of citizens. It therefore seems that heteronormativity alone does not account for the reality of the Greeks in the construction of the social order. It may be necessary to resort to a different concept and talk about politonormativity in addition to heteronormativity: the values and practices of citizens (*politeis*) are the norm, while women, and all non-citizens, deviate from this norm to various degrees.

According to this politonormativity, the best way to use oil is to follow the example of Athena, the virile female deity protecting Athens. Though female, Athena uses pure olive oil for her body, as Athenian citizens use oil contained in aryballoi in the gymnasium. Images show us how perfume vases were used by both sexes to perform their gender, as part of their "identity". On the images, the aryballos is linked with the citizen-athlete, while the alabastron and the plemochoe appear mainly in scenes of bathing, dressing and adornment of women and brides. Yet, a close examination of images and archaeological contexts can help to nuance this interpretation and reveal a more subtle use of perfume vases and their content in Athenian society. Neither alabastra nor plemochoai were exclusively symbols of the female world, as they could also serve as containers of expensive products reminiscent of luxury and eastern values that are obvious in iconography. Thus, perfume vases in iconography were not only gendered but could also denote men and women's socio-economic status. Vases often show the world of the wealthier citizens and their wives, a world of leisure, luxury and lavish expenses made, among others, on costly perfumes and their containers.

Acknowledgements

I would like to thank Uroš Matić for asking me to participate in this volume. I would also like to thank Vivi Saripanidi, Jean-Manuel Roubineau and Alexandre Mitchell, as well as the anonymous reviewers, for their valuable advice and comments.

Bibliography

Algrain, I. (2014) *L'alabastre attique. Origine, formes et usages.* Bruxelles, CReA-Patrimoine.
Algrain, I. (forthcoming) Images for the dead: the symbolic value of figured offerings in Athenian graves. In W. van de Put and D. Paleothodoros (eds), *Oikos-Taphos-Temenos. Iconography in Greek Context. Proceedings of the Conference, 26–27 February 2016.*
Algrain, I., Brisart, T. and Jubier-Galinier, C. (2008) Les vases à parfum à Athènes aux époques archaïque et Classique. In A. Verbanck-Piérard, N. Massar and D. Frère (eds) *Parfums de l'Antiquité. La rose et l'encens en Méditerranée. Catalogue d'exposition*, 145–164. Mariemont, Musée royal de Mariemont.
Badinou, P. (2003) *La laine et le parfum. Epinetra et alabastres: forme, iconographie et fonction.* Louvain, Peeters.
Bodiou, L. and Mehl, V. (2008) Parfums de passage: naissance, mariage et funérailles en pays grec. In A. Verbanck-Piérard, N. Massar and D. Frère (eds) *Parfums de l'Antiquité. La rose et l'encens en Méditerranée. Catalogue d'exposition*, 165–173. Mariemont, Musée royal de Mariemont.
Boix, A. (2013) Der attische Aryballos. *Kölner und Bonner Archaeologica* 3, 41–82.
Boehringer, S. (2010) La sexualité a-t-elle un passé ? De l'érôs grec à la sexualité contemporaine : questions modernes au monde antique. *Recherches en psychanalyse* 10 (2), 189–201.
Bozon, M. (2013) *Sociologie de la sexualité.* Troisième édition. Paris, Armand Colin.

Isabelle Algrain

Brumfiel, E.M. (2007) Methods in feminist and gender archaeology: a feeling for difference and likeness. In S.M. Nelson (ed.) *Women in Antiquity. Theoretical Approaches to Gender and Archaeology*, 1–28. Plymouth, AltaMira Press.

Bunch, C. (1987) *Passionate Politics: Essays 1968-1986. Feminist Theory in Action*. New York, St. Martin's Griffin.

Carter, J.C. (1998) Historical development. In J.C. Carter, J. Morter and A. Parmly Toxey (eds) *The Chora of Metaponto. The Necropoleis*, 167–236. Austin, University of Texas Press.

D'Acunto, M. (2012) I profumi nella Grecia alto-arcaica e arcaica: produzione, commercio, comportamenti sociali. In A. Carannante and M. D'Acunto (eds) *I profumi nelle società antiche. Produzione, commercio, usi, valori simbolici*. Paestum, Pandemos.

Dorlin, E. (2006) *La matrice de la race. Généalogie sexuelle et coloniale de la nation française*. Paris, La Découverte.

Duru-Bellat, M. (2017) *La tyrannie du genre*. Paris, Presses de la Fondation nationale des sciences politiques.

Filser, W. (2017) *Die Elite Athens auf der attischen Luxuskeramik*. Berlin/München/Boston, De Gruyter.

Foucault, M. (1984) *Histoire de la sexualité 3. Le souci de soi*. Paris, Gallimard.

Foxhall, L. (2012) Gender. In K.A. Raaflaub and H. Van Wees (eds) *A Companion to Archaic Greece*, 483–507. Chichester, Blackwell Publishing Ltd.

Gherchanoc, F. (2008) Nudités athlétiques et identités en Grèce ancienne. *Mètis* N.S. 6, 75–101.

Gherchanoc, F. (2016) *Concours de beauté et beautés du corps en Grèce ancienne. Discours et pratiques*. Bordeaux, Ausonius.

Heinemann, A. (2009) Bild, Gefäss, Praxis : Überlegungen zu attischen Salbgefässen. In S. Schmidt and J.H. Oakley (eds) *Hermeneutik der Bilder. Beiträge zur Ikonographie und Interpretation griechischer Vasenmalerei*, 161–175. München, Verlag C.H. Beck.

Héritier, F. (1996) *Masculin/Féminin I. La pensée de la différence*. Paris, Odile Jacob Poches.

Hill, D.K. (1965) To perfume the Etruscans and Latins. *Archaeology* 18, 187–190.

Houby-Nielsen, S. (1995) "Burial language" in Archaic and Classical Kerameikos. *Proceedings of the Danish Institute at Athens* 1, 129–191.

Keuls, E. (1985) *The Reign of the Phallus. Sexual Politics in Ancient Athens*. Berkeley, University of California Press.

King, H. (1993) Bound to bleed: Artemis and Greek women. In A. Cameron and A. Kuhrt (eds.) *Images of Women in Antiquity*, 109–127. Second edition. London, Routledge.

Kreilinger, U. (2007) *Anständige Nacktheit: Körperpflege, Reinigungsriten und das Phänomen weiblicher Nacktheit im archaisch-klassischen Athen*. Rahden/Westf, Leidorf.

Lanni, A. (2009) Social norms in the courts of ancient Athens. *Journal of Legal Analysis* 9, 691–736.

Laqueur, T. (1992) *La fabrique du sexe. Essai sur le corps et le genre en Occident*. Traduction de M. Gautier. Paris, Folio essais.

Lewis, S. (2006) Iconography and the study of gender. In S. Schroer (ed.) *Images and Gender. Contributions to the Hermeneutics of Reading Ancient Art*, 23–39. Göttingen, Vandenhoeck & Ruprecht.

Lissarrague, F. (1990) *L'autre guerrier. Archers, peltastes, cavaliers dans l'imagerie attique*. Paris/Rome, La Découverte-Ecole française de Rome.

Maggiani, A. (1972) Aska eleivana. *Studi Etruschi* 40, 183–187.

Miller, M.C. (1997) *Athens and Persia in the Fifth Century. A Study in Cultural Receptivity*. Cambridge, Cambridge University Press.

Mitchell, A.G. (2015) Humor, women, and male anxieties in Ancient Greek cisual culture. In A. Foka and J. Liliequist (eds) *Laughter, Humor, and the (Un)Making of Gender, Historical and Cultural Perspectives*, 214–240. Basingstoke, Palgrave Macmillan.

Newman, A.N. (2018) Queering the Minoans: gender performativity and the Aegean color convention in fresco painting at Knossos. *Journal of Mediterranean Archaeology* 30 (2), 213–236.

Ogden, D. (1996) *Greek Bastardy in the Classical and Hellenistic periods.* Oxford, Clarendon Press.

Parker, R. (1983) *Miasma. Pollution and Purification in Early Greek Religion.* Oxford, Clarendon.

Parker, H. (2012) Women and medicine. In S.L. James and S. Dillon (eds) *A Companion to Women in the Ancient World*, 107–124. Chichester, Wiley Blackwell.

Peschel, I. (1987) *Die Hetäre bei Symposium und Komos in der attischrotfigurigen Malerei des 6.-4. Jhs v. Chr.* Frankfurt am Main, Peter Lang.

Pomeroy, S. (2002) *Spartan Women.* Oxford, Oxford University Press.

Rodríguez-Pérez, D. (2016) Evocative objects. The Attic black-glazed plemochoai (exaleiptra) between archaeology and vase-painting. In J. Boardman, A. Parkin and S. Waite (eds) *On the Fascination of Objects. Greek and Etruscan Art in the Shefton Collection*, 17–30. Oxford, Oxbow Books.

Scheibler, I. (1964) Exaleiptra. *Jahrbuch des Deutschen Archäologischen Instituts* 79, 72–108.

Scheidel, W. (2011), Monogamy and polygyny. In B. Rawson (ed.) *A Companion to Families in the Greek and Roman Worlds*, 108–115. Chichester, Wiley Blackwell.

Schmidt, S. (2005) *Rhetorische Bilder auf attischen Vasen. Visuelle Kommunikation im 5. Jahrhundert v. Chr.* Berlin, Reimer.

Scott, J. (1986) Gender: a useful category of historical analysis. *American Historical Review* 91, 1053–1075.

Shelmerdine, C.W. (1985) *The Perfume Industry of Mycenaean Pylos.* Göteborg, Åström.

Shelmerdine, C.W. (1995) Shining and fragrant cloth in Homeric epic. In J.B. Carter and S.P. Morris (eds.) *The Ages of Homer. A Tribute to Emily Townsend Vermeule*, 99–109. Austin, University of Texas Press.

Smith, N.D. (1983) Plato and Aristotle on the nature of women. *Journal of the History of Philosophy* 21 (4), 467–478.

Topper, K. (2012), Approaches to reading Attic vases. In S.L. James and S. Dillon (eds) *A Companion to Women in the Ancient World*, 141–152. Chichester, Wiley Blackwell.

Chapter 7

Mirrors in the funerary contexts of Moesia Superior: Roman hegemony, beauty and gender?

Vladimir D. Mihajlović

Abstract

The paper considers burials that contained mirrors in two Roman period necropolises from the province of Moesia Superior – Viminacium and Demessus. Using the qualitative and quantitative analysis and comparisons of grave assemblages I address the issue of the roles mirrors had played within the provincial social setting. By examining the archaeological contexts of mirrors in burials I question if the widespread supposition about connection between mirrors and specific gender and age is as obvious and straightforward as generally held. Although the literary, visual and archaeological evidence from Rome and Italy suggests that mirrors were the prominent piece of the female beauty kit (mundus muliebris), the discussed case studies do not completely conform to the presumed rule. This raises several important questions that I tackle in the paper: how and to what extent the idea of mirrors as a device for feminine beauty had spread in the province of Moesia; was the bond of mirrors and certain age cohorts of females indeed so clear-cut; did the graves containing mirrors exclusively belonged to young unmarried or newly married females; could we speak of general social and gender class of "women" or such categorisation actually misses very important nuances of identity and oversimplifies the picture; were there other social and gender categories associated and buried with mirrors.

Key words: *mirrors, Upper Moesia, mundus muliebris, gender, Roman power and culture*

Introduction: androcentrism, beauty and mirrors in the Roman world

The Roman world, like other ancient Mediterranean societies, was markedly androcentric, with male-dominated perspectives pervading its entire functioning and structure. The ideas of female natural inferiority, passivity and dependency on men denied women a share of political decision-making, restricted them from regular and direct access to political and economic power, and considerably limited their modes of participation in public life. As women were generally understood as "creatures" that lack both the capacity and skills for severe intellectual endeavours, physical action, economic enterprise and political efforts, they were considered beings of superficiality and limited agency. This ideological "passivisation" and marginalisation of female gender was coupled with the expectation that women had to assume a submissive position (within the private domestic realm) and that the intrinsic potential of their "kind" should be articulated through the roles of obedient wives and caring mothers (see D'Ambra 2007; Evans Grubbs 2002; Milnor 2011).

The Roman gender system was formulated by the idea of natural predispositions (that were partially derived from biological sex), and corresponding power relations whereby (a properly constructed and accurately determined type of) manhood assumed the superior rank. Certainly, this was an ideal (primarily known from elite contexts), and it is not reasonable to expect that it continually and invariably functioned throughout space, time and social circumstances. In other words, we should always remember to question whether the elite normative that shaped literary representations applied in reality to all social contexts of the Roman Empire. Hence, we should by no means understand "women" in the Roman period as an entirely passive, static and homogenous group that lacked social agency and did not subvert the overall framework of androcracy (Dolansky 2012; Ferris 2015, 199; Harlow and Laurence 2002, 84; Hemelrijk 2015, 201; Revell 2016, 120–125; Tokarek LaFosse 2017). Instead, we must consider the diversity of particular female roles that actively worked their ways through and around orthodox societal schemes, manipulated and bypassed conventions, acquired various sorts of power and negotiated individual positionings (as some cases clearly show – Cooley 2013; D'Ambra 2007, 16–22, 142–166; Fantham 1995; Ferris 2015, 31–83). Nevertheless, the continual rule of masculine discourses and a generally unaltered (*i.e.*, marginal) position of women in antiquity make the Roman social environment prominently a "man's world", and this should be borne in mind in any attempt to shed some light on female histories.

One of the discourses stemming from the Roman period andronormativity was the concept of female beauty and proper appearance. Although it is best known from the upper parts of Roman society, it most probably cut through the entire socio-cultural structure. The idea of convenient display of femininity to (principally) male gaze seems to be so deeply embedded within the Roman Empire's habitus that it operated as a standard notion, normalised enough to be generally (even subconsciously) accepted by many women themselves (see Berg 2002; D'Ambra 2007, 111–128; Harlow 2013a; 2013b, 333; Shumka 2008; 2016; Swift 2012; Wyke 1994). However, while some women might have enjoyed the imposed standards of behaviour or looks, or took advantage if their appearance closely resembled the ideal, there is no doubt that these social norms would have been different if it were not for the dominance of the male gaze. In short, the male-dominated social expectations dictated that a woman should take care of her appearance (*cultus*) by utilising the cosmetic/toilet set (encompassed by the concept of *mundus mulieribus*) that enabled her to "upgrade" natural looks and transform this into an image fitting to men's pleasure and taste (Berg 2002; Dolansky 2012, 269; Johnson 2016, 8–12; Shumka 2008, 173, 177–178; Wyke 1994). The toilet apparatus consisted of dress, jewellery, cosmetics, cosmeceuticals and make-up (of various sorts, including creams, ointments, perfumes, etc.), suitable instruments (probes, spoons, palettes, etc.), mirrors, boxes for the equipment and containers (*e.g.*, flasks and bottles) for liquid or paste contents. All of these became so strongly associated with female identities and roles (Berg 2002; Ferris 2015, 86–93, 110; Martin-Kilcher 2000, 70; Oliver 2000, 115–116; Shumka 2008; 2016; Swift 2012), and were even extrapolated to imagining the world of goddesses (most notably Venus – Ferris 2015, 88; Hales 2008; Swift 2012, 54; Taylor 2008, 39–47), that it is safe to assert that acquiring fully-fledged femininity was not possible without associating with the aforementioned objects and behaviour. Hence, becoming and performing the ideal-typical female in the Roman world was possible only through tying-up with specific materiality, practices and ideas (*cf.* Berg 2002, 30–31) that enabled self-styling/fashioning and articulation of "truly feminine nature", and allowed subsequent linking to the wider networks of gender and social discourses.

However, such a transformation of appearance was the mechanism of male control, for it was socially acceptable only if done correctly and approved by the patriarchal standards. The men-dominated society set the conventional border between a tasteful and wanted image, achieved with the full awareness of the (all-encompassing) principle of chastity/virtue (*pudicitia*) and the one that was stigmatised as excessive, and publicly condemned. In simple terms, there was a subtle and somewhat ambiguous line (drawn by the ideas about female morality) between the appropriate care of woman's appearance and inappropriately extravagant and overdone looks. The former was regularly associated with the world of *matronae* and chaste girls (chiefly of citizen and higher status), whereas the latter was (stereo)typically paralleled with the *infames,* such as prostitutes, courtesans, actresses and women of the lower social orders, who are believed to be unchaste, adulterous and promiscuous (Berg 2002, 24–25; D'Ambra 2007, 48, 111–113; Dolansky 2012, 270–274; Johnson 2016, 6–12; Langlands 2006; Shumka 2008; Wyke 1994). Consequently, the proper cultivation of female appearance, defined by the ruling taste of men from the upper ranks, and judged upon by their moralising convenience, was mainly linked to the construction and performance of higher social status (Dolansky 2012, 287; Harlow 2013b; Milnor 2011, 616; Shumka 2008, 186–187; Wyke 1994, 141), regardless of whether it was already achieved or an aspired one. Thus, the conceptions of gender, social positioning, morality, adequate behaviour and beauty/physical display were interrelated and mutually conditioned (*cf.* Montserrat 2000), which should be remembered when any of these categories are reviewed in particular cases.

The ideology of female care for appearance is most closely connected with mirrors, the objects instrumental for achieving the beauty convention. As such, they became the quintessential symbol of femininity, which is evident in the range from iconography of the goddess Venus, to representations of "ordinary" women in art, to gendered burial customs (Cohen 2010; Hales 2010; Martin-Kilcher 2000; Oliver 2000; Shumka 2016; Swift 2012; Taylor 2008, 32, 36, 39–47; Wyke 1994, 135) or dolls found within girls' burials (Dolansky 2012; Harlow 2013b, 329–334; Newby 2019). Of course, men also used mirrors but, as far as the written sources and archaeological records indicate, on a much smaller scale. The social norm for men, at least among the higher social echelons, dictated that one should restrain himself from involvements with the mirror and use the object only for "manly" purposes of self-improvement that excluded beautification, adornment and the triviality of self-indulgence in one's own looks. Deviance from the rule risked the negative reputation of effeminacy, and in such cases, mirrors assumed the role of both an aid-to and a symptom-of moral corruption. In the case of a male, an over-entanglement with mirrors triggered the reversion, confusion, disruption or degradation of the expected gender construction, a fact that adds to the objects' relevance to the concept of womanhood (Berg 2002, 27–30; Taylor 2008, 20; Wyke 1994, 137–138).

Additionally, mirrors had multivalent roles and meanings, and were comprehended as objects with special powers and features. As mediators par excellence (*sensu* Latour 2005), mirrors acted as nods that transformed the state of being and self, and converted it from one sort of relations to another. They played the pivotal part in various metamorphoses and passages, and symbolised a threshold between the worlds and ontological conditions, which ensured them the connotation of objects of rites and magic (Hales 2010; Mihajlović 2011a; Taylor 2008, 7, 102–103). Simply put, by employing the mirror, one was crossing between different roles and spheres: private-public, girl-woman, virginal-nuptial, untidiness-tidiness, unappealing-attractive, manly-effeminate, etc. Accordingly, a mirror could acquire the capacity of an actor that facilitated the emerging of different social personae and states of being. A mirror's capacity to emit one's image contributed to it the aspect of a moral device (Taylor 2008). It empowered the individual to literally face her/himself, compare what was seen against the referential backdrop of governing habitus, and respectively accept or reject the reached assessment. However, reflexivity is never an objective and value-free process: it happens through re-evaluation and reconsideration of self and the relationalities one has towards other people, socio-cultural structure and various ideas about the world (*cf.* Adams 2006; Archer 2010; Holmes 2010). Each time a person was generating her/his corporeality with the help of a mirror, the process has been carried out in reference to the commonly accepted models, norms and expectations (that were determined by concepts of gender, status, age, beauty, occasion appropriateness, religion, etc.). Therefore, when one fashioned visual identity and social persona for the outer world and public display, s/he conducted this concerning particular ideological inclinations. This is why mirrors were not the mere tools for (re)shaping individual appearance, but active enablers and constitutive elements of roles and identities of people who used them. In other words, they were the mediators of one's becoming a personality with declared (physical and ideological) features, and of achieving the preferred social condition (gender role, appropriate looks, sexually appealing individual, socio-economic standing, etc.), which makes them one of the tangible centrepieces of the "technology of self" (*cf.* Foucault 1988).

Having in mind all of the aforementioned, there is a little doubt that research on mirrors in the Roman world could considerably contribute to comprehensions of several questions and phenomena, including the topic at the core of this volume. Indeed, this realisation is not new, and mirrors already have been the focus of very inspiring studies that set the basis and defined main trajectories for further investigation (*e.g.*, Berg 2002; Shumka 2008; 2016; Taylor 2008; Wyke 1994). Therefore, this chapter is an attempt to continue the work and broaden the arguments by addressing the role of mirrors within the funerary domain of the province of Upper Moesia. The following discussion should add to current scholarship, as it directs attention towards the edge of the Roman Empire, to an area that was outside the interests of ancient literary sources and has limited attention of international Roman scholarship. Whereas important research has been done on the Upper and Middle Danube regions and western provinces of the Empire, notably the analyses of visual representations (*e.g.*, Carroll 2013; 2015; Hales 2010; Rothe 2012a; 2012b; 2013), the Lower Danube and Balkan provinces are prominently missing from Roman period dress and gender literature. Recently, there has been some work by scholars from Serbia, but it is of an overview character and insufficiently informed in theoretical and methodological terms, thus risking the oversimplification of complex phenomena (Danković 2019; Danković, Milovanović and Marjanović 2018).

Mirrors in the graves of Roman Moesia: two case studies

Here I consider the burials from two Upper Moesian necropolises that were used from 1st to 3rd centuries CE near Viminacium (Stari Kostolac, Serbia) and the castrum of Stojnik (Demessus?), respectively (Fig. 7.1).

In both cases, the graves and their contents are analysed according to the published reports (Glumac 2014; Korać and Golubović 2009; Zotović and Jordović 1990) and data from a book in preparation that Tatjana Cvjetićanin kindly permitted me to consult (Cvjetićanin and Glumac forthcoming). In both burial grounds, the interment of a cremated deceased predominated and the graves were of the local *Mala Kopašnica-Sase* type (hereafter MKS; see Cvjetićanin 2016; 2018; Jovanova 2016, 58–61; Jovanović 2000; Korać and Golubović 2009, 541–546; Stamenković, Ivanišević and Pešić 2016). There are two subtypes of this kind of grave: MKS 1 – a simple, variously shaped (oval, square, rectangular) burial pit with burned walls; and MKS 2 – a more elaborate step-grave construction with burned walls, consisting of an upper-level pit (that usually contains grave-goods/offerings), within which the lower level/inner shaft (for cremated remains) is dug. The incineration of the deceased poses severe difficulties for anthropological analysis, and even if there is some assessment (such as the case with Viminacium material), it cannot be treated as reliable, as it was done only according the surviving bone fragments. Hence, data that can usually be extracted from skeletal evidence (age, sex, paleopathology) are beyond reach for the burials discussed in this chapter. Another limiting feature is the very general chronological determination of the graves, since the majority of these are vaguely dated within a half-a-century-span or conforming to the coins found inside them (*i.e.*, there is neither a more delicate typological determination of material nor has absolute dating been conducted). Having in mind these general restrictions, let us review the graves that contained mirrors by addressing first the case of Viminacium and then of Stojnik.

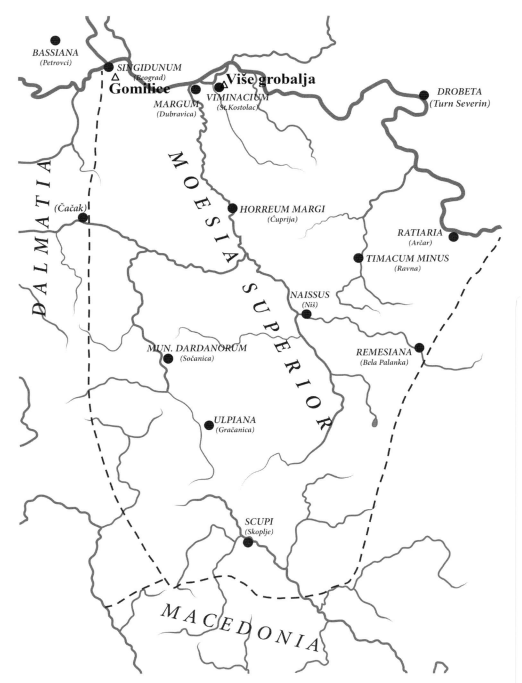

Fig. 7.1 Territory of Moesia Superior with the two discussed necropolises (marked with triangles) and settlements mentioned in the text (Map designed by Jelena Premović, reproduced with her permission)

Viminacium – "Više grobalja"

Viminacium was the most important settlement and the metropolis of Moesia Superior that was founded next to the legionary fortress and further developed from the second half of the 1st century CE. It was an administrative, military, economic and cultural centre of regional significance, and one of the most populous cities in this part of the Empire (Mirković 1986; Spasić Đurić 2002; 2015, 133–145). Up to now more than 13,000 burials from the early to the late Roman period (1st–5th c. CE) have been excavated at different sites around the city (Spasić Đurić 2002, 183; Zotović and Jordović 1990, 36). However, only 1,047 graves from the site of "Više grobalja" (Fig. 7.2) are published so far (Korać and Golubović 2009; Zotović and Jordović 1990), whereas the greatest portion of burials remains unknown. It should also be emphasised that published grave units equal to *c.* 25% of burials from the site of "Više grobalja" (Zotović and Jordović 1990, 122) and any interpretation is hence far from being conclusive.

The group of 26 burials with mirrors discussed here (Table 7.1) comes from the "Više grobalja" site which was the part of the southern necropolises of Viminacium.

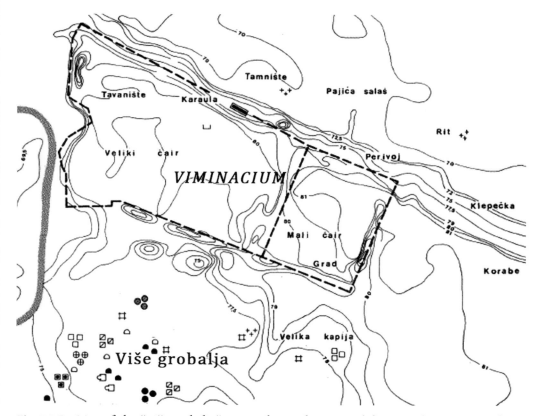

Fig. 7.2 Position of the "Više grobalja" necropolis, settlement and fortress of Viminacium (after Mirković 1986)

Table 7.1 Viminacium, Više grobalja necropolis, graves with mirrors (according to Zotović and Jordović 1990; Korać and Golubović 2009). The mirrors are all of the round type and made of bronze unless otherwise stated. Designation G_1 stands for cremation while G marks inhumation burials

	Grave no.	Grave type	Mirror	Box/case	Toilet/cosmetic equipment	Glass flask(s)	Lamp	Ceramic vessel(s)	Other	Age, sex	Date
1	G_1-192	MKS 2 cremation	fragment (silver)		fragmented bone needle			cup		adult female	I c.
2	G_1-170	MKS 2 cremation	fragment of bronze mirror with silver amalgam	iron sheet fittings, decorative bronze rivet				bowl, pot	fragmented bone distaff, coin (Trajan)	adult female	Trajan
3	G_1-167*	MKS 1 cremation	1 (rectangular, bronze with silver amalgam)				1		bronze bowl	undetermined	Trajan-Hadrian
4	G_1-44**	MKS 1 cremation	1 (bronze)		bone spoon	1	1	jug	2 bone sewing needles, coin (Hadrian)	undetermined	Hadrian (or later)
	G_1-47	MKS 2 cremation			fragments of bronze strigil			2 pots, 2 jugs	handle of glass vessel	undetermined	
5	G-75	simple pit inhumation	1 silver (bronze handle)	bronze fittings and plate	2 bone needles (found on each shoulder)	2	1	jug, beaker, pot	string of beads, coin (Trajan), glass beaker	8–10 years girl	first 1/2 of II c.

(Continued)

Table 7.1 Viminacium, Više grobalja necropolis, graves with mirrors (according to Zotović and Jordović 1990; Korać and Golubović 2009). The mirrors are all of the round type and made of bronze unless otherwise stated. Designation G_1 stands for cremation while G marks inhumation burials (Continued)

	Grave no.	Grave type	Mirror	Box/case	Toilet/cosmetic equipment	Glass flask(s)	Lamp	Ceramic vessel(s)	Other	Age, sex	Date
6	G_1-132	MKS 2 cremation	1 bronze (with silver amalgam)		bronze spatula	2	2	bowl, 3 jugs	2 coins	undetermined	first 1/2 of II c.
7	G_1-270	MKS 1 cremation	two fragments of bronze mirror				1	jug, 2 bowls, pot		adult, undetermined	mid II c.
8	G_1-273	MKS 2 cremation	fragments, bronze		bronze needle		1	2 jugs	frag. iron knife, coin (A. Pius)	adult female	A. Pius
9	G_1-23	MKS 1 cremation	1 bronze (with silver amalgam)		bronze needle			bowl, cup, beaker	2 coins (burnt), bone tube-handle, ceramic spindle whorl, 2 calcite beads attached by corrosion to amorphous bronze	Undetermined female	II c.

(Continued)

Table 7.1 Viminacium, Više grobalja necropolis, graves with mirrors (according to Zotović and Jordović 1990; Korać and Golubović 2009). The mirrors are all of the round type and made of bronze unless otherwise stated. Designation G_1 stands for cremation while G marks inhumation burials (Continued)

	Grave no.	Grave type	Mirror	Box/case	Toilet/cosmetic equipment	Glass flask(s)	Lamp	Ceramic vessel(s)	Other	Age, sex	Date
10	G_1–228 double burial	MKS 1 cremation inhumation	bronze with silver amalgam, 5 glass decorative inlays at the backside	bronze and iron sheet-plating, fragments of wood, decorative bronze rivet	fragmented slate cosmetic palette (decomposed)			Pot	fragmented bone sewing needle, coin	cremated adult female and inhumed infant	II c.
11	G_1–281*	MKS 2 cremation	3 fragments of bronze mirror				1 (fragments)	fragments of censer, bowl,	bronze brooch, bead	adult, undetermined	II c.
12	G_1–290	MKS 2 cremation	fragments of bronze mirror	circular bronze plate, handle, rim fittings with rivets			1	3 jugs	coin	adult male	II c.
13	G_1–321* double burial	MKS 2 cremation	damaged bronze round plate (initially not recognised as mirror)		2 bone needles			jug	coin (A. Pius), perforated coin, silver earring, bone bead, glass bead, 2 bone sewing needles	adult male + ±20 years undetermined	II c.

(Continued)

Table 7.1 Viminacium, Više grobalja necropolis, graves with mirrors (according to Zotović and Jordović 1990; Korać and Golubović 2009). The mirrors are all of the round type and made of bronze unless otherwise stated. Designation G_1 stands for cremation while G marks inhumation burials (Continued)

	Grave no.	Grave type	Mirror	Box/case	Toilet/cosmetic equipment	Glass flask(s)	Lamp	Ceramic vessel(s)	Other	Age, sex	Date
14	G_1-355	MKS 2 cremation	fragments of silver mirror	iron rim-fittings, bronze rivets, bronze handle, lock		4 (one fragm.)	1	fragments of censer, 3 jugs, pot, fragments of 2 plates	coin, fragments of iron knife	undetermined	II c.
15	G1-367	MKS 2 cremation	bronze round plate (initially not recognised as mirror)	rectangular iron sheet, iron lock, handle, 2 nails	small bone pyxis		2	fragments of beaker, fragment of amphora-lid, 3 jugs	2 frags bone bases (each with decorated legs - toy-bed? box plating?), iron key	undetermined	II c.
16	G_1-393*	MKS 1 cremation	fragment of round bronze mirror						iron nails	adult male	II c.
17	G_1-492	MKS 2 cremation	1 silver			1 frag., deformed		fragments of pot	fragmented golden-wire earring with pendant, coin (Domitian)	undetermined	II c.

(Continued)

Table 7.1 Viminacium, Više grobalja necropolis, graves with mirrors (according to Zotović and Jordović 1990; Korać and Golubović 2009). The mirrors are all of the round type and made of bronze unless otherwise stated. Designation G_1 stands for cremation while G marks inhumation burials (Continued)

	Grave no.	Grave type	Mirror	Box/case	Toilet/cosmetic equipment	Glass flask(s)	Lamp	Ceramic vessel(s)	Other	Age, sex	Date
18	G_1-517*	MKS 2 cremation	fragment of silver mirror	fragmented bronze plating with decorative rivets		1 fragmented	1	frag. of beaker, frag. of pot, 3 fragmented censers	coin, fragment of bronze rivet(?) with head filled with white paste, frag. iron key	undetermined	II c.
19	G_1-528	MKS 2 cremation	1 bronze				1	3 jugs	coin	adult female	II c.
20	G-281	pit, chest inhumation	1 fragmented rectangular					beaker	coin	adult female	II c.
21	G-498	pit, chest inhumation	1 silver				1 frag.	beaker	coin (Trajan)	adult undetermined	II c.
22	G_1-396	MKS 2 cremation	1 silver		bone needle, fragmented bronze needle			pot, fragments of a pot, beaker	coin (Hadrian), iron knife, coin (L. Verus),	male up to 40 years	second 1/2 of II c

(Continued)

Table 7.1 (Continued)

	Grave no.	Grave type	Mirror	Box/case	Toilet/cosmetic equipment	Glass flask(s)	Lamp	Ceramic vessel(s)	Other	Age, sex	Date
23	G₁-398	MKS 1 cremation	1 bronze	bronze plate with rivets, handle, iron lock	fragments of bone needle	1 fragmented			bone distaff, 3 coins (2 Hadrian, 1 A. Pius), glass slug (gaming counter?)	undetermined	second 1/2 of II c.
24	G₁-363*	MKS 1 cremation	fragments of bronze mirror with unclear relief representation		fragments of bronze needle (9.8 cm)				golden-wire earring, fragments of bronze bracelet, half of seashell	adult male	end of II c.
25	G₁-470	MKS 2 cremation	1 bronze (with relief representation of 2 seated figures)		bone needle (fragmented, possibly for sewing)		fragments (step)		deformed key finger-ring	adult female	end of II c.
26	G₁-329*	MKS 2 cremation	fragment of rectangular silver mirror	iron handle (of wooden box?)					bronze brooch	undetermined	first 1/2 of III c.

* – damaged graves, usually by later interments.
** – graves G₁-44 and G₁-47 intersected (the latter's shaft was most probably purposefully placed within the former's shaft) and their grave inventories cannot be precisely and completely differentiated.

The great majority of specimens (23) belong to the type of small (7–15 cm in diameter) round hand-mirror (see Fig. 7.2), whereas only three are rectangular (graves G_1-167, 128, 329) and also small in size (up to 10 x 9 cm). Most of the mirrors are made of copper alloy (18 in total: 16 round and 2 rectangular), but there is also a considerable number of those manufactured in silver (8 in total; 7 round and 1 rectangular: G_1-192, 355, 492, 517, 396, G 75, 498). Considering subtypes, there are only two instances of mirrors with a backside gilded relief-representation (G_1-363, 470) that are generally regarded as rare (Cohen 2010: 76; Spasić Đurić 2001 points out there are only seven such specimens from all of the Viminacium necropolises). One mirror (G_1 228) is of a type with five elliptic appliqués of jasper and glass inserted on the reverse side. All the others are of a simple production involving variously processed metal plates coated with an amalgam of silver that served as a reflective surface. Most of the simple-plate mirrors have a plain posterior, but in some cases, there are circle indentations on the back and/or perforations along the rim. Regarding chronology, almost all burials are dated to the 2nd century CE, while only one grave belongs to the 1st (G_1-192), and one (G_1-329) to the first half of the 3rd century (see Table 7.1). Such a temporal distribution corresponds very well with the most intensive usage of the "Više grobalja" burial site (this ended in the 3rd century CE), which is, in turn, linked to the impetus of Viminacium prosperity (after Emperor Hadrian granted it municipal status).

The number of 26 burials with mirrors amounts to *c.* 2.48% of the entire published assemblage originating from "Više grobalja". It has been noted that the rescue research of Viminacium yielded only 229 well-preserved mirrors of copper alloy (176), silver (43), and lead (10) (Krunić 2000, 6; Spasić Đurić 2002, 71, 143; this count excludes the numerous fragments of mirrors). If this refers to the entire funerary evidence (*i.e.*, ±13,000 graves), it reveals the minimal presence of mirrors within the burial grounds of Viminacium (*c.* 1.80%) and suggests that the practice was not a common one. Whatever the general trend might have been, the numbers derived from the "Više grobalja" sample demonstrate that mirrors were relevant only to particular deceased and, compared to, *e.g.*, oil lamps or ceramic vessels, cannot be regarded as a frequent funerary item. This however, does not mean that the mirrors at "Više grobalja" were necessarily a type of exclusive object that could be understood as markers of economic standing or privileged social position. Although reports explicitly state seven burials with a silver mirror (*i.e.*, not silver-amalgam coated copper alloy ones), these cases do not differ by any other funerary feature and cannot be straightforwardly seen as emblems of higher status. The same is true for the graves that contained copper alloy mirrors: none prominently diverges from others within the group or in comparison to the rest of the burials at the site. Of course, some of the buried people probably were of wealthy background, as this is indicated by the graves containing golden jewellery (G_1-492, 363) and the exceptional relief mirrors (G_1-363, 470). Nevertheless, the point is that we lack supportive evidence that mirrors, as a category of grave inventory, automatically signified the interment of persons from the upper scale social or economic echelons. On the other hand, the logic behind their usage might have been associated with specific ideological stances that could be paired with status aspirations (as it is argued in the concluding section of the paper).

Furthermore, there seems to be no correlation between the presence of a mirror and the grave type since both MKS 1 and MKS 2 are roughly equally represented within the analysed group (MKS 1: 9 graves, MKS 2: 13 graves). Graves with the deceased inhumated in a simple pit (G-75, 281, 498) are also not revealing in this respect, as the necropolises of Moesia Superior were generally bi-ritual with treatment of the dead body being the matter of preference and general trend that encompassed diverse social categories (*cf.* Jovanova 2016, 61; Mihajlović 2011b).

In some cases, age and sex of the deceased have been determined, but especially with the cremated remains, there is a problem with assessment of the heavily fire-damaged and fragmented bones (Bruzek and Murail 2006; Holck 2008, 50–76). Consequently, even the modest number of age and/or sex evaluated burials (Table 7.1, column *Age, Sex*) should be taken with the greatest caution and as highly inconclusive. The group of 26 graves considered here contained 29 individuals, as graves G_1-288 and G_1-321 were double interments, whereas graves G_1-44,47 were purposefully superimposed (the latter being cut-into the former), and their inventories cannot be entirely accurately sorted out. The rest of the graves are all single burials, although later interments have damaged some of them (marked with * in Table 7.1) and thus have compromised context. The largest number of burials (10) does not have determined age and sex. In five cases, the age has been assessed in general terms as a juvenile (G_1-228) or adult (G_1-270, 281, 321, G-498), but sex remained undefined. Only in one case (G_1-23), the situation is reversed, *i.e.*, the sex is determined as female, while the age is not specified. For half of the buried within the analysed group both general age and sex are estimated: eight were adult females (G_1-192, 170, 273, 23, 228, 528, 329, G-281), five were adult males (G_1-290, 321, 393, 396, 363), and one deceased was a female child (G-75). Only in three instances the more precise estimation of age is given: G-75 (8–10 years girl), G_1-321 (±20 years male), and G_1-396 (up to 40 years male). According to the cited data, mirrors are associated with adult persons in 16 cases (G_1-270, 281, 321, 192, 170, 273, 228, 528, 329, 290, 321, 393, 396, 363, G-281, G-498), and only in one (G-75) with a child (the inhumed infant in G_1-228 is purposefully excluded, as the mirror most probably belonged to the cremated adult within the same grave, see the discussion in the next section). As for the sex, an association with females (both adult and children) predominates, with nine instances in comparison to four adult male burials with mirrors. If this ratio were beyond methodological doubt, it would spark very interesting implications (of male-sex individuals being associated with mirrors) that are further examined in the discussion.

Furthermore, there is a question of whether the mirrors inside the examined group of burials show any particular association with other sorts of grave inventory. The categories of ceramic vessels (jugs, beakers, cups and bowls), coins, oil lamps, iron knives and nails should be excluded from further consideration, since they regularly appear inside the *Mala Kopašnica-Sase* type of burials. To the previous group of "ordinary" grave objects, one may also add various types of glass flasks (so-called unguentaria and balsamaria) that most probably contained liquids such as oil, ointment, perfume, balsam, etc. These are found in both cremation and inhumation burials, with no obvious consistent correlations to other kinds of objects or funerary features, and it is impossible to discern any special link they might have had with mirrors. It is likely that in some cases, the presence of a mirror and a glass flask was an outcome of the same funerary convention, but since glass flasks are found in a much larger number of burials without mirrors, the general ruling association between the two cannot be presupposed.

Hence, there remain several other classes of objects to review in relation to mirrors: jewellery, boxes/cases, cosmetic/toilet items and spinning/sewing equipment. Jewellery was present inside eight burials of the examined group (Table 7.1, G_1-23, 281, 321, 329, 363, 470, 492, G-75, column *Other*), but none contained a set consisting of several different items. In four graves (G_1-23, 281, 321, G-75), single, pairs, or several beads of different inexpensive materials (calcite, bone and glass) were found, and they probably belonged to necklaces or bracelets formed as strings of beads. The next most frequent type of jewellery, encountered in three graves, is earrings: in two instances (G_1-363, 492), a single golden-wire earring was found, while in one case, a silver specimen of a loop-type (G_1-321). Interestingly, none is found as a pair, which could mean that they, attached to the owner's ears, underwent the process of cremation (thus the fragmentation of the one from G_1-492), and their matches were not retrieved upon collecting the remains from the pyre; or that there was some sort of custom of wearing only one earring; or else that one was kept by the living/bereaved (in other cases at "Više grobalja" – G_1-59, 90, 104, 173, 193, 196, including one inhumation – G-251, only one gold earring was found, which suggests that such a situation is not exclusive for the group of burials examined here). In any case, the cited earrings are the most precious pieces of jewellery as far as the material of production is concerned and, consequently, the buried individuals might have been from an affluent backdrop. This possibility is especially valid for G_1-363 and 492, as the former contained the rare backside-relief mirror while the latter included a silver one.

The other pieces of adornment are not telling: in two graves there was a single copper alloy brooch (G_1-281, 329), in one burial a fragmented copper alloy bracelet (G_1-363) and one grave unit contained a key-shaped finger-ring (G_1-470). The double burial G_1-321 accommodated a perforated coin that most probably served as a necklace or bracelet pendant. If compared to some other cases of contemporary graves or necropolises, the assemblage scrutinised here lacks the burials with opulent jewellery and, subsequently, there are no grounds to assert an association of mirrors and lavish bodily adornment. Excluding the graves with golden earrings within the burials discussed here, the published portion of the "Više grobalja" necropolis gave 20 more interments with pieces of golden jewellery. Among these, there are only two cases with more than one sort of adornment: G_1-345 (necklace, finger-ring, two earrings) and G_1-481 (finger-ring and two earrings), whereas the other contained single or a pair of earrings. This is in stark contrast in comparison to, *e.g.*, the non-urban necropolis in Mala Kopašnica where a considerable number of gold and silver jewellery (diadems, necklaces, rings and earrings) was unearthed (Stamenković, Ivanišević and Pešić 2016, 30–34). In conclusion, the "Više grobalja" sample does not demonstrate a strong correlation between mirrors on the one hand and jewellery (both as a whole and as particular types of bodily ornament) on the other. The picture is perhaps somewhat biased if we consider the possibility that items of personal decorum were burnt with the deceased and eventually did not end up in tombs.

The metal components of wooden boxes (*capsae, cistae*), such as handles, rivets, lock-plating, side-sheets, rim-fittings, hinges and keys, were found in nine burials of our assemblage (Table 7.1, G_1-170, 228, 290, 355, 367, 517, 398, 329, G-75). Along with these, the metal remains of boxes were identified in only 20 more graves (G_1-99, 101, 112, 116, 149, 175, 179, 193, 196, 246, 718, 336, 395, 442, 481, 487, G-85, 209, 472, 487), which count a total of 29 instances (or *c.* 2.76%) of the published portion from "Više grobalja". The number is possibly biased, as some boxes could have been made entirely of wood and did not survive, while some highly fragmented and/or corroded pieces of metal fittings and plating are not recognised as belonging to boxes at all. Nevertheless, as far as the clear examples are concerned, the share of the burials with mirrors inside the total number of those containing remains of boxes measures a little over one third (*i.e.*, 9 of 29). Such a relationship may be telling and it is addressed at a later point of the paper.

The exact shapes, types and sizes of boxes from the "Više grobalja" site have not been determined, but the more important unknown feature of these objects is their exact purpose. While often regarded as jewellery caskets, no pieces of adornment were found next to or close to the boxes' metal segments in any of the 29 cases (*i.e.*, both in burials with mirrors and those without). Even if the boxes had been intended for such a function, at the occasion of a funeral, the actual ornaments were not placed inside them. The published reports and sketches of burials with boxes do not show the concentration of any other kind of material among or alongside the fragments of boxes either. For example, although mirrors could have had boxes, in no instance has a spatial-contextual link between a mirror and the elements of a box been recorded. Similarly, the supposed purpose of small wooden cases for keeping the flasks of cosmetics and cosmeceuticals, or items of toilet and personal grooming, has not been documented by the close association of these kinds of grave inventory in the "Više grobalja" sample. This situation allows for a very wide spectrum of interpretations (see Cebrián Fernández 2017), from empty jewellery boxes with a symbolic role, to small chests for personal belongings of different kinds that were however made of perishable materials (*e.g.*, cloth, books, letters?), to contents (of whatever kind) that were withheld by the living after the person's death (and leaving the interior of the case vacant). Thus, the exact role of boxes cannot be resolved with certainty, both in general and considering the burials with mirrors in particular.

The only regularity related to 29 graves with boxes is their prominently higher presence in the graves of allegedly female deceased. The total of 14 burial remains are identified as female (1 child, 1 young and 12 adult individuals) which is markedly over the number of individuals defined as a newborn (1), child (1), male (3), unspecified adult (4) and undetermined (6). The picture is more distorted when we consider the group of nine graves with mirrors, due to the number of remains of undetermined sex (G_1-329, 355, 367, 398, 517). On the other hand, among the remaining cases, females (adult – G_1-170, 228, and juvenile – G-75) have slight precedence over the single case of a male burial (G_1-290). Again, if the employed anthropological methodology was reliable, this situation would be compelling.

The next category of inventory found in larger number within the burials that contained mirrors is various items of toilet and cosmetic equipment. These are reviewed as closely related, since both are a part of corporeal care and appearance. Such artefacts were unearthed in 12 graves of the analysed assemblage, and include bone needles found in six burials (in pair: G-75, G_1 321, or as single: G_1 192, 396, 398, 470), copper alloy needles retrieved from three graves (G_1 273, 363, 396), a bone spoon (G_1 44), copper alloy spatula (G_1 132), slate palette (G_1 228) and bone pyxis (G_1 367). Bone and copper alloy needles are tentatively defined here as sartorial items since there is no certainty what their original purpose could have been. While they were not sewing needles (as such cases are explicitly stated in the published reports thanks to an eye at the thicker part of a body), it remains uncertain whether they could serve as dress-pins, hairpins or for some other purpose. It is perhaps indicative that none of the cited burials contained brooches, which is also the case with graves with such "needles", but without mirrors. This situation might suggest that objects of this kind indeed had a function as dress-pins. Additionally, the girl buried in G-75 had one of these on each shoulder, which strengthens the possibility that they were the part of her attire. On the other hand, such pins could have served for fastening the burial wrappings. Similarly, the exact purpose of the most frequent type of needle (with a conical head and up to 10 cm in length) cannot be securely identified. The same is valid for copper alloy specimens that are, in the absence of an eye in their bottom ends, supposed to be pins. Looking at the "Više grobalja" necropolis as a whole, bone and copper alloy pins of different subtypes were found in 21 and six cases respectively, with no apparent regularities that might be indicative: they were present both in inhumation and cremation burials, in the graves of juvenile, young and adult individuals, and both with allegedly female and male remains. However, it could be significant that out of 26 burials with mirrors nine had pins, whereas out of 1,021 graves without mirrors only 27 included such objects. In short, there appears to be a direct and meaningful relation between mirrors and pins, at least in some cases, if not in general.

The rest of the toilet/cosmetic elements are reasonably straightforward: spoon, spatula and palette most probably served for preparing and applying make-up or other paste/cream contents, whereas the pyxis could have been used for keeping such substances. In the "Više grobalja" sample these kinds of objects are rare, since a palette is found in four graves ($G_1$77, 193, 210, 476), spatulas in five ($G_1$77, 193, 362, 459, bone: G_1-518), and small bone ($G_1$263) and copper alloy ($G_1$276) spoons in one case each. In such small numbers, it is impossible to recognise any patterns.

Finally, in the assemblage examined here, six graves contained pieces of equipment for textile processing ($G_1$23, 44, 170, 228, 321, 398). In two graves ($G_1$170, 398) bone distaffs were encountered, one grave ($G_1$23) contained a tube-shaped bone handle (possibly of a distaff with the timber body) and a ceramic spindle whorl, while three burials had sewing needles in pairs ($G_1$44, 321) or single ($G_1$228). Taking into consideration the "Više grobalja" evidence as a whole (*i.e.*, 1,021 graves without mirrors), it can be asserted that such objects are not typical: bone "sewing" needles are found in 17 more cases, copper alloy specimens in five, while bone distaffs were unearthed in three. More so, as already hinted above, the purpose of needles as stitching instruments cannot be assumed with complete confidence, since they could have had other functions as well. For example, they could serve for arranging or adjusting dress and/or hair (see Stephens 2008), could have been used for fixing the burial shroud, or could have had some unknown symbolic role. Also, their capacity as tailoring tools is ambiguous, bearing in mind that needles with an eye at the bottom end were found in the graves of newborns or very young children (up to one year old). In such a situation, it is indeed challenging to narrow down the roles of needles, and it is highly probable that they had diverse purposes within funerary practices and rationale.

Stojnik (Demessus?) – "Gomilice"

Unlike Viminacium, the castrum in Stojnik is not well known from a historical and archaeological perspective. Although it has been investigated on and off since the beginning of the 20th century, that research did not answer a whole range of very important questions. It has been proposed that Roman auxiliary fortress at the site should be identified as *Demessus* (known from late Roman literary accounts), and it is almost certain that it had a direct link to the ore exploitation (Dušanić 1976, 94–117; Tomović 1995). The latter fact undoubtedly produced deep social impact, since it has been argued that mining territories of the Roman Empire had notable economic, demographic and cultural specificities due to their administrative extraterritoriality and mode of functioning (see Dušanić 2004; Hirt 2010). While there is no evidence that Stojnik/Demessus had municipal status, it probably was a (micro)regional centre for mine exploitation, with combined administrative, military and economic power concentrated within the fort and nearby settlement. In such a setting, the necropolis excavated at the site of "Gomilice" close to the Stojnik fort (Fig. 7.3) could be related to a population that was directly or indirectly linked to mining activities, and that could come from various status groups, and military, administrative and civilian backgrounds alike (see Cvjetićanin 2016; 2018).

At the site of "Gomilice" 370 graves were excavated in the period 1960–1978, all of which are the burials of a cremated deceased (MKS 1: 88, MKS 2: 254, lead sarcophagus: 2, urn: 1, and unknown type: 25). The major frustration regarding "Gomilice" is the loss of the journal of excavations, the considerable number of the terrain drawings of graves and 110 finds from the tombs. What is known and has been studied comes from the surviving excavation notes, sketches and grave inventories that are kept in the National Museum in Belgrade (Cvjetićanin 2018; Cvjetićanin and Glumac forthcoming; Glumac 2014, 25). No anthropological analysis of human remains was done, while the relative chronology of the graves is known by coin finds and the general typological attribution of diagnostic artefacts. The burial site was used from the end of the 1st up to the mid-3rd century, and it has not been estimated whether this is only a portion of the necropolis, or the larger part of the original perimeter of the cemetery has been investigated.

Considering burials that accommodated mirrors, 24 such cases were discovered (Table 7.2) and they amount to 6.48% of all the graves excavated at the site. As in the case of "Više grobalja", the majority of mirrors (15) found in "Gomilice" are made of copper alloy (graves nos. 126, 352, 24, 60, 177, 180, 229, 235, 243, 311, 318, 341, 257, 309, 230).

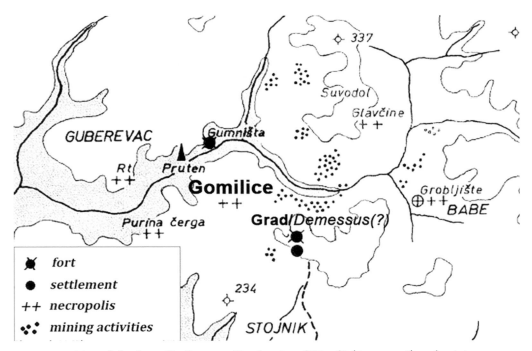

Fig. 7.3 Position of the "Gomilice" necropolis, the site of "Grad" (Demessus?) and mining area at Kosmaj (after Mirković et Dušanić 1976).

Table 7.2 Stojnik (Demessus?), Gomilice necropolis, graves with mirrors (according to Glumac 2014; Cvjetićanin and Glumac forthcoming). The mirrors are all of the round type and made of bronze unless otherwise stated

	Grave no.	Grave type	Mirror	Box/case	Toilet/cosmetic equipment	Glass flask(s)	Lamp	Ceramic vessel(s)	Other	Date
1	**22**	MKS 2 cremation	1 silver		2 bronze probes, 2 bronze hairpins, bronze needle,	1		3 jugs	bone sewing needle, bronze earring, frag. of iron needle, coin	end of I–beg. of II c.
2	**126**	MKS 2 cremation	1 bronze	fragment + holder, rings, chain of entwined bronze wire		12 + glass slug	2	2 jugs, cup-beaker, pot, cup, bowl	coin (Domitian), nail	end of I – mid II c.
3	**139**	MKS 2 cremation	1 silver (deformed, burnt)	iron lock, bronze plate, handle, bronze nail, bronze furnishing	bone rasp ("nail file")	1	1	3 jugs	bone dice, 5 melon-shape beads, bronze finger-ring, bronze earring, bronze bracelet, iron nails, coin (Nero), 3 fragmented terracotta figures (seated goddess, partridge and fig)	end of I–beg. of II c.
4	**352**	MKS 2 cremation	1 bronze (with lead handle)	handle, plate		1		2 jugs	bone sewing needle, coin (Nero)	end of I–beg. of II c.
5	**10/1960**	MKS 2 cremation	1 silver (representation of three Graces)	bronze plating	fragmented bone needle, bronze needle,	2	1	3 jugs	coin	II c.

(Continued)

Table 7.2 Stojnik (Demessus?), Gomilice necropolis, graves with mirrors (according to Glumac 2014; Cvjetićanin and Glumac forthcoming). The mirrors are all of the round type and made of bronze unless otherwise stated (Continued)

	Grave no.	Grave type	Mirror	Box/case	Toilet/cosmetic equipment	Glass flask(s)	Lamp	Ceramic vessel(s)	Other	Date
6	24	MKS 2 cremation	1 bronze (silver plated)	bronze handles, iron hinges and sheets, 5 nails		1		3 jugs		II c.
7	35	MKS 1 cremation	1 silver	iron fittings (?)				1 beaker-cup, 3 jugs	coin	II c.
8	60	MKS 2 cremation	1 bronze (burnt)			3	5	4 censers, bowl	2 coins (Trajan)	II c.
9	152	MKS 2 cremation	1 silver with bronze handle		bone hairpin (female-bust shaped head)	1		3 jugs	bronze buckle; 17 iron nails	II c.
10	177	MKS 2 cremation	1 bronze (silver plated)					3 jugs	perforated gaming token, coin (Hadrian), nails	II c.
11	180	MKS 1 cremation	1 bronze (silver plated)				4	3 beakers		II c.
12	229	MKS 2 cremation	1 bronze			1		4 jugs		II c.
13	230	MKS 2 cremation	1 silver			3 + glass slug	1	3 jugs	coin (Hadrian), gem (for a ring)	II c.
14	235	MKS 2 cremation	1 bronze (silver plated, with handle)			3		3 jugs	coin, nails	II c.

(Continued)

Table 7.2 (Continued)

	Grave no.	Grave type	Mirror	Box/case	Toilet/cosmetic equipment	Glass flask(s)	Lamp	Ceramic vessel(s)	Other	Date
15	**243**	MKS 2 cremation	1 bronze	lock, lock-plating, nails	2 bone spatulas/probes, bone distaff			3 jugs, beaker-cup	bone sewing needle, coin (Faustina I), iron nails	II c.
16	**311**	MKS 2 cremation	1 bronze (silver plated)	bronze plating			1	3 jugs, censer		II c.
17	**318**	MKS 2 cremation	1 bronze (silver plated)	fragments of plating, lock, fragments of entwined bronze wire with a hook (?)			1	3 jugs	2 melon beads, *bulla*, coin	II c.
18	**341**	MKS 2 cremation	1 bronze	handle, plating, rivets	bronze cylindrical box ("theca vulneraria")	1	2	2 cup-beakers	pair of golden earrings	II c.
19	**348**	MKS 2 cremation	1 silver		bone hairpin			3 jugs	coin	II c.
20	**257**	MKS 2 cremation	1 bronze			1 + glass slag		2 jugs, beaker-cup, small bottle, 2 bowls		mid II c.

(Continued)

Table 7.2 Stojnik (Demessus?), Gomilice necropolis, graves with mirrors (according to Glumac 2014; Cvjetićanin and Glumac forthcoming). The mirrors are all of the round type and made of bronze unless otherwise stated (Continued)

	Grave no.	Grave type	Mirror	Box/case	Toilet/cosmetic equipment	Glass flask(s)	Lamp	Ceramic vessel(s)	Other	Date
21	**309**	MKS 2 cremation	1 bronze (fragmented)	handle, fragments of bronze plating		4 + glass slag	2	3 jugs, amphora, 2 beakers, 2 censers, bowl	3 bone plates (for lace spinning), part of bone object, coin (A. Pius), nails	second 1/2 of II c.
22	**37**	Pit, urn cremation	1 silver							II–III c.
23	**140**	MKS 2 cremation	2 polygonal convex mirror glasses (with traces of lead on the backside)		3 bone hairpins, bone spatula, 2 fragmented bone needles		1	2 jugs	2 bone sewing needles, bronze sewing needle, finger-ring with *gemma*	II–III c.
24	**232**	MKS 2 cremation	1 bronze (silver plated, with handle)		fragm. of bronze needle	2	1	bowl	bronze sewing needle	II–III c.

* – damaged grave.

In some cases, it is reported that specimens are silver-plated, but these are probably mirrors with a preserved silver amalgam that served as a reflective surface. In eight cases silver mirrors are reported (graves nos. 22, 139, 10/1960, 35, 152, 230, 348, 37), which by all probability means they are entirely made of silver plate and polished. Some of the mirrors, both of copper alloy and silver, have concentric circle incisions and small perforations on their rims, while only one (now lost) silver specimen (grave no. 10/1960) had a gilded back that bears a representation of three female figures (possibly the three goddesses from the *Judgement of Paris* mythological episode). There is a singular find from grave no. 140 of two polygonal convex glasses, one of which had traces of a layer of lead that was foiled on the reverse side (Glumac 2014, 152). This type of glass mirror, that usually had a lead frame, was common in the late Roman period (thus the late date of the grave) and, to my best knowledge, it has not been found in any other published grave of the Mala Kopašnica-Sase type. The fact that there are two glasses and no lead frames is peculiar, although one could think of a few possible explanations for the missing casing (fragmentation/breakage/melting on the pyre, frame made of wood, etc.). On the other hand, the presence of a pair of mirrors is certainly a unique example in comparison to other graves of Moesia Superior that always contained one speculum, and it is difficult to think of a straightforward interpretation.

The "Gomilice" burials with mirrors predominantly date to the 2nd century CE (in 17 cases), with four graves placed at the end of the 1st and the beginning of the 2nd century, and three burials attributed to the end of the 2nd and beginning of the 3rd century. Such a chronological distribution closely resembles one at "Više grobalja", and perhaps suggests that the practice of placing mirrors in graves reached its peak and was the most widespread during the 2nd century CE. As in the case of "Više grobalja", the "Gomilice" sample does not show obvious correlations between mirrors and luxury or exclusive grave goods. Apart from the graves containing silver mirrors, and one with the gilded relief, in only one case (grave 341) was there a pair of golden earrings that could be regarded as indicative of the deceased's economic standing. The copper alloy cylindrical box ("theca vulneraria") found in the same burial further supports this possibility, as such a type of container is a rare funerary find in Moesia Superior. Other graves did not accommodate any kind of object, or indeed some other characteristic (spatial position, burial construction and marker) that would allow the claim of higher status or an affluent deceased. If such instances indeed existed among the group of burials with mirrors, they are not emphasised by the grave features and inventories. The grave types are also not helpful in this regard, since the majority of burials at "Gomilice" are of MKS 2 type, which is reflected in the assemblage with mirrors, as well (MKS 1: 2, MKS 2: 21). There is a unique case of burial (no. 37) in a ceramic urn that besides cremated remains contained a silver mirror as the only grave good. However, it is impossible to tell if this is in any way indicative, and generally, the whole situation does not suggest a particular association between mirrors and specific types of burials.

Considering other kinds of objects, as in the case of "Više grobalja", it is worthwhile to review jewellery, boxes with metal parts, cosmetic/toilet items and objects for textile processing, since other finds are within the usual repertoire of grave goods. It could be relevant to note that glass receptacles (predominantly various types of flasks) are more common in "Gomilice" than in "Više grobalja": 149 burials out of 370 accommodated different numbers of glass containers (1 to 12 pieces). This situation resolutely suggests that glass flasks were not specially linked with mirrors and instead belong to common funerary material. The observation that the flasks found at "Gomilice" were simple and of hasty production, and thus could have been specially made for burial (Glumac 2015, 280) is indicative: there could have been a custom to set these (with whatever contents inside) in the graves as a type of a "farewell gift" to deceased. Of course, in some cases, they could have served as cosmetic containers *i.e.*, as personal grooming material.

Pieces of jewellery and dress accessories are found in seven graves of the assemblage (graves nos. 22, 139, 152, 230, 318, 140, 341). In only one case (no. 139) there were four different kinds of items (earring, finger-ring, bracelets, and beads), in one grave (318) there were two sorts of adornment (bulla and beads), while all the other burials contained only one class of jewellery (graves nos. 22 – earring, 152 – copper alloy belt buckle, 230 – gem for a finger-ring, 140 – finger-ring, 341 – pair of golden earrings). Except for grave 341 with a pair of golden earrings, all the others were of non-precious materials (mostly copper alloy and in the case of beads, glass and ceramic). The group of burials with mirrors, therefore, does not show stronger associations with jewellery and accessories, neither in respect to sets and the higher concentration of pieces of the same kind, nor in regard to materials. In general, except for the mentioned seven burials with mirrors, the "Gomilice" necropolis had only 23 more graves with jewellery or accessories, which makes the total of 30 burials with items of adornment (or 8.10% of the "Gomilice" graves). Among these, there are only three instances with slightly more diverse sorts of adornment (g. nos. 127 – finger-ring, earring, bead; 240 – copper alloy bracelet, copper alloy wire with a bead, two copper alloy wire pendants; 334 – copper alloy belt buckle, bone pendant, copper alloy earrings, nacre plaque, nine glass beads), while the rest usually contained one type and one piece of jewellery (most frequently various beads, brooches, earrings and finger-rings). As for materials, only in two cases (297, 336), was a single golden earring found, while one grave (168) contained an amber finger-ring. Other graves usually accommodated copper alloy items and, in the case of beads, glass and ceramic pieces. As a whole, the "Gomilice" burials do not reveal an inclination towards the accumulation of jewellery and accessories, and no regularities (in terms of their occurrence or links to other funerary features) can be supposed. By extension, it is not possible to assert any associative patterns of adornment and other items within the group of burials with mirrors, or to advocate consistent, meaningful and special correlation between mirrors and jewellery/accessories in general.

The presence of wooden boxes, recognised by surviving metal elements, were found in 11 graves inside the group examined here (Table 7.2, column 4). The remains of boxes were unearthed in 15 more graves at the "Gomilice" site (graves nos. 18, 34,

151, 168, 234, 251, 264, 266, 295, 305, 329, 334, 336, 339, 359), which makes the total of 26 interments with boxes or 7.02% of the burials at the necropolis. This number is proportionally higher than at "Više grobalja" and suggests that the boxes, or at least those with metal elements, were somewhat more common as a grave inventory at "Gomilice". It might be relevant that 11 burials with boxes and mirrors come close to representing a half of the total number of graves with boxes. In other words, the association between these two categories of objects is to some extent stronger than at "Više grobalja" and could point to their even closer ideational connotation. As shapes, sizes and types of the boxes found at "Gomilice" are not reconstructed, and no contextual associations of their remnants and other funerary items (jewellery, tailoring/spinning equipment, *crepundia*, etc.) have been accounted for, it is unknown what precise purpose they had served. In all probability, they could have been used for the storing of diverse kinds of trinkets that in the meanwhile have decayed or, alternatively, these were placed empty to convey some symbolism.

In nine instances of the assemblage, cosmetic/toilet instruments were found (graves nos. 22, 139, 10/1960, 152, 243, 341, 348, 140, 232; Table 7.2, column 5), which is over a third of burials with mirrors. Four graves accommodated elongated bone items that were explicitly defined as hairpins (nos. 152, 348, 140) or more vaguely as bone needles (nos. 10/1960, 140 – these were certainly not of a sewing kind and could serve as some sort of pin). Grave 140 had five such objects (3 hairpins and 2 pins/needles), while the rest contained one piece each. Copper alloy needle-like objects were found in three burials (22, 10/1960, 232): in one case, a hairpin was recognised (22), whereas three items are generally regarded as pins. Two burials contained a pair of probes each, made of copper alloy (no. 22) and bone (no. 243), while one grave (no. 139) included a bone nail-rasp, and another (341) a bone pyxis (presumably for cosmetic contents). Although limited in respect of variety and number per grave, the cosmetic/toilet implements show a relatively steady association with mirrors at "Gomilice". By comparison, in the rest of 346 burials (*i.e.*, those without mirrors) only six accommodated cosmetic/toilet items: five had pins (3 of copper alloy and 2 of bone) and one a copper alloy probe. Such a proportion implies that interments with mirrors were more likely to include pins and other grooming/beautification items and could point to a meaningful link between the two (as in the case of "Više grobalja").

In the group of graves with mirrors, there are six cases where equipment for spinning and sewing was found. Five graves (nos. 22, 352, 243, 140, 232) contained needles with an eye at the bottom end, thanks to which they are interpreted as sewing implements. These are made of copper alloy (nos. 22, 140, 232), iron (22) and bone (352, 243, 140), and in two burials a pair was found (140 – 2 bone specimens, 22 – iron and copper alloy needle). As in the case of "Više grobalja", it is not certain that these objects were used for sewing, and it is possible they were part of the attire, hairdressing or shroud. It is perhaps suggestive that four graves (nos. 22, 243, 140, 232) from the assemblage contained both "decorative" pins and "sewing" needles, in some cases as many as nine, six and four pieces each (*cf.* Stephens 2008). In this light, it is difficult to assert without doubt the exact role such objects had in their original contexts. Besides needles, there are only two cases (nos. 243, 140) that probably accommodated bone distaffs (while in the reports these are interpreted as decorative dress pins, the mentioned loop-handles and dimensions better match the characteristics of a distaff). In one more burial (no. 309) spinning equipment was found, but these were the triangular bone plates for lace twirling. Looking at the "Gomilice" sample as a whole, there are only seven more burials with equipment for textile processing (needles in six cases and distaffs in two), which could imply a stronger correlation between mirrors and sewing/spinning instruments.

Mirrors in the graves of Roman Moesia: roles and meanings

Before discussing the two presented case studies and possible significance of mirrors in the funerary sphere of Moesia Superior, it is worthwhile to emphasise that the practice of placing mirrors in burials did not exist before integration within the Roman world. In the region's Late Iron Age mirrors are thus far known only from the site of Židovar in Banat (the area that stayed outside the Empire when the Danube became a frontier zone). One of the two mirrors from Židovar, made of high-tin bronze alloy and rectangular, originated from a hoard containing precious objects, such as silver and amber jewellery (*c.* mid-1st century BCE), while the fragment of a copper alloy round specimen was found in the Late Iron Age layer at the site (and thus might be from the 1st c. CE or later; see Jevtić, Lazić and Sladić 2006, 62, 158). It is interesting that the hoard also contained two silver folding-razors that, together with the mirror, could have formed a toilet set. Indicatively, both categories of objects were imported from the Roman world (Jevtić, Lazić and Sladić 2006, 166). Although there is no evidence of the local Iron Age production of mirrors, this case indicates that communities at the fringes of the Romano-Mediterranean Empire were familiarised with such objects, albeit limitedly and perhaps as rare and exclusive goods. However, so far there has been no finding of a mirror in any of the excavated graves in the Late Iron Age burial grounds, which suggests that these items were not internalised to the pre-Roman funerary systems in the region. Additionally, the group of ten graves from the Karaburma necropolis (Belgrade) that are recently dated to the first decades CE (Egri 2016), and could be regarded as the oldest Roman period burials of the local population, did not contain mirrors, although Roman-provenance objects were part of their inventories. Such a situation strengthens the argument that mirrors became an element of funerary customs only after the tighter integration of Moesia (Superior) into the Roman socio-political structure. Of course, this does not mean that there was no local practice of corporeal care aided with the means of self-reflection (in mirrors or otherwise), but that the introduction of mirrors in graves was a part of the general changes of burial customs that happened in the course of the second half of the 1st century CE.

Indeed, the "Više grobalja" and "Gomilice" samples show there were no burials containing mirrors earlier than the end of 1st century CE, and the majority of these belong to the 2nd century CE (which does not imply that mirrors are present in graves only up to the beginning of 3rd century CE, as they are found in later graves as well). This period coincides with the deeper extent of the Empire's socio-political system as reflected by the grants of municipal and colonial rights during the Flavian (*Scupi*) and Antonine dynasties (*Ratiaria, Viminacium, Singidunum, Ulpiana, Municipium Dardanorum, Margum, Naissus, Remesiana*), intensified economic exploitation (mining in the first place) and formation of non-municipal settlements next to auxiliary fortresses and along the main roads (*Demessus, Tricornium, Pincum, Timacum Minus, Horreum Margi*). In such a constellation it is likely that the usage of mirrors and their inclusion in burial inventories was directly linked to the spread of templates that were part of and/or inspired by the "global" imperial (elite and "middle ground") culture. In other words, it is possible to work under the assumption that the communities of Moesia, made up of a heterogeneous (local and immigrant) population, became deeply entangled with the imperial order and started to follow and adapt at least some of the trends that were gradually emerging as widespread socio-cultural features (*cf.* Hingley 2005; Mihajlović and Janković 2018; Pitts and Versluys 2015). In the case of mirrors, it seems evident that these have been included in the funerary domain at roughly the same time across the Empire (see Berg 2002; Bózsa 2017; Hales 2010; Martin-Kilcher 2000; Oliver 2000; Shumka 2008; 2016; Swift 2012; Taylor 2008; Wyke 1994) and that Moesian examples conform to this pattern. This situation further poses the question of whether the ideologies and practices that involved mirrors were shared by the people in Moesia as well. In the first place, do the Moesian cases match the generally accepted stance on mirrors as an integral part of a "beauty kit" (*mundus muliebris*)? Before addressing these issues, it is relevant to underline that the settlements of Moesia are minimally researched and household contexts are extremely limitedly known. Consequently, we lack meaningful insight in finds of mirrors within houses and villas, and there is therefore no chance to cross-reference and compare patterns from funerary and domestic backdrops.

Mirroring the "proper looks" in Moesia

As stressed in the previous section of the paper, upon examination of burials with mirrors at "Više grobalja" and "Gomilice", it is immediately obvious that such types of grave are not common: they account for 2.48% and 6.48% respectively. The slightly more frequent occurrence of these at "Gomilice" can be an outcome of sample bias, as the necropolises of Viminacium are extremely limitedly published. Alternatively, their more common presence could reflect a different profile of the buried population in comparison to "Više grobalja", or distinct local funerary customs. In any case, the low numbers in both necropolises suggest that a small portion of the buried population was associated with mirrors and that there had to be a reason for such a situation. However, as we have seen, although relatively rarely found, there is no clear link between social ranking and/or welfare and mirrors, and they cannot be generally regarded as obvious status markers (albeit in few cases where specific luxurious pieces most probably were).

Furthermore, according to the analysed evidence, it is not possible to directly and without difficulties point to the most probable social group(s) as the most likely candidate(s) for correlation with mirrors. Although ancient literary evidence and contemporary scholarship usually emphasise the intimate link of mirrors with feminine beauty and womanhood, archaeological contexts from the two discussed sites are not so straightforward (see also Chapter 4 by Kira Zumkley and Chapter 8 by Bo Jensen). First of all, not all the mirrors were accompanied by items that could have played a role in the making of the preferable female beauty image. At "Više grobalja" eight (out of 26) burials had neither traces of boxes (that could be connected with keeping make-up or toilet articles) nor the equipment of toilet or cosmetic provenance. Additionally, if the finds of pins are excluded from the tally on the grounds of their uncertain purpose, the number rises to 15 burials that except for the mirrors had no clear material association with body care and beautification. In the case of "Gomilice", the ratio is roughly similar: eight (out of 24) graves did not contain boxes or toilet/cosmetic items, and when bone and copper alloy pins of uncertain purpose are omitted from the count, the number increases to ten burials with no obvious reference to the practice of adornment. In such light, it is not possible to generalise that mirrors are regularly found together with other beautification assortments which, of course, does not *per se* exclude such a role for them.

Secondly, the correlation of mirrors with jewellery is not explicit, as could be expected having in mind some published examples (*e.g.*, Harlow 2012; Martin-Kilcher 2000; Oliver 2000; Swift 2012). The relatively low percentage of burials with mirrors that also contained pieces of jewellery ("Više grobalja" – 8, "Gomilice"– 7) does not suggest a consistent, contextual tie between the two. Moreover, unlike some graves that contained mirrors and luxurious adornment, no such case is discovered at the examined necropolises. In other words, the deceased buried with mirrors at "Više grobalja" and "Gomilice" were rarely equipped with jewellery and only in few cases with pieces made of precious metals. Apart from one case at "Gomilice" (grave no. 139) no other burial contained varied types of jewellery that could be referred to as a set. On the other hand, the graves at "Više grobalja" (G_1-345) and "Gomilice" (334) that included apparent jewellery sets did not accommodate mirrors. Hence, the "display convention" that alongside mirrors engaged elaborated ornamentation, seems to be missing from the analysed cases. An explanation for this could be found in a range of possibilities: "Više grobalja" and "Gomilice" were the burial grounds used by the non-elite and less wealthy population; expensive jewellery pieces were kept as heirlooms; it was not a custom to richly embellish the dead, at least during the 2nd century CE. In any case, the considered Moesian examples do not accord with the supposed intrinsic correlation of mirrors and jewellery, and cannot be unambiguously linked to the conceptualisation of feminine image implied by such a correlation.

Nevertheless, the remaining categories of objects found in the graves with mirrors, such as boxes, toilet/cosmetic items and instruments for textile processing, appear to be much more instructive. As has been shown, the metal components of wooden boxes had a considerable degree of association with mirrors in both of the necropolises (9 of 26 at "Više grobalja", and 11 of 24 at "Gomilice"). Albeit the remains of boxes are not reported as being mixed with pieces of jewellery or cosmetic items, and there are no reliable clues of what was kept in them, the funerary pairing of mirror-box corresponds with the persistent representation of women with (jewellery) caskets and mirrors that was probably the widespread metaphor of womanhood (Ferris 2015, 86–93, 191–192; Shumka 2008, 183). This situation perhaps suggests that burials that contained both categories of objects belonged to individuals who accepted (or had imposed in death, if not during life) the ideal of female corporeal care and appearance/beauty. In other words, it is these nine burials from "Više grobalja" and 11 from "Gomilice" that could be considered to echo at least some elements of the *mundus mulieribus* concept found in literary and artistic works.

The same is true if we allow the possibility that bone and copper alloy long needles (without an eye) indeed had a function of hair- and dress-pins. At "Više grobalja" 37 (out of 1,047) burials contained these sorts of pins, and nine of these also accommodated mirrors. At "Gomilice" there had been 11 (out of 370) graves with bone and copper alloy pins, six of which also contained mirrors. Consequently, the more frequent presence of pins inside graves that contained mirrors in both "Više grobalja" and "Gomilice", entails that these dressing accessories mediated the same idea about the display of femininity (Ferris 2015, 193–194; Shumka 2008, 182). This was the case with graves that accommodated items, such as cosmetic palettes and probes, whose function and association with mirrors is rather straightforward. Finally, there is also an interesting correlation between the objects for textile processing ("sewing" needles, distaffs, spindle whorls and bone lace-twirling plates) and mirrors. In both "Više grobalja" and "Gomilice" the former were more commonly found within graves that also comprised the latter, than in the burials without mirrors. It is important to remember that such instruments had a capacity as signifiers of womanhood (D'Ambra 2007, 59–61; Ferris 2015, 111; Martin-Kilcher 2000, 70; Pasztókai-Szeöke 2011), and being found together with mirrors might have indeed followed the principle of a femininity ideal.

The precise replication of the notion of "proper female looks" is the most probable in the cases that involved multiple objects of *mundus muliebris* and other elements that appealed to the concept of womanhood. Such graves usually encompassed a mirror, box, pin(s), jewellery, cosmetic apparatus, instruments for tailoring/spinning and artefacts that invoked the discourse of beauty/femininity (*e.g.*, by referring to Venus or other mythological characters). However, drawing from the above analysis, it becomes clear that the burials containing all or most of the cited components are markedly rare in both burial grounds. At "Više grobalja" only four out of 26 graves with mirrors fit this picture (G75, G_1-228, 367, 398),

Vladimir D. Mihajlović

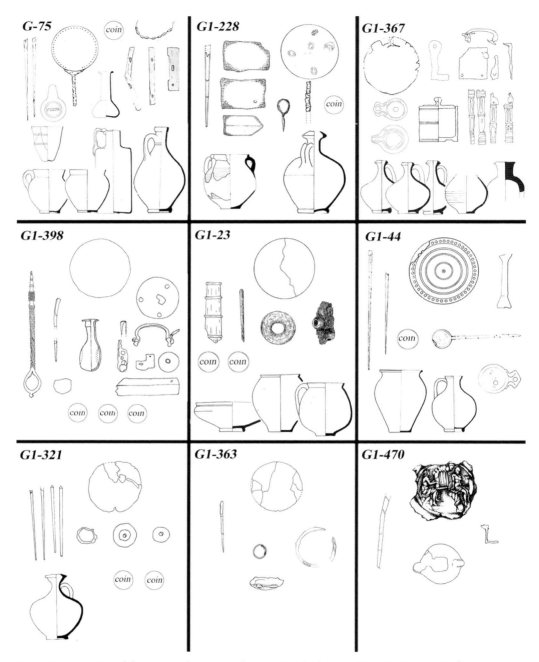

Fig. 7.4 Inventories of the graves that come close to the ideal-typical female beauty kit (items are not to scale) (© National Museum in Požarevac (excavation drawings) with permission of the custodian Dragana Spasić Đurić)

whereas 5 (G$_1$-44, 23, 321, 363, 470) come close to it (by containing at least three of five kinds of relevant objects – see Fig. 7.4).

The "Gomilice" sample gives a similar ratio: four of 24 burials realised the "norm" (nos. 139, 10/1960, 243, 341), while seven complied with it approximately enough (22, 352, 152, 318, 309, 140, 232). Thus, the cases where the inventory most likely constituted the "female beauty assemblage" made up less than half of the number of graves with mirrors and, when the total number of graves is considered, amounted to 0.85% at "Više grobalja", and 2.97% at "Gomilice", respectively. Of course, it should be remembered that the "Više Grobalja" necropolis is not published in its entirety, but only *c.* 25% of the excavated burials, whereas other Viminacium necropolises are not published at all. Consequently, the numbers will certainly change when eventually all the graves are made public. Nonetheless, taking into account the low percentage and relatively long periods (120 years at least) of the two discussed samples, it is safe to assert that there were not many examples of the standardised funerary content referring to a "proper female appearance/beauty", and that such cases cannot be regarded as a common phenomenon. Even if the idea of the correct/preferable female appearance was more widespread than indicated by the examples that most closely adhered to it, there was no extensive funerary adoption of the strictly uniform set of objects that is supposed to embody the conception. In simple terms, the ideal of *mundus muliebris* constructed in literary and visual spheres was not regularly followed within the two samples examined here, either in terms of recurrence, or in the rigidly defined cluster of material mediators.

To conclude, mirrors were associated with the full material assemblage of feminine appearance only in a limited number of cases, and hence cannot be treated as an indisputable reification of the elite notion of female beauty in each case. Although they could have played a role in arranging the desirable appearance, even without other ideally required elements, the point is that mirrors were not necessarily and in every single case manifesting a person's affinity for an optimal version of gendered fashion. Having this in mind, I now turn to the question of whether girls and young women could be understood as the chief population associated with mirrors.

Mirroring gender and age: were there general consistencies?

Several discussions of the burials containing precious bodily adornment (such as gold jewellery), accessories, toilet items, mirrors and (sometimes) dolls concluded that these items were explicitly linked to untimely deceased females of an adolescent or young-adult age. The explanations of this correlation, although varying in details, basically cite girls' coming of marriageable age, accompanying care for physical beauty and arranging the looks and costume to fit the idea of a betrothed or a bridal appearance. It is proposed that girls' entrance into the age of sexual reproduction and their eligibility to marry was followed by shifts in their outfit and equipment for corporeal care, which was in turn reflected in the funerary treatment of the deceased from this gender-age group. Furthermore, some authors have suggested that girls and young women buried with elaborate attire elements, boxes, toilet instruments and mirrors were fashioned in this manner to signify an unmarried state (see further in the text). Such a treatment of dead girls supposedly staged the unattained wedding and appealed to the social status that was not accomplished due to the interruption by a premature end of life (D'Ambra 2007, 117, 124–127; Harlow 2012; Newby 2019; Oliver 2000; Olson 2008, 148). In short, as they could not complete the intended role of becoming wives and mothers while alive, these girls and young women were adorned to emulate the wedding outfit in death. Therefore, it is supposed that this type of burial is primarily concerned with females from girlhood to young adulthood (5–20 years), which is corroborated with the cases of an inhumated deceased whose age could be ascertained (Harlow 2012; Martin-Kilcher 2000, tab. 7.1; Oliver 2000). The cited perspective poses the question of how the Moesian cases stand in comparison, and are there some difficulties with such a straightforward link between the presence of mirrors and a specific age-gender cohort?

As indicated throughout the paper, the majority of burials discussed here contained the remains of an incinerated deceased, which deem them mostly unfit for sex and age assessments. In the cases from "Više grobalja", where such a determination is conducted, we do have some information, but of markedly uncertain nature due to difficulties in methodology. If we are to believe the results, the graves with mirrors indeed contained persons of female sex more frequently than male (9 to 5 cases), and more adults than children (16 to 1). As for the supposed stronger connection between mirrors and females aged 5–20 years, the "Više grobalja" sample generally conforms to the framework, as eight (G_1-192, 170, 273, 23, 228, 528, 329, G-281) of nine allegedly female remains are defined as adult and one (G-75) as a female child, but since there is no precise and secure data on age this evidence is far from helpful. However, two cases stand out as quite indicative.

The first is the inhumated deceased from G-75, reliably defined as a female child buried with all of the elements of "female-beauty paraphernalia", which fall nicely within the abovementioned funerary convention. The second case concerns the cremated person from G_1-228, who was likewise accompanied with the (mostly) "standardised" feminine panoply. Crucially, this person was interred together with an inhumated infant, which opens the possibility we are looking at the grave of a mother and her child who met simultaneous or subsequent deaths. Hence, it seems that these cases corroborate the idea that female children on the brink of puberty, as well as young women of freshly wed and/or newly parental status, were susceptible to burials with a set or parts of *mundus mulieribus*. This, however, brings us to the very important general complication: that the several subcategories of feminine identity could be prone to this type of funerary fashioning and, consequently, we cannot automatically claim what exactly is hidden behind the mediators of female beauty ideology. In other words, without reliable data on sex and age, the mere objects for female corporeal care are impossible to link with more specified female gender and status category, no matter how convincing particular cases might have been (as those cited in Harlow 2012; Martin-Kilcher 2000; Oliver 2000).

This situation is the outcome of discrepancies between the several criteria that constitute individual female identity and stages of a life course, and that could be roughly outlined as gender, status, individual biological development, age categorisation, legal positioning, and socially expected assumption of roles and behaviour. In simple terms, chronological, physiological and social age did not necessarily match (Revell 2016, 128). They were determined by different frames of references and could be in mutual disagreement or even conflicting (see Harlow 2012; Harlow and Laurence 2002, 86–90; 2010). Therefore, we should be aware of critical differences between the biological features of an individual organism, lawfully or socially defined age (*i.e.*, maturity and minimal number of years for its fulfilment), and the social condition of a person (such as unmarried, betrothed or married), because these did not naturally come together and could have been in idiosyncratic relations in particular cases. In this light, we should not be surprised that reality in the Roman world regularly functioned with transitional states of individual identities: *e.g.*, a female person could have reached some of her capacities, but may not have achieved others, and thus was situated in a phase of incompleteness and pending finalisation of social metamorphosis.

An illuminating example is the category of girls aged *c.* 12 to 20 years who were not children anymore, physiologically they probably differed from case to case, and socially (probably in most cases) did not yet reach the full marital/parental and thus adult status. This period of "adolescence" and unfinished state could be however combined with the betrothal as a social condition that introduced the process of passage and announced the upcoming transformation (by marriage) into fully wed and adult women (Alberici and Harlow 2007; Dolansky 2008; 2012; Harlow 2012; 2013b; Harlow and Laurence 2010). Furthermore, we should also consider the immediately following status of mother, attained by giving birth to child(ren), which was the ultimate social recognition of a successfully performed adult state, as far as the literary evidence is concerned (D'Ambra 2007, 12, 46, 59–74; Harlow and Laurence 2002, 84–90; Tokkarek LaFosse 2017). Although these categories could be understood as essentially similar and not imperatively important from the archaeological perspective, ancient written accounts suggest that they constituted decisive nuances (see Table 7.3) in the range from a female child (*puella*) to an unmarried but possibly engaged girl (*virgo*), to betrothed young women (*sponsa*), to an adult married wife (*coniunx*) and mother (*matrona*). A further complication is that this idealised scheme could vary by geographical, chronological and societal criteria as well, meaning that we should be additionally cautious when examining contexts away from Rome and Italy.

Table 7.3 (opposite) Diversity of female roles and positionings defined by various criteria (the categories are defined according to Alberiri and Harlow 2007; D'Ambra 2007; Dolansky 2008; Evans Grubbs 2002; Harlow 2012; Harlow and Laurence 2002; Huebner 2019; Laurence and Harlow 2010; Montserrat 2000; Petrova 2019; Revell 2016; Tokkarek LaFosse 2017)

The discussed situation urges us to think in terms of the intersectionality of gender construction, which means that there was not an absolute and unrefined category of "women", stable and immune to other characteristics and social capacities that a person could acquire. Instead, this theoretical framework considers that there is a wide fluctuation of female modes that could share some general traits (*e.g.*, biological sex) but significantly differed in others (*e.g.*, privileges/restrictions derived from status, age, profession, ethnicity, etc.). Intersectionality calls for consideration that different social roles, categories and positionings mutually correlate and influence each other in various ways, producing outcomes that are specific and depend on the co-constitutive qualities of particular individuals and/or groups (see Montserrat 2000, 155; Cho, Crenshaw and McCall 2013). In simple terms, it was a very different experience being a woman from an imperial family, of senatorial background, free, freed or slave, while all of these further diverged with different economic capacities, professions and stages of life, such as young, adult or old; unmarried, married, widowed or divorced; childless, with children and grandchildren, etc. This is why we should beware of overarching gender categories, such as "women" (D'Ambra 2007; Ferris 2015, 199; Hemelrijk 2014, 158–159; Revell 2016, 121) and appreciate contextual conditionality and the situational character of particular cases, especially when dealing with communities beyond elite Greco-Roman environments. Hence, the archaeological gendering of certain kinds of objects as typically or chiefly female could be deeply essentialist (as demonstrated by *e.g.*, Allason-Jones 1995; Allison 2015), fail to recognise the difference between textual/visual meaning and actual practice, and miss very important nuances of femininity. Rather than exclusively stemming from the discourse of imagined gender bipolarity, the diverse ways of being female were a process of constant becomings and negotiations that revolved around multiple social aspects.

Mirroring betrothed girls and young wives?

Recent scholarship has argued that the coming of age for girls in the Roman world meant evolving into a sexually, maritally and reproductively available female and that, as in other passages, this was accompanied by specific conduct. Literary evidence indicates that by entering puberty or the socially determined age of adolescence, girls/young women were urged to tend to their corporeality and appearance. The transfer of competence for how to configure the looks in order to achieve the publicly most desirable image was a gradual process that introduced girls to their proper femininity. Especially in the upper social echelons, it was expected that a girl/young woman should learn the ways of a *mundus muliebris*,

Female

	Infancy	Childhood	Adolescence	Adulthood — early	Adulthood — middle	Adulthood — late
Social positioning	Slave / Free: upscale citizen (equestrian, senatorial, imperial); citizen-born (with occupational, economic, geographic variations); non-citizen freeborn (with occupational, economic, geographic variations); freed (with occupational, economic, geographic variations); *infames* (disgraced categories of free and freedwomen)					
Physiology	Infancy	Childhood	Adolescence	Adulthood (early)	Adulthood (middle)	Adulthood (late)
Age cohorts*	Babies	Girls	Young women	Women (junior)	Women (senior)	
Legal status	Not marriageable		Marriageable			
Marital status	Unmarriageable	Non-betrothed/married; Betrothed (Revolves around *pudicitia*)		Unwed; Contubernalis (slaves); Concubina (freedwomen); Matrona (free); Married with children; Married, without children	Married with grown children	
Repute**	Appropriately unmarried (*puella*)	Betrothed (Revolves around *pudicitia*)		Married, without children; Married with children; Married with grown children, exemplar (Revolves around *pudicitia*, number of marriages and children, morality and motherhood); Widowed; Divorced; Concubines; Appropriately unwed (as Vestals); Inappropriately unwed ("old maids" *infames*)		

* Divisions by years are not given as they are conventional and vary; quoted categories often overlap.

** Depends on social positioning and its variables.

Note that different categories are purposefully left vertically unaligned to indicate they do not mutually match in full.

delicately cultivate appearance and make herself as beautiful as possible (D'Ambra 2007; Dolansky 2012). Thus, the technology of self-construction into a beautiful female youth was an outcome of transgenerational initiation, and mothers (or other senior women) were held as instigators of their daughters' embellishments that were aimed to attract suitors (Olson 2008, 147–149; Tokkarek La Fosse 2017, 212).

For this reason, there is a tendency to interpret burials with a "female beauty kit" as graves of these early deceased betrothed girls or of childless newlywed women. It has been supposed that fine clothes, jewellery, mirror and cosmetics were *insignia sponsalarium* (Harlow and Laurence 2010, 65–66) given to a future bride, either as a gift by a fiancé (Harlow 2012; Martin-Kilcher 2000, 69–70), or as a parental dowry (D'Ambra 2007, 65; Oliver 2000, 120), or else as a donation of their wealthy female kin (Tokkarek La Fosse 2017, 212–213). In other words, burials containing cited articles are not only comprehended as strongly linked to a specific age group (*c.* 5–20 years), but also to the particular social condition of being betrothed or freshly married. Does this view sit well with evidence from Moesia?

First, let me point to a study that analysed tombstones with representations of sets or elements of the *mundus muliebris* from Roman Italy, and that discovered no regularities between the age of the commemorated females, their marital status and an association with the depictions of a beauty kit. As Shumka (2016) has demonstrated, among the 16 cases where the age of the deceased is stated, there were girls under the age of ten, those in their teenage period, young women in the twenties, women in the thirties, and even ones that died at later points of life. Although there is a potential bias caused by the possible lack of choice of monument types, this warns us not to be too rigid when it comes to the correlation of age and the symbolism of womanhood. Moreover, the same analysis revealed that among the females commemorated with *mundus muliebris* motifs there is a much larger number of dedications made by spouses than parents (30 to 9 respectively), while some were honoured by their offspring as well (Shumka 2016, Appendix). Hence, the association between betrothed or married but childless females and signifiers of femininity does not appear to be as straightforward as some scholars have previously argued, at least when it comes to the realm of monumental commemoration.

Having this in mind, the Moesian burials with mirrors are very difficult to evaluate as particularly strongly connected with the category of deceased fiancées. In the first place, considering several known funerary monuments with depictions of mirrors and other sartorial items, it becomes apparent they are not strongly associated with a specific age or marital-status group. In the only case from Singidunum, a girl of very young age (two years and eight months) was buried under a tombstone showing sandals, mirror and box (IMS 1, no. 43). In four monuments from Scupi (IMS VI, nos. 92, 122, 131, 146), a mirror (and related items) is the motif associated with women of 28, 35, 50, and even 80 years of age, which does not support any regularity in terms of the stage of a life course. In three instances the dedicators are named and they were either a husband (IMS VI, no. 92: the woman is shown together with her child) or children (IMS VI, nos. 131, 146). Although very limited in quantity, these examples, all the same, undermine the thesis for the susceptibility of betrothed or childless young women to the symbolism of female instruments of ornamentation.

Furthermore, as stated before, when we look at the samples discussed in this paper, there is no case containing artefacts that could be unambiguously linked to the status of betrothal or marriage (such as *e.g.*, engagement/wedding rings or elaborated jewellery). While it is true that in both "Više grobalja" and "Gomilice" a number of burial assemblages refer to the concept of femininity (9 and 11 cases respectively), only few could be seen as interments of engaged or newlywed females. The most obvious is the already discussed case of a potential mother buried with an infant ("Više grobalja" G$_1$228), albeit it is impossible to speculate if the dead child was her first newborn and it is hence inconclusive of whether she was indeed a freshly married young woman. Another candidate is "Gomilice" grave no. 139 that, along with the jewellery set, mirror, box and rasp, contained terracotta figurines of a seated goddess, a partridge and a fig (?). If the goddess is to be interpreted as the incarnation of Venus similar to Verticordia, whose aid was supposed to lead to marriage (D'Ambra 2007, 173–176; Staples 1998, 103–112), we are looking at the grave of a girl or a young female who was potentially betrothed or newly married. Some degree of probability for similar interpretation exists in the case of burial no. 140 at "Gomilice". This funerary unit accommodated mirror glasses, a spatula and eight needles/pins together with a *gemmata* bronze ring that could be understood as an engagement gift.

Of course, there are few examples outside the analysed samples that are interpreted similarly (*cf.* Mihajlović 2011a; Spasić Đurić 2006), but the point is that these are markedly scarce and too vague to be held as confirmation of an alleged connection between mirrors and untimely departed betrothed girls and/or recent brides. For this reason, I am very sceptical that such a link was the general rule and instead would suggest less fixed relations for mirrors and certain female identities (*cf.* Olson 2008, 150). Namely, if we again consider the heuristic scheme in Table 7.3 and the variety of ideal-typical (literary-centered) modes of being female, a mirror (or other toilet and adornment items) is an object eligible for many particular cross-sections of gender, age, social position, legal and marital status and economic standing. Any of the ideologically gendered objects did not have to exclusively signify categories, such as girl available for marriage, betrothed girl, or wedded woman, as much as they did not automatically mark a specific age group (*e.g.*, adolescents). Rather, mirrors could be generally related to a range of states, from girlhood at the very end of juvenility, to the liminal stage of adolescence or transitional phase of betrothal, to young adult married female with or without children, up to fully-fledged senior wife and mother.

The mirror and associated objects can be comprehended as actors in attaining maturation and establishing/maintaining a capacity of feminine adulthood, but they cannot indicate the specific form of female gender-age-status subcategory. While, of course, there were generally shared qualities of femininity, it is crucial to bear in mind the delicate distribution of female identities as they could illuminate the complexity of life in the Roman period, which surpassed the simple division of men and women. It is in this light we should conceptualise mirrors and the practices they involved, from shaping and fashioning the self, to rites of passage and achieving gender and social roles. More precisely, a mirror could imply the accordance with or internalising of the dominant discourse of beautification, appearance and idealised femininity, but it certainly cannot automatically and per se provide the more precisely defined social positioning of a buried female. This liability of mirrors to engage a variety of individuals also triggers the question of whether these objects were strongly bound only to a palette of femininity or that there might be other plausible options as well.

Reflecting the margin: males, gender-benders and ghosts?

How does all of the aforementioned concern the mirrors in the burials of Moesia Superior? First, this should warn us that it is tricky to pinpoint mirrors (and other associated mediators of "female beauty") as absolutely gender-specific objects (compare with Chapter 4 by Kira Zumkley). They were generally emblematic of the ideal of femininity, but it is notably problematic to spontaneously tie all particular cases to the discourse of female beauty, since numerous burials lack other articles to match the full "woman's toilet set" and the cultural value it involved. More importantly, if any of the burials with mirror accommodated a person of male sex (and if any of the anthropological assessments of incinerated remains as male are valid), this would imply that mirrors were not exclusively associated with biologically female individuals. Such a situation would further suggest a few striking possibilities.

The first is that local burial customs (and perhaps life practices) opposed the (Roman) elite cultural norms of accurately gendered behaviour and construction of self as a generic man or woman. In this scenario, the usage of a mirror, and association with it in the funerary context, might not have borne the meaning of a discursive (in)correct femininity or masculinity. In other words, the standard known from literary and visual representations was not strictly followed, but rather adapted in a more relaxed manner, giving way to more haphazard gender activities and less fixed attachments to "normally" masculine or feminine items. In simple terms, some practices (e.g., self-fashioning) and objects (e.g., mirrors) did not have to be as rigidly gender-specific as their general connotation would lead us to conclude (see Revell 2016, 109–110). An excellent Moesian example of this kind comes from Singidunum (Belgrade) and concerns the grave (no. 54) of MKS 2 type that, along with two ceramic vessels, a coin and a lamp, contained a terracotta horse-shaped rattle, a fragment of a copper alloy mirror and a small iron axe head (Fig. 7.5; Simić 1997, 39; T. V).

This grave defies straightforward interpretation on more than one level. As the deceased was cremated, s/he most likely was not of juvenile age, since children less than 15 years were predominantly inhumated at the urban necropolises of Moesia (Korać and Golubović 2009, 532; Mihajlović 2011b; Zotović and Jordović 1990, 111–113).

This makes the presence of a toy within the grave somewhat peculiar, and possibly indicates a person who just has exited childhood, or a child who was interred in an atypical way for its age. Furthermore, the coupling of an iron axe and a mirror within the same grave is exceptional, since it has not been reported in any other published burial from Moesia. If both artefacts belonged to the buried individual (*i.e.*, one of them was not some kind of a farewell gift by the grievers), this combination downplays the expected comprehension of an axe and a mirror as evidently gendered articles and perhaps hints at some sort of liminality.

The case is similar with grave 170 from the NE necropolis of Scupi (Skopje). The grave built of bricks and mortar, with the base and cover formed of large bricks, contained the skeletal remains of what is reported as a male-sex individual. This grave was purposefully cut into an older one of MKS 2 type and was immediately next to a small marble sarcophagus containing the remains of a child, which gives reason to suspect a family connection between the three. The inventory of grave 170 included a copper alloy cylindrical box ("theca vulneraria"), lead pyxis, small iron pestle, unidentified deformed iron blade, glass strigil, silver mirror, coin (Hadrian), and three allegedly chirurgical items (probe, knife/scalpel and chisel) made of iron (Fig. 7.6; Mikulčić 1975).

Due to the presumed medical nature of instruments, as well as, surprisingly, the mirror, the deceased was initially interpreted as a physician (Mikulčić 1975, 100). Later, it has been proposed that the deceased was a barber/hairdresser buried with the tools of his trade (Krunić 2000, 68, 233), or that these items could also serve for bathing and body care (Jovanović 2006, 33; Krunić 2000, 233). If the sexing of the skeletal remains is accurate, the former interpretation is very instructive, since there is also literary evidence that barbers used mirrors for their business (Boon 1991, 24–25; Toner 2015, 95, 98). No matter if we accept this possibility for the Scupi burial, it all the same impels us to realise that this profession could cut through normative gender roles and their usual material agents. By extension, if mirrors are to be understood not only as a part of *mundus muliebris* but as mediators of what is typically male personal grooming (*e.g.*, face shaving) their pairing with the masculine deceased ceases to be an unexpected phenomenon. Consequently, Scupi burial 170 could have easily contained a male interred with his gear for body care (strigil, *theca*, pyxis, pestle) and toilet (mirror and blades), which indicates that some graves with cremated individuals possibly accorded with the similar funerary logic (for alternatives see further in text). As Laurence (2010, 69–70) and Olson (2014, 194–205) have argued, the adoption of a specific fashion or "sub-cultural" trend (such as the one of Roman youth "dandies") could have caused the inversion of normative gendered practices and associated materialities (see also Toner 2015, 95–100). Consequently, the association with some things typically understood as "womanly"/"manly" could imperil the state of fully normative femininity/masculinity without entirely collapsing it, but "only" making it incomplete/imperfect or peculiar. In any case, the instructive examples, such as the two cited,

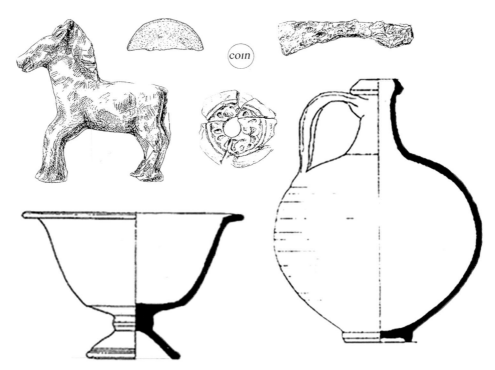

Fig. 7.5 The inventory of grave 54 from the Kosovska Street, Belgrade (Singidunum) (Objects are not to scale) (after Simić 1997, 39; T. V, with permission of the Cultural Heritage Preservation Institute of Belgrade)

advise us not to expect neatly carved gender divisions of material culture and the practices it entangled.

The second implication of a possible male-sex deceased with mirrors is the existence of people who may have challenged conventional gendering and occupied the state of blurriness and betweenness. Such cases have been reported, albeit rarely (Montserrat 2000, 156–161; Revell 2016, 110), and could indicate gender ambiguous positions or fluid experiences and persons who, because of the lack of closer evidence, we might place within a wide range covered by the contemporary terms such as non-binary, "third gender", gender-bender, cross-gender or transgender (of course, modern concepts certainly will not correspond accurately to categories and comprehensions of antiquity, but again, the absence of reliable data deprives us of precise understandings – see Budin 2020; Matić 2012; Power 2020). Social actors of this kind could manipulate and subvert anything from dress codes, posture and gesture, to governing discourses, accepted practices and materialities, in order to construct their own sense of self, even if it was at odds with domineering "genderology". For all we know from the surviving elite literature, such behaviours were considered deviant, and persons thus categorised were represented as abnormal

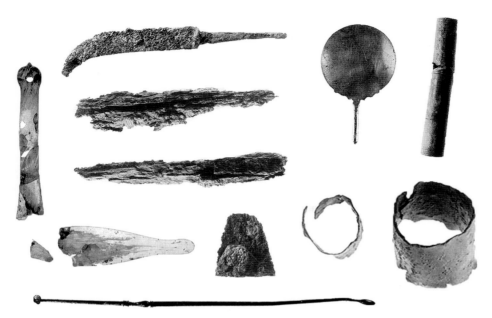

Fig. 7.6 The inventory of grave 170 from the eastern necropolis of Scupi (objects are not to scale) (© The City Museum of Skopje, with permission of the custodian Lenče Jovanova)

and morally corrupt (Kamen and Levin-Richardson 2015; Latham 2012; Laurence 2010, 67–73, 84–86; Montserrat 2000; Olson 2014, 184–193; Williams 2015). On the other hand, stigmatisation did not have to bring total separation, since the functioning of normative order requires eccentric phenomena, and defamed individuals could cohabit in their social environments, albeit with difficulties. For the Roman world, such a likelihood is increased by the immense local cultural varieties that, although operating within the global imperial structure, could distort the ruling customs (but stayed outside the thematic scope covered by elite writers).

Considering mirrors, they were indeed strongly tied to feminine aspects and women both in literary and visual discursive practices, and even individualised mediators of personhood, such as funerary monuments, associated these with females without a single exception (see Shumka 2016 for Roman Italy and IMS I, 42; VI, 122, 131, 146 for Moesia). Notwithstanding, all the aforementioned kinds of media constructed a public image of self, and if unconventional, could risk additional deterioration of one's repute in life or death. Alternatively, the materiality of burial and objects associated with a deceased could have been seen as a relatively more intimate realm and hence enabled manifestation of the aspects of persona that would otherwise have been covert. Thus, male-sex individuals buried with mirrors, who possibly transgressed gender conventions in a manner of "unmanly men", could have been a "tolerable anomaly" in some local communities, which in turn could explain some of the interments from Moesia (remember *e.g.,* grave no. 170 from Scupi).

However, even if they existed, it is currently impossible to securely recognise such cases, let alone to give any estimation of their commonness.

Speaking of localised practices, there is a third plausible explanatory line for tackling the potential burials of males with mirrors. At least in the case of the "Više grobalja" sample, there are repeated records of fragments and fragmented mirrors: 14 (G_1 192, 170, 270, 273, 281, 290, 321, 355, 367, 393, 517, 363, 329, G 281) out of 26 cases. This situation might have its cause in the practice of burning the dead body together with personal belongings, and hence the fragmentation and damaging of mirrors. On the other hand, the fragmented rectangular specimen from G-281 is found with the remains of an inhumated individual, which makes it hardly probable that it was exposed to a funeral pyre. Additionally, it has been argued that mirrors had significance in funerary rituals and were regarded as objects associated with the realm of the dead and otherworld (Taylor 2008, 90–136). Since a mirror was a strikingly personalised item that enabled the catching of one's likeness and was involved in various transformations a human could undergo (including death), this object could have been comprehended as an integral part of an individual's persona (in a similar manner as the deceased's clothes and other personal items – Hope 2011; 2019). The entanglement with a person and possible daily-basis role of reflecting its image could have created the understanding that a mirror entrapped part of an individual within it. However, as the image of the living person it once reflected stood in stark contrast with the benumbed and decaying body after death, this could create profound ontological tension. In turn, uneasiness of this kind could have generated a belief that a mirror was a potentially perilous object after its owner's passing away. In other words, mirrors were possibly seen as having the unwanted capacity to summon the deceased and act as a sort of a passage between the two realms, especially given the evidence of catoptromancy (mirror-divination), their role in contacting the divine and revealing something which could not be regularly seen (see Bur 2020; Ogden 2004, 195–196; Seaford 1998, 104–105, 112; Taylor 2008, 94–98, 102–104). This opens up the possibility that mirrors were buried with the deceased, and in some cases purposefully broken (as were other objects used during the burial and funeral process), in order to prevent invoking the dead back into the world of the living. Thus, the broken mirror had an effect of a closed portal in which a part of the deceased was still captured, and whose fragmentation disabled the performance of yet another, but this time unwanted, reversed and threatening passage.

Of course, if it existed, this was certainly not a widespread practice (*e.g.*, it is not reported at "Gomilice" in any of the graves with mirrors). Additionally, even if it was indeed an ongoing phenomenon localised to Viminacium, it was obviously of limited character, as the burials with mirrors had the markedly minor share at "Više grobalja". Nevertheless, if this notion operated at least in a portion of the population, the placing of mirrors within graves of any gender or age category could have had an agency linked to the spheres of magic rites, funerary ideology and cultic relations with otherworldly entities. In that case, a mirror inside a grave cannot straightforwardly be seen as an index for gender, especially in the instances that lack any tangible reference to gendered roles and practices.

Concluding remarks: passing on the "beauty code", hegemonising the province

Employing compelling reasons, it has been categorically claimed that body care, toilet and adornment were conspicuously linked to the performance of status (on which generally, see Morley 2019) and were an integral element of the culture of urban elites in Roman society. The conceptualisation behind this connection defined a member of higher society as a cultivated human (as opposed to "wild barbarians" or people from lower orders) who gave an example by showing proper manners, behaviour and appearance. Therefore, the use of a mirror, cosmetics, jewellery and adequate dress in becoming the publicly appreciated version of a female was not a neutral endeavour, but one with an embedded ideological driving force (Berg 2002, 24, 41; D'Ambra 2007, 111–113; Dolansky 2012, 275, 287; Shumka 2008, 186–187; 2010; Swift 2012, 55; Wyke 1994).

Having this in mind, let us open up the final question of whether we can recognise the elitist discourse of femininity in shaping the funerary assemblages reviewed in this chapter. First, it is good to recall that in both necropolises the number of burials with mirrors is quite limited ("Više grobalja" – 2.48%, "Gomilice" – 6.48%). Second, of these low percentages, only nine graves at "Više grobalja" (or 0.85%) and 11 at "Gomilice" (or 2.97%) gave enough evidence to be regarded as a close manifestation of feminine beauty concept. Such a situation goes in favour of the thesis that mirrors, together with other sartorial items, were associated with a limited group of people (at least in the funerary sphere), probably more closely with females, and possibly from a privileged background. Consequently, the practice of mirroring and self-fashioning could be seen as an outcome of the habitus of praising the proper physical appearance that was created under the influence of Roman "citizen ideology".

The term stands for the advance of social and cultural inclinations that happened in the course of the intensive involvement of local communities with the imperial structure. The ordering of provincial life through administrative units, such as *coloniae*, *municipia*, *peregrinae civitates* or *territoria metallorum*, the penetration of Roman law, the creation of institutions according to imperial models, the new economic and demographic unfoldings, and the continually present army, had a profound impact on provincial communities. All of these happened synchronously with the establishment of new privileged groups that were part of the hierarchically structured imperial network of elites (*cf.* Mihajlović and Janković 2018). These transformations included affinities and practices that were circulating among these privileged groups and, thanks to their relation to power and elite favouritism, acted as agents of cultural hegemony. Epitomised in the spread of municipal rights and Roman citizenship in Moesia Superior, the aforementioned developments coincided with the introduction of mirrors (and related objects) into the funerary sphere, and can be comprehended as an overall socio-cultural framework. It then seems plausible to argue that the female beauty code and specific corporeal care were among the practices linked to wide socio-cultural flows in Moesia, and part of the imperial urbane cultural preferences (others being *e.g.*, public space and architecture, housing, baths, monumental-epigraphic practice, consumption habits, etc.; *cf.* Janković 2012; 2018). It is also important to emphasise that by passing down and around such a conceptualisation of "proper femininity", the elite "genderology" was reproduced in local contexts, which generated a feedback effect of strengthening the overall normative androcracy.

The same can be said about the (possible) utilisation of mirrors by men who, from the perspective of dominant imperial elite expectations, acted in gender-vague and inappropriate ways: they might have been marginalised and stigmatised to make an example and discipline public opinion about the correct masculine roles. Thus, the practices and connotations stemming from the involvement with mirrors could be regarded as a hegemonic socio-cultural phenomenon, as they were in accordance with the commanding discourses. In a nutshell, this could explain the mechanism of dissemination of ideas about and technology of becoming a conventional (male-elite-preferred) female, or an odd (male-elite-unpreferred) male. On the other hand, if the local social and cultural environments indeed tolerated the male usage of mirrors in a wider range than the attitudes of Mediterranean high society would allow, we could be looking at some divergence from Graeco-Roman standards and a "vernacular" adaptation of the agency of mirrors. In such a scenario, Roman elite norms would be downplayed in favour of local ideas about personal toilette, *i.e.*, the preferred imperial cultural traits were not simply replicated in the provincial settings, but were rather negotiated and modified.

In any case, regardless of the plausibility of the suggested interpretation, there are no grounds to assume that mirrors had an exclusive correlation with high status or even "ordinary" Roman citizens. In other words, the Moesian examples are not apparently linked to high-ranked individuals and could have come from the "middle" and lower layers of society as well. As already emphasised, only in rare instances can we assert that the buried individuals belonged to an affluent environment, while some other cases warn us not to jump to a conclusion about status by referring to objects made of precious metals (Berg 2002, 46, 49). Additionally, as Shumka (2016) points out, a considerable number of women commemorated with *mundus muliebris* motifs came from freed or even slave classes. Although this kind of evidence is sporadic in Moesia, several known examples also adhere to freed people circles (Dragojević-Josifovska 1982, 35). Moreover, as indicated, there is a chance that the published portion of "Više grobalja" necropolis was used by the residents of Viminacium who were of limited economic and/or unprivileged social capacities. The situation is similar at "Gomilice" necropolis, but with the marked distinction that Demessus is not confirmed as a town of municipal status. Unlike Viminacium, the settlement in the vicinity of Stojnik fortress must have had a comparatively lower number of Roman citizenship holders over the course of the 2nd century, but simultaneously yields a proportionally higher quantity of burials with mirrors.

This leaves us with the curious situation that the occurrence of mirrors went along with the promotion of general social and cultural trends while, at the same time, these objects were not associated with an obvious funerary expression of high(er) social positioning. Such a constellation suggests that Roman "citizen ideology" (or its elements) could have freely progressed downscale (*cf.* Wallace-Hadrill 2008, 370), and operated regardless of social status. In other words, even the people who did not enjoy Roman socio-political privileges could adhere to cultural templates defined and set by the elite and commoner bodies of society. In the case of mirrors, this would mean that their engagement indicated the aspired social positioning and performativity, *i.e.*, the status which was not necessarily achieved or already possessed but desired, strived for and/or pending (with special relevance for the categories such as freed people or freshly promoted citizens – *cf.* Hales 2010). As the mediator of favoured manners, self-fashioning and assumed role(s), as the attribute of preferable worldviews and, possibly, learnedness (implied by the pieces with mythological scenes), a mirror was a device that reified multivalent discourses and aided hegemonic structuring. This is why it cut across status distinctions and various social classifications, passing on the beauty code and enabling reflexive technologies of the self.

Acknowledgements

I am deeply grateful to many people who helped me with the research and production of the text. Uroš Matić honoured me with the invitation to be a part of the project, had considerable patience and recommended insightful recent work on archaeology of gender. Tatjana Cvjetićanin and Mirjana Glumac from the National Museum in Belgrade enormously contributed the research by allowing me to use their still unpublished analysis of the "Gomilice" necropolis. Dragana Spasić Đurić from the National Museum in Požarevac kindly permitted me to use the excavation drawings of material from "Više grobalja". Nela Mićović from the Cultural Heritage Preservation Institute of Belgrade and Lenče Jovanova from the City Museum of Skopje collegially let me reproduce illustrations of material kept in their institutions. Leslie Shumka and Ada Cohen thoughtfully shared their papers which were unavailable to me at the moment. Comments and suggestions of two anonymous readers aided me to improve the paper and express some ideas in a much clearer manner. Not least, I am grateful to Milica Vasiljić for the thought-provoking discussions and enlightenment in the areas of feminism and intersectionality. Naturally, all errors and omissions are mine own.

Abbreviations

IMS I: Mirković, M. and Dušanić, S. (1976) *Inscriptions de la Mésie Supérieure I. Singidunum et le Nord-Ouest de la Province*. Beograd, Centre d'Études Épigraphiques et Numismatiques.

IMS VI: Dragojević-Josifovska, B. (1982) *Inscriptions de la Mésie Supérieure VI. Scupi et la région de Kumanovo*. Beograd, Centre d'Études Épigraphiques et Numismatiques.

Bibliography

Adams, M. (2006) Hybridizing habitus and reflexivity: towards an understanding of contemporary identity? *Sociology* 40 (3), 511–528.

Alberici, L.A. and Harlow, M. (2007) Age and innocence: female transitions to adulthood in late antiquity. In A. Cohen and J.B. Rutter (eds) *Construction of Childhood in Ancient Greece and Italy*, 193–204. Athens, The American School of Classical Studies at Athens.

Allason-Jones, L. (1995) 'Sexing' small finds. In P. Rush (ed.) *Theoretical Roman Archaeology: Second Conference Proceedings*, 22–32. Aldershot, Avebury/Ashgate.

Allison, P.M. (2015) Characterizing Roman artifacts to investigate gendered practices in contexts without sexed bodies. *American Journal of Archaeology* 119 (1), 103–123.

Archer, M.S. (2010) Routine, reflexivity, and realism. *Sociological Theory* 28 (3), 272–303.

Berg, R. (2002) Wearing wealth: *mundus muliebris* and *ornatus* as status markers for women in imperial Rome. In R. Berg *et al.* (eds.) *Women, Wealth and Power in the Roman Empire*, 15–73. Rome, Institutum Romanum Finlandiae.

Bruzek, J. and Murail, P. (2006) Methodology and reliability of sex determination from the skeleton. In A. Schmitt, E. Cunha and J. Pinheiro (eds) *Forensic Anthropology and Medicine: Complementary Sciences from Recovery to Cause of Death*, 225–242. Totowa, NJ Humana Press Inc.

Boon, G.C. (1991) 'Tonsor humanus': razor and toilet-knife in antiquity. *Britannia* 22, 21–32.

Bózsa, A. (2017) Instruments of beauty care from the Hungarian part of Pannonia. *Dissertationes Archaeologicae ex Instituto Archaeologico Universitatis de Rolando Eötvös nominatae* 3 (5), 423–438.

Budin, S.L. (2020) Sex and gender and sex. *Mare Nostrum* 11 (1), 1–59. https://doi.org/10.11606/issn.2177-4218.v11i1p1-59.

Bur, T. (2020) Mirrors and the manufacture of religious aura in the Graeco-Roman world. In M. Gerolemou and L. Diamantopoulou (eds) *Mirrors and Mirroring: From Antiquity to the Early Modern Period*, 107–117. London, Bloomsbury Academic.

Carroll, M. (2013) Die Kleidung der Eravisci und Azali an der Donau in römischer Zeit. In A. Wieczorek, R. Schulz and M. Tellenbach (eds) *Der Macht der Toga. DressCode im Römischen Weltreich*, 194–198. Mannheim, Schnell & Steiner.

Carroll, M. (2015) Projecting self-perception on the Roman frontiers: the evidence of dress and funerary portraits. In D.J. Breeze, R.H. Jones and I.A. Oltean (eds) *Understanding Roman Frontiers: A Celebration for Professor Bill Hanson*, 154–166. Edinburgh, John Donald

Cebrián Fernández, R. (2017) Las *capsae* de la necrópolis de incineración de las parcelas números 45 y 46 de *Segobriga* (Saelices, Hispania Citerior). *Archivo Español de Arqueología* 90, 29–51.

Cho, S., Crenshaw K.W. and McCall, L. (2013) Toward a field of intersectionality studies: theory, applications, and praxis. *Signs* 38 (4), 785–810.

Cohen, A. (2010) Mistress' bronzes from the Classical World. In A. Brauer (ed.) *Teaching with Objects: The Curatorial Legacy of David Gordon Mitten*, 76–91. Cambridge, MA, Harvard University Art Museums.

Cooley, A.E. (2013) Women beyond Rome: trend-setters or dedicated followers of fashion? In E. Hemelrijk and G. Woolf (eds) *Women and the Roman City in the Latin West*, 23–46. Leiden and Boston, Brill.

Cvjetićanin, T. (2016) Mala Kopašnica – Sase graves: narrative of continuity. *Issues in Ethnology and Anthropology* 11 (3), 711–730 (in Serbian with an English summary).

Cvjetićanin, T. (2018) Roman pottery from Kosmaj: being about something or being about somebody. In M.A. Janković and V.D. Mihajlović (eds) *Reflections of Roman Imperialisms*, 214–235. Newcastle, Cambridge Scholars Publishing.

Cvjetićanin, T. and Glumac, M. (forthcoming) *Gomilice Necropolis*. Belgrade, National Museum.

D'Ambra, E. (2007) *Roman Women*. Cambridge, Cambridge University Press.

Danković, I. (2019) Burial of a woman with an amber distaff at Viminacium. *Starinar* 69, 215–229.

Danković, I., Milovanović, B. and Marjanović, M. (2018) From a girl to a *matrona*: the life course of the women on the limes. In M. Korać and S. Pop-Lazić (eds) *Roman Limes and Cities in the Territory of Serbia*, 73–81. Belgrade, Serbian Academy of Sciences and Arts and Archaeological Institute – Belgrade.

Dolansky, F. (2008) *Togam virilem sumere*: coming of age in the Roman world. In J. Edmondson and A. Keith (eds) *Roman Dress and the Fabrics of Roman Culture*, 47–70. Toronto, Buffalo and London, University of Toronto Press.

Dolansky, F. (2012) Playing with gender: girls, dolls and adult ideals in the Roman world. *Classical Antiquity* 31 (2), 256–292.

Dragojević-Josifovska, B. (1982) Scupi et la région de Kumanovo. In *IMS VI*, 13–46.

Dušanić, S. (1976) Le Nord-Ouest de la Mésie Supérieure. In *IMS I*, 95–120.

Dušanić, S. (2004) Roman mining in Illyricum: historical aspects. In E. Urso (ed.) *Dall' Adriatico al Danubio, L'Illirico nell' età greca e romana Atti del convegno internazionale Cividale del Friuli 25-27 settembre 2003*, 247–270. Fondazione Niccolò Canussio.

Egri, M. (2016) The Beograd 4 Horizon in the Scordiscian environment. Chronological delimitation and interpretation. In S. Berecki (ed.) *Iron Age Chronology in the Carpathian Basin*, 339–355. Cluj-Napoca, Editura Mega.

Evans Grubbs, J. (2002) *Women and the Law in the Roman Empire: A Sourcebook on Marriage, Divorce and Widowhood*. London and New York, Routledge.

Fantham, E. (1995) Aemilia Pudentilla: or the wealthy widow's choice. In R. Hawley and B. Levick (eds) *Women in Antiquity: New Assessments*, 220–232. London and New York, Routledge.

Ferris, I. (2015) *The Mirror of Venus: Women in Roman Art*. Stroud, Amberley Publishing.

Foucault, M. (1988) *Technologies of the Self: A Seminar with Michel Foucault* (L. H. Martin, H. Gutman and P. H. Hutton eds). Amherst, University of Massachusetts Press.

Glumac, M. (2014) *Roman Necropolis Guberevac - Gomilice at Kosmaj. Social Structure of Inhabitants from I to III century A.D.* Unpublished PhD thesis, University of Belgrade (in Serbian with an English summary).

Glumac, M. (2015) Rock crystals as grave goods at the Gomilice necropolis at Guberevac. *Recueil du Musee National* 22 (1), 279–287 (in Serbian with an English summary).

Hales, S. (2008) Aphrodite and Dionysus: role models for Romans? In S. Bell and I.L. Hansen (eds) *Role Models in the Roman World: Identity and Assimilation*, 236–255. Ann Arbor, University of Michigan Press.

Hales, S. (2010) Tricks with mirrors: remembering the death of Noricum. In S. Hales and T. Hodos (eds) *Material Culture and Social Identities in the Ancient World*, 227–251. Cambridge and New York, Cambridge University Press.

Harlow, M. (2012) Death and the Maiden: reprising the burials of Roman girls and young women. In M. Carroll (ed.) *Dressing the Dead in Classical Antiquity*, 148–157. Stroud, Amberley.

Harlow, M. (2013a) Dressed women on the streets of the ancient city: what to wear? In E. Hemelrijk and G. Woolf (eds) *Women and the Roman City in the Latin West*, 225–241. Leiden and Boston, Brill.

Harlow, M. (2013b) Toys, dolls, and the material culture of childhood. In J. Evans Grubbs and R. Bell (eds) *The Oxford Handbook of Childhood and Education in the Classical World*, 322–340. Oxford, Oxford University Press.

Harlow, M. and Laurence, R. (2002) *Growing Up and Growing Old in Ancient Rome. A Life Course Approach.* London and New York, Routledge.

Harlow, M. and Laurence, R. (2010) Betrothal, mid-late childhood and the life course. In L. Larsson Lovén and A. Strömberg (eds) *Ancient Marriage in Myth and Reality*, 56–77. Newcastle, Cambridge Scholars Publishing.

Hemelrijk, E.A. (2014) Roman citizenship and the integration of women into the local towns of the Latin West. In G. de Kleijn and S. Benoist (eds) *Integration in Rome and in the Roman World, Proceedings of the Tenth Workshop of the International Network Impact of Empire*, 147–160. Leiden, Brill.

Hemelrijk, E.A. (2015) *Hidden Lives, Public Personae: Women and Civic Life in the Roman West.* Oxford, Oxford University Press.

Hingley, R. (2005) *Globalizing Roman Culture: Unity, Diversity and Empire.* Cambridge, Cambridge University Press.

Hirt, A.M. (2010) *Imperial Mines and Quarries in the Roman World: Organizational Aspects 27 bc–ad 235.* Oxford, Oxford University Press.

Holck, P. (2008) *Cremated Bones: A Medical-Anthropological Study of an Archaeological Material on Cremation Burials* (Reprint of the third revised edition). Oslo, Anatomical Institute, University of Oslo.

Holmes, M. (2010) The emotionalization of reflexivity. *Sociology* 44 (1), 139–154.

Hope, V.M. (2011) Remembering to mourn: personal mementos of the dead in Ancient Rome. In V.M. Hope and J. Huskinson (eds) *Memory and Mourning. Studies on Roman Death*, 176–195. Oxford, Oxbow Books.

Hope, V.M. (2019) Dead people's clothes. Materialising mourning and memory in ancient Rome. In Z. Newby and R.E. Toulson (eds) *The Materiality of Mourning: Cross-Disciplinary Perspectives*, 23–39. London and New York, Routledge.

Huebner, S.R. (2019) Single men and women in pagan society: the case of Roman Egypt. In S.R. Huebner and C. Laes, C. (eds.) *The Single Life in Roman and Later Roman World*, 37–56. Cambridge, Cambridge University Press.

Janković, M.A. (2012) The social role of Roman baths in the province of Moesia Superior. In M. Żuchowska (ed.) *Archaeology of Water Installation*, 27–39. BAR International Series 2414. Oxford, Archaeopress.

Janković, M.A. 2018. Archaeology of taste: board and dice games of Moesia Superior. In M.A. Janković and V.D. Mihajlović (eds) *Reflections of Roman Imperialisms*, 236–263. Newcastle, Cambridge Scholars Publishing.

Jevtić, M., Lazić, M. and Sladić, M. (2006) *The Židovar Treasure: Silver Jewelry Hoard from the Settlement of Scordisci.* Vršac and Belgrade, City Museum of Vršac and Faculty of Philosophy Belgrade.

Johnson, M. (2016) *Ovid on Cosmetics: Medicamina Faciei Femineae and Related Texts.* London, Bloomsbury Academic.

Jovanova, L. (2016) Colonia Flavia Scupinorum – The world of the dead. In V. Sekulov (ed.) *Acta Musei Tiberiopolitani I*, 54–74. Strumica, NI Institute for Protection of Monuments of Culture and Museum.

Jovanović, A. (2000) Romanization and ethnic elements in burial practice in the southern part of Pannonia Inferior and Moesoa Superior. In J. Pearce, M. Millett and M. Struck (eds) *Burial, Society and Context in the Roman World*, 204–214. Oxford, Oxbow Books.

Jovanović, A. (2006) Prologue to the research of inhumation in Moesia Superior in the first to third centuries A.D. *Journal of the Serbian Archaeological Society* 22, 23–44.

Kamen, D. and Levin-Richardson, S. (2015) Revisiting Roman sexuality: agency and the conceptualization of penetrated males. In M. Masterson, N. Sorkin Rabinowitz and J. Robson (eds) *Sex in Antiquity: Exploring Gender and Sexuality in the Ancient World*, 449–460. London and New York, Routledge.

Korać, M. and Golubović, S. (2009) *Viminacium Više Grobalja 2.* Belgrade, Archaeological Institute.

Krunić, S. (2000) *Römische Medizinische, Pharmazeutishe und Kosmetishe Instrumente in der Provinz Moesia Superior.* Unpublished PhD thesis, University of Belgrade (in Serbian with a German abstract).

Langlands, R. (2006) *Sexual Morality in Ancient Rome.* Cambridge, Cambridge University Press.

Latham, J. 2012. "Fabulous clap-trap": Roman masculinity, the cult of Magna Mater, and literary constructions of the *galli* at Rome from the Late Republic to Late Antiquity. *The Journal of Religion* 92 (1), 84–122.

Latour, B. (2005) *Reassembling the Social. An Introduction to Actor-Network-Theory.* Oxford, Oxford University Press.

Laurence, R. (2010) *Roman Passions: A History of Pleasure in Imperial Rome.* London and New York, Continuum.

Martin-Kilcher, S. (2000) *Mors immatura* in the Roman world – a mirror of society and tradition In J. Pearce, M. Millett and M. Struck (eds) *Burial, Society and Context in the Roman World*, 63–77. Oxford, Oxbow Books.

Matić, U. (2012) To queer or not to queer? That is the question: sex/gender, prestige and burial no. 10 on the Mokrin necropolis. *Dacia* NS 56, 169–185.

Mihajlović, V.D. (2011a) Adultery in the mirror: Roman mirror from Viminacium, myth, moral and rite(s) of passage. In K. Maricki Gadjanski (ed.) *Antiquity and Modern World: Religion and Culture*, 178–193. Belgrade, The Serbian Society for Ancient Studies.

Mihajlović, V.D. (2011b) Inhumation in the Early Roman Period in the Central Balkans: the reflection of socio-ideological changes? *Istraživanja* 22, 13–31 (in Serbian with an English summary).

Mihajlović, V.D. and Janković, M.A. (2018) Reflecting Roman imperialisms. In M.A. Janković and V.D. Mihajlović (eds) *Reflections of Roman Imperialisms*, 1–29. Newcastle, Cambridge Scholars Publishing.

Mikulčić, I. (1975) Tombes de haute époque romaine à inhumations de Scupi. *Starinar* 24–25, 89–102. (in Serbian with a French summary)

Milnor, K. (2011) Women in Roman society. In M. Peachin (ed.) *The Oxford Handbook of Social Relations in the Roman World*, 609–622. Oxford, Oxford University Press.

Mirković, M. (1986) *Inscriptions de la Mésie Supérieure II: Viminacium et Margum.* Beograd, Centre d'Études Épigraphiques et Numismatiques.

Montserrat, D. (2000) Reading gender in the Roman world. In J. Huskinson (ed.) *Experiencing Rome: Culture, Identity and Power in the Roman Empire*, 153–181. London, Routledge and The Open University.

Morley, N. (2019) Status as performance in Roman Society. *Istraživanja JHR* 30, 7–23.

Newby, Z. (2019) The Grottarossa doll and her mistress. In Z. Newby and R.E. Toulson (eds) *The Materiality of Mourning: Cross-Disciplinary Perspectives*, 77–101. London and New York, Routledge.

Ogden, D. (2004) *Greek and Roman Necromancy.* Princeton and Oxford, Princeton University Press.

Oliver, A. (2000) Jewelry for the unmarried. In D.E.E. Kleiner and S.B. Matheson (eds) *I Clavdia II*, 115–124. Austin, University of Texas Press.

Olson, K. (2008) The appearance of the young Roman girl. In J. Edmondson and A. Keith (eds) *Roman Dress and the Fabrics of Roman Culture*, 139–157. Toronto, Buffalo and London, University of Toronto Press.

Olson, K. (2014) Masculinity, appearance, and sexuality: dandies in Roman antiquity. *Journal of the History of Sexuality* 23 (2), 182–205.

Pasztókai-Szeöke, J. (2011) "The mother shrinks, the child grows. What is it?" The evidence of spinning implements in funerary context from the Roman province of Pannonia. In C.A. Giner, M.J. Martínez García and J. Ortiz García (eds) *Mujer y vestimenta: aspectos de la identidad femenina en la antigüedad*, 125–140. Valencia, Sema.

Pitts, M. and Versluys, M.J. (eds) (2015) *Globalisation and the Roman World.* Cambridge, Cambridge University Press.

Petrova, M. (2019) Single as a *Lena*: the depiction of procuresses in Augustan literature. In S.R. Huebner and C. Laes (eds) *The Single Life in Roman and Later Roman World*, 165–178. Cambridge, Cambridge University Press.

Power, M. (2020) Non-binary and intersex visibility and erasure in Roman archaeology. *Theoretical Roman Archaeology Journal* 3 (1), 1–19. DOI: https://doi.org/10.16995/traj.422

Revell, L. (2016) *Ways of Being Roman: Discourses of Identity in the Roman West.* Oxford and Philadelphia, Oxbow Books.

Rothe, U. (2012a) Clothing in the Middle Danube provinces. The garments, their origins and their distribution. *Jahreshefte des Österreichischen Archäologischen Institutes in Wien* 81, 137–231.

Rothe U. (2012b) The "third way": Treveran women's dress and the "Gallic ensemble". *American Journal of Archaeology* 116, 235–252.

Rothe, U. (2013) Whose fashion? Men, women and Roman culture as reflected in dress in the cities of the Roman north-west. In E. Hemelrijk and G. Woolf (eds) *Women and the Roman City in the Latin West*, 243–270. Leiden and Boston, Brill.

Seaford, R. (1998) The Mirror of Dionysus. In S. Blundell and M. Williamson (eds) *The Sacred and the Feminine in Ancient Greece*, 128–146. New York and London, Routledge.

Shumka, L. (2008) Designing women: the representation of women's toiletries on funerary monuments in Roman Italy. In J. Edmondson and A. Keith (eds) *Roman Dress and the Fabrics of Roman Culture*, 172–191. Toronto, Buffalo and London, University of Toronto Press.

Shumka, L. (2016) Inscribing agency? The mundus muliebris commemorations from Roman Italy. *Phoenix* 70 (1), 77–103.

Simić, Z. (1997) Results of protective archaeological research in the area of the south-eastern Singidunum necropolis. *Singidunum* 1, 21–56 (in Serbian with an English summary).

Spasić-Đurić, D. (2001) Relief mirrors from Viminacium. *Viminacium* 12, 159–178 (in Serbian with an English summary).

Spasić-Đurić, D. (2002) *Viminacium: The Capital of the Roman Province of Upper Moesia.* Požarevac, The National Museum of Požarevac.

Spasić-Đurić, D. (2006) *Lectus genialis* from Viminacium. *Journal of the Serbian Archaeological Society* 22, 295–310 (in Serbian with an English summary).

Spasić-Đurić, D. (2015) *The City of Viminacium.* Požarevac, The National Museum of Požarevac (in Serbian with an English summary).

Stamenković, S., Ivanišević, V. and Pešić, J. (2016) A Roman cemetery at Mala Kopašnica. In S. Perić and A. Bulatović (eds) *Archaeological Investigations Along the Highway Route E75 (2011-2014)*, 17–45. Belgrade, Archaeological Institute.

Staples, A. (1998) *From Good Goddess to Vestal Virgins: Sex and Category in Roman Religion.* London and New York, Routledge.

Stephens, J. (2008) Ancient Roman hairdressing: on (hair)pins and needles. *Journal of Roman Archaeology* 21, 110–132.

Swift, E. (2012) The archaeology of adornment and the toilet in Roman Britain and Gaul. In M. Harlow (ed.) *Dress and Identity*, 47–57. Oxford, Archaeopress.

Taylor, R. (2008) *The Moral Mirror of Roman Art.* Cambridge, Cambridge University Press.

Tokarek LaFosse, M. (2017) Age hierarchy and social networks among urban women in the Roman east. In S.R. Huebner and G. Nathan (eds) *Mediterranean Families in Antiquity: Households, Extended Families, and Domestic Space*, 204–220. Oxford, Wiley Blackwell.

Tomović, M. 1995. Roman mines and mining in the Mountain of Kosmaj. In B. Jovanović (ed.) *Ancient Mining and Metallurgy in Southeast Europe. International Symposium, Donji Milanovac, May 20-25, 1990*, 203–212. Belgrade, Archaeological Institute – Museum of Mining and Metallurgy Bor.

Toner, J. (2015) Barbers, barbershops and searching for Roman popular culture. *Papers of the British School at Rome* 83, 91–109.

Wallace-Hadrill, A. (2008) *Rome's Cultural Revolution*. Cambridge, Cambridge University Press.
Williams, C. (2015) The language of gender: lexical semantics and the Latin vocabulary of unmanly men. In M. Masterson, N. Sorkin Rabinowitz and J. Robson (eds) *Sex in Antiquity: Exploring Gender and Sexuality in the Ancient World*, 461–481. London and New York, Routledge.
Wyke, M. (1994) Woman in the mirror: the rhetoric of adornment in the Roman world. In L. Archer, S. Fischler and M. Wyke (eds) *Women in Ancient Societies: An Illusion of the Night*, 134–151. London, Macmillan Press.
Zotović, Lj. and Jordović, Č. (1990) *Viminacium 1, Nekropole „Više Grobalja"*. Beograd, Arheološki institut, Republički zavod za zaštitu spomenika kulture (in Serbian with a German summary).

Chapter 8

Washed and well-kempt, pale and red-eyed: ideal bodies in Viking Age Scandinavia, *c.* 750 to 1050 CE

Bo Jensen

Abstract

Viking Age bodily ideals were strangely disembodied: the ideal body was an abstract type, of no particular age, size or build. Gender seems to have played a very minor role in bodily aesthetics, with the same ideals applied to a different degree to men and women. Textual sources mention eye-shadow, tattoos, hair and washing, swaddled children and staring eyes. We have only two sources for eye shadow and one for possible tattoos, so these may have been rare. Iconography supplies information about hairstyles and beards, and burial archaeology reveals a very uneven distribution of combs, toilet sets and other relevant artefacts. This may say more about burial customs than about living populations. Burials also reveal modified teeth, something never mentioned in textual sources. A combination of texts and iconographic sources may hint that elites cultivated a hard stare, which was not considered attractive, but aggressive and scary. This was less about looking good than about rejecting the gaze of observers altogether. On the whole, bodily aesthetics in Viking Age Scandinavia appear negative, understood in terms of not having obvious flaws or blemishes. There is little evidence that pagan Scandinavians looked very different from their European, Christian peers, but there is some evidence of regional variation within Scandinavia.

Key words*: Viking Age, Scandinavia, eyes, hair, historical archaeology*

Introduction

A popular quote in Viking Age studies (discussed below) tells that the Danish Vikings shocked England – not by their paganism, not by their brutality, not by their politics, but by washing regularly. Bodies mattered in Medieval Europe, and regimes of bodily discipline and body-maintenance varied from population to population, from period to period. This paper focuses on the archaeological evidence for body maintenance in Viking Age Scandinavian culture. I draw on texts and images where relevant, but focus archaeological artefacts. These are sources for what people actually did, texts and images only for what they wanted to communicate. I shall not try to do any justice to osteoarchaeology here. There is a vast body of analyses, but, understandably, osteoarchaeologists focus on the lived realities of bodily health, notably as they affected bone anatomy. There is a significant gap between osteoarchaeologists' factual information about actual variations in bodily health, and archaeologists' interpretations of what this means for understanding society and culture. This is a gap I cannot close in this paper.

Sources

Between roughly 750 and 1050 CE, communities from South Scandinavia expanded overseas east and west. By the year 1000 there were satellite settlements from South Greenland to the Black Sea. These shared a common language and much of their material culture. Expansion and Christian missions brought Scandinavians into contact with more literate groups and with book-making crafts. By the 1200s Icelanders had created an extensive, vernacular literature. We have a number of Viking Age texts describing Scandinavians from outsiders' perspectives and a number of later manuscripts providing local retrospective. Unfortunately, most texts are very isolated in space and time. Quite apart from problems of author bias and factual mistakes, this raises questions about how homogenous Scandinavian culture ever was. (A huge number of introductions to the period exist, some tendentious, many outdated, all biased towards one perspective or another; Graham-Campbell 1980 is a good starting point; for a good example of source-critical issues, see Montgomery 2003, 1*ff.*)

Viking Age iconography is limited. Much is stylised, standardised animal ornament, with some types copied in their thousands (*e.g.*, Urnes openwork brooches). Human figures are less frequent, often appearing in narrative scenes. They are simplified, often to ambiguity. For example, we often cannot tell hair from headwear. Carved and painted wood, embroidered textiles and painted stones existed, but much is lost. Monochrome stone carvings and metalwork survive better. Specifically, we have the so-called tapestries from five sites (Oseberg, Rolvsöy, Rennebu, Overhögdal and Skog), carved wood from anaerobic conditions, especially in Oseberg, Dublin's Wood Quay, Staraya Ladoga, Novgorod and Bergen (see *e.g.* Lang 1988), 78 chess pieces in ivory from Lewis, perhaps two dozen more or less recognisable human or divine figures on runestones (see Jensen 2017) and some 50 Viking Age picture stones from Gotland (types C, D and E, in Lindqvist 1941) as well as a smaller body from Northern England and the Isle of Man (Table 8.1).

Table 8.1 Images on stone

Human figures on the Gotland C, D and E stones	Bearded men	Long-haired women – with hair in knots/ without visible knots	Other figures	References (figures in Lindqvist 1941 unless otherwise indicated)
Alskog K.	9	2/1	9 unclear	Figs 135–136; Jensen 2017, passim.
Alskog Tjängvida	9	1/1	5 unclear	Figs 137–138; Jensen 2017, 209; Graham-Campbell 2013, figs 39, 181
Ardre I	3		2 unclear, partial	Figs 160, 166
Ardre II	2		1 child?	Figs 162, 167
Ardre III			2 ambiguous, one interpreted as Wayland (Oerhl 2009)	Figs 153, 169; Jensen 2017, 205
Ardre IV	2		1 child?	Figs 161, 165 Jensen 2017, 211
Ardre V			1 swordsman, no obvious beard	Figs 159, 163, 164
Ardre VIII	8	2/0	23 unclear; 2 of these are likely to be badly eroded women with hair in knots	Figs 139–140; Jensen 2017, passim. Graham-Campbell 2001, fig. 192.
Buttle Änge I	9		15+ unclear	Figs 125–127
Buttle Änge V	1			Fig. 123
Garda Bote	4		9 unclear. 8 in skirts (feminine dress) but no indication of long hair	Figs 141–144; Ewing 2008, fig. 4.
Hablingbo K	1		6	Fig. 183
Halla Broa III			5 (poorly preserved; composition suggests five men)	Fig. 108
Halla Broa IV			9 (poorly preserved; composition suggests one woman and eight men)	Fig. 105, 116, 117
Hangvar II	1			Fig. 95
Hemse Annexh.			2	Figs 172, 179

(Continued)

Table 8.1 Images on stone (Continued)

Human figures on the Gotland C, D and E stones	Bearded men	Long-haired women – with hair in knots/ without visible knots	Other figures	References (figures in Lindqvist 1941 unless otherwise indicated)
Hjernum Riddare	11		2	Figs 79, 80
Klinte Hunninge I	13	0/3	5 unclear	Figs 128–131; Jensen 2017, passim. Graham-Campbell 2001, fig. 194
Klinte Hunninge III	3			Fig. 132
Klinte Ksp.	1	0/1	3	Fig. 134
Levide K.		0/2		Figs 176, 178
Lokrume K	2		5 (unclear, bearded or beadless men)	Figs 93, 94
Lärbro St. Hammars I	20	0/1	15 (likely 14 bearded men and one bird, but poorly preserved)	Figs 81, 82; Jensen 2017, 209; Ewing 2008, fig. 2.; Graham-Campbell 2013, figs 36, 37
Lärbro St. Hammars III	9	0/2		Figs 84, 85; Jensen 2017, 209
Lärbro St. Hammars IV	4	0/1		Fig. 83
Lärbro Tängelgårda I	27			Figs 86, 87, 88; Ewing 2008, figs 49, 50.
Lärbro Tängelgårda II	9			Figs 89, 90; Jensen 2017, 209
Lärbro Tängelgårda IV	2		4 (unclear, bearded or beardless men)	Fig. 91
När Bosarve (side B)			2 unclear, possibly bearded men	Fig. 175
När Smiss I	2		4 unclear, very stylised.	Figs 142, 143
Sanda I	2	1/0	3	Figs 171, 177
Sanda Sandegårda II	5?			Figs 106, 118, 119

(Continued)

Table 8.1 (Continued)

Human figures on the Gotland C, D and E stones	Bearded men	Long-haired women – with hair in knots/ without visible knots	Other figures	References (figures in Lindqvist 1941 unless otherwise indicated)
Stenkyrka Lillbjärs I	1			Figs 103, 109, 110, 113
Stenkyrka Lillbjärs III	4	0/1? (poorly preserved)		Figs 104, 111, 112, 114, 115; Jensen 2017, passim.
Stenkyrka Lillbjärs XVII	4			Fig. 107
Stenkyrka Smiss I	28	0/2	9 (most of these badly eroded, probably men and women both): one possible, beardless man	Figs 97–102; Jensen 2017, passim. Graham-Campbell 2013, fig.38
Total	196	6/16	142+	
The Sigurd stones	Bearded men	Long-haired women – with hair in knots/ without visible knots	Other figures	References (Svenska runverket)
Drävla		0/2	2 unclear, supposed to be Sigurd and the Valkyrie	U 1163; Jensen 2017, 208 and fig. 10.1
Gök			2 unclear, supposed to be Sigurd and Regin	Sö 327; Jensen 2017, 208
Norum Church	1			Bo NYIR 3; Jensen 2017, 211
Ockelbo			4, possibly two men and two women	Gs 19
Ramsundsberget	1		2 beardless men, both interpreted as Sigurd	Sö 101; Jensen 2017, 208; Graham-Campbell 2001, fig. 195
Stora Ramsjö	1			U1175; Jensen 2017, 208
Västerljung	1		1 beardless man (interpreted as Sigurd)	Sö 40; Jensen 2017, 208
Årsunda			2 unclear	Gs 9
Åsunda			2 very unclear figures	Gs 9

(Continued)

Table 8.1 Images on stone (Continued)

The Sigurd stones	Bearded men	Long-haired women – with hair in knots/ without visible knots	Other figures	References (Svenska runverket)
SUM	4	0/2	15	
Hørdum Stone	1		1 unclear	
Snaptun Stone	1			Jensen 2017, 202, fig. 10.1, and Madsen 1990

British Scandinavian stone monuments	Bearded men	Long-haired women – with hair in knots/ without visible knots	Other figures	
Gosforth Cross	7	0/3	2 unclear, both dressed like men	Jensen 2017, 203; Graham-Campbell 2013, figs 13, 200
Gosforth stone			2 unclear	Graham-Campbell 2013, fig. 186
Kirby Hill			2; one headless and one vague man, probably beardless	
Kirby Stephen	1			Jensen 2017, 203
Kirk Andreas, Siguard's cross			1 unclear, likely Sigurd	Graham-Campbell 2001, fig. 196
Kirk Andreas, Thorwald's cross	2			Graham-Campbell 2001, fig. 199
Skipwith stone	4		2 unclear, may also be bearded men	Buckland 2010, fig. 4.4 and 51ff.
Total	13	0/3	9	
	Bearded men	Long-haired women – with hair in knots/ without visible knots	Other figures	
	211	6/21	164+	

We have uncounted hundreds of small finds in non-ferrous metal – I have catalogued 45 human figures and 42 so-called mask pendants in Jensen 2010; no-one has ever catalogued all the masks decorating other artefacts (for examples, see Lemm 2010; Kjærum and Olesen 1990). More stylised human figures can be found in the animal style ornament, *e.g.*, three bearded men on a cross-piece from Oseberg

(Graham-Campbell 2013, 52), on oval brooches, strap ends and on ornamental panels for horse equipment (see Kjærum and Olsen 1990, 172ff.).

Two sites deserve special mention here: Birka and Haithabu. Both were early towns, both had cosmopolitan populations of perhaps 1000 people at any one time. On both sites, huge excavation campaigns in the 1800s produced enormous burial records, but the settlements themselves have only been explored to a very limited degree. However, the Birka graves are vastly richer than those of Haithabu, and of any other site known in Viking Age Scandinavia. In any quantitative analysis, Birka attains a dominance entirely out of proportion with how unusual the site is, as I shall illustrate below.

In recent years, archaeologists have compiled national databases of old and new finds. Unfortunately, the Scandinavian countries have adopted very different strategies, making comparison difficult. The Swedish SHM has provided researchers with a wonderful, searchable online catalogue (http://mis.historiska.se/mis/sok/start.asp). Officially, only some 21% of the collections are yet registered here, but the coverage for Viking Age archaeology seems far better. In Norway, the main centralised database is that provided by Universitetes Oldsakssamling (www.dokpro.uio.no/arkeologi/oslo/hovedkat.html), more basic but similar to the Swedish database. Confusingly, the same museum provides a different database for all Norway (https://www.khm.uio.no/forskning/samlingene/oldsak/), with different strengths and weaknesses. Denmark has largely failed to make its finds similarly accessible. Until recently, we had a limited overview through Museernes samlinger, which actively discouraged excavators from sharing contextual information. Recently, even this service been discontinued. New solutions have been promised, but not yet realised. Consequently, it is frustratingly difficult to obtain any confident, international overview of unpublished material.

With these reservations in mind, let us turn to the evidence: different sources mention eye shadow, tattoos, hair and washing, attitudes to nakedness and swaddled children. Archaeology supplements this with a few observations unmatched in the written sources.

Eye shadow

"There is also an artificially made eye make-up ['k-h-l]; when they use it, their beauty never decreases but rather increases, both among men and women" (my translation from German; see Jacob 1927, 29). The quote comes from Zaharija al-Qazwînî's description of "Šlšwîq", usually identified as Haithabu/Schleswig, written in the 13th century. Al-Qazwînî cites Akhmad al-'Udri who in turn cites a lost report by Ibrâhîm at-Tarṭûshî (before c. 962 CE). Al-Qazwînî's text describes public animal sacrifices and widespread paganism, suggesting that this editor did not update this 300-year-old information. Eye shadow is also mentioned in Hallfreðar saga (14): "Hallfreðr then put on beggar's gear. He had color put on his eyes, and turned his eyelids back, which changed his appearance greatly" (translation after Whaley 2002, 88). These two sources are clearly independent of each other, one produced in Western Asia, the other in the North Atlantic. While they suggest different purposes (beauty and disguise), the basic technology seems identical. In Al-Qazwînî, both men and women use eye shadow, in the Hallfredr saga, the whole point is that the one man mentioned did not normally use it, but someone else (men or women) presumably did. Eye shadow has not been identified in iconography (but see below) and no relevant material artefacts have been identified. At best, then, these sources may suggest that this technology was known and became notably fashionable in at least one settlement at one time in its history. Hægstad suggests an even more damning critique: he suggests that al-Qazwînî mixed information from different sources and misunderstood ambiguous words. Hægstad argues that the original information did not refer to Schleswig but to Wolin (Poland), and did not describe eye shadow but amber jewellery. He glosses 'k-h-l as kohl or resin, arguing that in Medieval Arabic, this could refer to amber (Hægstad 1964, 91). Other historians seem to have ignored this critique. Technically, kohl would have been quite easy to make, from a dark pigment, such as soot, and an adhesive. A society that could dye cloth and paint wood could certainly manage this. In gender terms, at-Tartûshî is unambiguous: if anyone wore eye shadow, both men and women did.

Tattoos (or body paint)

"Each man, from the tip of his toes to his neck, is covered in dark-green lines, pictures and such like." The quote is from one of the most famous texts in Viking studies, Akhmed ibn Fadlan's travelogue Rīsala (translated in Montgomery 2003, 6). It may describe tattoos or body paint. The Egtved runestone mentions an individual called Fainn, possibly "the painted one". Lisbeth Imer suggests that this may refer to the same phenomenon (Imer 2016, 246; DR 37). The Rīsala is widely regarded as trustworthy (see discussion in Montgomery 2003). Like at-Tartûshî, above, ibn Fadlan reports first hand from his own journeys, describing multiple ethnic groups. However, in ibn Fadlan's case, we have his original text. Yet, the same reservations apply as before: the 'Rus whom Ibn Fadlan met on the Volga may not be equally representative of all Scandinavians everywhere throughout the Viking Age, and they may not have been Scandinavians at all (Montgomery 2003, 1ff. and 23ff.). Again, the source is isolated: no other text mentions tattoos or body paint, and no image shows them. The lack of relevant images is particularly striking, since other cultures of tattooing have gone out of their way to illustrate their tattoos, as in Maori ancestral portraits, Japanese woodblock prints, modern western tattooing culture's magazines, websites, and representation in graffiti, on film and in graphic novels. In some of these cultures we find people depicted in surprising states of undress, simply to allow artists to illustrate their tattoos. If tattoos were common in Scandinavia, it is exceedingly odd that they were never depicted. We have plenty of human images from Viking Age Scandinavia, yet not one identified example of a possible tattoo. The closest thing are the joint spirals on the shoulders of the Rällinge and Aukereyi figurines, on the Ramsundsberget rock carving and the River Thames plaque (Tables 8.1. and 8.2; see also Graham-Campbell 2013, 110).

Even these are unlikely to represent tattoos: such spirals were a standard way of indicating joint anatomy in contemporary European iconography, and also widely used for images of bird and animal bodies. On Ramsundsberget, people, horse and wild birds all have the same spirals.

Table 8.2 Portable images, metalwork and small finds

Motif	Total number	Pieces (with references)
Long-haired women, hair in knots	20	Scania (Tegnér 2005; Jensen 2010, nr. 543); Tissø valkyrie brooch (Mannering 2006, pl. 4.4, no. 9); Bj. 825 pendant (SHM 34000: Bj. 825); Bj. 968 pendant (SHM 34000: Bj. 968); Grödinge pendant (Mannering 2006, pl. 4.6, fig. 16; Jensen 2010, nr. 614; SHM 20672); Tuna pendant (Mannering 2006, pl. 4.6, fig. 18); Gamla Uppasala pendant (Mannering 2006, pl. 4.6, fig. 19); Nygård pendant (Mannering 2006, pl. 4.6, fig. 21, NM I 7221/91) Öland pendant; (Mannering pl. 4.7, fig. 22); Lejre Valkyrie (Christensen 2015, 193 and cat. 149); Tissø pendant (Mannering 2006, pl. 4.7, fig. 23); Tissø pendant (Zeiten 1997, nr. 12, NM I FB 209/J. nr. 7701/94) Tissø "Freya" pendant (Mannering 2006, pl. 4.7, fig. 24, Jensen 2010, nr. 37, FG 3589); Norsborg pendant, two women (Mannering 2006, pl. 4.3, no. 7); Nygård, Bornholm (tall knot; Zeiten 1997, nr. 13; Jensen 2010, nr. 121. NM I C32009); Jensen 2010, nos. 19, 27, 62, 66, 243, 342, 351, 364, 555, 749, 775, 817, 903, 908, 1237, 1266.
Women with covered hair	5	Tissø valkyrie brooch (Mannering 2006, pl. 4.4, no. 5); Hagebyhöga pendant (Jensen 2010, nr. 1277; SHM 16429/16560); Klinta pendant (Mannering 2006, pl. 4.6, fig. 17 SHM 128; Jensen 2010, nr. 1237); Tissø Valkyrie pendant (Mannering 2006, pl. 4.7, fig. 25; Zeiten 1997, nr. 11; Jensen 2010, nr. 74, NM I KN 563/C 32167), Wickham Market Area valkyrie (Jensen 2010, no. 252)
Bearded men, including "mask amulets"	53+	Uppåkra pendant with drinking horn (Mannering 2006, pl. 4.8, fig. 29; Jensen 2010, nr. 551); Uppåkra pendant "Wayland" (Graham-Campbell 2003, fig. 193; Jensen 2017, 205*ff.* with references); Vester Egespor Brooch (Mannering 2006, pl. 4.3, no. 5); Gudme figurine (Zeiten 1997, nr. 14; Jensen 2010, nr. 165, NM I j. nr. 4620/82); masks: Jensen 2010, nos. 7, 11, 14, 20, 46, 63, 73, 105, 106, 107, 123, 140, 144, 156, 160, 164, 174, 178, 229, 240, 269, 273, 296, 297, 321, 332, 333, 338, 382, 534, 550, 729, 761, 762, 965, 1276, 1287, see also *Ibid.* nos. 74, 165, 455, 457, 508, 551, 553, 720, 730, 752, 753, 909, 1133, 1134, 1252, 1283, 1290). Nørre Åby figurine, Lejre figurine, Rällinge Figurine, Eyrarland figurine, Lund figurine, Feddet figurine, Baldursheimur figurine, Chenya Moglia figurine, Gnëzdovo figurine Lindby figurine (all these Perkins 2001, *passim.*, and *op. cit.*), Trønning figure (Jensen 2003, 353), Birka "smiling Viking" (*e.g.* Graham-Campbell 2001, fig. 217)
Beardless, short hair	1	Haithabu (Zeiten 1997, nr. 16; Jensen 2010, 1299)

The minimum material culture of tattooing is minimal indeed: a needle, pin or thorn and a stable pigment, such as sooth. Sooth tattoos are black when fresh, but often fade to shades of blue, green or grey, perhaps explaining the "dark green lines" in Ibn Fadlan's text. Although tattooing equipment could easily be undetectable to archaeology, one iron artefact from a grave at Vendel, Sweden has been interpreted as such (Arrhenius 2005, 314). It looks like a chisel with a serrated edge. If the serrations once ended in fine needles, it would resemble "combs" used in e.g., Japanese or Nagaland tattooing (e.g., Pitt-Rivers Virtual Collections 2011, not paginated). If the points were instead slightly wider, the tool would resemble the spacer punches used in leatherwork to make holes for lacing and stitching. Given the poor preservation of the working edges, the object is ambiguous.

In any case, history suggests caution: when modern Europeans encountered tattooing in Polynesia, South Sea sailors quickly acquired tattoos from local masters, but for more than a century, the phenomenon was almost entirely limited to sailors, criminals, royals and others beyond normal society. Tattooing only became reasonably mainstream much later (see Gell 1993, 22ff.). Thus, tattooed sailors may have been as exotic in Bulgar or Birka in the 900s as they were in London or Amsterdam in the 1800s, and just as unknown a few kilometres inland. Ibn Fadlan's comments only refer to men. He offers no information for or against tattooed Viking women.

Head hair

Our best evidence for hairstyles comes from textual sources. A few examples stand out. In 793 CE, following the Viking attack on Lindisfarne, Alcuin of York admonished Æthelred of Northumbria against sin and luxury: "Look at your trimmings of beard and hair, in which you have wished to resemble the pagans" (trans. Whitelock 1955, 776). Two centuries later, in De Sanguine, Abbot Ælfric warned his brother against "Danish fashion with a shaved neck and blinded eyes" ("ableredum hneccan and ablendum eagum", Clayton 2007, 36). This kind of wordplay is much valued in contemporary learned culture, and often results in precisely this kind of ambiguously flowery language. Clayton suggests that this refers to the hairstyle depicted for the Normans in the Bayeux tapestry (Clayton 2007, 36). Importantly, as Alcuin stresses, hairstyles could be copied. One generation's "Viking" hairstyle might become the next fashion in England and eventually lose its ethnic association.

No other contemporary text describes hairstyles in as much detail as Ælfric's letter, but some texts suggest that men might wear their hair long: the notoriously fantastic Jómsvíkinga saga describes a warrior with hair so long that his executioners had to lift it aside for his decapitation; when he jerked his neck, the blow severed one executioner's hands instead (Jomsvikinga saga, ch. 47). I am unconvinced this would work in reality, and the anecdote is clearly a brutal joke, but the hairstyle may have existed.

Non-Scandinavian textual sources are silent on women's hair, but the Old Norse corpus offers a few mentions: in Skáldaskárpamál, the goddess Sif wakes up with her head shorn, and the trickster god Loki is sentenced to compensate her and replace her hair with living gold (Skáldaskárpamál 1). In Locesenna, Loki claims to have been Sif's lover (verse 54). Arwill-Nordbladh suggests that the hair-cutting might imply that they were indeed very intimate (see Arwill-Nordbladh 2016, 1). Brennu-Njáls saga implies a similar association between women's hair and bodily autonomy. In this account, Gunnar married Hallgerd, and gave her his word that he would never hit her. He broke this promise once; much later, when they were surrounded by his enemies, he asked Hallgerd for hair to repair his bowstring. She refused him, explicitly because he had once hit her. Gunnar died in that fight, a victim of his wife's pride and his own respect for her autonomy (ch. 77). The episode implies a symmetry between hair-cutting and violence, so that for Hallgerd to surrender even one strand of her hair would be a major concession, much more serious than remaining in an apparently unhappy marriage. Both episodes (Sif, Hallgerd) imply that women's hair was socially extremely important and not cut lightly. Conversely, they may also imply that perfect hair in public might hide and elide all manner of private misery and compromise. The Brennu-Njáls saga episode also implies that women's hair was better for bowstrings than men's, most obviously perhaps because it was longer. Viking Age bows could be as long as the 185 cm bow from Haithabu but even making a shorter bow's string would require very long hair indeed (for the Haithabu bow, see Paulsen 1999).

We have good iconographic evidence for hairstyles: a large number of Viking Age images show obviously bearded men in trousers and long-haired women in skirts. A smaller number of images differ from these stereotypes, including several images of Sigurd Völsung, who famously killed the dragon when still a beardless boy (Table 8.1) and the peculiar "bird-men" on Oseberg tapestry 10. In iconography, men's hair may be so short as to be invisible, hidden by hats, or cut short "Roundhead" style. At least one image clearly shows a completely bald man, possibly elderly (Feddet, Denmark; see below). Other men's hair is somewhat longer, but always short of the shoulders. On the Viking Age Gotland stones alone, there are at least 196 examples of bearded men with short or slightly longer hair (Table 8.1). When men's faces are shown en face, they very often have a vertical line down the crown of the head suggesting either a severe centre-part or a close-fitting cap with a central seam (*e.g.*, Uppåkra, Graham-Campbell 2003, fig. 193). This is often accompanied by a headband. Ælfric's description of "blinded eyes" cannot be recognised in iconography. Here, hair always ends above the height of the eyebrows (examples in Table 8.2). The "Viking" hairstyle so beloved of cartoonists and Romantic artists, with two braids hanging to mid-chest, is nowhere in evidence.

Women's hair is shown in a few different styles, all based on long hair: long ropes of hair, which may indicate ponytails; ornate knots, either atop or behind the head; and a unified mass, sometimes clearly collected in some sort of head-covering (hairnet or headscarf, Fig. 8.1). I have found only one image of apparently short-haired women, on the Garde Bote stone, where seven of the eight women are hanged. They may

Fig. 8.1 Images of Viking Age bodies. Top row, left to right, woman with hairnet, silver (Birka grave 825, Uppland, Sweden); swaddled child, amber (Haithaby, Schleswig, Germany); woman with ornate hairstyle, silver (Tissø, Denmark); and chess pawn with staring eyes, walrus ivory (Lewis, Scotland). Bottom row: bearded men with shoulder-length hair, carved limestone (Lärbro Tängelgårde, Gotland, Sweden); and woman with her hair in a knot and horseman with a jutting beard, carved limestone (Alskog Tjängvida I, Gotland, Sweden) (Drawings by author, not to scale)

represent some unusual category of people whose hairstyle was not typical. Gansum (2003, 201) cites an Anglo-Saxon law that mentions "a free woman with long hair", suggesting perhaps that short-haired women are not free (Laws of Ethelberth of Kent, ch. 33). Women are never shown wearing proper hats, though a few of the so-called Valkyries wear helmets (Table 8.2). The most frequently illustrated hairstyle for women is a simple ponytail, occasionally with one large knot shown at the back of the neck (Table 8.1: six images on stone clearly show the knot, 21 more show the ponytail). A few images show women with their hair in two knots, on each side of the neck (see Arwill-Nordbladh 2012, 48). A single three-dimensional image from Vårby, Denmark, clarifies that the usual hairstyle could not look like that from any perspective, so we may have evidence of three different hairstyles based on long, straight hair. A few pieces show different hairstyles: the Nygård and Öland pendants shows women with their hair apparently piled up above their heads, and the Gosforth cross-shaft shows two people with their hair twisted into long ropes or braids. I have found one clear illustration of a hairnet (Fig. 8.1), two images of women whose hair seems covered with decorated cloth (headscarves or bonnets) and a handful of

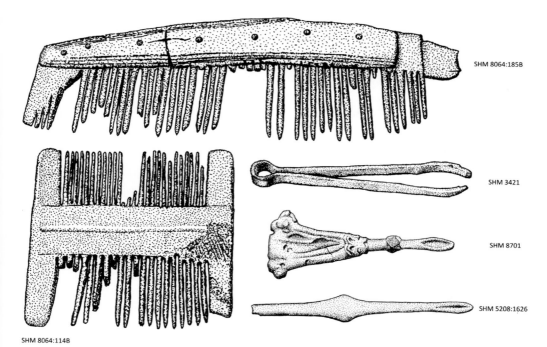

SHM 8064:185B

SHM 3421

SHM 8701

SHM 5208:1626

SHM 8064:114B

Fig. 8.2 Tools for body-maintenance. Top: one-sided three-layer comb (Harvor, Gotland, Sweden; SHM 8064:185B). Grave find. Antler and metal rivets (iron?). Lower left: one-layer, two-sided comb with fine and coarse teeth (Harvor, Gotland, Sweden; SHM 8064:114B). Grave find. Antler. Lower right, top to bottom: tweezers (Rone, Gotland, Sweden; SHM 3421). Stray find. Copper alloy. Ear-spoon (Birka, Uppland, Sweden; SHM 8701). Settlement find. Copper alloy. Ear-spoon (Birka, Uppland, Sweden; SHM 5208:1626). Settlement find. Antler (Drawings by author, not to scale)

ambiguous images that may also show women with covered hair (Tables 8.1 and 8.2). The archaeology of Viking towns, notably Dublin, suggests that bonnets were more common in real life than in iconography (Wincott Heckett 2003). This selective representation may perhaps suggest that most images only show a few specific, very formal occasions, including perhaps weddings (see Steinsland 1989).

We have little idea whether iconography represents typical or ideal persons, kings or commoners. Combs and other artefacts bring us much closer to the realities of everyday Viking Age life (Fig. 8.2). Of these finds, combs are far the most common. Viking Age combs are very similar in design, with few types dominating the record from the Baltic to Iceland. The standardised designs suggest that there was a shared culture of haircare throughout the Viking world. The common three-layer combs are occasionally found with sheaths, indicating that they were used to comb hair, and not worn as hair-ornaments; the rarer two-sided combs often have very fine teeth on one side, suggesting that they were made to remove headlice (though Ashby 2014, 162 disagrees). Lice likely became a bigger problem with urbanisation and long-distance trade. Many combs seem to have been worn on belts or in pouches, allowing owners to touch up their hair during the day. Combs have been found in huge numbers all over the Viking world. The SHM database lists some 1780 examples of Viking Age combs, the Oslo databases some 4000 combs from all periods, and even the Danish database lists 163 Viking Age combs. A quantitative survey of all this is beyond the scope of this paper. Instead, I shall rely on previous syntheses (see Table 8.3).

The burial evidence is frustratingly varied from site to site, and may say more about burial customs than about comb use among the living: Ambrosiani (1981, 73f.) catalogues 259 graves with (preserved) combs from Birka, out of *c.* 1000 excavated graves. In Haithabu, excavation of 1350 graves yielded just one comb, and that one from the richest burial on the site (Arents and Eisenscmidt 2010, Taf. 10:4:1). Yet, the very small settlement excavations, covering some 5% of the area inside the wall, produced tens of thousands of waste fragments from comb-making (Ashby 2014, 162), suggesting that combs were readily available. Thus, the burial evidence does not directly reflect living realities.

On Birka, Ambrosiani (1981, 73ff.) reports combs from 29% of the (gendered or sexed) men's graves and 29% of the women's graves, suggesting no strong association with either gender. There are another 1200 finds of comb fragments from the settlement, meaning that Birka alone accounts for about 3/4 of the Viking Age combs in the SHM database. One hundred and sixty-seven are from Gotland, 45 from Södermanland, just south of Birka, and there are no more than 16 combs from any other province in this database. We can supplement that evidence with Svanberg's catalogue of graves in South-East Scandinavia (Svanberg 2003). Svanberg reports combs from 55 graves, including seven osteologically identified males and four osteologically identified females. Grave goods allow us to gender the deceased from another six graves with combs as feminine and one as possibly feminine. Again, combs are not exclusive to either sex. Nor do combs have strong status associations, being found with extremely rich graves (*e.g.*, Svanberg 2003, cat. 142:A:59:2, with ship and animal sacrifices) and in graves with no other goods at all (*e.g.*, Svanberg 2003, cat. 54:39). More than half these graves with combs are from Öland, a number entirely out of proportion with that island's small size and limited presence in the catalogue. Much larger Scania yields only five examples. Even outside Birka, there is much regional variation, then. Here, the evidence from children's graves is striking: Öland offers four examples (three from Alby, one from Kastlösa), while children's graves with combs have not been recognised anywhere else in South-Eastern Scandinavia. Again, burials with combs tell us more about burial customs than about lived realities. Typologically, men's and women's combs are quite similar. Therefore, different gendered hairstyles did not affect comb design.

Settlement evidence suggests that combs were mass-produced. In Scandinavia, combs and comb-making are much more in evidence on settlements in the Viking Age than in the previous Iron Age (before *c.* 750 CE). This is but one of many examples of how cultural artefacts, and presumably behaviours, spread from elites to a much broader segment of society during this period.

Table 8.3 Grave goods

Type	Context	Region	Number	Reference
Combs	Osteologically female graves	South Sweden	4	Svanberg 2003, cat. 54:4, 142:D:4, 142:D:20, 151: Räa:115
	Culturally feminine graves	Birka	74	Ambrossianni 1981, 73*ff.*
		South Sweden	6	Svanberg 2003, cat. 53:3, 54:15, 86:32, 99, 186, 197
	Σ women		*84*	
	Osteologically male graves	South Sweden	7	Svanberg 2003, cat. 142:A:59:2, 142:D:10, 143:4, 151:Raä 51: 18, 176:1994:1, 181:1941,258; female: cat. 54:4, 142:D:4, 142:D:20, 151: Räa:115
	Culturally masculine graves	Birka	48	Ambrossianni 1981, 73*ff.*
		South Sweden	1 possible	Svanberg 2003, cat. 87:2
	Σ men		*56*	
	Gender balance: 84/56= 60 % women			
	Children's graves	Öland	4	Svanberg 2003, cat. 142:D.3,188:1971:3, 188:1971:46, 188:1971:47
Tweezers	Culturally femine graves	Birka	37	Waller 1984, 189
		Gotland	4	Waller 1984, 189
		South Sweden	2	Svanberg 2003, 172:1964:2, 174:1873; 10:3, 103:9, 163: 1896, 165
		Norway	6	Petersen 1951, 503; C5463, C 1283–85 & C1671–72, St 2192, and Ytre Arna.
		Haithabu and Denmark	3	Arents & Eisenschmidt 2010, grab 497, Eisenschmidt 2004, 203
	Σ women		*52*	
	Osteologically male graves	South Sweden	1	Svanberg 2003, cat. 142:D:4;
	Culturally masculine graves	Norway	2	Petersen 1951, 503; Ts 5374
		Haithabu and Denmark	3	Eisenschmidt 2004, 203
	Σ men		*6*	
	Gender balance: 52/6= 76 % women			

(Continued)

Table 8.3 Grave goods (Continued)

Type	Context	Region	Number	Reference
Ear spoons	Culturally femine graves	Birka	9	Gräslund 1984, 181
		Gotland (NB: Late Iron Age, not Viking Age)	23	Gräslund 1984, 181
		The rest of Sweden	8	Gräslund 1984, 181 and SHM 8154:6, 10211, 15482, 2394, 19802:1, 31001, though these last two may not be ear-spoons
		Karelia	6	Gräslund 1984, 181
		Norway	1	Petersen 1951, 503
	Σ women		*47 (24 Viking Age)*	
	Culturally masculine graves	Norway	1	Petersen 1951, 503
	Σ men		*1*	
	Gender balance: 24/1= 96 % women			
Shears and scissors	Culturally femine graves	Birka	98	Arwidsson 1984b, 195
		Rest of Sweden	10	SHM 4689, 8277, 8791, 10243:XV, 11570, 13804:4, 19052, 19732:2a, 19802:1, 22765:10, 25840:59:3:37
		Norway	136	Petersen 1951, 318
		Denmark	8	Eisenschmidt 2004, 199
	Σ women		*252*	
	Culturally masculine graves	Birka	3	Arwidsson 1984b, 195
		Rest of Sweden	5	SHM 12300, 12360:10, 12475, 22293:1, 30962:F14
		Norway	194	Petersen 1951, 318
		Denmark	3	Eisenschmidt 2004, 199
	Σ men		*205*	
	Gender balance: 252/205= 55 % women			

Hairpins are not in evidence, a striking fact compared to Roman Iron Age archaeology (see *e.g.*, Jensen 2003, 330; for examples of RIA hairpins, see *e.g.*, Boye 2009, 283; Ethelberg *et al.* 2000, *62ff.* and 181; Hansen 1995, 237*ff.*; 2008, 168*f.*; the standard typology is Beckmann 1966). Ambrosiani remarks that in graves, Iron Age hairpins and combs are frequently found behind the head of the deceased, suggesting that they were worn as ornaments, whereas Viking Age combs are found at belt-height, as if carried.

In metalwork, hair and beards are usually indicated with straight lines, and the long ponytails on *e.g.*, the Vårby figurine would require very straight hair. On stone, a few images suggest rather more curly hair, *e.g.*, the Snaptun stone. Eyebrows are occasionally mentioned in written sources, but are rarely evident in iconography. Other body hair is never even mentioned and seems not to have been socially important. Unlike many ancient cultures, there is no evidence that body hair was shaved. From all sources, hairstyles seem clearly associated with gender, but technologies of haircare much less so.

Beards

"Njal was wealthy and handsome but he had this peculiarity: he could not grow a beard". This is Brennu-Njáls saga's entire description of its protagonist (ch. 20). We learn nothing about his colouring, build or height, but Njál's beardlessness is mentioned twice in lampoons, calling him "Old beardless". The last of these lampoons challenges Njál's masculinity, and helps rekindle the feud that eventually kills him. On picking up Njál's peace offering, a silk shirt, Flosi tells Njál's sons "I think it was your father who gave it, 'Old beardless', for few can tell just by looking at him if he is a man or a woman" (ch. 123). This leads to immediate violence. In the story, Njál's beardlessness becomes a social handicap, invoked to explain how this supposedly wise and peace-loving leader and his family were tragically destroyed through no fault of his own.

Unsurprisingly, beards are associated with men. Gylfaginning (ch. 34) says "You must have noticed that a woman has no beard", explaining that women's beards, fish's breath and other strange phenomena were all used up to make the legendary chain used to chain the Fenris Wolf. Full beards can set adult men apart from women and children. Under Old Norse law, adult men were full legal actors, women and children had limited legal agency. Only in exceptional circumstances did women have as much agency as men (notably as widows or adult orphaned, unmarried women; see also Sanmark 2014). Yet, beardless Njál was accepted as a man and was a husband, a father and a grandfather, a lawyer and a political leader. Flosi's sudden distrust seems to be as much a strategic move as it is a display of well-established cultural prejudice.

In iconography almost all men have beards (as noted already, there are hundreds of examples; see *e.g.*, the "masks" in Jensen 2010). There are multiple styles to these beards, from goatees and short, full beards, to big, flowing full beards and impressive ropy beards falling below the waist. There is no clear chronology to this. Very long beards are limited to one small group of so-called idols (see below). Therefore, this style seems not to have been common. The only recognisable, beardless man in iconography is young Sigurd Völsung (for images of Sigurd, see Jensen 2017, Staecker 2006, and Table 8.1).

Despite modern and Romantic imaginations, Viking Age images always show beards as well groomed, carefully combed or dramatically curly, but not braided or tied in tufts. Viking Age finds include no obvious razors. It is likely beards were trimmed with something, but specialised small blades are not in evidence.

Toilet sets and shears

A number of graves contain tweezers, pins or points ("nail-cleaners", "tooth picks") and so-called ear-spoons (Fig. 8.2). They are frequently associated with keys, strike-a-lights and other small objects. As Gräslund (1984, 187) notes, even on objects from the same grave, suspensions are often quite differently made, suggesting they were not made in sets, nor do sets seem very standardised. Burial evidence suggests that they were worn hanging from necks or belts. These are overwhelmingly associated with women (gendered, or sexed). They are far less common than combs or shears.

Some tweezers may have been used for managing eyebrows and other minor hairs. Other tweezers could have been used for fine crafts or even for surgery. Four Norwegian finds have ring sliders, typical of modern surgical tweezers (see Table 8.3). SHM has catalogued 71 finds of Viking Age tweezers. Fifty are grave finds, 41 of these feminine and none clearly masculine graves. Birka alone has produced 44 grave finds and four settlement finds (see Arbman 1943; Waller 1984, 189; and the SHM database). Thirty-seven of these are from feminine graves, the others from graves without obvious gender indicators (contra Arbman 1943, 320, there is no gender evidence for Bj 861). Gotland yields 16 finds, 10 of these from graves, four of these are feminine, the rest unclear. Seventeen tweezers are reported from the rest of eastern Sweden, from Jämtland to Öland. Interestingly, Birka's rural uplands (Uppland and Södermanland) yield only three examples. In mainland Sweden, burial with tweezers was an urban phenomenon and rare in the countryside. On Gotland, this pattern is not evident. We can perhaps speculate, but only speculate, that just as Haithabu may have seen a brief fashion for eye shadow, so Birka may have seen a fashion for carefully managed body hair, unmatched by most other Viking Age settlements. In South Sweden, Svanberg reports finds of "pinchers" (likely tweezers) in seven graves, containing one sexed male and two gendered women (Svanberg 2003, cat. 142:D:4; 172:1964:2, 174:1873; 10:3, 103:9, 163: 1896, 165). Overall, Swedish tweezers are strongly associated with women, and concentrated at Birka and Gotland. For Norway, Petersen (1951, 503) lists tweezers from six feminine, one masculine, and two double graves. The updated databases add one masculine grave (Ts 5374). Two of these feminine graves contained tweezers with ring-sliders, possibly for surgery. In Haithabu, there is just one grave find, from a feminine grave (Arents and Eisenschmidt 2010, Grab 497) and for Denmark, Eisenschmidt (2004, 203) lists 15 examples, tentatively labelling three graves as masculine and two as feminine. Clearly, this is a very different pattern from Sweden, suggesting that tweezers may have associated with different tasks in different regions.

The so-called toothpicks or nail-cleaners are entirely uncharacteristic. Presently, they cannot be distinguished from common dress-pins, and it is pointless to try to enumerate them until more typological and contextual work has been done.

The final type of artefact characteristic of these sets is the "ear-spoon". Gräslund (1984, 181) suggests that some may have been used to clean ears of wax, some perhaps to remove foreign objects from children's ears, and some to remove make-up or medicine from narrow flasks. On Birka there are nine examples, all from feminine graves. Gräslund lists three more examples from feminine graves in Viking Age Sweden, six from Karelia, and 23 from Late Iron Age Gotland. The SHM catalogue adds up to five feminine graves and two graves without gender indications, three stray finds and a hoard find (Table 8.3). All are copper alloy, except one of silver from Birka grave Bj. 507 and a bone ear-spoon from the Birka settlement (SHM 5208:1626). Bone artefacts may have been far more common, lost to acidic soils. Out of the 13 examples in the SHM catalogue, seven are from Gotland and four from the Birka settlement. The Norwegian databases provide just three examples of grave finds, all found with tweezers, but without clear gender indicators (B3731, B8991 and Ts 1053). Petersen (1951, 503) lists two more Norwegian graves with two ear-spoons each, one masculine and one feminine grave. The Danish database contains one possible example, apparently a stray find and ambiguous due to poor preservation (NFHA 0706x00185-C35298). Metallic ear-spoons seem to have been a peculiar local fashion. Either the artefacts were not very necessary for everyday body-care or most people used organic versions that are now lost.

Shears show regional differences: in Sweden, they are strongly associated with women, in Norway not so. On Birka, 98 feminine graves contained shears, and three masculine graves contained scissors (Arwidsson 1984b, 195). This may suggest that these two different designs were associated with different activities, scissors perhaps with some "masculine" craft or other. Some shears could potentially be used to style hair, but they are often associated with needles and may be textile tools instead. Clearly, they were made in several sizes and only the smaller ones were worn on the person. Arents and Eisenschmidt interpret all three shears from the Haithabu graves as wool shears. Two of these lay in wooden containers well away from the bodies (Arents and Eisenschmidt 2010, 166). Another 60 or so shears were found in the Birka settlement area and a mere 28 Viking Age shears are known from the rest of Sweden (SHM database). Ten are from feminine, five from masculine graves (Table 8.3). Many of these graves are remarkably rich, with bridles, stirrups, weapons and wagon parts, suggesting that burial with shears was an elite rural phenomenon, far more so than burials with toilet sets. Two graves from Dalarne stand out, one with a shear and a chain ornamented with iron clappers shaped like shears, the other with a typical shear and three extra shears on a ring (SHM 22293:1 and 2). Clearly, these were elite individuals who really treasured their shears. Perhaps they were sheep magnates. Two feminine graves with shears also contain those iron rods that it is currently fashionable to associate with shamanism (SHM 10234:XV, 25840:59:3). Petersen (1951, 318) lists 194 masculine graves and 136 feminine graves with shears from Norway, observing that short "embroidery" shears, under 15 cm, are almost exclusive to women and that shears are more common in feminine graves than are most other tools. He interprets all these as wool and textile shears. Sheep were historically a major part of the Norwegian economy. The Norwegian databases add 16 masculine graves and 15 feminine graves to this, but do not change the overall pattern. In Denmark, Viking Age shears are rare. There are three examples from Haithabu (Arents and Eisenschmidt 2010, Grab 81, Grab 479 and Kammergrab 5). Eisenschmidt lists a total of 19 graves with shears, and identifies eight feminine and three masculine graves. All these are were richly furnished (Eisenschmidt 2004, 199). Just as with tweezers, the remarkable geographical differences may suggest that shears were used for different tasks in different regions.

Overall, the record for toilet items is entirely dominated by Birka. Here, they were strongly associated with women. Gräslund suggests that some may have been used by women to maintain children's health and appearance, as well as their own. Be that as it may, there seems to be a fairly strong association between women and the work of care needed to maintain ideal bodies. The burial evidence is largely limited to Birka and Gotland. Although scattered finds show that the artefacts and the association existed throughout Sweden, only in this small area were they important in burial ritual. Shears show an entirely different pattern and seem much less narrowly tied to beautiful bodies. Many of these may be textile tools, and in Norway at least, they show masculine associations, similar to those for other craftwork tools.

Washing

"They are the filthiest of all Allāh's creatures: they do not clean themselves after excreting or urinating or wash themselves when in a state of ritual impurity (*i.e.*, after coitus) and do not [even] wash their hands after food" reports ibn Fadlan, later saying that the 'Rus washed their faces every day, reusing the same water amongst an entire crew and spitting in it (Montgomery 2003, 7*ff.*). Ibn Fadlan reports on other pagan groups with no comment on their hygiene, so 'Rus washing habits must have been remarkable, even in the local context. Centuries after the fact, John of Wallingford's Chronicle discusses the Brice's days massacre, and claims that the Danes seduced many Anglo-Saxon women because "they were – according to their country's customs – in the habit of combing their hair every day, to bathe every Saturday, to change their clothes frequently and to draw attention to themselves by means of many such frivolous whims." (Trans. William Hunt). The point is clearly that such relations between Danes and Anglo-Saxon women were politically undesirable and that only strange Danish customs may explain why women made such bad choices. On Iceland, Landnámabók claims that in pagan times Helgafell Mountain was considered so sacred that no one was allowed to look at it before they had washed their faces in the morning (Landnámabók ch. 33). The point of this anecdote may be to explain the place-name, Holy Mountain. Strikingly, these three very different texts, with different agendas, agree that people washed and groomed every morning. This is a rare case of an aspect of everyday Viking Age behaviour that can actually be confirmed from credibly independent, written sources.

In the last century of the Viking Age (*c.* 950–1050 CE), we find a few furnished graves with imported washbasins, and possibly with cloths, reflecting an aristocratic culture of morning toilette also known from Continental Europe (*e.g.*, Mammen, Jutland; see Pedersen 2014, 136f.). People outside of this late elite may well have washed without expensive metal washbasins, and failed to bury their washbasins with the dead. These graves hint that washing may have elite associations. This may also be hinted at in Rígsthula's description of the parallel lives of three archetypical boys, named Slave, Farmer and Lord (Þræl, Karl and Jarl), and their wives. The poem emphasises that slaves are dark and brown, aristocrats pale and elite women very pale (compare Rígsthula verse 7, 21, 35). This could perhaps imply that cleanliness was an elite privilege and that slaves would bathe last and get dirty again soonest. However, it more likely suggests that elite women spend less time out of doors. Pale aristocrats are a universal trope of European medieval literature, probably reflecting economic realities: although elite medieval women worked hard, overseeing farm economy, raising children and producing cloth, dairy and beer, much of this could be indoor work. Farmhands probably tanned more than did housewives, no matter how often they washed. There are no references to washing clothes or cleaning houses in the literature. We can conclude nothing on that basis: plenty of other everyday chores are equally invisible, and nobody remarked on either the filthiness or cleanness of Scandinavian clothes or homes. The evidence does not allow interpreting washing as a strongly gendered practice.

Swaddled babies

A single figurine from Haithabu shows a swaddled baby (Fig. 8.1), possibly the Infant Christ (Jensen 2010, no. 1305). In Rígsthula, two of the three archetypical boys, Farmer and Lord, were swaddled at birth. Slave, on the other hand, was not swaddled, and grew up bent-backed and bowlegged, but strong. From Ancient Greece to early modernity, swaddling has used in hopes of making babies grow straight and upright (Dasen 2010, 302), and Rígsthula may hint at similar beliefs.

Unfortunately, historians suggest that Rígsthula may be very late and/or atypical (see Simek 1993, 264f.). Moreover, Christians in cosmopolitan Haithabu may have had novel or exotic ideas of childcare; even if they swaddled their babies, it does not follow that anyone else did. Thus, there is little doubt that some babies were swaddled at least by the late Viking Age, but it is unclear how frequently, where, or when. Physical anatomy does not seem ready to address this issue. We lack reference studies of historic populations to show how or if swaddling affects bone anatomy. The examples above are boys, but other swaddling cultures fairly consistently swaddle both sexes, and we have no evidence that girls were not swaddled.

Tooth modification

Twenty-nine finds reveal modified teeth (see SHM database, Arcini 2005; 2018, 73*ff*.; Loe *et al.* 2014, 53 and 63; Sparevohn 2013, 48 *ff.*). All had parallel, horizontal grooves filed into the front of their incisors. Presumably, this would be quite painful. Its visibility must have depended on personal behaviour. Of 29 examples in literature, 18 are from Gotland, four from Öland, two from Scania and four from Denmark (Galgedil and Snubbekorsgård). The final example is from the Ridgeway Hill mass grave in Dorset, convincingly interpreted as executed Scandinavians (Loe *et al.* 2014). Here, one person has filed teeth, five more have modified teeth.

Most of these individuals are male adults. None have been identified as female, but one of the Danish individuals is a teenage boy (Sparevohn 2013, 48 *ff.*), suggesting, perhaps, some regional variation. Strontium isotope analyses of the Swedish individuals suggest that 13 of these may originate from Gotland (Arcini 2018, 80), but that five did not.

There are no written sources for this phenomenon. It may have been more common than we know: bone preservation is poor in much of Scandinavia, and the phenomenon may have been overlooked. Without text references, we have no way of knowing if such modifications were considered beautiful. The practice seems exclusive to men.

Iconographic bodies

Written sources offer very limited evidence for any discussion of Viking Age beautiful bodies, or indeed for beauty as a concept. We have a number of texts where the plot is clearly driven by sexual attraction or desire for marriage, but in most cases, we can only infer people's attractiveness from the fact that others were attracted to them. A telling example is this non-description of Frey and Freya: "[they] were beautiful and powerful... Frey is the most splendid of the god... Freya is the most splendid of the goddesses" (Gylfaginning, ch. 24). There is no information how these splendid gods looked, in this text or anywhere else. Adam of Bremen does inform us that the image of Fricco (Frey) in Uppsala was *cum igenti priaopo*, with a mighty phallus (Adam of Bremen, 4:26). If this is the signal mark of male beauty in the Viking Age, it is only signalled in this one text and one surviving image (Rällinge, below).

Iconographic sources are far more numerous, if individually less informative. One group that deserves special mention are the so-called idols. There are ten known examples (information on most of these has been collected in Perkins 2001, with references; however, for Trønning, see Jensen 2003, 353; for Lejre, see Christensen 2010). Each is unique, but they share some characteristics. They range in size from 2.2 to 10.9 cm and are made of gold, silver, copper alloy, lead, amber and walrus ivory. Two come from burials with gaming boards (Baldursheimur, Chernaya Moglia/Chernigov), one is a hoard find (Gnëzdovo) and all others are stray finds.

These figurines show their subject standing (Norra Åby, Feddet, Lindby, Gnëzdovo) or seated, either on the ground (Rällinge, Baldursheimur, Chernaya Moglia) or on chairs. Chairs range from the simple (Aukereyi, Trønning), to the ornate (Norra Åby, Lejre). An ornate chair with no preserved figurine is know from Haithabu. The Lejre chair has birds on the armrests and an ornate backrest with two animal heads. The ornate Haithabu chair has two swan-like birds on the backrest and animals on the armrests (for more on chair amulets, see Jensen 2010 and Kalmring 2019). The figure from Trønning seems beardless and Lejre is ambiguous. All other figurines have beards, either forked (Aukereyi, Baldursheimur), rope-like (Norra Åby, Feddet, Gnëzdovo) or short (Lindby, possibly Rällinge). Most hold their beards with both hands, either side by side (Aukereyi, Baldursheimur) or over and under (Norra Åby, Feddet, Chernaya Moglia, and likely the damaged Rällinge piece). Lejre and Trønning have no indication of hands and Lindby definitely does not touch his own beard. Two figurines wear broad triangular hats (Aukereyi, Lindby; from the shape, these are not helmets), two wear tall, narrow triangular caps or helmets (Gnëzdovo, Rällinge), two wear close-fitting caps or headbands (Lejre, Trønning) and three are bareheaded (Norra Åby, Feddet, Chernaya Moglia,). Baldursheimur is too poorly preserved to say if headwear is shown. Below the hat, Rällinge man is naked, Aukereyi seems to be, too (see Perkins 2001, 95 for a detailed discussion) and Baldursheimur is very ambiguous. All other figures are clearly clothed. Lindby wears a short coat reaching to the thigh, the rest wear long robes or big coats that reach the shin. The Chernaya Moglia image, only, has a variety of tools hanging from the belt (Murasheva 2010).

Clearly, the figurines do not show exactly the same motif. Lindby, especially, stands apart. If they are idols, they could represent several different gods. They may be idols. They may not. This argument has taken several forms. Most obviously, the phallic man from Rällinge may resemble Adam of Bremen's description of the phallic pagan idol of "Fricco" (above). For Lejre, only, Tom Christensen has argued that the birds are Odin's two ravens, the animals on the backrest his two wolves and that therefore the figure is Odin (*e.g.*, Christensen 2010). The birds and animals cannot be clearly identified by species, but no other mythological figure is associated with a throne and two birds. On the Haithabu throne, the birds strongly resemble swans. Swans were not associated with Odin. Perkins has argued at length that Aukereyi represents Thor and, less convincingly, that other images also do. He reconstructs a lost legend about Thor creating wind by blowing in his beard (Perkins 2001, 61).

He also claims, unconvincingly, that naked figures in precious materials are likely idols (Perkins 2001, 95 and 101), and even less convincingly, that Aukereyi man's ornate beard represents Thor's hammer. Some ten years ago, I catalogued some 250 representations of Thor's hammer and a further 390 Thor's-hammer rings. The vast majority of these show one consistent shape, with a triangular or pentagonal head and a tapered shaft, nothing like Aukereyi man's beard (*cf.* Jensen 2010, 65*f.*). Idols or not, clearly these images represent bodies and reflect a body-ideal. We can supplement this with a number of narrative scenes, mainly on the Gotland stones (see Lindqvist 1941). Many of these have been tentatively identified as illustrations of legendary stories and thus of named gods or heroes (see discussion in Jensen 2017, 200*ff.*). Fortunately, the identification of the characters is unimportant for any discussion of bodily beauty. Whether two- or three-dimensional, Viking Age iconography reveals a consistent aesthetic of all bodies, but not necessarily any ideas about what made some bodies more attractive than others.

Nearly all figures are shown fully dressed. This clothing neither folds nor drapes, but completely masks the body's silhouette in smooth cylinders of hanging cloth. Dress conceals buttocks and breasts, bellies and waists. This might remind readers of modern Islamic dress, but western conservative suits, Japanese multilayer kimonos, Indian saris and Roman togas can be equally concealing. By contrast, there are only a handful of examples of likely naked bodies: the "idols" from Aureyki and Rällinge and two of the hanged men from Lunda (see Andersson, Beronius Jörpeland and Dunér 2003; Perkins 2001, 95). Rällinge man is a phallic figure and the two Lunda men have indications of genitals, possibly erect, but stylised to ambiguity. The third Lunda individual seems sexless. All these three-dimensional figurines show a striking lack of interest in anatomy. The bodies have joints, but no indication of individual muscles, veins, folds or anatomical landmarks, nor even a tapper of limbs from proximal to distal end. On the Aukereyi image, only, abstract spiral patterns on the back probably indicate shoulder joints, following a convention well-known in images of animals (Perkins 2001, 95 and above). Otherwise, the nude body is just a simpler version of the clothed body, composed of smooth cylinders. Pagans had little reason to associate nakedness with sin, and Ibn Fadlan claims that they were shamelessly open about sexual acts (as are the sagas). However, clothing may have functioned as a status marker. This would explain the hats worn by Rällinge man and Aukereyi man. The only completely naked figures are the hanged men from Lunda. These are likely to represent sacrifices, which may have been all the social information anyone needed about them.

Muscularity also seems not to have been a factor in Viking Age bodily aesthetics, as no human figure in this iconography is notably muscular. This calls to mind Rígsthula's disparaging remark that Slave was bent, but strong (verses 8 and 9). In contrast, his betters are never described as strong, but rather as skilled. A number of legendary heroes perform superhuman feats, but again, raw strength is rarely even mentioned – for example, Sigurd chops anvils in two, but needs his family heirloom sword to do this, and he kills the dragon though guile, not strength (Völsung Saga, chs 5 and 18). This heroic ideal is less about force, more about skill. Almost all images show people of the same size and apparent age. Only Ardre VI clearly shows a size difference between child and adult (Lindqvist 1941, Taf. 165). Everyone else is depicted as adult sized. The long-bearded idols must logically be men of some years, but otherwise, depicted adults are of no particular age, much like most people in the written sources. Nor are they recognisably fat or thin, short or tall. Almost all bodies seem intact. Old Norse mythology contains a number of episodes of maiming (Odin lost an eye, Tyr a hand, Völundr was hamstrung, and so on), and the laws are obsessed with compensations for amputation (see Jensen 2014), but in iconography, missing limbs and organs are never indicated, nor are figures normally recognisably wounded, although a very few scenes show decapitated bodies (*e.g.*, Ramsundsberget – Jensen 2017, 208).

There is currently a fashion in Viking Age research for interpreting various images as Odin, due to supposedly damaged eyes (*cf.* Lindby, Lejre, Ribe, Torslunda, Staraya Ladoga; summarised in Arwil-Nordbladh 2012; Price and Mortimer 2014). The same interpretative fashion has produced many claims that various images display damaged eyes. Even keenest supporters of this claim seem to find far more and far better examples of this phenomenon before the Viking Age, especially in Anglo-Saxon Britain (Price and Mortimer 2014, 531). Two of the best Scandinavian examples are the Torslunda matrices and the woven Högom image, both centuries earlier than the material discussed here (see Jørgensen 2003, 65). All the Viking Age examples are questionable, at best. I have examined the Ribe image first hand, and I cannot see the supposed injury at all. On the high-quality photo in Jensen (1990, 178*f.*), there may be an indication of a pupil in the right eye, but no injury. On the very poor photo in Ewing (2008, 98, fig. 36), the supposed injury is obvious, but this is not how the real piece actually looks. The injury in that photo seems an artefact of poor copying. I have examined Lejre, too, and did not notice the injury which Tom Christensen describes as "practically microscopic" (quoted in Arwill-Nordbladh 2012, 51). If this detail was meant to identify the image, it seems illogical to make it so hard to see. From photographs of the Lindby find, I cannot even decide which eye my colleagues see as damaged. Clearly, the two are different, but equally clearly, the workmanship is crude. Much more obviously, Lindby man is missing a foot and half an arm. Neither of those injuries are attributes of Odin, but rather of Tyr and perhaps Völundr. If we dismiss these obvious injuries as irrelevant to interpretation, I cannot accept that the much less evident eye injury conclusively establishes identity. Instead, I suggest that this is an image of an unidentified bearded man, with several injuries inflicted after its creation and likely irrelevant to its original meaning. Of course, Odin is not the only one-eyed figure in the world, or even in Viking Age literature. Indeed, Arwill-Nordbladh reports similar supposed eye injuries for several women's figurines which clearly cannot represent Odin (Arwill-Nordbladh 2012, 45*ff.*). Simek claims that the idea of the one-eyed Odin is only documented in 13th- and 14th-century manuscripts

(Simek 1993, 240). I submit that iconography does not suggest a strong association between Odin and eye injury in the Viking Age, either. Attempts to find it in iconography seem to be wistful thinking.

Much less evidence has been mobilised for the other handicaps mentioned by the textual sources (but see Oerhl 2009). I have argued elsewhere that maiming was considered entirely negative, and that the whole point of legislation was to erase it socially and restore the legal integrity of the person (Jensen 2014). Thus, a beautiful body was not visibly maimed, scarred or otherwise marked, and there is very little evidence that maimed, living bodies were ever depicted in Viking Age iconography. This lack of detail (age, injury, build) is interesting in the light of manuscript sources. In Rígsthula, Slave's children are all named with nicknames, describing their appearance or behaviour (Stout, Badbreath, Fatty; verses 12–13); Farmer's sons are named for their work, and perhaps skills (Smith and Soldier; verse 24), their personalities or their beards; and Lord's children are named for their heritage and birth (Firstborn and Baby; verse 41). This might suggest that lower-class ugliness was specific, whereas elite beauty was generically, indescribably flawless. Centuries later, historiographers made up nicknames for kings and leaders, to tell apart people with the same name from different generations. Contemporaries had no such trouble, and many of these names are fairly unflattering. On the Great Jelling Runestone (DR 42), King Harald refers to himself as "King Harald... that Harald who collected all Denmark and part of Norway and made the Danes Christian". Later generations invented the nickname "Bluetooth" to tell him apart from the other, later Haralds.

I suggest, then, a Viking Age negative aesthetic of the body: overwhelmingly, text and image agree that ideal bodies are nondescript, of no obvious age, build or history, with perfect, unmarked skin, untouched by dirt, scars and sunburn. The only positive characteristics that are named are straight builds, height, skill and hard, staring eyes.

Iconography has a paradoxical relationship to gender: nearly all figures can be gendered, but gender is expressed through a minimum of highly standardised codes (clothes, hair). The inattention to anatomy and bodily difference is equal for both genders. This may tie in with the nondescript, somewhat asexual ideal already described: if beauty is negative, defined by a lack of flaws, then men and women may be beautiful in much the same way, by lacking the same flaws. Clean, unbroken skin is not gender specific, and the same clothes that clearly communicate an iconographic figure's place in stereotyped genders also hides the specific anatomy of the body. In Viking Age Scandinavia, cultural gender completely overwrites biological sex and we find a culture with no pornography and no erotica, neither written nor iconographic.

Staring eyes

One element that recurs in the Old Norse sources is the idea that warriors and aristocrats have hard, staring eyes. Rígsthula claims that Lord's sons (or all his children;

the text is ambiguous) had eyes like young snakes. I read this as a confused reference to the fact that snakes, with fixed eyelids, never blink (see CZAR, n.d.), and that human eyes may develop all sorts of problems with old age (see, *e.g.*, Khalaj, Barikani and Ghasemi 2012, 79). A young snake, then, might be imagined as unblinking and clear eyed. Thýmskvida gives us a description of these eyes: when Thor disguised himself as a veiled bride to enter Giantland, one giant drew back the veil to steal a kiss. On seeing "her" eyes, the giant was so shocked that he backed halfway down the hall. Thor's sly companion, Loki, stepped in and explained that the bride was red-eyed from lack of sleep, so eager was she to marry. So, it seems that fictive Viking Age aristocrats consistently look angry or sleep deprived, glaring at everyone. Though aristocratic, this feature is never identified as attractive. Indeed, in Skírnirsmál, stares become a form of aggression, when Skirnir curses Gerd: "May you become a spectacle when you go out, may Hrimnir glare at you, may everything stare at you" (verse 28). Again, literary convention may owe something to real-world behaviour. Humans, dogs and other animals engage in stare-down contests (see Weick, McCall and Blascovich 2017, 1188, with references). For humans, staring behaviours are one of those "techniques du corps" first defined by Marcel Mauss (2006). Like other techniques of the body, they must be learned, and they may be gendered. Thus, Vincent (2006, 2f.) describes how her attempts pass as a man in the modern US required her to learn to gaze differently. She reports that US women drop their eyes immediately when seeing men, while men drop their eyes more slowly. Similarly, Brian Bouldrey describes how US men are on visual display only in uniform, "invisible" as individuals, reduced to types and roles, *e.g.*, in sports (Bouldrey 2004, 84). Out of their protective uniform, US men are gazing subjects, not objects of the gaze. I suggest, then, that aristocrats may have trained specifically to glare angrily at everyone, and everyone else may have learned to drop their eyes in deference. The Viking Age idea of hard, staring eyes may also reflect theories of vision. Going back at least to Plato, Europeans have believed that the eye throws "rays of vision" towards the object of observation. This theory was adopted by the great medical authority Galen, by St. Augustine of Hippo, and a number of Arabic writers contemporary with the Viking Age (see Wilcox 2008, 204f.). Thus, the gaze could be imagined as almost equivalent to poking people with a stick, and potentially an act of aggression or even magic, as in the evil eye.

Staring eyes may be represented in Viking Age iconographic sources. Eyes are among the few anatomical features consistently shown, often exaggerated and oversized (Fig. 8.1), for example, on all the long-bearded figurines (above). Some of the wide-eyed Lewis chessmen bite their shields, a well-established code for berserker rage (see Caldwell, Hall and Wilkinson 2010, 38). The long-bearded figurines may be idols and rage may have been a divine attribute, notably of Odin (*cf.* Adam of Bremen's remark: "Wotan id est furor", "Odin, that is, rage"; Adam 4:26). More generally, a wide-eyed figurine could surely outstare anyone, establishing divine superiority. Interestingly, contemporary Anglo-Saxon images represent vision differently. Here, pupils are usually slightly to one side, to indicate direction of attention. More generally, Lemm (2010, 339*ff.*) notes that Viking Age iconography is full of faces, often placed on weak points where two different components join. He argues that these staring faces were likely apotropaic. If eye shadow was ever an established part of Viking Age Scandinavian culture, it may tie in with this idea: eye shadow does draw attention to the eyes. I have argued elsewhere that Viking Age society saw a struggle between old warrior aristocrats and new merchant elites, and that the latter took shortcuts to claim the privileges that old elites had established over generations (Jensen 2010, 160*f.*). Merchants may have reused old burial mounds, because they had neither access to mounds inherited from ancestors, nor the massive following needed to build new ones, and perhaps some merchants in Schleswig used eye shadow as a shortcut to a striking stare like that of aristocrats trained since childhood. In Old Norse literature, staring eyes are clearly a class marker. They are often described for men, less often for women.

Conclusion – indescribable beauty and flawless perfection

Most of the variables mentioned in the written sources are not gender specific. Men and women washed, may have worn eye shadow and tattoos and learned the hard, aristocratic stare. These last two variables are better documented for men than for women, but not unambiguously gendered. Only hair and beards were obviously highly gendered. Archaeology reveals a different picture: the artefacts of hair care are not gender specific, whereas toiletries are feminine and filed teeth are masculine. Archaeology also shows a degree of regional variation not obvious in the textual sources.

The hegemonic body ideal seems to have relied on a negative description: beauty was an absence of marks, flaws and injuries. Positive descriptions ignore beauty and instead centre on skills and possessions. A degree of, and a certain definition of, cleanliness seems to have been idealised, but may have applied only to exposed, visible skin, notably faces. Descriptions of appearance often stress imperfections, a technique possibly employed to objectify slaves. Viking Age Scandinavians seem to have thought far more about marked, flawed bodies than beautiful ones. Flaws were rarely gender specific. Compared to their contemporaries across Northern Europe, Scandinavians hardly stood out. Only tattoos and eye shadow would mark them as different, and these features are poorly documented and may have been rare. Hairstyles differed, but were readily copied.

Viking Age text sources are remarkably unconcerned with actual bodies. Appearances are all on the surface, and there is no indication that surfaces reveal any kind of depths, of either anatomy or character. A flawless appearance and a flawless performance were paramount, and all flawless people were the same. There was remarkably little attention to improving bodies through any kind of physical regime. Body care seems limited to avoiding or mitigating physical flaws, creating a strangely anodyne ideal. Looking for differences was looking for trouble, and the competitive aesthetic of Ancient Greece and modern fitness culture was worlds away.

Bibliography

Primary sources
Brennu-Njál's saga: Magnusson, M. and Palsson, H. (trans.) (1960) *Njál's Saga*. London, Penguin.
Chronica Iohannis Wallingford: Vaughan, R. (ed.) (1958) *The Chronicle Attributed to John of Wallingford*. Camden Miscellany 21. London, Royal Historical Society.
De sanguine: Clayton, M. (trans.) (2002) De sanguine/Letter to Brother Edward. In E. Treharne and S. Rosser (eds) *Early Medieval English Texts and Interpretations Studies Presented to Donald G. Scragg*, 263–283. Arizona, Tempe.
Clayton, M. (2007) Letter to Brother Edward: a student edition. *Old English Newsletter* 40 (3), 31–46.
Gesta Hammaburgensis Ecclesiae Pontificum: Schmeidler, B. (trans.) (1917). *Adam von Bremen, Hamburgische Kirchengeschichte*. Scriptores Rerum Germanicarum in Usum Scholarum Separatim Editi 2. Hannover, Monumenta Germaniae Historica.
Hallfredr saga: Whaley D. (ed.) (2002). *Sagas of Warrior-Poets. Kormak's Saga. The Saga of Hallfred Troublesome-poet, The Saga of Gunnlaug Serpent-tongue. The Saga of Bjorn, Champion of the Hitardal People. Viglund's saga*. London, Penguin Classics.
Ibn Fadlan, Ahmed: Rīsala: Montgomery, J.E. (trans.) (2003) Ibn Fadlān and the Rūssiyya. *The Journal of Arabic and Islamic Studies* 3: 1–25.
Jómsvíkinga saga: Rafn, C.C. (trans.) 1829. *Jomsvikinga saga og Knytlinge Saga tillige med Sagabrudstykker og Fortællinger vedkommende Danmark*. Copenhagen, Det Kongelige Nordiske Oldskriftsselskab.
Landnámabók islands: Jónsson, F. (ed.) (1925) *Det kongelige Nordiske Oldskriftsselskab*. Copenhagen.
Lokesenna: Larrington, C. (trans.) (1996) *The Poetic Edda*. Oxford, Oxford University Press.
al-Qazînî: Jacob, G. (trans.) (1927) al-Qazînî. In G. Jacob (ed.) *Arabische quellen van Gesandten an germanische Fürstenhöfe aus dem 9. und 10. Jahrhundert*. Quellen zur deutsche Volkskunde 1. Berlin, Walter de Gruyer.
Rígspula: Larrington, C. (trans.) (1996) *The Poetic Edda*. Oxford, Oxford University Press.
Skáldaskarpamál: Byock, J.L. (trans.) (2005) *The Prose Edda*. London, Penguin Classics.

Secondary sources
Andersson, G., Beronius Jörpeland, L. and Dunér, J. (2003) *Gudarans gård: Tre fallosfigurer från Lunda i Stängnäs socken, Södermanland*. Fornvännen 98. Stockholm, Kungliga Viterhets Historie och antikvitetsakademien.
Arbman, H. (1943) *Birka I. Die Gräber. Text*. Uppsala, Kungliga Viterhets Historie och antikvitetsakademien.
Arcini, C. (2005) The Vikings bare their filed teeth. *American Journal of Physical Anthropology* 128, 727–733.
Arcini, C. (2018) *The Viking Age. A Time of Many Faces*. Oxford, Oxbow Books.
Arents, U. and Eisenschmidt, S. (2010) *Die Gräber von Haithabu. Die Ausgrabungen in Haithaby 15*. Neumünster, Wachholtz Verlag.
Arrhenius, B. (2005). Three riders coming to Vendel. In K.A. Bergsvik and A. Engevikjr (eds) *UBAS. Universitetet i Bergen Arkeologiske Skrifter. Nordisk 1. Fra funn til samfunn. Jernalder studier tilegnet Bergljot Solberg på 70-årsdagen*, 307–317. Bergen, Universiteteti Bergen.
Arwill-Nordbladh, E. (2012) Ability and disability on bodily variations and bodily possibilities in Viking Age myth and image. In I.M. Back Danielsson and S. Thedéen (eds) *To Tender Gender: The Pasts and Futures of Gender Research in Archaeology*, 33–59. Stockholm, Stockholms Universitet.
Arwill-Nordbladh, E. (2016) Viking Age hair. *Internet Archaeology* 42.

Arwidsson, G. (ed.) (1984a) *Birka II:1*. Stockholm, Kungliga Vitterligheds och Antikvarie Akademien.

Arwidsson, G. (1984b) Scheren. In G. Arwidsson (ed.) Birka II:1, 195–199. Stockholm, Kungliga Vitterligheds och Antikvarie Akademien.

Ashby, S.P. (2014) Technologies of appearance hair behaviour in Early-Medieval Britain and Europe. *Archaeological Journal* 171, 151–184.

Ambrosiani, K. (1981) *Viking Age Combs, Comb Making and Comb Makers in the Light of Finds from Birka and Ribe*. Stockholm studies in archaeology 2. Stockholm, Institutionen för arkeologi, Stockholms Universitet.

Beckmann, B. (1966) Studien über die Metalnadeln der römischer Kaiserzeit im freien Germanien. *Saalburg-Jahrbuch* 23, 5–100.

Bouldrey, B. (2004) *Monster: Gay Adventures in American Machismo*. Los Angeles, Alyson Books.

Boye, L. (2009) Catalogue of burial sites. In L. Boye and U.L. Hansen (eds) *Wealth and Prestige: An Analysis of Rich Graves from Late Roman Iron Age on Eastern Zealand, Denmark*. Kroppedal, Albertslund.

Buckland, P. (2010) Ragnarök and the stones of York. In J. Sheehan and D. Ó Corráin (eds) *The Viking Age. Ireland and the West. Proceedings of the fourth Viking Congress, Cork, 18-27 August 2005*, 47–59. Dublin, Four Courts Press.

Caldwell, D.H., Hall, M.A. and Wilkinson, C.M. (2010) *The Lewis Chessmen Unmasked*. Edinburgh, National Museums Scotland.

Christensen, T. (2010) Gud, konge eller...? *Arkæologisk forum* 22, 21–25.

Dasen, V. (2010) Childbirth and infancy in Greek and Roman antiquity. In B. Rawson (ed.) *A Companion to Families in the Greek and Roman Worlds*, 291–314. London, Blackwell.

Eisenschmidt, S. (2004) *Grabfunde des 8. bis 11. Jahrhunderts zwischen Kongeå und Eider*. Neumünster, Wachholtz.

Ethelberg, P., Lund Hansen, U., Demant, I., Bennike, P., Alexandersen, V., Hating, T., Adomat, A. and Nebich, G. (2000) *Skovgårde. Ein Bestattungsplatz mit reichen Frauengräbern des 3.Jhr. n.Chr. auf Seeland*. Copenhagen, Det kongelige Nordiske Oldskriftsselskab.

Ewing, T. (2008) *Gods and their Worshippers in the Germanic World*. Stroud, The History Press.

Gansum, T. (2003) Hår og stil og stilig hår. In P. Rolfsen and F.-A. Stylegar (eds) *Snartemofunnene i nytt lys*, 191–222. Oslo, Universitetet i Oslo.

Gell, A. (1993) *Wrapping in Images. Tattooing in Polynesia*. Oxford, Oxford University Press.

Graham-Campbell, J. (1980) *The Viking World*. London, British Museum.

Graham-Campbell, J. (2013) *Viking Art*. London and New York, Thames and Hudson.

Gräslund, A.-S. (1984) Ohrlöffel. In G. Arwidsson (ed) Birka II:1, 177–182. Stockholm, Kungliga Vitterligheds och Antikvarie Akademien.

Hansen, U.L. (1995) *Himlingøje – Seeland –Europa. Ein Gräberfeld der jüngeren Kaiserzeit auf Seeland, seine Bedeutung und internationalen Beziehungen*. Copenhagen, Det kongelige Nordiske Oldskriftsselskab.

Hansen U.L. (2008) Runen in Frauengräber. In H. Beck, D. Heuning and H. Steuer (eds) *Erganzungsbände zum Reallexikon der Germanische Altertumskunde 15*, 237. Berlin, Van der Gruyer.

Hægstad, A. (1964) Har At-Tartuschi besøgt Hedeby (Slesvig)? *Aarbøger for Nordisk Oldkyndighed og Historie*, 82–91.

Imer, L. (2016) *Danmarks runesten. En fortælling*. Copenhagen, Nationalmusseet and Gyldendal.

Jensen, B. (2010) *Viking Age Amulets in Scandinavia and Western Europe*. Oxford, British Archaeological Reports International Series.

Jensen, B. (2014) Kroppen som samlesæt. *CHAOS. Skandinavisk Tidsskrift for Religionshistoriske Studier* 57, 37–58.

Jensen, B. (2017) Skull-cups and snake-pits. Men's revenge and women's revenge in Viking Age Scandinavia. In U. Matić and B. Jensen (eds) *Archaeologies of Gender and Violence*. 197–222. Oxford, Oxbow Books.

Jensen, J. (2003) *Danmarks oltid: yngre jernalder ogvikingetid*. Copenhagen, Gyldendal.

Jensen, S. (1990) Odin fra Ribe. In P. Kjærum and R.A. Olsen (eds) *Oldtidens ansigt*, 178–179. Copenhagen and Højbjerg, Det kongelige nordiske oldskriftsselskab and Jyskarkæologisk selskab.

Jørgensen, L.B. (2003) Krigerdragten i folkevandringstiden. In P. Rolfsen and F.-A. Stylegar (eds) *Snartemofunnene i nytt lys*, 53–80. Oslo, Universitetet i Oslo.

Kalmring, S. (2019) A new throne-amulet from Hedeby. First indication for Viking-age barrel-chairs. *Danish Journal of Archaeology* 8, 1–9.

Khalaj, M., Barikani, A. and Ghasemi, H. (2012) Eye disorders in older people. *Global Journal of Health Science* 1, 79–86.

Kjærum, P. and Olesen, R. (eds) (1990) *Oldtidens ansigt*. Copenhagen and Højbjerg, Det Kongelige Nordiske Oldskriftsselskab and JyskArkæologisk Selskab.

Lang, J.T. (1988) *Viking Age Decorated Wood*. Dublin, National Museum of Ireland.

Lemm, T. (2010) Die Positionierung von Gesichtsdarstellungen auf vendel- und wikingerzeitlichen Bildträgern – ein Schlüssel zum Verständnis ihrer Funktion? In W. Heizmann and S. Oehrl (eds) *Publikation zur Tagung Bilddenkmäler zur germanischen Mythologie und Heldensage Autopsie - Dokumentation - Deutung*, 333–349. Berlin and Boston, Siemens-Stiftung.

Lindqvist, S. (1941) *Gotlands Bildsteine I*. Stockholm, Wahlström and Widstrand.

Loe, L., Boyle, A., Webb, H. and Score, D. (2014). *Given to the Ground: a Viking Age Mass Grave on Ridgeway Hill, Weymouth*. Dorset Natural History and Archaeological Society Monograph Series No. 2. Oxford, DHAS and Oxford Archaeology.

Madsen, H.J. (1990) Loke fra Snaptun. The god Loki from Snaptun. In P. Kjærum and R. Olesen (eds) *Oldtidens ansigt - Faces of the Past*. Copenahegn and Højbjerg, Det Kongelige Nordiske Oldskriftsselskab and Jysk Arkæologisk Selskab.

Mannering, U. (2006). *Billeder af dragt. En analyse af påklædte figurer fra yngre jernalder i Skandinavien*. Unpublished PhD thesis, Copenhagen University.

Mauss, M. (2006) *Techniques, Technologies and Civilization*. New York and Oxford, Blackwell.

Murasheva, V. (2010) Gods from pouch? Gaming pieces? Presentation at the 2010 EAA conference in den Haag, Netherlands.

Oerhl, S. (2009) Wieland der Schmied auf dem Kistenstein von Alskog Kyrka und dem Runenstein Ardre Kyrka III zur partielle Neulesung und Interpretation zweier gotländischer Bildsteine. *Analecta Septentrionalia* 65, 540–566.

Paulsen, H. (1999) Pfeil und Bogen in Haithabu. In H. Gelbing and H. Paulsen (eds) *Das archäologische Fundmaterial IV. Berichte über die Ausgrabungen in Hathabu 33*, 93–143. Neumunster: Wachholtz Verlag.

Pedersen, A. (2014) *Dead Warriors in Living Memory*. Copenhagen, Nationalmuseet.

Perkins, R. (2001) *Thor the Wind-Raiser and the Eyrarland Image*. London, University College London.

Petersen, J. (1951) *Vikingetidens redskaber*. Oslo, Det Norske Videnskabsakedemi and Jakob Dybwad.

Price, N. and Mortimer P. (2014). An eye for Odin? Divine role-playing in the age of Sutton Hoo. *Journal of European Archaeology* 17 (3), 517–538.

Sanmark, A. (2014) Women at the Thing. In N. Coleman and N.L. Løkka (eds) *Kvinner i vikingtid*, 85–100. Lund, Scandinavian Academic Press.

Simek, R. (1993) *Dictionary of Northern Mythology*. Stuttgart, Alfred Körner.

Sparevohn, L.R. (2013) Gravgods, ritualer og svenske forbindelser. In H. Lyngstrøm and L.G. Thomsen (eds) *Vikingetid i Danmark*, 47–50. Copenhagen, Saxo-insituttet.

Staecker, J. (2006) Heroes, kings and gods. Discovering sagas on Gotlandic picture stones. In A. Andrén, K. Jennbert and C. Raudvere (eds) *Old Norse Religion in Long Term Perspectives*, 363–374. Vägar till Midgård 8. Lund, Nordic Academic Press.

Steinsland, G. (1989) *Det hellige bryllup og norrøn kongeideologi en undersøkelse av hierogamimyten i Skírnismál, Ynglingatal og Hyndluljód*. Oslo, Universitetet i Oslo.

Svanberg, F. (2003) *Decolonizing the Viking Age 2. Late Iron Age Burial Customs in South-East Scandinavia*. Acta Archaeological Lundensia 24. Stockholm, Stockholm Almqvist and Wiksell International.

Vincent, N. (2006) *Self-made Man. My Year Disguised as a Man*. London, Atlantic.

Wincott Heckett, E. (2003) *Viking Age Headcoverings from Dublin. National Museum of Ireland. Medieval Dublin Excavations 1962-81. Ser B, vol. 6.* Dublin, Royal Irish Academy.

Whitelock, D. (ed. and trans.) (1955) *English Historical Documents Vol. I. c. 500–1042*. London and Oxford, Routledge.

Waller, J. (1984) Nadlen/Pfreime und Pinzetten. In G. Arwidsson (ed.) *Birka II:1*, 188–192. Stockholm, Kungliga Vitterligheds och Antikvarie Akademien.

Weick, M., McCall, C. and Blascovich, J. (2017) Power moves beyond complementarity: a starring look elicits avoidance in low power perceivers and approach in high power perceivers. *Personality and social psychology bulletin* 43 (8), 1188–1201.

Wilcox, M. (2008) Alfred's visual metaphors. *Anglo-Saxon England* 35, 179–217.

Websites
CZAR (n.d.) Snake Ocular Anatomy. Companion to zoological vetenary medicine. UC Davis University. https://czar.vetmed.ucdavis.edu/research/snake-ocular-anatomy.

Pitt-Rivers Virtual Collection (2011) Naga tattooing tools. Pitt Rivers Museum, Oxford. http://web.prm.ox.ac.uk/bodyarts/index.php/permanent-body-arts/tattooing/169-naga-tattooing-tools.html Accessed on 04.04.2020.

Chapter 9

From moon-faced *amrads* to *farangi*-looking women: beauty transformations from the 19th to early 20th century in Iran

Maryam Dezhamkhooy

Abstract

The Qajar Dynasty (1786–1925) is the last Iranian royal monarchy before the rise of the modern state in Iran. In 1786, Agha Mohammad Khan-e Qajar defeated Lotfali Khan, the young king of the Zand dynasty, and took control of the whole country. The Qajars were nomadic tribes of Turkoman origin (not to be confused with Turkish Turkey) who mostly lived in north-east Iran, particularly Astarabad. Qajar Iran is mainly recognised as a transitional phase when modern Western values modified Iranian society. The Qajar monarchy transformed into a constitutional monarchy when Mozaffar al-Din Shah issued the constitution's decree on the 6th of August 1906. This constitutional monarchy catalysed the adoption of Western norms, including those of gender and sexuality. This paper investigates gendered transformations of beauty from Qajar to early Pahlavi Iran. The author attempts to apply beauty as an analytical concept and considers how this changes throughout history. Hence, beauty will be questioned concerning gender, class, and socio-political changes during the late Qajar. Beauty underwent considerable transformations in the late 19th and early 20th century. Economic circumstances enforced by imperial/colonial encroachments were also involved in cultural changes and in reshaping notions of beauty. Finally, the Pahlavi government's body project, as a significant part of the modernisation project, in the early 20th century, dismantled plural understandings of gender and beauty, and considered Westernisation and feminisation of beauty. Materially speaking, visual evidence plays a vital role in this study. Thanks to rich archival data, such as photographs and paintings, this paper can trace the transformations of beauty in one of Iran's most challenging episodes of contemporary history. Textual evidence and material culture provide us with eminent engagements on beauty and its social and even political implications.

Key words: *beauty, women, Qajar and early Pahlavi Iran, gender, heterosexulisation*

Introduction: is gender the primary principle in the construction of beauty?

Rising to power after the Zand dynasty (1751–1794), the Qajar dynasty (1786–1925) is officially the last monarchy before the nation-state's rise in Iran. Under the Qajars, Iran experienced a gradual transition and the adaption of Western social and political values (Afary 2009, 111–112; Zahirinejad 2014, 72), such as democracy, nation, liberty and equality (Najmabadi 2005b, 167). During Fathalishah's reign (1797–1834) and after Iran's disastrous defeat in the wars with Russia, known as the Russo-Persian Wars (1804–1813 and 1826–1828; Mikaberidze 2011; Shafiyev 2018), Abbas Mirza, the crown prince and prince regent of Iranian Azerbaijan, called for reforms and modernisation of his country. Coupled with intellectuals' and reformists' polemical contentions for the main reasons of regressiveness, the country evoked modernisation. Contextually, modernisation refers to rapid changes from above. The notion of modernisation usually includes Westernisation (see Afary 2009, 146; Keddi 1981, 111).

Interestingly Naser al-Din Shah (r. 1848–1896) enthusiastically welcomed urban modernisation in the capital city Tehran, and partially restructured it by introducing European elements, such as gas lights, pavement, and modern public spaces, such as parks, green areas and an amphitheatre. "Iran was becoming more global in its architecture, clothing, cityscape, and the increased presence of foreigners" (Scheiwiller 2012, 26).

Nevertheless, the country still preserved indigenous characteristics and cultural traditions, particularly in the provinces. Finally, in 1906 the autocratic Qajar government transformed into a constitutional regime. The Constitutional Revolution catalysed transformations of gender and sexuality. The investigation of historical texts and visual material (see Najmabadi 2005b, 6), particularly newspapers, paintings, wall paintings and photos, indicates that Qajar Iran appreciated multiple and changing gender identities, among others. Far beyond modern gender dualism, women, men, *amrads*, eunuchs and *mukhannas* lived in non-modern Iranian society. "In premodern and early modern Persian male homoerotic culture, an amrad was more often a young male, so long as he did not have a fully visible beard" (Najmabadi 2005b, 15). For amrads to be an object of desire for adult men was considered unavoidable. Mukhannas were adult men who made themselves look like young beardless men (amrads) in order to remain the object of desire of adult men. The latter was strongly condemned, as it depicted unmanliness (Najmabadi 2005b, 16). Some research has discussed eunuchs as the third gender (Khazaei 2019). Investigating sexuality and gender in precolonial Latin America, Michael Horswell (2003) states that a third gender does not mean that there are three genders. It is rather a way to transcend sex and gender dualities. Being castrated, eunuchs were a regular feature of harem life (Afary 2009, 90), but also the royal court and Qajar bureaucracy, as their services and duties went beyond the harem (see Etemad al-Saltaneh 2000).

It is worthy of note that there is no equivalence for the word "gender" in Persian. Influenced by modern social science and gender studies, the word *jensiyat* has been in recent decades suggested for gender. Najmabadi (2008, 275) has nicely formulated this for Qajar Iran: "I have found this refusal of the hailing categories useful for studies gender in Qajar Iran, where genders do not respond to the question of being a man or a woman". Some gender identities, such as amrad, were temporary and transient, while others were eternal. Almost all groups mentioned above could live within society without having stigma attached to them. According to Afary (2009, 104) in the era of Naser al-Din Shah (r. 1848–1896) and Mozaffar al-Din Shah (r. 1896–1907), Iranian society remained accepting of many male and female homoerotic practices, among these the staging of dances by *mukhannathun* (effeminate men) in coffee shops (Fig. 9.1). Accordingly, people could engage in different sexual practices without taking on a distinct sexual identity. Hence, the modern discrepancy between homosexuality and heterosexuality (and between homosexuals and heterosexuals) had no meaning for Qajar Iran (see Najmabadi 2006; 2008, 275).

At the turn of the 20th century, same-sex practices were considered problematic. In the eyes of Europeans who travelled or were missioned to the county, same-sex practices were a grave sin. This anxiety over Europeans' judgment of Iranian sexual mores and practices remained a preoccupation throughout the 19th century (Najmabadi 2005b, 37). As a result, leading constitutionalists enthusiastically joined the campaign against homosexuality. Sex with adolescent boys became culturally less acceptable than before (Afary 2009, 162). By the end of the 19th century, in a closely connected development, depictions of male beauty and male-male loving couples completely disappeared (Najmabadi 2005a, 50). Hence "a new regime of sexual and gender regulations emerged in Iran that was deeply connected with the concept of achieving modernity" (Najmabadi 2005a, 55). Thus, one marker of Iranian modernity became the transformation of homoeroticism into masqueraded hetero-eros (Najmabadi 2005a, 62). Lugones (2007, 186) considers the modern gender system as a colonial and violent introduction which consistently and contemporarily used to destroy peoples, cosmologies, and communities as the building ground of the "civilised" West. In this sense, the modern gender system is profoundly European, white-centred and advocates heterosexuality.

Fig. 9.1 Amorous couple with ambiguous gender identity (Olga Davidson Collection, http://www. qajarwomen.org)

This gender plurality and different notions of femininity and masculinity led to various beauty assumptions in general and regarding royal beauty, notably. Generally, the recognition of gender, or its absence, play a crucial role in beauty characteristics. Archaeological research shows how gender and bodily expressions of gender were the "dominant principle" and building blocks in some ancient cultures and societies (see Meskell and Joyce 2003; Montón-Subías 2019; Najmabadi and Babayan 2008). This paper explores the question: can gender as an organising principle be applied to beauty culture in Qajar Iran? It also examines the notion of beauty among women of the royal and urban upper classes. Beauty is a cultural constitution and body, far from being "a given or natural fact" (Turner 2003, 15), which is an unfinished organ and "to some extent socially fashioned" (Nettleton 2001, 44) would be given a final touch with costumes, make-up, specific accessories and jewellery, changes in body appearance, and even bodily practices and postures.

Visual evidence can shed light on the beauty standards of past societies. Visual representations, such as material culture, not only represent beauty and its transformations, but also actively engage in the constitution and changes of beauty ideals. Fortunately, there are extensive photo and painting archives that reflect numerous engagements on Qajar beauty. Specifically, until the end of Naser al-Din Shah's reign, the Qajar court had patronised artists and painters. Moreover, an immense number of photographs have been taken of the kings, courtiers and harem. Mesmerising harem personnel include eunuchs, nannies, ladies in waiting, wet nurses, dry nurses and servants, who have appeared in some photographs of royal women.

Besides photographs and paintings, other forms of material culture, documents and memoirs have also been studied for this paper. Archaeologically speaking, material culture includes cosmetic containers, mirrors, fans and lacquer-worked jewellery boxes. To contextualise the objects particular attention was given to the background data related to different classes and genders. For this reason, middle- and lower-class urban women will be studied in a comparative frame "as in records of the 18th and 19th century Ottoman Empire, considerably less information is available on the poorer sectors of Iranian society than on the elites" (Afary 2009, 20).

Bearing in mind the nature of the data consisting mainly of visual evidence and scrutinising the concept of beauty, this essay considers six main body and body-related factors: face make-up, hairstyle, clothing style, jewellery, the shape of the body and body postures. Transformations of beauty ideals will also be traced based on the changes and inventions in mentioned factors (*cf.* Papoli-Yazdi and Dezhamkhooy 2021).

Chronological framework

According to evidence, the research suggests three phases of beauty transformations among royal and upper-class women from the late 18th to the early 20th century:

1. Genderless beauty: Zand to the early decades of Naser al-Din Shah (late 18th to the mid-19th century).
2. Gendered beauty: from middle Naseri era to 1909. The term Naseri refers to the long reign of Naser al-Din Shah, who is distinguished by a passion and interest in the West and modernisation.
3. Feminisation of beauty: post-constitution era (1909–1941).

In this research, the early Pahlavi era (1925–1941) is considered the last part of post-constitution. Phase 3 should be considered the continuation of phase 2; during phase 3, the connection of beauty to the feminine body can be found in visual material. The author suggests a further phase 4 of beauty and femininity for the 1940s, which will not be discussed here, as it goes beyond the scope of this paper.

Phase 1: Early Qajar royal art and the representation of genderless beauty

In post-Islamic epochs artists engaged in fresco, portraiture, landscape, and an exemplary form of Iranian painting known as miniature. The latter has been usually part of manuscripts, either lyric or heroic literature, with its characters introduced through narration. The beginnings of Islamic book illustration in Persia are still very little known, since no actual examples have been preserved that can be authoritatively dated earlier than the end of the 13th century (Dimand 1941). Oil painting and lacquer (*lāk-kāri*) were the forms introduced to Persian art in the Safavid era. This art flourished and became popular in the Zand era (Esfandiari and Salehi Kakhki 2015). Diba argues (1989, 148) that "lacquer work as such – that is, painted and varnished bookbindings, boxes, and pen cases – is an adaptation and extension of the art of traditional miniature painting". Most of the early Qajar paintings belonged to the portraiture tradition. The art of painting in the early years of the Qajar era was affected by the painting traditions of Zand and the high resemblance between the late Zand and the early Qajar paintings brings about difficulty in differentiating Zand and Qajar paintings from each other (Esfandiari and Salehi Kakhki 2015, 101).

Qajar Iran, Najmabadi states (2001, 89) "began with notions of beauty that were largely gender-undifferentiated; that is, beautiful men and women were depicted with very similar facial and bodily features. Sometimes the only way one can tell who is male or female is through the style of headgear" (Fig. 9.2). This is a feature that Qajar visual and literary representation shares with pre-Qajar Persian (particularly Sufi-inspired) literary and painting traditions (Najmabadi 2001, 90).

Gender-distinctive features are absent from most of the paintings. Beard and moustache for adult men and the breast for women have rarely been depicted. However, the exception to this rule was adult males, specifically kings and courtiers,

Fig. 9.2 Qajar amorous couple with gender undifferentiated beauty features, early 19th century, The Hermitage Museum VP-1156 (https:// commons.wikimedia.org/wiki/File:Amorous_ Couple_V%D0%A0-1156.jpg)

who have been sometimes portrayed with a gender-distinguishing feature of bushy beard or thick and bold moustache. With a beardless face it is difficult to recognise if the figure is a woman, a man, a eunuch or an amrad. Moreover, features like henna, a herbal dye producing a red color, slim waist, make-up, red cheeks and long hair have been used in portraits for men and women far beyond modern gendered stereotypes. Such images also have a direct equivalent in literature; the same adjectives, such as moon-faced, bow-eyebrows, narrow waist, narcissus eyes and cypressed stature, are used to describe male and female beauty (Najmabadi 2001, 89).

A portrait of Mohammad Shah (r. 1834–1848) preserved in Golestan Palace serves as an example. The king appears with bow-shaped connected eyebrows, big eyes, bushy beard and prayer beads in his hand, but his nails have been coloured red, probably with henna. In early portraits of Naser al-Din Shah, the son and successor of Mohammad Shah, the young king also appears with a slim waist, red cheek and lips and bow-shaped eyebrows, although, with a thick moustache (Diba and Ekhtiar 1998; Najmabadi 2001, 90–91; 2005a, 74).

In these paintings, the ones who can be most likely recognised as women have been presented in rich clothing, jewellery and different headgear. Interestingly, some have been depicted as balancers while smoking a water pipe, drinking wine and holding flowers, or putting some fruit in front of the scene. Najmabadi (2005b, 39) categorised this group as women of pleasure. Bodies in these paintings have been depicted as slim and with narrow waists. The red cheeks, big dark eyes and arched eyebrows can be inviting for an adult male. The thin red lips have been made more enchanting with a beautiful black mole above the lips or the cheek. The nails are usually red, probably coloured with henna. A strand of black short tressed hair on the forehead, *torreh*, and around the face connects to long hair at the back. These women have been represented either in portrait style or in scenes depicting romantic couples (see Najmabadi 2005a and 2005b). Najmabadi (2005a, 59) discusses that both women and amrads could be interpreted as figures of desire for adult men, "two figures of pleasure that were promised to male Muslim believers in a heavenly afterlife". And it is worth noting that the viewers and the painters, particularly in the royal service, were adult males (see Diba 1989).

The early Qajar portrait tradition of genderless beauty and the amorous scenes in which the gender identity of couples is ambiguous lasted almost until the end of the 19th century, but on a minimal scale. This style of representation of amorous couples or festivity scenes also embellished decorative boxes, pen boxes, decorative pitchers and even water pipes. Transformations of beauty characteristics and the rise of gender-differentiated features can be observed in visual evidence at least from the middle of the 19th century (the middle of the Naseri era). For instance, in the visual field, royal portraits of the late and post-Naseri period do not have the slim waists and facial features associated with the beautiful male bodies of earlier decades (Najmabadi 2005b, 26). Regarding female figures, for the first time, we encounter plump women with plump round faces.

Phase 2: Gender-differentiated beauty

Photography and the new genre of feminine beauty

The gradual changes to beauty features and gender norms were responsible for transformations to gender and beauty standards in early modern Iran. Also, photography has not only documented but contributed to these transformations. Thousands of photos have survived from Qajar Iran. These have been taken either by Naser al-Din Shah or by royal and other photographers, foreign politicians and even merchants. Recent studies also emphasise the role of women photographers (Scheiwiller 2017; Zoka 1997), as historical texts also claim that women of the royal harem and upper classes learned photography from their male relatives and photographed women, among other subjects (Hasan Beigi 2003, 431). Among these women, Ashraf al-Saltaneh is considered the first Iranian female photographer.

Fortunately, photography was not only active documenting the royal court. Photographers, such as Antoin Sevruguin, have taken numerous photos of citizens. Sevruguin was one of the pioneer photographers of Qajar Iran (Scheiwiller 2018, 145) and spent most of his long life in the country, producing and selling many photographs. He has been described as a "scenes and types" photographer, ethnographer and portraitist (Scheiwiller 2018, 154). Photography granted travellers, researchers and curious people a new medium to document the world of ordinary people and the quotidian life of different social classes. These photos covered almost all social classes, including royal and upper-classes, middle class, the poor and prostitutes, even nomads and rural women. Still, quantitatively, the number of photographs of upper-class women prevails. The photos present a wide variety of subjects, from Jewish wedding ceremonies to barber shops, Persian carpet workshops, street puppet plays and street vendors.

Naser al-Din Shah's photos of the royal harem, which is the most extensive collection recording women, Antoin Sevruguin's and other photographers' images of ordinary women should be considered as significant visual evidence on women. Royal officials, such as Ali Khān-e Vāli, among the others, have taken also photographs. Vāli was interested in photographically documenting traditions, local cultural customs and ceremonies during his missions and official trips throughout the country. He also took a considerable number of photos of women. It is also worth noting here that the male photographers, mainly Europeans, rarely had access to the royal harem.

Fig. 9.3 Portrait of two ladies (Institut for Iranian Contemporary Historical Studies (IICHS))

Regarding women, the photographs can be divided into three main groups:

1. Portrait photography
This group includes individual portraits, collective photographs, and family photos. Both groups usually belong to the royal harem in the early years of photography (Fig. 9.3).

2. Photo modelling
This group consists of both individual and collective images of women who have posed as portrait models, probably as a part-time job (Fig. 9.4). In these photos, young, sometimes middle-aged and senior women wear elegant traditional clothing and jewellery. Sometimes they are dressed in very modest clothing. They are presented either in photographic studios or in open areas. Even more striking some examples show young women appearing in front of the camera half-naked or naked and in various poses.

Jennifer Yee (2004, 14) puts forward an interesting debate about this kind of photography in the French colonies, stating that they are representations of ethnographic "types", and were objects to be collected. The same has been discussed, for example, regarding Sevruguin's photography by some scholars (see Behdad 1999; 2001, 144). European photographers, like Sevruguin, polemically discussed as being Iranian, Russian or Armenian-Georgian (see Scheiwiller 2018), and Ernst Holtzer (a German telegraph operator employed by the British in Isfahan), offered their European audiences an extensive archive of exotic, picturesque and erotic images: dervishes, ethnic figures, bazaar scenes, shots of "primitive" village life, women posed in traditional dress, staged pictures of the harem's lascivious world. These photographs, taken mostly in line

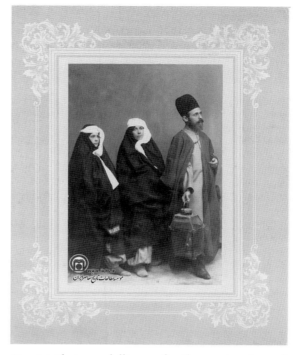

Fig. 9.4 Photo modelling, a family passing through a street at night (Institut for Iranian Contemporary Historical Studies (IICHS))

with European desire, inspired a fantasy that implicated them in colonial relations of power (Behdad 2001, 144).

3. Daily life

Different aspects of Iranian everyday life have inspired both local and European photographers. Interestingly, in many examples, individuals are shown directly looking at the camera but continue working, as if they have not been asked to pose. Carpet-weaving girls in Kashan gazing into the camera and Savojbolaq's Sufi women, who have appeared with their musical instruments, *daf,* a kind of Persian drum, bring these images to life (Fig. 9.5). Other images show women in relaxed postures, smoking a water pipe or lounging by a *korsi,* a traditional Iranian heater.

Some, specifically Sevruguin's photographs, were exhibited at international exhibitions in Paris and Brussels at that time (Scheiwiller 2018, 145). Many of these photographs can now be found in museums and collections worldwide and have been instrumental in creating and disseminating discursive knowledge on Iran (Scheiwiller 2018, 145).

Fig. 9.5 Carpet-weaving girls from Kashan with fringe cut hairstyle and traditional headgear (Institut for Iranian Contemporary Historical Studies (IICHS))

Naser al-Din Shah: the private photographer of the royal harem
Photography was invented in 1839 and introduced to the Qajar court between 1839 and 1842, but cameras and their equipment were given to Naser al-Din Shah's father Mohammad Shah as gifts by diplomatic missions from Queen Victoria and the Russian Czar Nicholas I (Behdad 2001, 144; Diba 2013, 87). Having the patronage of the Qajar ruler, Naser-al-Din Shah, had a vital role in introducing and adapting photography in Iran. "He, as crown prince, was at thirteen the first principal indigenous photographer of Iran and was trained by leading photographer Richard a French educator" (Behdad 2001, 145).

Criticising the colonial lens, Scheiwiller states that "many countries had already had an indigenous tradition of photography that percolated very quickly after photography's official announcement in Paris in 1839, such as in Iran and Japan" (Scheiwiller 2018, 162). After 1859, Carlliane taught Naser al-Din Shah more advanced methods of photography (*i.e.*, developing pictures from negatives), enabling the young king to pursue his interest in taking photos and developing them (Behdad 2001, 145). Naser al-Din Shah's contribution to the development of photography culminated in establishing a photographic institute, *Akkas-khanah-I Mubarak-i*

Humayuni, in one of the buildings of the Golestan Palace (Behdad 2001, 145). Under Naser al-Din Shah, photography became popular, at least among the royal family and noble classes. While portrait painting was a strong tradition in Fath-Ali Shah's reign and he supported and encouraged artists in his court, Naser al-Din Shah replaced the portrait with photography and developed this contemporary art in Iran (Behdad 2001).

The passionate Qajar king was also interested in history, geography, foreign languages, particularly French, poetry and painting (see Etemad al-Saltaneh 2000). Golestan Palace preserves Naser's drawings, usually rendered with pencil, of his harem ladies. However, after the adoption of photography, the king started a project which was to continue until his death in 1896. He decided to take photographs of his harem. The Shah even trained a boy, Gholam Hossein Khan, to help him take private pictures of himself and his harem (Behdad 2001, 145).

Based on the personal experience of the author of this paper, there are thousands of photographs in Golestan Palace, but the authorities refuse to declare the whole number and access to the archive is very restricted. However, Scheiwiller (2012, 19) believes that by the end of the Shah's reign in 1896, he had amassed a collection of over 40,000 photographs, of which 20,000 were taken himself, in more than 1,000 albums at the Golestan Palace in Tehran. A considerable number belongs to the royal harem, known as *Boyutāt* (Taie 2008, 168). The king precisely categorised and numbered almost all the photos himself. Moreover, he has inserted captions for photos which usually include the names of women or short notes about their health or death. Sometimes the captions get close to memoirs in their form, especially when they point to short biographies of women, their health, a day to remember, an event or the general mood, like being tired.

Golestan Palace was the main official building of the Qajar dynasty, where the king accepted foreign diplomats and delegates, and where official and national ceremonies were held. The palace served as both royal residence and administrative base, and emphasised stability within Tehran's development as Iran's capital. The Palace was a vehicle for the expression of Qajar power and a residence for the royal family with a spectacular architectural and decorative environment (Scarce 2001, 104). It was part of the *arg,* royal citadel, a small town located in the northern part of the capital city and surrounded by a wall.

The royal harem, *haramsarā* or *andarun,* was in the arg; although, other palaces outside the arg, summer pavilions, such as Niavaran and Shahrestanak, had their andarun for royal ladies. The surrounding wall itself was a telling one, as it physically separated the royal town from the city, and it also symbolised a recognisable distinction between royal residents and regular citizens, between royal ladies and ordinary urban women. In short, the royal harem comprised of the king's spouses, his daughters, under-aged boys, the queen-mother and occasionally other female relatives, such as aunts and grandmothers. Eunuchs, nannies, waitresses, nurses and maids of honour also lived in or had access to the harem.

Royal taste of beauty?
"Being rather short-height and plump she [Princes Esmat al-Dowleh] is considered beautiful according to Iranian's criteria for feminine beauty" (Serena 1983, 229).

In the middle Qajar photographs, we can recognise an almost unexpected change in feminine beauty features compared to the early Qajar paintings. By the end of the 19th century, we come across a gendered representation of beauty. Likewise, female figures are now more individualised and gender-differentiated in facial and bodily features (Najmabadi 2005a, 59). Women with round faces and double chins appeared in front of the camera. Their thick black eyebrows, sometimes connected, have been made thicker and blacker using make-up. Describing the events of Naser al-Din Shah's 50th kingdom anniversary in her memoirs, Taj al-Saltaneh (1982, 63), the daughter of Naser al-Din Shah, explains how harem women made mascara to darken their eyebrows:

> It was a recent invention in the royal harem to make special use of Nitrate d'argent (Nitrate silver acid) to blacken eyebrows. As you know, this chemical compound is light-sensitive. As soon as it exposes to the light it acts double and, it is difficult to remove it. It takes a few days until it fades.

In the account of her 1877 journey to Iran, Carla Serena (1983) describes a woman's feast arranged by Esmat al-Dowleh, the daughter of Naser al-Din Shah, and her interest in putting make-up on Carla. She explains that the princess had a thin line over her lips and drew the same over Carla's lips as a symbol of feminine beauty. According to the photographs, women and young girls, such as Afsar al-Dowleh, the daughter of Naser al-Din Shah, also put a large mole of colour between their eyebrows. Chronologically, this make-up style of adding a mole appeared in early photos and gradually vanished in later photographs, indicating a change in make-up style. Many historical texts confirm that the Qajar royal women were not only obsessed with putting on too much make-up, but also with expensive clothing and high fashion (see Azad 1979; Fauvrier 2006). Serena (1983, 229) describes the young princess Esmat al-Dowleh with such heavy make-up that it made her look much older than she was. Taj al-Saltaneh (1982, 106) also mentions that upper-class women were interested in applying the cosmetic powder that was available in cosmetic shops in the city. Among others, the French merchants, Monsieur and Madam Eugenie Pillot's shop, regularly introduced new trends and offered the royal harem and noblewomen luxurious products, such as fine clothes, shoes, perfumes and cosmetics (Azad 1979, 395).

Make-up, body care and self-adornment have a long tradition in Iran notably among the ruling and upper classes. The lifestyle of women of the upper classes plays a leading role in creating and cultivating superb tastes of beauty. Women's gathering and events were held regularly as part of the royal harem's cultural life in the homosocial lifestyle of the upper class (see Astarabadi 1993; Etemad al-Saltaneh 2000). It is supposed that the presence of a sense of body freedom, intimate bodily contacts and putting on elegant and open dresses, which was quite common in homosocial women's spaces, made it possible for ladies to display their trendy clothing and accessories. Thus, ladies presented and shared ideas and experiences on recent fashions in such gatherings.

According to the Dust Ali khan Mo'ier al-Mamālek's report, urban women were always interested in the new fashions invented by the ladies of the royal harem, and eager to test and imitate new dresses and cosmetics (Mo'ir al-Mamālek 1983, 21). Over the years, Anis al-Dowleh, Naser al-Din Shah's queen and head of the harem, had a significant influence on the sense of fashion and cosmetics of Iranian women. She successfully replaced the heavy make-up with the light European style and she played a crucial role in changing women's clothing style in Iran. In his memoirs, Qahreman Mirza Ein al-Saltaneh (1997, 1070), one of the Qajar courtiers (1871–1945), describes the queen's role as follows:

> Most changes in women's clothing styles are Her Majesty ideas and innovations. Everybody, men and women, owe her much. These changes made women prettier, and those old-fashioned clothes vanished. For example, this new fashion; the gauze scarf is far different from the former cretonne, cashmere, or calico scarfs. Also, this new simple and delicate makeup is better than the old makeup with those stripes and speckles and little hair loops made the ladies look like painted elephants. They used to paint the whole body with multiple speckles, like barbarians. Also, the new European curler heats up and makes the hair curly or straightens it beautifully. These new hairstyles made women a thousand times prettier and more delicate.

According to photos, besides face make-up, hairdressing was a distinguished beauty marker of upper-class women. The long back part of the hair has been made either into dreadlocks, braided or left open around the face or back (Fig. 9.6). In early Naseri, the front part was usually kept long and parted at the centre. Another popular haircut in early Naseri photographs is *zolf*, a strand of cheek-length short hair which is usually made centre-parted and has been carefully cut and combed (Fig. 9.7). Again, this has been made stable with the use of a gel-like material. It was usually made a fringe in the late Naseri era, a little curly and short enough to reveal eyebrows. According to the photos, there is no doubt that a unique gel-like material was used to fix the fringe or short hairs on the forehead. Azad (1979, 395) states that women put quince seeds in water, and after a few hours, the result was a sticky substance that was used as hair gel.

The very common headgear is the *chārqad*, that was made of fine textiles, such as gauze, brocade or knitted fabric. Describing her make-up by Princess Esmat al-Dowleh, Carla Serena (1983, 236) explains that:

> after drawing a thin down over my lips, the princess made my headgear. She put on a white scarf, afterwards, she gave it to me as a gift, on my head covering my hair as Iranian style. Then the makeup was finished. Certainly, the best part of the party was when she put an Iranian scarf on my head.

Fig. 9.6 Baghban Bashi (left), Naser al-Din Shah's wife, and a Circassian (Cherkesy) bondwoman with fringe cut hairstyle and dreadlocks. Original caption by Naser al-Din Shah: photo 10-2, on the marble stairs, Bashi and Cherkesy in Chinese clothing (Institut for Iranian Contemporary Historical Studies (IICHS))

Chārqad was part of the make-up, a prominent piece of hairdressing, and an aesthetic and fashionable element that changed accordingly to suit new fashions. Generally, different headgears were highly decorated, usually on the forehead and under the chin, with jewellery (Serena 1983, 230) and sometimes flowers and blossoms (Azad 1979, 395).

According to the photos, paintings and historical documents, royal women had access to a wide range of elegant clothing and jewellery. Several quotes of travellers or Iranian men and women point out the importance of fashion and aesthetic. Serena (1983, 229–230) states that their jumpers and blouses are exquisite and thin to reveal their beautiful feminine bodies. Describing princess Esmat al-Dowleh's clothing, she explains how her fashionable lightweight orange blouse was elegantly decorated with finely polished pearls and handmade embroideries. Visiting hundreds of women in fascinating clothing, she was so enchanted that she stated that this scene reminded her of Calypso and the other nymphs living on the island of Ogygia (Serena 1983, 229). A vast number of photographs in Golestan Palace confirm Serena's report. Prominent women, including the crown prince's mother, Shokuh al-Saltane, and Anis

Fig. 9.7 Queen Shekouh al-Saltaeh in chārghad and shaliteh with zolf hairstayle. Original caption: Shekouh-e Ozma, the mother of Mozaffar al-Din Shah and the dauther of Qavānlou, the commander-in-chief

al-Dowleh appear in a jumper of silk or gauze that revealed their naked breasts and bellies while putting their hands either on their breasts or bellies. Polak's report (1989, 116) confirms that harem women used a thin jumper of silk, of blue or pink, embroidered with golden margins that only reached the navel, so that half of the belly remained naked. Describing her official journey to Tabriz, Taj al-Saltaneh (1982, 95) explains that before her departure she had to pay 2,800 toman, Iranian currency, to Seyyed Ebrahim, a merchant of silk cloth, who usually offered her the best quality and most fashionable textiles. Regarding the lower part of the costume, women have been shown in short wrinkled classy skirts, a *shaliteh*, short white socks and dark shoes, probably black. Azad (1979, 395) claims that rubber trousers later replaced these short socks. It is worth mentioning that European dress models influenced royal harem costumes, and it would be interesting to know whether the shaliteh was designed after Naser al-Din Shah's travels to Europe, as the Shah was interested in short ballet outfits.

Alexis Soltykoff (1957, 94), the Russian traveller, who visited Iran during Mohammad Shah's reign in 1828, passionately describes the beauty of women and their clothing style:

> Iranian women, especially Shirazi women, dye their thick black hair with henna; they do the same with their fingers and feet. They put on makeup on their faces and draw a black or blue fine line of mascara or kohl, *sormeh*, around eyelashes. Tall and beautiful, their body movements are charming. They wear a blue or red dress of fine material specifically tight on shoulders, waist and arms but leaves breasts and belly free. This clothing is so close-fitting that they must keep their shoulders back. This pushing back of the shoulders gives them an enchanting posture when walking around.

Judging by the photographs, ladies have also adopted a wide range of gestures. Some of the gestures would have been proposed by Naser al-Din Shah, particularly the ones which can be categorised as a series. The best example is a series showing ladies, young and old, sitting on the same chair to get photographed in turn. These women appear in front of the lens individually or in a group, sometimes accompanied by their spouses and children, and even with their pets, particularly cats and dogs, as keeping pets was usual in Iran. Holding an elegant mirror in the woman's hand was a typical posture. This posture has been already recognised in Safavid miniatures, where not only women, but also young men and amrads have beautiful book-shaped mirrors in their hands, with the cover painted with herbal motifs. Nevertheless, in the late Qajar photos a mirror was considered a feminine symbol by those whose gender was associated with femininity. Still equivalent to early Qajar, the postures such as smoking the water pipe, holding a bowl of wine or a flower, usually roses and pink flowers (also common among men, amrads and eunuchs) in the hand, and putting one hand on breasts or belly are also recognised in paintings.

However, a series of obviously erotic postures can also be recognised among the royal harem's photographs. There are several photographs of Anis al-Dowleh and other Qajar harem and ordinary women, with or without a scarf, with the curls of their forehead hair peeking out, or even pictures with naked thighs and legs which can not be covered by their short skirts, shaliteh and socks. Lasciviously and invitingly sitting on knees with naked legs wide apart, these women have adopted erotic and playful postures. More strikingly, their body hair has not been removed, as one can easily recognise the hairy legs of the women in some photos. According to Safavid texts, such as Aqayed al-Nesā (Khansari 1976) and Old Tehran, a late Qajar-early Pahlavi text (Shahri 1992, 528), women used to remove all body hair, with a unique component which is called *nureh*. The question therefore would be if these hairy legs were of a sexual appeal for the king or not.

Still, some beauty marks among harem women do seem to reflect the peculiar taste or erotic fantasies of Naser al-Din Shah. Competition for the king's favour among women and keeping up with each other played a prominent role in defining and altering beauty ideals. Also, Ein al-Saltaneh's (1997) account reveals implicitly that harem make-up styles and fashion were not necessarily charming and according to men's taste. And it is important to note that women spent most of the day together in the homosocial space of harem or participating in various feasts, ceremonies, events and even trips together. Taj al- Saltaneh's description of such events is considerable:

> The royal court and harem were centers for gathering the most beautiful women. And I was always considered as the most beautiful one. Competing, these ladies always did their best and chose the best jewellery, clothing and make-up style to attract the king and satisfy his royal taste. As each evening, all the ladies were busy with putting on make-up and selecting precious colourful clothing. The whole process took between two and three hours (Taj al-Saltaneh 1982, 19).

Alongside photography, the beauty ideals of women in paintings also transformed significantly. In a limited number of female portraits, overweight women with a chārqad are shown. Royal court painters also used photographs in devising their paintings. A convincing example is a portrait of Queen Anis al-Dowleh by Mohammad Qaffari, who received the noble title Kamal al-Molk, in which Anis is shown with a plump round face, while her chārqad is ornamented with a row of flowers around her face and a branch of jewellery under her chin. Iranian modern artists, such as Kamal al-Molk, achieved a naturalist aesthetic in painting. "Thus, the effects of modernisation were also prevalent in Iranian painting and reflected the desire to record what was and what was to be no more" (Scheiwiller 2012, 19).

Concerning the female harem personnel's appearance and their beauty ideals, sources are poor. In some photographs, nannies, nursemaids and housemaids are also shown. Their hairdressing is assumed to be completely different, perhaps simpler; moreover, they wore colourful *chādor*, a veil, but without a *rubandeh* (face cover) that might point to their lower social status (Fig. 9.8).

Correspondingly, in the middle of the Naseri era, a slight shift in style and royal paintings' subjects occurs. The use of gender undifferentiated beauty marks from early paintings, such as coloured nails, slim waist and red cheeks, particularly in royal and political figures, almost completely disappeared for men. A facial hairstyle, particularly bushy beards and incredibly thick handlebar moustaches, instead became the distinguishing features of masculinity in the constitution and post-constitution

Fig. 9.8 Princess Akhtar al-Dowleh among harem female personnel (Institut for Iranian Contemporary Historical Studies (IICHS))

paintings. Therefore, by this time, one could recognise adult males and females almost precisely.

Ordinary women in the eye of the camera
Until the middle of the Qajar era, visual evidence rarely represented ordinary women. Enjoying royal patronage, painters scarcely chose ordinary citizens as the subject of their artwork. The reports of the modern Tehran Police, established on the 11th of November 1878 (Motamedi 2002, 576), provide researchers with considerable information about all classes' urban women (see Shaykh Rezaie and Azari 1999). Photography also granted the opportunity to document women's everyday lives.

Scrutinising the word, "ordinary women", in short, refers to a wide range of middle and lower urban classes, rural women, nomad women, Sufi and dervish women (see Soltykoff 1957, 95), Armenians, Zoroastrians, Christians and Jews. The photographs show little girls, infants, young, middle-aged and older women of different age classes. Unexpectedly, and perhaps in opposition to the stereotype of veiled Muslim women seen in the West as oppressed (Abu-Lughod 2002; Bullock 2010, 5), women have sat in front of the lens with a sense of comfort. Even more surprising, women have consented to be models for nude photography.

Many women and young girls followed the royal hairstyle, including dreadlocks at the back and a fringe cut on the forehead. This group must have been mainly urban (Tehrani) women. It was also completely normal to wear a chārqad. Contrary to the royal and upper classes, who used delicate and thin fabrics, urban women utilised relatively cheap and thick materials for the chārqad.

In photographs that have been taken outside Tehran, a wide range of local headgears and jewellery, instead of the chārqad, and different hairstyles can be distinguished. Traditional costume, headgears and local hairstyles are considered as beauty features, among other social functions, in different groups of ordinary women, and jewellery has been adapted accordingly. However, poverty and misery can be explicitly observed in some photographs, as the appearance and body shape of ordinary women differ from those of the royal harem. Heavy make-up, exaggerated black and thick eyebrows, short skirts and socks are rarely attested. The royal women have distinctly overweight bodies and faces with double chins, while urban, rural and nomad women have relative slim bodies. One can easily distinguish this difference in the slim bodies of nude models.

Parallel to photography, the daily life of ordinary people only gradually received the attention of painters. Kamal al-Molk, who was at the royal court as the head painter, is among those pioneer masters whose paintings replicate mundane scenes from everyday life (Scheiwiller 2012, 20) and the ordinary women's world. He trained in Iran and later (1897–1900) in Europe, where he established a close friendship with Henri Fantin-Latour (Scheiwiller 2012, 20). He was interested in democracy and intellectual viewpoints, and was familiar with Jean-Jacques Rousseau's ideas on society, even with French poet Anatole France (Parsaie 2001, 61).

Kamal al-Molk's works before his travels to Europe represent the contemporary world, instead of traditional motifs. He was a realist painter drawing portraits and details in a realistic style (Dezhamkhooy and Massoudi 2014, 597). After having spent a few years in Iraq, Kamal focused on the people and their daily lives, hopes, wishes and beliefs. Thus, people have come to the foreground for Mohammad Qaffari. In the painting "Baqdadi Fortuneteller", women uncover their faces while laughing and talking to the fortune-teller (Dezhamkhooy and Massoudi 2014, 600), whereas the royal harem beauty characteristics are almost absent. In another painting by Sani' al-Molk, Kamal al-Molk's uncle, Mirza Abolfazl, the physician, is shown examining his patients. Urban veiled women in this painting have black eyes and bow-shaped eyebrows, but the coloured nails and red cheeks are absent.

Phase 3: Feminisation of beauty

The term feminisation of beauty has already been introduced for this topic by A. Najmabadi (2001, 101; 2005a: 65). This phase chronologically coincided with the Iranian Constitutional Revolution. Since the Naseri era, the development of distinctive feminine beauty marks was influenced by Western beauty ideals. Beauty transformations should therefore be considered to have been part of social, political and even economic circumstances that rapidly changed Iranian society at the turn of the 20th century.

During the Mashruteh (the Persian word for the constitution) Revolution (1906–1911), intellectuals, avant garde religious leaders, and people actively evoked modern Western concepts of law and progress, calling for socio-political reforms. Women's rights were mainly demanded by women themselves, although some intellectuals also encouraged women's rights, particularly for education (Afary 2009, 114). Consequently, gender and sexual norms were also criticised, particularly by intellectuals and women activists. The new Western-inspired and rising regime introduced women as men's companions, sexual and emotional partners. Hence, heterosexuality was implicitly emphasised. Education, changes in housekeeping methods, husband's companionship and motherhood, were now the focus. Therefore, gradually, dressing styles and women's appearance were also subjected to criticism (Taj al-Saltaneh 1982).

During the Constitutional Revolution and particularly during the post-constitution era, which begins after Mohammad Ali Shah (r. 1907–1909) and covers the early years of the Pahlavi Dynasty, gender and sexuality transformations intensified, as women activists, free thinkers and women's journals called for change. Afary (2009, 111) has formulated this nicely: It was in this period (mid 19th century) that three broad and overlapping political discourses on gender and modernity emerged in elite urban circles: scientific domesticity, social-democratic discourse and conservative religious discourse.

The constitution's socio-political context and post-constitution were so tense and turbulent that we cannot reduce its female agents to predefined groups. Accordingly, diverse groups of women (and intellectuals) pursued the improvement of women's condition. We could mention prominent women activists, influenced by social democratic discourse, who advocated women's rights and political reforms on a national scale. However, to discuss the issue in detail goes far beyond the scope of this paper. In short, this group published women's journals, such as *Zabān-e Zanān*, encouraged the establishment of girls' schools, held political events, organised lectures and even demonstrations in favour of the constitution and independence of the country. Hence, we should speak of different points of views and interests and consequently the birth of "various forms of modern women", but women who were still interested in traditional norms were in the majority, particularly outside Tehran.

Other groups of activists followed nationalist discourse. Afary (2009, 111) describes it as:

> A new nationalist discourse of "scientific domesticity" embraced modernity in the areas of health, hygiene, and education. It emphasized industrialization, education, and new health measures that improved living standards, reduced child mortality, and gave women greater authority within the home, all to turn Iran into a modern country. Most proponents of this view did not want to radically alter existing gender or sexual patterns or question the sharia in terms of family and personal law.

The scientific domesticity discourse gave rise to a specific figure of a modern woman. This category was predominantly occupied by royal princesses or women from noble families, upper classes, including merchants, religiously prominent families and probably also some traditional middle-class women. The advocates of this new figure of a woman were either educated in missionary schools in European countries or were privately tutored by Western teachers. This group also managed to publish women's journals. They clarified in their flyers, announcements and cover pages that they do not follow a political agenda in their journals. The journals *Alam-e Nesvān* and *Dānesh* are good examples of this. *Dānesh* is officially distinguished as the first women's magazine, and was first published in 1910 (Brown 1975, 383). It introduced its policy as applicable to girls and women, and entirely away from contemporary politics (Babran 2002, 35). Generally, *Dānesh* put the focus on household and domestic issues related to middle- and upper-class urban women (Afary 1996, 266).

These journals developed a modern urban women's lifestyle, in which more emphasis was put on how the quotidian life of a "real lady" should be. This new lifestyle considered body and beauty as significant elements of the daily life of a modern woman. Modernity introduced a new notion of femininity, primarily concerned with the body, gesture and appearance (Afary 2009, 119). Accordingly, beauty marks were gradually changing according to Western ideals; more remarkably, they were defined as feminine. Being a woman was considered to be delicate and charming. The term "fair sex" even appeared in a women's newspaper, Peyk-e Sa'ādat-e Nesvān (Massoudi and Mohajer 2011, 121). These modern feminised beauty features were formed in Tehran and in major cities, such as Shiraz, where women's journals were also released. Therefore, modern, feminine beauty in Iran was an urban phenomenon.

Also noteworthy, as discussed above, is that by the beginning of the 20th century, there were several contesting discourses on women's rights and status in modern society. Some women's activists, for example, criticised women's obsessive interest in a modern appearance. Rowshanak Now'dust, who published Peyk-e Sa'ādat-e Nesvān in Rasht, north Iran, denounced upper-class women for their interest in glamorous Western products and formal changes in women's life. Calling women the "forgotten majority", she argued for improving women's conditions, especially in rural areas (Massoudi and Mohajer 2011, 98–100).

Interestingly, these journals accepted advertisements whose primary addressees were rich and upper-class urban women. European imported commodities, such as silk socks, perfumed soaps, cosmetics, perfumes, fine textiles and European tailor shops were heavily advertised by these journals. Alam-e Nesvān allocated several pages of every issue to women's fashion by publishing European dress patterns and the latest trends in hats that were updated according to the season. It can therefore be said that an economy related to the feminine body and body care gradually developed. Its consumers were bourgeois and petit-bourgeois women, the rising classes. Contextually, the government's economic policies supported Western consumer goods, particularly from England, France and Russia (see Nategh 1990). A provocative issue that caused waves of protests and dissatisfaction among Iranian merchants and later women's activists. However, Homayoun Katouzian (2012, 92) has argued the Iranian economy was principally underdeveloped as the demands of upper classes for Western luxury and consumer goods were increasing. Women (and men) with royal or noble backgrounds passionately acknowledged the new beauty ideals. Taj al-Saltaneh's (1982, 109) narrative, for example, is engaging:

> My French language teacher kept talking about materialists. Being influenced, I first changed my clothing to European style, *farangi*, and went completely unveiled. But throughout the country, traditional clothing was still common. My new dress included a corset and had tight sleeves.

According to Taj, historical photographs and texts, traditional and local costumes, and beauty characteristics, particularly in rural areas, small cities and among the nomads, continued even after the veil ban, the European Dress Code Act, in 1935. After the Constitutional Revolution, it was more common to appear without a hijab and in a European style in front of the lens. Taj al-Saltaneh had several photographs taken without a scarf, in European dress with a European hat (Fig. 9.9).

Historically, some noblemen who had visited Europe had already started criticising women's appearance and behaviour, as well. They desired women, not only with European appearance, but also humble and companionable like these. In this regard, a pioneering work is a surviving essay by a member of the Qajar aristocracy, written in the early 1880s, and appropriately entitled Ta'dib al-Nesvān (Disciplining of Women). It reveals how some aristocrats used their knowledge of Western culture to construct a contemporary and more confining discourse concerning the proper behavior and dress of upper-class Iranian women (Afary 2009, 119). The author suggested that the book should be taught in girls' schools. In this the girls were given detailed suggestions on make-up and attire, such as how a woman should use eyeliner and rouge on her face, henna on her hair, polish on her nails, and rosewater on her body, and whether she should wear her hair long or short. Additionally, a proper woman wore the kind of clothes her husband liked and changed her outfit once a

Fig. 9.9 Princess Taj al-Saltaneh in European dress (http://www.qajarwomen.org)

day. She never touched dirt, and she washed her hands with perfumed soaps instead of ordinary ill-smelling ones. She kept her hands in silk gloves, even if she was sitting by a korsi, so that her hands would always remain attractive and smooth (Javadi, Marashi and Shekarloo 1992, 54–55, 61–63).

The Qajar aristocrat also presented detailed rules of conduct for proper behavior in bed. For example, a husband and wife should sleep in separate beds unless they were having sex, since sleeping in the same bed reduced affection. The woman should wear gowns made of a soft cloth and come to bed fully perfumed and clean. During the day, the woman was expected to be weak and submissive, but in bed, she should use erotic and provocative language and carry on with utter shamelessness. More importantly, she was not supposed to deny her husband's demands for sex at any time or in any place (Afary 2009, 120). Continuing to be published more and more after the constitution and in the Pahlavi era, the sections that read like advice manuals were not unlike the 1890s' Ta'dib al-Nesvān. Women were expected not only to have modern docile bodies, but also docile minds, which would assure their lifelong obedience to their husbands (Afary 2009, 120).

In a long-term process, beauty features and body standardisation developed for modern urban women. In late Qajar photographs, the heavy make-up, particularly thick connected eyebrows, soft down over upper lip, and heavy jewellery of royal women disappeared. The chārqad has also been used infrequently. Postures like smoking a waterpipe and holding a bowl of wine, flower or mirror, that were common in the early and middle Qajar period, almost vanished. Lacquer work on different objects, such as ceilings and book covers, continued to be used until the late Qajar when women's figures in European dress and make-up appeared in it.

By analogy, almost until the middle Qajar period, the use of jewellery, hair colours and probably some basic cosmetic materials, such as kohl and henna, were common between adult men, eunuchs, women and amrads. Soltykoff (1957) describes how young men and especially male dancers put on make-up and made their hair. Noteworthy, transformations of beauty features also affected modes of masculinity, and traditional male beauty marks were partly dismantled. Also, there were other gendered clues, such as gestures (Najmabadi 2005a). Postures like holding a flower in the hands and men's costume with light, fresh colours, such as lemon, white, blue and red, or wearing luxuriant garments ornamented with traditional arts such as *maftul duzi* became slightly outmoded (Etemad al-Saltaneh 2000).

After the constitution, new values, such as bravery and defence of the motherland, *mām-e vatan* (see Najmabadi 1997), honour, *nāmus* in Persian, and protection of Iranian women as national sisters, represented the new forms of masculinity. Constitutional newspapers encouraged men to show their zeal for Vatan (see Najmabadi 2005b), and the term *Sarbāz-e Vatan*, soldiers of the homeland, was widely applied, which put men in charge of both national sisters and the homeland. Therefore, the new construction of masculinity was highly tied to loyalty to the constitution and the nation.

In post-constitution times, clothing style and "etiquette" were considered as codes of elegance and of being a gentleman, especially by upper classes and journals which mostly propagated a modern appearance and lifestyle. The press and especially women's newspapers called for men's proper treatment of respectful ladies (Safavi 1933, 3–5). In a nutshell, behaving like a gentleman was considered the ideal of masculinity among the middle and upper urban classes.

Conclusion

Unfortunately, the number of studies on beauty in general and feminine beauty in Qajar and early Pahlavi Iran is minimal (see Chekhab-Abudaya and Sobers-Khan 2016; Fellinger 2018). Notably, the interplay of gender, beauty and class in the late Qajar socio-political context has mostly been ignored. Lugones (2007, 187), notably, criticises the persistence of "indifference" in feminist analysis. She appreciates the attempts of women of colour and Third World feminism to include race, gender, class and sexuality in feminist discussions.

Najmabadi (2006, 14) has subtly pointed out that the 19th century in Iran is a long period characterised by gender and sexuality transformations. Methodologically it is necessary to divide this into sub-periods to help the scholars contextualise data and historical trajectories. Given the co-existence of different forms of femininity and beauty in this article, the goal was to adopt social and political metamorphosis and its materiality to develop a proper chronological framework. It should always be borne in mind that the orthodox chronological frameworks based on political history, particularly for the middle Qajar onwards, do not work properly. This consideration is crucial when it comes to figuring out the image(s) of women in 19th- and early 20th-century Iran.

Almost to the middle of the Qajar era, beauty was just as related to class and social associations, such as ethnicity, religion, age, marital status and even localities, as only with gender. Concerning royal women, other beauty features indeed acted as symbols of social distinction. Therefore, the goal was to illustrate the difference between the royal harem and ordinary urban women. Moreover, beauty was sometimes the subject of competition and even cooperation within the homosocial harem.

After the constitution, a new notion of beauty, among the local, traditional and other modern ones, was introduced and claimed, particularly through the newspapers and essays, for all women regardless of their social status. It was connected to concepts such as male/female companionship and educated/trained housewife. The role of a group of women's newspapers and magazines, which explicitly or implicitly refused any political engagements and their contribution to new aesthetic criteria and modern femininity was critical. However, to a large extent, this aspect has still not been thoroughly investigated.

Much more emphasis on women's bodily care and daily life was found in these journals; the new guides for etiquette prohibited women (and men) from many actions that were now considered uncivilised. It is supposed that this etiquette guide also reduced the mobility and physical activity of women. Adopting the European dress code, Taj al-Saltaneh (1982, 109) complains that the European corset and sleeves were so tight and unpleasant that she couldn't do anything (see also Afary 2009, 119). Whereas women in the traditional context used to engage in different levels of physical activities, agriculture and animal husbandry.

In short, after the constitution, we encounter different and contesting notions of modern women. Being a modern woman was considered by some women activists and organisations as an active engagement in the country's destiny and claiming of women's rights. For some classes, on the other hand, being modern was more a matter of fashion, modern appearance, prestige and social distinction. To exemplify this, activists, such as Sediqeh Dowlatabadi, appreciated women's participation in the public sphere. She was one of the pioneers of women's campaigns against Western commodities and particularly textiles. Her newspaper, Zabān-e Zanān, followed an explicitly political agenda, however, it changed its policies after the rise of the Pahlavi government.

Nonetheless, a women's beauty code cannot be adequately grasped unless we conduct a systematic investigation of the constitution of modern masculinity. Qajar Iran marked a radical change in sexual morals and erotic sensibilities toward feminising beauty and correspondingly toward the heteronormalising of love (Najmabadi 2005a, 61). Men also began to show public affection toward women, to serenade them in poems and to write about such experiences in detail (Najmabadi 2005a, 54). While the beloved one in classic Persian poems was predominantly male, not female (Shamisa 2003), male homoerotism subsequently appeared as deviance. The latest beauty features should thus bring consensus to men as partners. Later, a link between the feminine body, beauty and male erotism was implicitly inaugurated. Foucault (1990, 103) has demonstrated how sexuality as a modern apparatus densely transformed power relations between men and women. Modern politics of gender and heterosexualisation influenced perceptions of beauty and established a connection between the feminiation of beauty and placing women in an inferior position.

As Lugones (2007, 206) has detailed "the dark side of gender system" is fully violent (see also Matić and Jensen 2017). In the 1920s, Reza Shah accepted only his own women's organisations and oppressed many female activists and closed their newspapers. The centralisation and suppression of other independent women's movements also acted in favour of homogenisation. Under Reza Shah, women had to adopt the European Dress Code and could wear make-up in public (*cf.* Papoli-Yazdi and Dezhamkhooy 2021). As Foucault (1990, 139) states, "the disciplines of the body and the regulations of the population constituted the two poles around which the organization of power over life was deployed". Women were reduced to their body, which was highly politically charged and adhered to the subjugation of women as beautiful creators, not only to their male relatives, but also to the current patriarchal regime. However, the Revolution claimed modern Western democratic ideals and justice for the entire nation; just as it had implicitly encouraged a patriarchal order. Several documents show that National Parliament did not support women's organisations, particularly financially (see Afary 1996); sometimes, it was only with empty promises while women supported the Revolution politically, financially, and sometimes at the expense of their lives.

To the contemporary eye Qajar women's moustaches made them look like men and made them ugly. Nevertheless, in its own time, the moustache was a cherished sign of a woman's beauty (Najmabadi 2005a, 55). Modern gender and sexual regimes and aesthetic criteria have led to a negative evaluation of Qajar female beauty as obese, ugly and hairy without taking other aspects of women's life in Qajar Iran into consideration. The new criteria gradually led to the manipulation of the feminine body. Heterosexualisation and the domination of male sexuality resulted in obsessive interest in a slim body, Western hairstyle, make-up and dress (*cf.* Papoli-Yazdi and Dezhamkhooy 2021). For women the latest beauty codes symbolised being modern, civilised and a deserving companion for gentlemen. Under Mohammad Reza Shah, slim bodies with a European look were defined as ideal femininity in the mass media.

Acknowledgement

Malek National Library and Museum Institution provided access to its documents and press archives. The author is thankful to the museum staff: Mohammad Nowruzi and Hojatollah Qorbani. Ghoncheh Habibiazad, Uroš Matić and Andrea Sinclair have thoroughly proofread my English.

Bibliography

Abu-Lughod, L. (2002) Do Muslim women really need saving? Anthropological reflections on cultural relativism and its others. *American Anthropologist* 104 (3), 783–791.

Afary, J. (1996) *The Iranian Constitutional Revolution, 1906–1911: Grassroots Democracy, Social Democracy, and the Origins of Feminism*. New York, Columbia University Press.

Afary, J. (2009) *Sexual Politics in Modern Iran*. New York, Cambridge University Press.

Astarabadi, B. (1993) *Ma'ayeb al-Rejal [Men's Imperfection]*, A. Najmabadi (ed.). Chicago, Midland Press.

Azad, H. (1979) *Behind the Harem Curtain*. Urmia, Anzali Publishing (in Persian).

Babran, S. (2002) *Women's Journals*. Tehran, Roshangarān va Motaleat-e Zanān Publishing (in Persian).

Behdad, A. (1999) Sevruguin: orientalist or orienteur? In F. Bohrer (ed.) *Sevruguin and the Persian Image: Photographs of Iran, 1870–1930*, 79–98. Seattle, Arthur M. Sackler Gallery, Smithsonian Institution and the University of Washington Press.

Behdad, A. (2001) The power-ful art of Qajar photography: orientalism and (self)-orientalizing in nineteenth-century Iran. *Iranian Studies* 34 (1–4), 141–151.

Brown, E. (1910) *The Press and Poetry of Modern Persia*. Trans. into Persian by M. Abbasi. Tehran, Nashre Elm.

Bullock, K. (2010) *Rethinking Muslim Women and the Veil: Challenging Historical and Modern Stereotypes*. Herndon, the International Institute of Islamic Thought.

Chekhab-Abudaya, M. and Sobers Khan, N. (2016) *Qajar Women: Images of Women in 19th-Century Iran*. Milan, Silvana Editoriale.

Dezhamkhooy, M. and Massoudi, A. (2014) The painter in two frames: an archaeological investigation of Kamal-ol Molk's agency in the field of art and politics. *International Journal of Historical Archaeology* 18 (4), 591–611.

Diba, L.S. (1989) Persian painting in the eighteenth century: tradition and transmission. *Muqarnas* 6, 147–160.

Diba, L.S. (2013) Qajar photography and its relationship to Iranian art: a reassessment. *History of Photography* 37 (1), 85–98.

Diba, L. and Ekhtiar, M. (1998) *Royal Persian Paintings: The Qajar Epoch, 1785–1925*. New York, Brooklyn Museum of Art in association with I.B. Tauris of London.

Dimand, M. (1941) *Persian Miniatures: A Picture Book*. New York, Metropolitan Museum of Art.

Esfandiari, Z. and Salehi Kakhki, A. (2015) Painting in Qajar epoch. *Cultural Researches* 1 (1), 99–119 (in Persian).

Etemad al-Saltaneh, M.H. (2000) *Ruznāmeh-ye Khāterāt-e Etemad al-Saltaneh [Etemad al-Saltaneh's Memoirs]*. I. Afshar (ed.). Tehran, Amir Kabir (in Persian).

Ein al-Saltaneh, Q.M.S. (1997) *Ruznāmeh-ye Khāterāt-e Ein al-Saltaneh [Ein al-Saltaneh's Memoirs]*. M. Saloor and I. Afshar (eds) Tehran, Asatir (in Persian).

Fauvrier, J. (2006) *Trois ans a'la cour Perse*. Trans. into Persian by Abbas Eqbal Ashtiani. Tehran, Nashr-e Elm.

Fellinger, G. (2018) *L'Empire des roses: chefs-d'œuvre de l'art persan du XIXe siècle*. Gand, Snoeck Publishers.

Foucault, M. (1990) *The History of Sexuality I. Introduction*. Trans. into English by Robert Hurley. New York, Vintage.

Hasan Beigi, M.R. (2003) *Old Tehran*. Tehran, Qoqnus (in Persian).

Homayoun Katouzian, M.A. (2012) *Iran, the Short-term Society*. Trans. Into Persian by Abdullah Kowsari. Tehran, Nei Publishing.

Horswell, M. (2003) Toward an Andean theory of ritual same-sex sexuality and third gender subjectivity. In P. Sigal (ed.) *Infamous Desire: Male Homosexuality in Colonial Latin America*, 25–69. Chicago, University of Chicago Press.

Javadi, H., Marashi, M. and Shekarloo, S. (eds) (1992) *Ta'dib al-Nisvan va Ma'ayeb al-Rejal*. Chicago, Historical Studies of Iranian Women.

Keddie, N. (1981) *Roots of Revolution: An Interpretive History of Modern Iran*. New Haven and London, Yale University Press.

Khansari, A. (1976) *Kolsum Naneh (Aqayed al-Nesā)*. Tehran, Morvarid (in Persian).

Khazaei, Y. (2019) The third sex: a conceptual and physiological examination of eunuchs in Qajar court (1796–1886). *Iran History* 12 (1), 167–184 (in Persian).

Lugones, M. (2007) Heterosexualism and the colonial/modern gender system. *Hypatia* 22 (1), 186–209.

Massoudi, B. and Mohajer, N. (eds) (2011) *The Payk-e Saadat Nesvan Journal*. Köln, Noghteh Books (in Persian).

Matić, U. and Jensen, B. (eds) (2017) *Archaeologies of Gender and Violence*. Oxford, Oxbow Books.

Meskell, L. and Joyce, R. (2003) *Embodied Lives. Figuring Ancient Maya and Egyptian Experience*. New York, Routledge.

Mikaberidze, A. (2011) *Conflict and Conquest in the Islamic World: A Historical Encyclopedia. Vol. 2*. Santa Barbara, ABC-CLIO, LLC.

Mo'ir al-Mamālek, D.A.Kh. (1983) *Notes on the Private Life of Naser al-Din Shah*. Tehran, Nashr-e Tarikh-e Iran (in Persian).

Montón-Subías, S. (2019) Gender, missions, and maintenance activities in the early modern globalization: Guam 1668–1698. *International Journal of Historical Archaeology* 23, 404–429.

Motamedi, M. (2002) *Historical Geography of Tehran*. Tehran, Nashr-e Daneshgahi (in Persian).

Najmabadi, A. (1997) The erotic vatan (homeland) as beloved and motors: to love, to possess and to protect. *Society for Comparative Study of Society and History* 39 (3), 442–468.

Najmabadi, A. (2001) Gendered transformations: beauty, love, and sexuality in Qajar Iran. *Iranian Studies* 34 (1–4), 89–102.

Najmabadi, A. (2005a) Mapping transformations of sex, gender and sexuality in modern Iran. *Social Analysis* 94, 54–77.

Najmabadi, A. (2005b) *Women with Mustaches and Men without Beards: Gender and Sexual Anxieties of Iranian Modernity*. Berkeley and Los Angeles, University of California Press.

Najmabadi, A. (2006) Beyond the Americas; are gender and sexuality useful categories of historical analysis? *Journal of Women's History* 18, 11–21.

Najmabadi, A. (2008) Types, acts or what? Regulation of sexuality in 19th century Iran. In A. Najmabadi and K. Babayan (eds) *Islamicate Sexualities: Translations across Temporal Geographies of Desire*, 275–296. Cambridge and Massachusetts, Harvard Center for Middle Eastern Studies.

Najmabadi, A. and Babayan, K. (eds) (2008) *Islamicate Sexualities: Translations across Temporal Geographies of Desire*. Cambridge and Massachusetts, Harvard Center for Middle Eastern Studies.

Nategh, H. (1990) *Iran dar Rahyabiy-e Farhangi [Persia Torn between Two Cultures]*. Paris, Khavaran and Pegah (in Persian).

Nettleton, S. (2001) The sociology of body. In W.C. Cockerham (ed.) *The Blackwell Companion to Medical Sociology*, 43–63. Massachusetts, Blackwell Publishers.

Papoli-Yazdi, L. and Dezhamkhooy, M. (2021) *Homogenization, Gender and Everyday Life in Pre- and Trans-modern Iran: An Archaeological Reading*. Münster, Waxmann.

Parsaie, K. (2016) *Kamal al Molk*. Tehran, Dabir (in Persian).

Polak, J. (1989) [1865] *Persien, das Land und Seiner Bewohner: ethnograpische Schilderungen*. Trans. into Persian by K. Jahandari. Tehran, Kharazmi.

Safavi, N. (Journal manager) (1933) *Journal of Alam-e Nesvān*. Tehran.

Scarce, J. (2001) The architecture and decoration of the Gulistan Palace: the aims and achievements of Fath 'Ali Shah (1797–1834) and Nasir al-Din Shah (1848–1896). *Iranian Studies* 34 (1/4), 103–116.

Shamisa, S. (2003) *Shahed bāzi dar adabiyāt-e Farsi [Shahed Bazi in Persian Literature]*. Tehran, Ferdows (in Persian).

Scheiwiller, S.G. (2012) Reframeing the rise of modernism in Iran. In M. Munro (ed.) *Modernism Beyond the West: a History of Art from Emerging Markets*, 11–32. London, Enzo Press.

Scheiwiller, S.G. (2017) *Liminalities of Gender and Sexuality in Nineteenth-Century Iranian Photography: Desirous Bodies*. London and New York, Routledge.

Scheiwiller, S.G. (2018) Relocating Sevruguin: contextualizing the political climate of the Iranian photographer Antoin Sevruguin (*c.* 1851–1933). In M. Ritter and S.G. Scheiwiller (eds) *The Indigenous Lens? Early Photography in the Near and the Middle East*, 145–172. Berlin, de Gruyter.

Serena, C. (1983) *Homines et choses en Perse*. Trans. into Persian by Ali Asghar Sa'idi as Adamha va a'inha dar Iran. Tehran, Zavvar.

Shafiyev, F. (2018) *Resettling the Borderlands: State Relocations and Ethnic Conflict in the South Caucasus*. Montreal and Kingston, McGill-Queen's University Press.

Shahri, J. (1992) *Old Tehran*. Tehran, Moien (in Persian).

Shaykh Rezaie, E. and Azari, Sh. (eds) (1999) *Police Reports of Tehran Districts*. Tehran, Iran National Archives Organization Records Research Center (in Persian).

Soltykoff, A. (1957) *A Journey to Iran*. Trans. into Persian by Mohsen Saba. Tehran, Bongah-e Nashr va Tarjomeh Ketab.

Taie, P. (2008) A study of the women photographers in Qajar Iran. *Binaab Journal* 12, 164–181(in Persian).

Taj al-Saltaneh, Z. (1982) *Ruznāmehye Khāterāt-e Taj al-Saltaneh [Taj al-Saltaneh's Memoirs]*. M. Ettehadieh (Nezam Mafi) and C. Sa'duniyan (eds). Tehran, Nashr-e Tarikh-e Iran (in Persian).

Turner, B.S. (2003) Foreward: the phenomenology of lived experience. In L. Meskell and R. Joyce (eds) *Embodied Lives. Figuring Ancient Maya and Egyptian Experience*, 13–20. New York, Routledge.

Yee, J. (2004) Recycling the "colonial harem"? Women in postcards from French Indochina. *French Cultural Studies* 15 (1), 5–19.

Zahirinejad, M. (2014) Implication of economic relations on political transitions during Qajar dynasty. *Hemispheres: Studies on Cultures and Societies* 29 (4), 67–79.

Zoka, Y. (1997) *The History of Photography and Pioneer Photographers in Iran*. Tehran, Nashr-e Elmi va Farhangi (in Persian).

Chapter 10

Afterword: a deep time perspective on bodily beauty

Katharina Rebay-Salisbury

It is not without a spot of envy that a prehistoric archaeologist engages with the chapters of this book and marvels at the wealth of iconographic and textual evidence Egyptologists and historical archaeologists have available to supplement the interpretation of their material evidence. This book gathers chapters that comment on notions of bodily beauty, and the way aesthetic ideas of the body may – or indeed may not – be gendered. Even with the knowledge that gender is always contextual and situational, it is never easy to look beyond the engrained notions of gendered beauty that characterise our own socialisation and upbringing. In many of the chapters, even small hints provided by images and texts prove decisive for a specific interpretation.

The advantage that prehistorians might have, however, is to look at bodily beauty from a somewhat different perspective, a perspective rooted in evolutionary thought that integrates the human body's biological basis to understand beauty. Underneath the cultural notions of what is beautiful, there are general evolutionary principles at work. Attraction is an evolutionary mechanism to identify a physiologically healthy mate (Brierley et al. 2016). A beautiful body is perceived as sexually attractive, and sexual attraction is linked to bodies that signal physiological heath to provide optimal conditions for reproduction in their specific environments. Even if there is substantial cultural variation, beauty standards are biologically based (Grammer et al. 2003).

Of course, there are also notions of bodily beauty beyond sexual attractiveness, but suffice it to say there are substantial overlaps. It is not only the facial features and build of the body that are important; bodily beauty also references skin tone and hair, a groomed appearance, graceful posture and elegant movements, even tone of voice and body scent (Eibl-Eibesfeldt and Sütterlin 2007; Swami and Furnham 2008). Beauty is an intrinsic property of the body that generates positive feelings and pleasure (Etcoff 1999). The quote "what is beautiful is good" (Dion, Berscheid, and Walster 1972) encompasses the notion that beauty is associated with more attention, success, wealth and social status for the lucky individuals that are perceived as better looking than others.

Humans are the only species who changed the path of their own evolutionary trajectory through the use of artefacts (Taylor 2010), and since the desire to alter and beautify the body is ancient, so is material culture associated with beautifying the body. Cross-culturally, much time and energy are expended to enhance bodily beauty. The earliest evidence for the use of pigment and body ornamentation is continuously pushed back in time, even beyond our current hominid species. Red pigment use has been discovered in a Neanderthal context at Maastricht-Bélvèdere, dating as early as 250,000 to 200,000 years ago (Roebroeks *et al.* 2012); a set of white-tailed eagle talons from Krapina, Croatia, which had been collected, processed and worn, are currently thought to represent the earliest personal ornaments in Europe, dating to about 130,000 years ago (Radovčić 2020).

Face

In social interactions, the face plays a decisive role, which is why it is often at the centre of the perception of attractiveness. Both men and women prefer faces on photos that have been manipulated towards greater symmetry (Rhodes *et al.* 1998). Facial symmetry is thought to reflect optimal conditions during development, because our genes encode perfect symmetry; during development, however, stress by diseases, infections, parasites and a lack of nutrients may cause growth disruptions and asymmetries. Fewer imperfections are thought to indicate developmental stability and a strong immune system to withstand external influences. Symmetry may then indicate heath and optimal genetic features to pass on to potential offspring (Thornhill and Møller 1997).

Differences in the shape of female and male faces mainly arise from the influence of circulating sex hormones. Men with higher testosterone levels develop larger jawbones, more prominent cheekbones and thinner cheeks; women with high levels of circulating oestrogen develop feminine, round and soft features. Exaggerated forms of this general sexual dimorphism are seen as attractive, because they advertise reproductive fitness through these visual signs of their hormonal status (Little, Jones and DeBruine 2011). However, there are always counterforces at play. In women, a face with too many baby features may not signal enough maturity to indicate fertility; in men, extreme masculine features may suggest too much aggressiveness in a mate (Grammer *et al.* 2003).

Beyond the individual level, it appears that average faces within a population are seen as the most attractive. This has been established by studies in which adults judged the attractiveness of individual faces against computer-generated composite images, suggesting evolutionary pressures led us to favour average characteristics of our own group (Langlois and Roggman 1990). This brings us to the question if beauty is in the familiar or the exotic – if we favour cultural sameness or difference in our choices of partners.

Body shape

In addition to the face, the mass and proportions of the body are important components of bodily beauty. Multiple studies have rated attractiveness in relation to body mass index and hip-to-waist ratio as indicators of bodily shape, consistently finding that what is considered healthy is also considered beautiful. Men usually find a hip-to-waist ration of 0.7 and the lower end of a healthy body mass index most attractive in women (Muñoz-Reyes *et al.* 2015), as they signal youthfulness and a fertile, non-pregnant body. Women's optimal age for reproduction is 24, which ensures enough maturity to become a competent mother and correlates with high ratings of attractiveness. A healthy level of female body fat, distributed in the right places, is important for reproduction; overall, heavier mothers tend to have more children (Grammer *et al.* 2003).

What actually qualifies as a healthy weight is not only physiologically determined, but also depends on environmental and cultural factors. Female fat storage ensures that a foetus can be brought to term, even in adverse conditions. Cross-cultural surveys thus find that some cultures prefer thin women, while others prefer fat women. The Moors of the Sahara Desert, for example, value extreme feminine fatness. Through confining girls and restricting their mobility, as well as through providing high caloric food, girls are deliberately fattened up for marriage (Popenoe 2004). Such preferences correlate with a number of factors – the reliability of food supply and climate, but also the relative social dominance of women, the value placed on women's work and the probability that the expression of adolescent sexuality will have adverse consequences on girls were found important (Anderson *et al.* 1992). Nevertheless, preferences are not fixed, but subject to relatively rapid changes of fashion, as Dezhamkhooy points out using the example of beauty transformations in 19th/20th-century Iran (Chapter 9 in this volume). The changing appearance of female figurines during European prehistory may be explained by a change in living conditions; the scarcity of food and cold climate during the Ice Age led to a female ideal of fatness, whilst slim and slender figurines of the metal ages indicate a much more stable food supply, in particular for the depicted elites (Rebay-Salisbury 2016).

Bodily integrity

Bodily integrity is another aspect of beauty that intersects with health. Injuries, lost teeth and amputated body parts might not only restrict the functions of the body, but generate social responses triggered by emotions ranging from repulsion to compassion. The archaeology of disability, including explorations into social responses to mental and physical handicaps, still leaves much to be explored (but see Boutin 2016, Finlay 1999, Perego and Scopacasa 2016). There are few, but significant, finds in the archaeological record that testify to medical treatment, the ingenuity of engineering material culture to aid and expand bodies' capabilities, and to the way people are able to adapt and adjust after life-changing injuries. The world's oldest artificial eye dates to 2900–2800 BCE and was found in the eye socket of a 30-year-old woman from a burial at Shahr-I Sokhta, Iran (Moghadasi 2014). A prosthetic big toe made of wood and leather found on the foot of an ancient Egyptian mummy, dating to 950–710 BCE, was discovered in the tomb of Tabeketenmut in the necropolis of Thebes (Archaeological Institute of America 2011), to name two examples. The bioarchaeology of care (Tilley 2017) has developed a systematic framework for analysing past caregiving practices by working from bones that show pathological changes to understand possible treatments in a contextualised manner, and it has yet to be widely applied.

Dental health seems trivial today, but abrasion, caries and associated root infections were not only painful and made food consumption more difficult, they could turn into life-threatening conditions. Body care may have included some form of cleaning teeth; wooden sticks to remove plaque have been used for millions of years, as interproximal grooves between the teeth of several species of our genus, including Neanderthals, suggest (Lozano *et al.* 2013). The removal of build-up of dental calculus, much to the delight of contemporary scientists, has often not been very thorough. The oldest evidence of dentistry, tooth fillings of beeswax, was discovered in a 6500-year-old human canine from Slovenia (Bernardini *et al.* 2012). Dentures that replace missing front teeth appear from the 7th century BCE onwards in Etruscan graves. The teeth are fixed with small gold bands and appear primarily in high-status female burials.

There is the suspicion that the teeth the dentures replace were not always naturally exfoliated, but deliberately removed, perhaps in the course of stage of life transition rituals. The replacements were barely functional and did no more than restore a beautiful smile (Becker and Turfa 2017). The modification of teeth, for example by filing grooves, has cross-cultural examples all over the world (see Jensen, Chapter 8 in this volume, for Viking Age Scandinavian men). It seems counter-intuitive that such obviously harmful practices with negative consequences for heath and survival were, at times, desirable and fashionable. One could add many more examples of body modifications for which this is the case; from Chinese foot-binding to female circumcision and from metal piercings to Brazilian lip plates, they almost always include a gender dimension. Like the peacock's tail, practices that come at a great energetic cost or reduce survival have not been eliminated in the course of evolution if they help in the attraction of mates. The male peacock that is able to produce a large, ornate train is preferred by females, as he is considered the fittest to sire healthy chicks. The disadvantages in reduced survival are compensated by the advantage of reproduction.

Skin

Unblemished skin signals a balanced hormonal status and general good health. During evolutionary history, humans lost their fur and became the only naked species of ape (Morris 1967). Humans were capable of sustained physical activity in hot climates because of better body temperature regulation through sweating, which provided an obvious advantage when outrunning their prey. In tandem, humans evolved dark skin through melanin pigmentation that protects against adverse effects of sun radiation in Africa (Jablonski 2004). Out of Africa, skin colour has adapted as a response to the environment and changed towards lighter pigmentation in the northern hemisphere. With less UV radiation, melanin pigmentation turns into a disadvantage for the synthesis of Vitamin D, the lack of which involves serious health implications such as rickets (Brickley *et al.* 2017, Chaplin and Jablonski 2009). Natural selection is therefore the most likely mechanism for the evolution of pigmentation-associated variation in West Eurasia (Ju and Mathieson 2021). Increasingly, however, clothing, shelter and less time spent outdoors became a factor in skin colour evolution.

Dark skin colour in combination with blue eyes have been found through genetic studies of European hunter-gatherers, such as a 7,000-year-old Mesolithic skeleton discovered at the La Braña-Arintero site in León, Spain (Olalde *et al.* 2014) or the 10,000-year-old "Cheddar Man" discovered in an English cave (Brace *et al.* 2019). The evolutionary advantage of the blue eye colour variation, which has developed exclusively in western Eurasia and some adjacent regions, is less well understood and may have arisen through sexual selection (Wilde *et al.* 2014).

Discussing notions of skin colour preference in antiquity is a particularly thorny issue in today's world, in which skin colour is primarily linked with perceptions of race and racism. Skin colour variations are, however, also associated with age and gender (Etcoff 1999). It is striking that skin colour was used in Late Bronze Age Aegean art to differentiate children by gender, with white indicating girls and red indicating boys (Franković, Chapter 5 in this volume). Light skin has the ability to tan under the influence of sunlight; the difference in skin colour may therefore reference where it was seen as appropriate to spend time for girls and boys – protected from the sun inside or exposed to it outdoors. Algrain (Chapter 6 in this volume) notices the importance of just the right skin tone for males in Ancient Athens – not too light so as not to appear effeminate, but not to dark so as not to appear foreign. Jensen (Chapter 8 in this volume) reports on how skin colour variations were perceived in the Viking Age, ranging from dark and brown slaves to pale aristocrats, and very pale elite women.

Here, we see how skin colour intersects with social status and class. Tanning is a body technique that can be deliberately employed in signalling social status, as the shifting connotations of tanned skin during the 20th century in Europe and the western World have demonstrated: a good tan had been associated with low-status and outdoor labour, as farmers and construction workers were not able to protect themselves from the sun. Women in particular protected most of the surface of their bodies with long sleeves and dresses, sun hats and parasols. At the turn of the 20th century, it became recognised that exposure to sun has some health benefits, such as preventing rickets. Soon, sun-bathing and journeys to the Mediterranean become fashionable, and a good tan started to indicate that the leisurely class could afford spending time doing sporting activities outdoors or trips to exotic locations rather than labouring in offices. Tanning studios for the masses and an increasing awareness of the adverse effects of too much UV radiation, the discovery of the Ozone hole in the 1980s, slowly brought a halt to the tanning trend.

The surface of the skin can further be altered through scarification and tattooing, both of which were practiced widely across cultures, with varying connotations (Schildkrout 2004). Similarly to what Jensen (Chapter 8 in this volume) reports about the Viking world, facial scarring is normally not considered beautiful in western societies, but non-severe facial scarring might make men more attractive to women (Burriss, Rowland, and Little 2009). Tattooing has a long history in European prehistory, with Ötzi, the Copper Age ice mummy from the Tyrolean alps as one of the few preserved individuals on which this practice can be investigated in detail (Zink *et al.* 2018). The tattoos appear in the form of single to seven parallel lines as well as crosses all over the body; their locations suggest a link to the treatment of painful injuries and degenerative diseases and may even result from an early form of acupuncture. It is clear that in this case, around 3300 BCE, the tattoos were employed as therapeutic treatment rather than as bodily ornamentation.

Scythian mummies of the Altai mountains in Sibera (Rudenko 1970), in contrast, testify to a different background of tattooing practices in the 5th century BCE. The elaborate, stylised motifs include elements from horses, rams, large cats and even fish to compose mythical beasts. The tattoos have been associated with shamanism (Hasanov 2016), but they are also ornamental; their apparent beauty makes them to one of the most popular ancient tattooing motifs in the modern world, with thousands, if not millions of copies on our contemporary's bodies (Krutak and Deter-Wolf 2017).

Tattooing is perhaps so elusive because it is not associated with a specific tool – several kinds of pointy objects may be used to puncture the skin, which can also function as awls, needles or pins, to name just a few (Gillreath-Brown *et al.* 2019). Human skin decays quickly, and only under exceptional circumstances do mummified human remains continue to display the tattoos that once adorned them (Deter-Wolf *et al.* 2016). Since the ancient Greeks, tattooing was employed to stigmatise and punish, and its negative connotation continued through Christianity until the 19th century (Jones 1987).

Scarification and tattooing are permanent alterations of the body, which makes them so powerful, whereas face and body paint are temporary. The application of pigments to the human skin transforms and changes appearance, but it is reversible. The excessive use of ochre for the first modern human burials (Pettitt 2014) begs the question of whether the covering of the body surface and clothes in red was not a feature of everyday life, in part necessitated by the need to ward off insects. But body paint may also have been employed in identity transformations, such as the transformation from civilian to warrior (Rebay-Salisbury 2017) through war-paint. It is possible that the Picts of northern Scotland (Noble 2020) painted themselves blue for battles, but the jury is out if this is just Roman and modern imagination or was indeed practiced. Native Americans used paint extensively, both for themselves and their horses; the paint and the symbols had power and were used to protect and to communicate to each other and the spirit world (Dubin 1999). More often perhaps are pigments employed as make-up, both to cover up and hide unwanted facial features, and to enhance others.

Reflections

Today, it is hard to imagine a world in which one rarely, if ever, sees one's own face. Mirrors and reflective surfaces of glass and metal are all around us, giving us ample opportunity to look at ourselves, tamper with our looks, correct our appearance, smile and have our reflection smile back at us. And yet, over most of human (pre-) history, people have lived in a world without mirrors. It was not impossible to see one's reflection, for instance in a natural pool of water like Narcissus in Ovid's fable or in the surface of a vessel filled with water, but it must have been a rare event.

That it used to be so difficult to see one's own face has been put forward as an argument to interpret Upper Palaeolithic female figurines (also known under the disputed term "Venus figurines") as self-portraits. Spread across Eurasia, from France to Siberia and dating predominately between 28,000 and 12,000 years ago, the female depictions share some common aspects, despite their wide variability. As mobile, portable forms of art, they are sized to fit into a human hand. The female bodies frequently display emphasised breasts, abdomens, hips and buttocks; some appear pregnant, others do not. The exaggeration of indicators of female fertility has led to the predominate interpretation of the figurines as mother goddesses. Other aspects of the female body are frequently downplayed or entirely missing from the representation, such as hands and feet, as well as faces. The Venus of Willendorf, Austria (Antl-Weiser 2008), is a good example of this prototype. LeRoy McDermott (1996) has argued that because of the missing face and the warped body proportions, the Upper Palaeolithic female figurines may have been made by women who looked down on their bodies and depicted what they saw.

The first known mirrors were made of obsidian. Ground and polished disks of *c.* 9 cm diameter were discovered in the context of the Neolithic proto-city Çatalhöyük in Turkey, and date to *c.* 6200 to 6000 BCE (Enoch 2006). With the use of metal, mirrors became more common, although they never became as ubiquitous and constantly available as today. Mihajlović (Chapter 7 in this volume) shows that evidence of mirrors in funerary contexts of Moesia Superior is only found in a very small percentage of female graves, perhaps referencing the beauty rituals connected to the wedding ceremony.

Reciprocity

The scarcity of mirrors has important implications for understanding bodily care and beauty maintenance. Grooming, the application of make-up, plucking eyebrows, removing facial hair and even shaving is difficult to impossible without having the reflection of one's own face at one's disposal, and may therefore have been done by others, either as an act of mutual care, or, in societies with social differentiation, by servants or professionals. Body maintenance, in this sense, is less to be understood as self-care than as care orchestrated through others; beauty can be understood as coming into being through the relationship between people.

For the discussion of the relationship between artefacts used for bodily care and gender, this has an important implication that is frequently overlooked: in particular when found in association with burials, it remains unclear if the particular beauty tool in question was intended to be used *by* or *on* the buried person – the user of toiletry items may not be the same as the recipient. Sets of toiletry items were common throughout the ancient world and included tweezers, picks and ear-spoons. In Bronze and Iron Age Europe, toiletry items are primarily associated with male warrior burials (Gedl 1988; Treherne 1995). In the Viking period, in contrast (Jensen, Chapter 8 in this volume), they are associated with buried women.

Which aspect of the triangle human-human-object relationship was in fact represented in the burial? Who used the tools for body care, and whose beauty did they help to enhance? Objects only become gender-typical through the practice of their use (Franković, Chapter 5 in this volume), which may or may not be preferably done by persons of a specific gender. Mere associations with buried bodies of male or female sex may lead to interpretational fallacies. The idea that toiletry items were used by the buried person on themselves might just be too simple, and we are not even yet asking in which spatial context they were used; if it was public or private, and if it had specific gendered connotations (Matić, Chapter 3 in this volume).

The ancient Egyptian tool most likely employed in wig-making and maintenance discussed by Zumkley (Chapter 4 in this volume) is an interesting case in this context, as it is hard to imagine the high-status men in whose graves they are found repairing their own wigs. But then, Egyptian funerary assemblages may include literally everything anybody may ever need in the afterlife, with service implied, as the tomb of Tutankhamun so vividly illustrates. The perfume vases of ancient Athens (Algrain, Chapter 6 in this volume) illustrate another point. Used by both sexes in quite different ways to perform gender (men used unscented oil in the context of training, women used scented oils as components of attraction), it is hard to determine their use in the funerary rite. They may be associated with the dead, but equally, with the person cleaning and preparing the body for the funeral. It is likely that using objects in such rituals rendered them taboo and unusable for other purposes – so why not dispose of them in the grave.

Status

Francis Galton, cousin of Charles Darwin and one of the founding fathers of eugenics, famously graded women on a scale from attractive to repulsive in his beauty map of Britain–the most beautiful women were found just outside the luxury department store Harrod's in London, whist the lowest point was Aberdeen (Jones 2008). This nicely illustrates the link between beauty and wealth. High-status women are expected to be beautiful, and have access to the necessary resources to maintain and care for their beauty. Beauty maintenance, training and controlling the body through diet can be time intensive and costly; overdone looks might, in contrast, signal too much time at hand. Beautification tools and body ornaments are frequently found in high-status graves, and they are thought to indicate the wealth and position of an individual in their society. Nevertheless, it is often quite difficult to compare female and male grave assemblages directly with each other, as the concepts of beauty and wealth may be quite different for men and women.

The evolution of mating strategies might play a role here, based on the unequal burden of reproduction for men and women. In principle, males can have as many offspring as available females, whereas the number of offspring for women is limited by the duration and costs of pregnancy, breastfeeding and childrearing (Dufour and Sauther 2002). Women therefore look for wealthy partners, who can provide for their children, whereas men are attracted to beautiful women, as beauty serves as a visual clue to youth and fertility (Buss 2016). The extent to which this principle plays a role for modern human societies has been shown to depend on the level of gendered labour division and inequality. In more gender unequal nations, women select partners for their earning potential, money and status, whereas in more gender equal nations, men and women are increasingly looking for the same qualities in partners such as high levels of education (Eastwick *et al.* 2006, Zentner and Eagly 2015).

In the past of our archaeological disciplines, the rich and elaborate grave goods found in women's graves have primarily been explained by their partner's wealth and status; gender and feminist archaeology has repeatedly questioned this interpretation and aimed to claim women's social status directly in their own right (Sofaer and Sørensen 2013). The discourse around the Lady of Vix in Burgundy, one of the most lavish Celtic burials ever found and dating to *c.* 500 BCE, illustrates that it had not been easy to accept that a female was afforded such riches (Arnold 2012; Pope 2021).

The Mesopotamian Queen with her elaborate hairdo and heavy gold accessories discussed in this book (Vogel, Chapter 2 in this volume), represents a quite similar case. The heavy objects on and around her head must have impacted her gate and composure and thus visually communicated that she is of high status. As Vogel stresses, leadership must be embodied, and the leader's body must be shaped according to social norms and values. This includes beautification techniques regarding make-up, jewellery and dress as well as the control of actions and gestures.

The boomerang-shaped sheet bronze objects around the head of few wealthy women in Early Bronze Age graves at Hafnerbach and Franzhausen, Austria (*c.* 2000 BCE), may have been instrumental in attaining the correct body position. Remains of striped textiles suggest that these objects were worn in conjunction with veils, framing the face and broadening the women's appearance. Curiously, it is unknown how exactly they were balanced and fixed on the head, but exactly this might have been the point: wearing the objects would lend the wearers a straight and upright posture and would have made it impossible to tilt the head or take a bow (Grömer and Neugebauer-Maresch 2017).

However, the focus on interpreting the individual in the grave in terms of their own gendered beauty, wealth and social status, perhaps makes us overlook an important aspect – the dynamics of power couples, who were able to work together and pool their resources, with beauty as one of the currencies. We need to see the relational interactions as the catalyst for success, and investigate relationships within and between families to understand the distribution of power in the wider social network.

Acknowledgements

I would like to thank Uroš Matić for the opportunity to read the chapters of this book and the invitation to write this afterword. I would like to acknowledge Marjolein D. Bosch and Roderick B. Salisbury for discussions on prehistoric beauty, and Roderick B. Salisbury for reading and commenting on this chapter. My project "The value of mothers to society: responses to motherhood and child rearing practices in prehistoric Europe" has received funding from the European Research Council (ERC) under the European Union's Horizon 2020 research and innovation programme (grant agreement No. 676828).

Bibliography

Anderson, J.L., Crawford, C.B., Nadeau, J. and Lindberg, T. (1992) Was the Duchess of Windsor right? A cross-cultural review of the socioecology of ideals of female body shape. *Ethology and Sociobiology* 13 (3), 197–227.

Antl-Weiser, W. (2008) The anthropomorphic figurines from Willendorf. *Wissenschaftliche Mitteilungen des Niederösterreichischen Landesmuseums* 19, 19–30.

Archaeological Institute of America. 2011. Artifact. *Archaeology* 64 (3) https://archive.archaeology. org/1105/artifact/egyptian_mummy_artificial_toe.html.

Arnold, B. (2012) The Vix Princess redux: a retrospective on European Iron Age gender and mortuary studies In L. Prados Torreira (ed.) *La Arqueología funeraria desde una perspectiva de género*, 215–232. Madrid, UA Ediciones.

Becker, M.J. and Turfa, J.M. (2017) *The Etruscans and the History of Dentistry. The Golden Smile through the Ages*. London, Routledge.

Bernardini, F., Tuniz, C., Coppa, A., Mancini, L., Dreossi, D., Eichert, D., Turco, G., Biasotto, M., Terrasi, F., De Cesare, N., Hua, Q. and Levchenko, V. (2012) Beeswax as dental filling on a Neolithic human tooth. *PLOS ONE* 7 (9), e44904.

Boutin, A.T. (2016) Exploring the social construction of disability: an application of the bioarchaeology of personhood model to a pathological skeleton from ancient Bahrain. *International Journal of Paleopathology* 12, Supplement C, 17–28.

Brace, S., Diekmann, Y., Booth, T.J., van Dorp, L., Faltyskova, Z., Rohland, N., Mallick, S., Olalde, I., Ferry, M., Michel, M., Oppenheimer, J., Broomandkhoshbacht, N., Stewardson, K., Martiniano, R., Walsh, S., Kayser, M., Charlton, S., Hellenthal, G., Armit, I., Schulting, R., Craig, O.E., Sheridan, A., Parker Pearson, M., Stringer, C., Reich, D., Thomas, M.G. and Barnes, I. (2019) Ancient genomes indicate population replacement in Early Neolithic Britain. *Nature Ecology and Evolution* 3 (5), 765–771.

Brickley, M.B., D'Ortenzio, L., Kahlon, B., Schattmann, A., Ribot, I., Raguin, E. and Bertrand, B. (2017) Ancient Vitamin D deficiency: long-term trends. *Current Anthropology* 58 (3), 420–427.

Brierley, M.-E. (2016) The body and the beautiful: health, attractiveness and body composition in men's and women's bodies. *PloS one* 11 (6), e0156722-e0156722.

Burriss, R.P., Rowland, H.M. and Little, A.C. (2009) Facial scarring enhances men's attractiveness for short-term relationships. *Personality and Individual Differences* 46 (2), 213–217.

Buss, D. (2016) *The Evolution of Desire*. New York, Basic Books.

Chaplin, G. and Jablonski, N.G. (2009) Vitamin D and the evolution of human depigmentation. *American Journal of Physical Anthropology* 139 (4), 451–461.

Deter-Wolf, A., Robitaille, B., Krutak, L. and Galliot, S. (2016) The world's oldest tattoos. *Journal of Archaeological Science: Reports* 5, 19–24.

Dion, K., Berscheid, K. and Walster, E. (1972) What is beautiful is good. *Journal of Personality and Social Psychology* 24, 285–322.

Dubin, L.S. (1999) *North American Indian Jewelry and Adornment: From Prehistory to the Present*. New York, Harry N. Abrams.

Dufour, D.L. and Sauther, M.L. (2002) Comparative and evolutionary dimensions of the energetics of human pregnancy and lactation. *American Journal of Human Biology* 14 (5), 584–602.

Eastwick, P.W., Eagly, A.H., Glick, P., Johannesen-Schmidt, M.C., Fiske, S.T., Blum, A.M.B., Eckes, T., Freiburger, P., Huang, L.-l., Fernández, M.L., Manganelli, A.M., Pek, J.C.X., Castro, Y.R., Sakalli-Ugurlu, N., Six-Materna, I. and Volpato, C. (2006) Is traditional gender ideology associated with sex-typed mate preferences? A test in nine nations. *Sex Roles* 54 (9), 603–614.

Eibl-Eibesfeldt, I. and Sütterlin, C. (2007) *Weltsprache Kunst: Zur Natur- und Kunstgeschichte bildlicher Kommunikation*. Wien, Brandstätter.

Enoch, J.M. (2006) History of mirrors dating back 8000 years. *Optometry and Vision Science* 83 (10) 775–781.

Etcoff, N. (1999) *Survival of the Prettiest: The Science of Beauty*. New York, Anchor Books.

Finlay, N. (ed.) (1999) *Disability and Archaeology. Archaeological Review from Cambridge* 15 (2).

Gedl, M. (1988) *Die Toilettegeräte in Polen. Prähistorische Bronzefunde Abteilung XV Band 1*. München, Beck.

Gillreath-Brown, A., Deter-Wolf, A., Adams, K.R., Lynch-Holm, V., Fulgham, S., Tushingham, S., Lipe, W.D., and Matson R.G. (2019) Redefining the age of tattooing in western North America: a 2000-year-old artifact from Utah. *Journal of Archaeological Science: Reports* 24, 1064–1075.

Grammer, K., Fink, B., Møller, A.P. and Thornhill, R. (2003) Darwinian aesthetics: sexual selection and the biology of beauty. *Biological Reviews* 78 (3) 385–407.

Grömer, K. and Neugebauer-Maresch, C. (2017) Inszenierung von Status und Identität–Gedanken zur Kleidung frühbronzezeitlicher Frauen aus Franzhausen I. In F. Pieler and P. Trebsche (eds) *Beiträge zum Tag der Niederösterreichischen Landesarchäologie 2017, Festschrift für Ernst Lauermann*, 145–162. Asparn, Niederösterreichisches Landesmuseum.

Hasanov, Z. (2016) A method for determining the practice of shamanism in archeological cultures. *Anthropology and Archeology of Eurasia* 55, 188–231.

Jablonski, N.G. (2004) The evolution of human skin and skin color. *Annual Review of Anthropology* 33 (1), 585–623.

Jones, C.P. (1987) Stigma: tattooing and branding in Graeco-Roman antiquity. *Journal of Roman Studies* 77, 139–155.

Jones, S. 2008. Is human evolution over? UCL Lunch Hour Lecture. London.

Ju, D. and Mathieson, I. (2021) The evolution of skin pigmentation-associated variation in West Eurasia. *Proceedings of the National Academy of Sciences* 118 (1), e2009227118.

Krutak, L.F., and Deter-Wolf, A. 2017. *Ancient Ink: The Archaeology of Tattooing*. Seattle, University of Washington Press.

Langlois, J.H. and Roggman, L.A. 1990. Attractive faces are only average. *Psychological Science* 1 (2), 115–121.

Little, A.C., Jones, B.C. and DeBruine, L.M. 2011. Facial attractiveness: evolutionary based research. *Philosophical Transactions of the Royal Society B: Biological Sciences* 366 (1571), 1638–1659.

Lozano, M., Subirà, M.E., Aparicio, J., Lorenzo, C. and Gómez-Merino, G. (2013) Toothpicking and periodontal disease in a Neanderthal specimen from Cova Foradà Site (Valencia, Spain). *PLOS ONE* 8 (10), e76852.

McDermott, L. (19969 Self-representation in Upper Paleolithic female figurines. *Current Anthropology* 37 (2), 227–275.

Moghadasi, A.N. (2014) Artificial eye in burnt city and theoretical understanding of how vision works. *Iranian Journal of Public Health* 43 (11), 1595–1596.

Morris, D. (1967) *The Naked Ape*. London, Cape.

Muñoz-Reyes, J.A., Iglesias-Julios, M., Pita, M. and Turiegano, E. (2015) Facial features: what women perceive as attractive and what men consider attractive. *PloS one* 10 (7), e0132979-e0132979.

Noble, G. (2020) The problem of the Picts. Searching for a lost people in northern Scotland. *Current Archaeology* 364, 28–35.

Olalde, I., Allentoft, M.E., Sánchez-Quinto, F., Santpere, G., Chiang, C.W.K., DeGiorgio, M., Prado-Martinez, J., Rodríguez, J.A., Rasmussen, S., Quilez, J., Ramírez, O., Marigorta, U.M., Fernández-Callejo, M., Prada, M.E., Encinas, J.M.V., Nielsen, R., Netea, M.G., Novembre, J., Sturm, R.A., Sabeti, P., Marquès-Bonet, T., Navarro, A., Willerslev, E., and Lalueza-Fox, C. (2014) Derived immune and ancestral pigmentation alleles in a 7,000-year-old Mesolithic European. *Nature* 507 (7491), 225–228.

Perego, E. and Scopacasa, R. (eds) (2016) *Burial and Social Change in First Millennium BC Italy: Approaching Social Agents. Gender, Personhood and Marginality. Studies in Funerary Archaeology 11*. Oxford, Oxbow Books.

Pettitt, P. (2014) The European Upper Palaeolithic. In V. Cummings, P. Jordan and M. Zvelebil (eds) *The Oxford Handbook of the Archaeology and Anthropology of Hunter-Gatherers*. Oxford, Oxford University Press.

Pope, R. (2021) Re-approaching Celts: origins, society, and social change. *Journal of Archaeological Research*. https://doi.org/10.1007/s10814-021-09157-1

Popenoe, R. (2004) *Feeding Desire. Fatness, Beauty, and Sexuality among a Saharan People*. London, Routledge.

Radovčić, D. (2020) Neandertal aesthetics? In M.R. Monti and D. Pećnjak (eds) *What is Beauty? A Multidisciplinary Approach to Aesthetic Experience*. 27–44. Newcastle, Cambridge Scholars Press.

Rebay-Salisbury, K. (2016) *The Human Body in Early Iron Age Central Europe. Burial Practices and Images of the Hallstatt World*. London, Routledge.

Rebay-Salisbury, K. (2017) Comments on Paul Treherne's 'The warrior's beauty: the masculine body and self-identity in Bronze Age Europe'. *European Journal of Archaeology* 20 (1), 5–9.

Rhodes, G., Proffitt, F., Grady, J.M. and Sumich, A. (1998) Facial symmetry and the perception of beauty. *Psychonomic Bulletin & Review* 5 (4), 659–669.

Roebroeks, W., Sier, M.J., Nielsen, T.K., De Loecker, D., Parés, J.M., Arps, C.E.S. and Mücher, H.J. (2012) Use of red ochre by early Neandertals. *Proceedings of the National Academy of Sciences* 109 (6), 1889.

Rudenko, S.I. (1970) *Frozen Tombs of Siberia: The Pazyryk Burials of Iron Age Horsemen*. London, J.M. Dent and Sons.

Schildkrout, E. (2004) Inscribing the body. *Annual Review of Anthropology* 33 (1), 319–344.

Sofaer, J. and Sørensen, M.L.S. (2013) Death and gender. In S. Tarlow and L. Nilsson Stutz (eds) *The Oxford Handbook of the Archaeology of Death and Burial*, 527–542. Oxford, Oxford University Press.

Swami, V. and Furnham, A. (2008) *The Psychology of Physical Attraction*. London, Routledge.

Taylor, T. (2010) *The Artificial Ape: How Technology Changed the Course of Human Evolution*. New York, Palgrave Macmillan.

Thornhill, R. and Møller, A.P. (1997) Developmental stability, disease and medicine. *Biological Reviews of the Cambridge Philosophical Society* 72 (4), 497–548.

Tilley, L. (2017) Showing that they cared: an introduction to thinking, theory and practice in the bioarchaeology of care. In L. Tilley and A.A. Schrenk (eds) *New Developments in the Bioarchaeology of Care. Further Case Studies and Expanded Theory*, 11–43. International, Springer.

Treherne, P.D.M. (1995) The warrior's beauty: the masculine body and self-identity in Bronze Age Europe. *Journal of European Archaeology* 3 (1), 105–144.

Wilde, S., Timpson, A., Kirsanow, K., Kaiser, E., Kayser, M., Unterländer, M., Hollfelder, N., Potekhina, I.D., Schier, W., Thomas, M.G. and Burger, J. (2014) Direct evidence for positive selection of skin, hair, and eye pigmentation in Europeans during the last 5,000 y. *Proceedings of the National Academy of Sciences* 111 (13), 4832.

Zentner, M. and Eagly, A.H. (2015) A sociocultural framework for understanding partner preferences of women and men: integration of concepts and evidence. *European Review of Social Psychology* 26 (1), 328–373.

Zink, A., Samadelli, M., Gostner, P. and Piombino-Mascali, D. (2018) Possible evidence for care and treatment in the Tyrolean Iceman. *International Journal of Paleopathology* 25, 110–117.